# Culture, Sociality, and Morality

# ECONOMY, POLITY, AND SOCIETY

The foundations of political economy—from Adam Smith to the Austrian school of economics, to contemporary research in public choice and institutional analysis—are sturdy and well established, but far from calcified. On the contrary, the boundaries of the research built on this foundation are ever expanding. One approach to political economy that has gained considerable traction in recent years combines the insights and methods of three distinct but related subfields within economics and political science: the Austrian, Virginia and Bloomington schools of political economy. The vision of this book series is to capitalize on the intellectual gains from the interactions between these approaches in order to both feed the growing interest in this approach and advance social scientists' understanding of economy, polity, and society. This series seeks to publish works that combine the Austrian school's insights on knowledge, the Virginia school's insights into incentives in non-market contexts, and the Bloomington school's multiple methods, real-world approach to institutional design as a powerful tool for understanding social behaviour in a diversity of contexts.

## Series Editors

Virgil Henry Storr, associate professor of economics, George Mason University; Don C. Lavoie Senior Fellow, F. A. Hayek Program for Advanced Study in Philosophy, Politics, and Economics, Mercatus Center at George Mason University

Jayme S. Lemke, senior research fellow, Mercatus Center at George Mason University

## Titles in the Series

*The Need for Humility in Policymaking: Lessons from Regulatory Policy*
    Edited by Stefanie Haeffele and Anne Hobson
*Commercial Society: A Primer on Ethics and Economics*
    Cathleen A. Johnson, Robert F. Lusch, and David Schmidtz
*Exploring the Political Economy and Social Philosophy of Vincent and Elinor Ostrom*
    Edited by Peter J. Boettke, Bobbi Herzberg, and Brian Kogelmann
*Nudging Public Policy: Examining the Benefits and Limitations of Paternalistic Public Policies*
    Edited by Rosemarie Fike, Stefanie Haeffele, and Arielle John
*Culture, Sociality, and Morality: New Applications of Mainline Political Economy*
    Edited by Paul Dragos Aligica, Ginny Seung Choi, and Virgil Henry Storr

# Culture, Sociality, and Morality

## New Applications of Mainline Political Economy

Edited by Paul Dragos Aligica,
Ginny Seung Choi, and Virgil Henry Storr

ROWMAN & LITTLEFIELD
Lanham • Boulder • New York • London

Published by Rowman & Littlefield
An imprint of The Rowman & Littlefield Publishing Group, Inc.
4501 Forbes Boulevard, Suite 200, Lanham, Maryland 20706
www.rowman.com

86-90 Paul Street, London EC2A 4NE

British Library Cataloguing in Publication Information Available

**Library of Congress Cataloging-in-Publication Data**

Names: Aligică, Paul Dragoş, editor. | Choi, Ginny Seung, editor. |
   Storr, Virgil Henry, 1975- editor.
Title: Culture, sociality, and morality : new applications of mainline
   political economy / edited by Paul Dragos Aligica, Ginny Seung Choi, and
   Virgil Henry Storr.
Description: Lanham : Rowman & Littlefield, [2021] | Series: Economy,
   polity, and society | Includes bibliographical references and index.
Identifiers: LCCN 2021035473 (print) | LCCN 2021035474 (ebook) | ISBN
   9781538150856 (cloth) | ISBN 9781538150870 (paper) | ISBN 9781538150863
   (ebook)
Subjects: LCSH: Schools of economics. | Economics—Sociological aspects |
   Economics—Moral and ethical aspects. | Economics—Study and teaching.
Classification: LCC HB75 .C849 2021 (print) | LCC HB75 (ebook) | DDC
   330.09—dc23/eng/20211005
LC record available at https://lccn.loc.gov/2021035473
LC ebook record available at https://lccn.loc.gov/2021035474

# Contents

# List of Figures and Tables

## FIGURE

## TABLES

# Introduction

Paul Dragos Aligica, Ginny Seung Choi,
and Virgil Henry Storr

The interdisciplinary chapters in this edited volume explore how the paradigm defined by the Austrian, Virginia, and Bloomington Schools of Political Economy, collectively the mainline political economy tradition, can help us to understand human action in a variety of social contexts while still seriously accounting for culture, sociality, and morality. Here, we provide a summary of each of the following chapters, each of which constitutes original research and novel efforts to apply insights from mainline political economy to a range of social problems. Each chapter applies, explores, or extends the mainline political economy approach to culture, sociality, and morality. In a sense, there are three parts to this volume. The first part of the volume presents critical assessment of the research on social processes in mainline political economy and attempts to reconcile tensions surrounding the mainline political economy approach and fact/data. The following part constitutes novel and interesting applications of the mainline political economy approach to culture, sociality, and morality to the indigenous people of the Pacific Northwest Coast in North America, hashtags, robots in Japan, museum narratives in Taiwan and the People's Republic of China (henceforth China), and politics in Austria. The chapters in the final part of this volume take inspirations from the underlying theme of this volume to guide their discussions on emergent (dis)orders, corruption, and the Reproductive Justice Framework. Together these chapters demonstrate the continuing relevance of the insights from mainline political economy to our understanding of human action embedded within cultural, social, moral, and historical processes.

The first chapter offers an overview of the approach to understanding culture, sociality, and morality pursued by mainline political economists. Arguably, the concept of culture has an ambiguous place in the classical liberal tradition. On the one hand, critics of liberalism contend that the extended order of a free society is destructive of culture. On the other hand, proponents of liberalism like F. A. Hayek maintain that a robust culture is necessary for the sustenance of a free society. In chapter 2, Lewis Hoss demonstrates that Hayek and the classical liberal tradition he represents embrace a nuanced understanding of culture as the nebulous middle ground that lies in between human nature and human reason. He argues that this approach to understanding social order is not unique to Hayek, but has deep roots reaching back through the history of western thought to classical political philosophy. Those who adopt this approach, Hoss explains, resist the urge to collapse disparate social phenomena into a monolithic conception of "culture," but instead try to treat each of those phenomena as individually important aspects of social order in their own right.

In chapter 3, James Goodrich examines the question of who owns our personal digital data using Israel Kirzner's neo-Lockean theory of private property rights and the finder-keepers ethics. He argues that while Kirzner's theory of private property may imply that large tech companies are entitled to profit from using personal digital data, the wider finders-keepers ethics does not so clearly give large tech companies the right to exclude others from also using that data. His argument is premised on the idea that personal digital data together constitutes a kind of common-pool resource over which people have rights to access. These rights to access must be, in turn, conditioned upon and constrained by the conventions we adopt to promote certain goals. According to finder-keepers ethics, the promotion and enabling of entrepreneurship constitutes one such goal. Therefore, conventional rights to access the common-pool resource of personal digital data must be conditioned upon and constrained by, among other things, the promotion and enabling of entrepreneurship.

Scholars of the mainline political economy tradition, including F. A. Hayek, James Buchanan, and Elinor and Vincent Ostrom, have long acknowledged multiple types of fact and knowledge: brute fact, historical fact, institutional fact, natural fact, scientific fact, and social fact. In his discussions of artisanship, Vincent Ostrom hinted at a seventh type of fact: aesthetic fact. In chapter 4, Jaime L. Carini argues that the ongoing conversation on artisanship and fact between the Bloomington and Virginia Schools of Political Economy benefits from Austrian insights on knowledge. In doing so, she urges us to develop a science of culture in the Ostromian framework, especially if it is to continue analyzing complex problems that concern human society.

Chapter 5 couples insights from Austrian economics with qualitative examples from the field of cultural anthropology. More specifically, Rosaleen McAfee elucidates the Austrian School's reframing of *property rights, wealth, production, and the market* using three Indigenous groups from the nineteenth- and early twentieth-century Pacific Northwest Coast of North America: the Tlingit, the Tsimshian, and the Nuu-chah-nulth. In this chapter, she provides specific examples of precolonial-contact economic and cultural systems along the Northwest Coast, such as salmon ranching and the potlatch, as well as postcolonial-contact engagement with the market economy, such as Tlingit women's entrepreneurial engagement with the tourism industry through the production and sale of handwoven basketry items. Insights on culture and economic activity in Austrian economics enhance her critique of early economists' and social theorists' misunderstanding of Indigenous social, political, and economic systems. In doing so, McAfee joins the Austrian economists in advocating for the further application of cultural studies within economic analysis.

Chapter 6 links insights on culture, human action, and social entrepreneurship to the new digital age. Ololade Afolabi explores the advancement of digital feminism as an affordance of the online space to allow women to converge across transnational borders and discuss similar issues that threaten their rights and existence. She focuses on how digital feminists can work across borders to dehegemonize social movements that have emanated from the West and allow women in disparate communities to localize the movement to produce maximum social change. While the internet has made the world seem a bit smaller ("global village"), globality cannot substitute the indigenous ways of life that help communication processes to be more effective. Afolabi thus warns that tensions and challenges will emerge in our new "global village" if local cultures are not given space within this new platform.

States facing a shortage of workers may facilitate the use of foreign labor (via liberalizing trade and immigration) or promote the use of labor-replacing machinery. Deciding on how to fill jobs is often not a straightforward economic calculus whereby marginal costs solely determine outcome. Cultural influences and historical legacies shape the concerns of the people, affect how they perceive their available remedies, and therefore could play important roles in determining the agenda and nature of the national discourse.

In chapter 7, Nicole Wu draws on Japan to demonstrate that popular and elite reluctance to accept immigrants may in turn motivate governments to promote workplace automation. She demonstrates that automation is a path of lesser resistance given Japan's positive attitude toward technology and its long history of restrictive immigration controls. An aggressive push toward automation helps the government to delay thorny public discussions about reforming the country's conservative immigration system. While close-mindedness about outsiders and perhaps prejudice might stifle discussions around open immigration, it could have the unintended effect of incentivizing private innovation and faster technological adoption.

Lee Moore, in chapter 8, bridges political systems and museum narratives. Utilizing James Buchanan's framework of the moral community and moral order and museums in China and Taiwan, he shows that different political systems can produce starkly district narratives in museums about ethnic minorities. In China, the Kashgar Urban Planning Exhibition Hall, a museum situated in a region mostly occupied by Turkic-speaking Uighurs (not by the ethnic majority Han Chinese), narrates regional history without discussing Uighurs. The history of Kashgar becomes an ethnic Han Chinese space, with Kashgar's majority-Uighur population eliding out of their own narrative. Moore argues that this narrative contributes to China's attempt to construct a Buchananian moral community, where moral subjectivity is only granted to those within the in-group. In Taiwan, the Ketagalan Cultural Center offers multiple narratives of what the nation is and where the Ketagalans, a Taiwanese aboriginal people, fit within that nation. Moore explains that the narrative demonstrates a Buchananian moral order, where allegiance to the state/law is important, not membership to an in-group. This chapter sheds light on how the museum can be a space that reproduces important elements of the state's ideology and understanding of what it means to be a part of the nation.

For chapter 9, we turn to politics in the country Austria. The rise of the far right in Austria during the 1990s is often described as the Haider phenomenon, named after the leader of the Austrian Freedom Party, Jörg Haider. Simultaneously, Austria experienced fundamental economic transformations with the decline of Austro-Keynesianism and the rise of neoliberalism. Valentina Ausserladscheider suggests that Haider's success as a political entrepreneur and the rise of Austrian neoliberalism are deeply intertwined phenomena. Haider's winning formula was based on a policy mix of authoritarian and culturally exclusive ideas and neoliberal policies, which was particularly successful during a time of economic turmoil and uncertainty. Using a descriptive analysis of Haider's political discourse, Ausserladscheider addresses how and when particular cultural and economic ideas of far-right parties become successful. In doing so, she illustrates the importance of the ideational and institutional context for far-right political entrepreneurship and the usefulness of the concept of political entrepreneurship in understanding ideational change.

In chapter 10, Brandon Hunter-Pazzara critiques F. A. Hayek's notion of emergent order and his theory of law by drawing attention to the problem of crime. Hunter-Pazzara argues that crime reflects society's inherent fractiousness, which raises an important tension within Hayek's notion of law as the equal and universal application of legal rules. For Hayek, uniform rules of just conduct are essential for ensuring each individual can effectively pursue their ends and is thus a prerequisite both for liberty and difference. In complex, pluralistic societies, however, law's capacity to be read as uniform is impossible, while the instantiation of a uniform set of rules carries the potential of undermining the possibility of difference. He turns to Émile Durkheim to resolve this tension and advances a notion of individuality grounded both in a sense of consciousness and conscientiousness toward others. As Hunter-Pazzara explains, Durkheim shares Hayek's liberal spirit but departs from Hayek, conceiving law as a pluralistic site of conflict between distinct moral communities. Durkheim believes law must not be uniform but relational and restorative. Hunter-Pazzara shows that these guiding values can help to orient social scientific investigations of law, thereby charting a way toward normative, yet open-ended, social inquiry. Hunter-Pazzara grounds his argument using ethnographic material he collected in Playa del Carmen, Mexico.

Mario I. Juarez-Garcia in chapter 11 argues that it is necessary to have a pluralistic approach to corruption and that understanding the problem of corruption can be aided by insights from the mainline approach to morality, sociality, and culture. Some scholars and experts in anti-corruption typically employ a principal-agent framework to frame and propose solutions to corruption in developing countries. Others have interpreted corruption as a collective action problem. Despite obvious differences between the two frameworks, both share one key assumption: laws must be enforced. Juarez-Garcia argues that, for some communities, the key to eradicating corruption may actually be the community to *not* enforce certain laws. Drawing from mainline political economy economists, he presents a Hayekian approach to corruption, which emphasizes what people do over what the law says: it focuses on the cultural practices. Ultimately, Juarez-Garcia concludes that there is no blueprint for the complex terrain of corruption: sometimes, corruption may be a moral problem of public officials; other times, it may a social problem resulting from undesirable norms; and, still more, it can also be a cultural response to inadequate laws.

The final chapter, written by Samantha Godwin, pushes even further the frontiers of the perspective and approach advocated by the volume and engages in a reassessment of the Reproductive Justice Framework through the lens of Hayekian social justice. She argues that the reproductive justice movement's case is initially compelling: the pro-choice movement's focus on legal abortion rights is divisive and primarily benefits wealthy women, while impoverished women lack real choices regarding the right to have or not have children, and to parent those children. With a focus on the ends of healthy and sustainable communities through positive rights rather than the limited means of negative rights against government interference, the message of reproductive justice is, at first glance, both more inclusive and more politically palatable. On closer examination, however, the shift in register in the pro-choice movement toward the Reproductive Justice Framework has implications quite opposed to those intended by its advocates. Applying Hohfeld's jural relations theory in concert with F. A. Hayek's analysis of social justice rhetoric, Godwin argues that the Reproductive Justice Framework's strategy of focusing on uncontroversial ends and not controversial means risks losing the possibility of a morally principled case. The Reproductive Justice insistence on placing the bodily integrity based right to terminate or prevent a pregnancy on a par with the right to the legal and financial resources to parent according to one's preferences further undermines the pro-choice movement by offering superficially progressive grounds for endorsing patriarchal norms.

In conjunction, the contributions to the volume offer a sample of the range, the depth, and the versatility of the mainline political economy framework for the study of culture, sociality, and morality. These contributions benefit the convergence of conceptual tools and insights derived from the Austrian, Bloomington, and Virginia Schools. At the same time, these insights and tools are employed to address a wide range of cultural phenomena, social processes, and normative dilemmas and to respond to problems and challenges that go in many ways beyond the themes, cases, and problems addressed traditionally by mainline political economy. As such, the volume may be seen as a tangible display of the promise and potential of the framework as well as an invitation to the readers to join the exploratory investigations taking place at the frontier of this research program.

## Chapter 1

# A Framework for Understanding Culture, Sociality, and Morality in Mainline Political Economy

Ginny Seung Choi, Paul Dragos Aligica,
and Virgil Henry Storr

In one sense, neoclassical economics operates on a peculiar understanding of individuals and the environments in which economic actions take place. For instance, economic agents are often assumed to have a perfect memory of all decisions that have been made and an accurate understanding of the underlying incentives, the economic situations they are operating in, and their expected net profits for each possible outcome. They are often assumed to occupy something of an institutional desert. They are also often assumed to be rational and to almost never miscalculate or make mistakes. And, to the extent that they do make a mistake or miscalculation, it is frequently assumed that the quantity of information to which they had access was somehow inadequate or the quality of the information shared with individuals was somehow inferior. Of course, these assumptions are sometimes relaxed, but much of the hyper-rational, omniscient agent typically remains. It is then perhaps unsurprising that economists have tended to view culture, at best, as a coordination device for individuals by aligning their beliefs or as a filter that predicts the success of particular institutions and groups in specific economic environments and, at worst, as a hindrance to achieving optimal economic outcomes. While there may be perceived benefits to sterilizing economic agents and environments in this manner for theory building, doing so has limited our understanding of the richness and vibrancy of people as well as the environments in which they reside and navigate.

Scholars in the Austrian, Bloomington, and Virginia Schools of Political Economy, including F. A. Hayek, Elinor and Vincent Ostrom, and James Buchanan, point to the importance of looking at context for understanding economic, political, and social phenomena. These traditions do not conceive of individuals as isolated figures without any social relationships who are believed to occupy an institution-less environment (i.e., an under-socialized view of individuals). Nor do they believe that individuals' social circumstances completely and automatically determine their actions and outcomes without any role for individual choice (i.e., an over-socialized view of individuals). Indeed, these approaches do not model human beings as social atoms or social robots. Instead, they appreciate that human action is simultaneously embedded in the economy, the polity, and the society and is shaped by the environments in which actors are rooted. For instance, culture acts as the lens through which people interpret their world that renders purposeful actions intelligible; social relations influence and guide human choices; and morality differentiates good behavior from bad behavior. Without looking to culture, sociality, and morality, then, it is almost impossible to fully understand how people are able to make sense of past events/actions, anticipate future circumstances, and formulate plans. Human action, these scholars believe, is embedded within and inseparable from cultural, social, moral, and historical processes.

The Austrian, Bloomington, and Virginia Schools (collectively understood as the mainline political economy) have offered critical insights into the embeddedness of human action and its implications. For instance, in the Austrian School, F. A. Hayek (1967, 1973) believed that the growth of civilization depended on what he called a cultural evolution; social cooperation depends on the evolution of rules of just conduct. Similarly, Don Lavoie (1986; [1991] 2015) argued that economic and political processes necessarily take place within a context of shared meanings and values. As such, economic processes like entrepreneurship were really the achievement of culturally embedded actors who picked up on the gist of ongoing conversations in the market. Likewise, Emily Chamlee-Wright (2010) highlighted the importance of social ties in helping individuals to overcome collective-action problems. She also stressed the heterogenous nature of the social capital structure (Chamlee-Wright 2008), which means that different configurations of that structure will be more or less useful for different functions. In addition, Hayek (1977), Israel Kirzner (1989), Peter J. Boettke (2004), and more recently Virgil Henry Storr and Ginny Seung Choi (2019) have utilized an Austrian perspective to explore the relationship between markets and morality. Building on the work of Adam Smith and Max Weber, often quite explicitly, thinkers within the Austrian School have imagined individuals as culturally situated actors, with meaningful social ties, guided by their values (see Storr 2008, 2013; Choi and Storr 2018, 2020).

Other scholars in the mainline political economy tradition have highlighted the challenges of collective decision making and social coordination as well as the limits of government and the potential of bottom-up solutions to social dilemmas. In their research, for instance, Elinor and Vincent Ostrom explored the extraordinary capacities of citizens to come up with rules on how to cooperate and associate with one another in a world rife with conflict and their ability to engage in self-governance (see E. Ostrom 1990; V. Ostrom 1991). Similarly, building on the Ostroms' work, Paul Dragos Aligica (2019) emphasized the valuable role that heterogeneity (of citizen's capabilities, preferences, beliefs, and information) plays in a society of self-governing and free individuals. Although best known for his work in constitutional political economy, James M. Buchanan ([1981] 2001) also spoke about how any society may be described as a mix of moral community, moral order, and moral anarchy. This mix, he contended, would directly determine the level of orderliness and the degree of governmental coercion observed in a society. Likewise, he stressed that liberty and responsibility lay at the core of the human development (Buchanan [1975] 2000). Stripping people of free choice and responsibility destined them to live out programmed existences predetermined by their genetic codes, their natural impulses, and historical processes; people, Buchanan stated, want to have the liberty to become the people they wish to be. Culture, sociality, and morality shape but do not determine the way individuals are governed and govern themselves.

This chapter overviews key contributions by scholars within the mainline political economy tradition to three vital areas: culture and economy, collective action, and the social and moral aspects of economic life. Unlike neoclassical economics, the mainline tradition does not view culture, sociality, and morality to be binding constraints for human behavior that limit individuals and societies from realizing great(er) achievements. Instead, this tradition appreciates them to be not only integral but also adding richness to our understanding of human behavior.

## ON CULTURE AND ECONOMICS

Austrian economists have long understood economics as a science of meaning. It is critical, they argued, to take the meanings people attach to their actions and their circumstances in order to fully appreciate individual action and behavior. For instance, Ludwig von Mises, one of the central figures in Austrian economics, believed that "the task of sciences of human action is the comprehension of the *meaning and relevance of human action*" (Mises [1949] 1963, 51; emphasis added). He explained that "[w]e cannot approach our subject if we disregard the meaning which acting man attaches to the situation, i.e., the given state of affairs, and to his behavior with regard to this situation" (ibid., 26). In other words, Mises simply thought that social scientists could not claim to study human behavior and action if they did not recognize the meanings actors attached to situations into their analyses.

F. A. Hayek, another key figure in Austrian economics, similarly high-lighted the importance of how people perceive and interpret their objective worlds in understanding human behavior. In *The Counter-Revolution of Science*, for instance, Hayek (1952) noted that there was a tendency for social scientists to impose behavioral assumptions onto their subjects and to assume that their subjects will perceive, interpret, react, and navigate through their worlds in the precisely identical manner as they (the social scientists) would and do. On the contrary, explained Hayek, people in real life react quite differently to the same external stimuli because these stimuli carry different meanings for them. Should knowledge and beliefs of different people have been identical, it would not have mattered whether a property (or character or fact) of a phenomenon was described as objective or subjective. But, so long as such knowledge is not identical across people, social scientists cannot sever their analysis of human behavior from the meanings people attach to their actions. In addition, he cautioned that social scientists cannot simply focus on the objective facts of social phenomena and must also be concerned with the subjective character of social phenomena because they study human beings. "So far as human actions are concerned[,] the things are what the acting people think they are" (ibid., 27), and, so, "[i]t would be impossible to explain or understand human action without making use of this knowledge" (ibid., 26). "Unless we can understand what the acting people mean by their actions," Hayek warned, "any attempt to explain them . . . are bound to fail" (ibid., 31).[1] While the early key thinkers in the Austrian tradition did not explicitly study the relationship between culture and economic action, their works suggest that they would have been deeply alarmed by the neoclassical economists' dismissal of culture (understood as shared meanings) from the economic analysis of human behavior.[2]

Don Lavoie, like Hayek, believed that the primary task of social scientists was to learn about how people interpreted their worlds—to decipher "*already interpreted* meanings" behind human action (Lavoie [1985] 2011, 106; emphasis in the original)—without imposing or presuming particular intentions onto the acting agents. To Lavoie, culture was "the level of meaning underneath social action" (Lavoie and Chamlee-Wright 2000, 23), "the language in which past events are interpreted, future circumstances are anticipated, and plans of action are formulated" and what "renders purposeful action intelligible" (Lavoie [1991] 2015, 49). Emily Chamlee-Wright, another influential Austrian thinker in cultural economics, also defined culture in similar terms. "Culture provides the interpretive framework that allows us to understand objects as symbols, actions as part of an overall plan, or interaction as social relationship. The world is never experienced directly. *It must be interpreted through the lens of culture*" (Chamlee-Wright 1997, 24; emphasis added).

Likewise, Virgil Henry Storr portrayed culture as "a lens through which economic actors make sense of the world and their options in it" (Storr 2013, 14). It "colors our decisions regarding which tools (strategies) are available to us and which tools we should utilize as we pursue our goals" (ibid., 55). Viewing culture in this manner—as a "complex of meanings that allows us to comprehend human action" (Lavoie [1991] 2015, 34)—economic action can never be fully comprehended without understanding the cultural context within which they occur.

In his paper, "The Discovery and Interpretation of Profit Opportunities: Culture and the Kirznerian Entrepreneur," Lavoie ([1991] 2015) argued that entrepreneurship necessarily takes place within a cultural context and demonstrated this point through his critique of Kirzner's theory of entrepreneurship. The Kirznerian story about the market being an entrepreneurial process often begins with market ignorance. Unlike their neoclassical counterparts (who, to use game-theoretic jargon, are often assumed to have perfect knowledge and complete information), real market actors are prone to making mistakes. For example, despite their best efforts, they simply may not know that there is another buyer around the corner who is willing to pay more for a good or that there is another vendor around the corner who is willing to sell the good at a cheaper price. Because these sorts of errors occur, there are numerous untapped profit opportunities to buy low and sell high (i.e., unexploited and available price discrepancies) in the market. And market actors who spot or discover these opportunities will take advantage of them. Consequently, by exploiting these opportunities, their entrepreneurial activities will nudge the market toward an equilibrium state. In this story of entrepreneurship, entrepreneurial alertness refers to the market actors' sensitivity toward untapped opportunities and their aptitude to spot them, or "an attitude of receptiveness to available, but hitherto overlooked, opportunities" (Kirzner 1997, 72).

Lavoie found Kirzner's description of alertness to be unsatisfactory. He argued that its description seems to invoke some sense of objectiveness, as if the successful discovery of a profit opportunity was a matter of who took the initiative and of who decided to be alert and act upon the gains that were simply out there to be found. For Lavoie, it seemed to take for granted that (1) any entrepreneur could have instantaneously recognized any and all profit opportunities, no matter who she was, and that (2) these opportunities have always existed right underneath the entrepreneur's nose, as if those who overlooked the opportunities before her just simply failed to see them. "Kirzner's theory . . . seems to treat the entrepreneur's actions as something 'called forth' by prior circumstances" and as "a passive reaction to the equilibrium dictated by the data [or objective facts]" (Lavoie [1991] 2015, 57). To Kirzner, "[a]lertness seems to be some kind of general-purpose attentiveness that is 'switched on or off'" and that being or becoming alert was simply a matter of "opening one's eyes" (ibid., 58). Lavoie explained that "it is misleading to treat [alertness] like an on/off switch or to say there is simply more or less of it" (ibid., 59). He recognized that alertness was context-dependent or, more specifically, culturally dependent and that being alert to certain types of opportunities implied that the entrepreneur cannot be alert to other types. According to Lavoie,

> all the old opportunities will suddenly look different, indeed may no longer be considered opportunities at all, when a new one is found. And of course the circumstances one has been alert to in the past help determine the kinds of situations one will be apt to notice in the future. That is, profit opportunities are not independent atoms but connected parts of a whole perspective on the world. And the perspective is in turn an evolving part of a continuing cultural tradition, constantly being reappropriated to new situations.[3] ([1991] 2015, 59)

By altering the way we understood alertness, Lavoie thought that it would render the process by which entrepreneurs perceive opportunities change more coherent:

> Entrepreneurship is not only a matter of opening one's eyes, of switching on one's attentiveness; it requires directing one's gaze. When an entrepreneur sees things others have overlooked, it is not just that he opened his eyes when they had theirs closed. He is reading selected aspects of a complex situation others have not read. And this raises the question of what gives a predirectedness to the entrepreneur's vision, of why he is apt to read some things and not others. I submit that the answer to this question is culture.[4] ([1991] 2015, 59)

Like Lavoie, Emily Chamlee-Wright believed that culture should not and could not be divorced from economic action. *The Cultural Foundations of Economic Development*, her investigation into the female entrepreneurship in Ghana, revealed how "indigenous cultural norms and institutions within the Ghanaian context may provide the foundation for an emerging entrepreneurial class" and how "female entrepreneurs do possess the potential to advance market-led development" (Chamlee-Wright 1997, 102). Here, Chamlee-Wright demonstrated how (1) the capitalist ethic and entrepreneurial mindset in urban Ghana was in fact an outgrowth of the local culture and (2) interpreting the Ghanaian context through a Western European lens could have missed or misunderstood the significance of female entrepreneurship and the role it played (and could play) in Ghanaian economic development. For instance, she detailed how Ghana holds (or at least held at the time of her study) distinctively different views about gender roles and relations than the West. In particular, she described how West Africans have traditionally viewed marriages to be akin to economic partnerships. According to these traditional notions, for instance, women were expected to grow vegetables on their gardens or farms and to cover the majority of the day-to-day household expenses, while men were expected to provide proteins (e.g., meat and fish) and to contribute to large household expenses. Chamlee-Wright remarked how these expectations and historical practices seemed to have shaped the types of economic activities in which people engaged along gender lines as Ghana grew urbanized: men tended to engage in more socially distant activities (e.g., international trade), while women tended to engage in activities in closer social proximity (e.g., local food markets). Furthermore, due to the general unreliableness of their husbands' contributions to household expenses, Chamlee-Wright noted how wives in Ghana seemed to consider their engagement in entrepreneurial activity (or securement of independent incomes) to be an essential part of their duty as primary providers for their children and their households. Due to these cultural forces (among others), it was not surprising to see urban Ghanaian markets (at least during this study) often dominated by female entrepreneurs. Chamlee-Wright concluded that a "cultural analysis can help us identify indigenous sources of wealth and development potential within an emerging economy" (ibid., 131). Incorporating culture in economic analysis can help us appreciate that economic development is not synonymous with a society or country becoming more Westernized, but that economic development is about harnessing key local cultural resources for economic prosperity.

Similarly, Virgil Henry Storr argued that culture can and does shape the types of attitudes and behaviors that emerge in markets. In *Understanding of the Culture of Markets* (2013), he criticized previous economic studies that tended to regard culture as a tool or a resource from which members of a society derived comparative advantages over members of other societies. Viewing culture in such light suggested that there were "right" and "wrong" cultures for economic success, or that a society required a precise set of configurations and combinations of cultural capital to achieve economic success. It is clearly misleading, claimed Storr, to think of culture as a tool, capital, or resource. He rationalized that culture was not a set of tools that a group of individuals had at their disposal. A person, he said, cannot deliberately decide to employ or pick a particular part of their culture at certain times and disengage it for others as one might choose a hammer from a tool kit. Rather, he conceived of culture as the framework through which people decide whether a given item is a tool and as the lens though which they read and make sense of the world in which they reside. Storr explained how culture can, at least partly, determine "who can buy and sell, when a deal between them is properly consummated, which items buyers and sellers can trade, and what counts as an acceptable unit of exchange" and "why entrepreneurs notice some opportunities and not others as well as why they chose to peruse certain paths to exploit the opportunities that they notice and not others" (ibid., 31). People inherit and form their beliefs and attitudes within the culture to which they were born (or to which they become enculturated). In turn, these beliefs and attitudes mold people's economic decisions and bias the way they understand the world, the way in which they communicate and act, and the opportunities they pursue. In this manner, for Storr, the market is necessarily overlaid with meaning, and understanding economic life in a particular context requires undertaking a cultural analysis.

Storr recommended that we adopt a Weberian approach to economic analysis, a qualitative approach to economic analysis that operationalized culture as a lens. Max Weber [1905] 2011 theorized that capitalism can take on a variety of forms and that each form or flavor of capitalism can be characterized by a particular set of attitudes and behaviors shared by the people who populate the economic space, which he called economic spirits. Storr (2004, 2013) extended Weber's approach to permit the coexistence of more than one economic spirit within an economy and for these multiple economic spirits to simultaneously shape economic actions and practices. Using the Bahamas as an example, Storr in *Understanding Culture of Markets* (2013) and *Enterprising Slaves and Master Pirates* (2004) showed how two economic spirits could explain and reconcile seemingly contradictory economic behaviors exhibited in the Bahamas: the spirit of Rabbyism (the belief that promoted cunning and deception over enterprise as strategies for economic success) and the spirit of Junkanoo (the view that celebrated hard work ethic, creativity, cooperation, endurance, and productivity). Storr argued that explaining economic life in the Bahamas with just one of these two economic spirits—or none, for that matter—would have been, at best, incomplete and, at worst, false and misleading. Similarly, John and Storr (2018) pointed to the possibility of a differential effect of a cultural environment on the identification or exploitation of profit opportunities, two distinct moments of entrepreneurship. Using Trinidad and Tobago as a case study, they demonstrated how a particular cultural and institutional environment of a particular place (and time) could encourage opportunity identification but discourage opportunity exploitation, and vice versa. Without understanding and accounting for these nuances, an analysis of entrepreneurship in Trinidad and Tobago would also be deficient, imprecise, and inaccurate.

The Austrian tradition understands economics as a science of meaning, not a predictive science. Like Storr wrote, "[t]he opinions and beliefs that guide the actions of individual under study cannot be ignored, even if those beliefs are wrong, or irrational, or based on superstition rather than reason" (2013,

25). Culture is the lens through which we understand and navigate our worlds and make sense of other people's actions. It can explain, for instance, why entrepreneurs notice and pursue some profit opportunities and the manner in which they exploit those opportunities.[5] It can also explain why prices of certain goods are high while others are not. As this section (hopefully) established, for mainline political economists, culture shapes our economic action and, therefore, markets and the entrepreneurial activities that take place within markets are necessarily cultural phenomena. So long as economics is a study of human behavior and actions, culture cannot be excluded from its analyses.

## ON COLLECTIVE ACTION

The academic conversation surrounding collective action arguably began with Alexis de Tocqueville. In *Democracy in America*, Tocqueville ([1835; 1840] 2010) endeavored to describe and analyze the democratic system of government. Furthermore, he hoped to convey what people may reasonably hope to expect or fear from the then-new form of government. In his second volume, he spoke about voluntary associations in the context of his discussion about the sustainability of the democratic form of government. Tocqueville clearly admired the American people's independent and proactive natures and their drive to pursue individual goals, dreams, and interests. However, he thought that individual pursuits came at the expense of people's concerns for their fellow citizens' well-being and the public life they shared. Thus, he worried that people in democracies would grow apathetic toward one another over time and become strangers to one another.

> As conditions become equal [in democratic societies], a greater number of individuals will be found who, no longer rich enough or powerful enough to exercise great influence over the fate of their fellows, have nonetheless acquired or preserved enough enlightenment and wealth to be able to be sufficient for themselves [i.e., isolate themselves from the majority of others in society]. (Tocqueville [1840] 2010, 884)

The true danger of this isolation, Tocqueville noted, was that it would ultimately lead to the people's submission to a despotic central government: a government that would have reduced a nation to "being nothing more than a flock of timid and industrious animals" with itself positioned as "the shepherd" (ibid., 1252).

Tocqueville believed voluntary associations can act as a defense against the despotism of democratic governments. He was deeply impressed by

American people's unique aptitude for organizing voluntary associations (ibid., 896) and by the extraordinary capacity they gave citizens to solve problems that they individually could not. He described how "all citizens are independent and weak; they can hardly do anything by themselves, and no one among them can compel his fellows to lend him their help. So they all fall into impotence if they do not learn to help each other freely" (ibid., 898). Yet, Tocqueville marveled, American people were accomplishing common goals and objectives, all because of their ability and propensity to form organizations.[6] "[T]he most democratic country on earth is, out of all, the one where men today have most perfected the art of pursuing in common the object of their common desires and have applied this new science to the greatest number of things" (ibid., 897). For Tocqueville, permitting and fostering the flourishing of voluntary associations within a democratic society would prevent it from falling prey to a despotic central government.

Tocqueville admitted that voluntary associations can be messy (as banded citizens fumble and grapple for the right solution or path to achieving a common objective) and can result in occasional failure. Understandably, a government would be greatly tempted to do away with voluntary associations and to supply a community's public needs and/or to attain their common objectives on its own. Tocqueville, however, was highly skeptical that there was a "political power [that] could ever substitute for the countless small enterprise which American citizens carry out daily with the help of associations" (ibid., 900). More critically, even if such a political entity existed, citizens could grow increasingly reliant on governments to provide their needs and grow less apt to solving problems, should governments replace voluntary associations. "The more [the government] puts itself in the place of associations, the more individuals, losing the idea of associating, will need it to come to their aid" (ibid., 900).

Furthermore, Tocqueville explained how voluntary associations can have civilizing effects on the citizens who actively participate in them. "The morals and intelligence of a democratic people," he wrote, "would run no lesser dangers than their trade and industry, if the government came to take the place of associations everywhere. Sentiments and ideas are renewed, the heart grows larger and the human mind develops only by the reciprocal action of men on each other" (ibid., 900). In short, in Tocquevillian thought, voluntary associations serve crucial roles in democratic societies. Of course, they serve as useful vehicles for citizens to effectively solve their own collective-action problems. But, more crucially, voluntary associations serve as spaces where people socially interact with one another and learn to cooperate and connect with one another; they keep people from growing apathetic toward one another and teach them to become better human beings. In this way, voluntary associations play an essential role in the defense against soft despotism and general democratic decay.

If Tocqueville's insights into democracies put emphasis on the power of communities (and the inadequacy of external authorities) to overcome collective-action problems, the models that came to dominate the literature on collective action in the 1960s and 1970s—the tragedy of the commons, the prisoner's dilemma, and even Olson's (1965) logic of collective action—highlighted the exact opposite. They saw situations of social dilemma as problems pertaining to the tension between individual and group incentives and the need to prevent individuals from benefiting from the contributions of others without themselves contributing (i.e., free-riding problems). These models concluded that the *only* way to overcome such problems was through an external authority. And, if one authority represented the correct solution, the other cannot ever be one too. These models, as well as many other scholars and policymakers, seemed to operate on little faith in the people's ability to get themselves out of social dilemmas.

In a sense, one could interpret the life research of Elinor Ostrom, one of the architects of the Bloomington School of Institutional Analysis and Development, as a fierce rejection of the helplessness of people to solve their own problems.[7] In *Governing the Commons*, Ostrom empirically explored "how a group of principals who are in an interdependent situation can organize and govern themselves to obtain continuing joint benefits when all face temptations to free-ride, shirk, or otherwise act opportunistically" (E. Ostrom 1990, 29). Here, she demonstrated that the success of adopted solutions (or successful outcomes of institutional arrangements) depended on their compatibility with the local communities (including their culture and social institutions) and the specifics of the common-pool resource (CPR) problem.[8, 9] "'[G]etting the institutions right' is a difficult, time-consuming, conflict-invoking process . . . that requires reliable information about time and place variables as well as a broad repertoire of culturally accepted rules" (ibid., 14).

Ostrom offered eight essential elements (to which she referred as design principles) for how to sustainably and equitably govern CPRs within a community. She summarized her first five design principles as follows:

> When CPR appropriators design their own operational rules (design principle 3) to be enforced by individuals who are local appropriators or are accountable to them (design principle 4), using graduated sanctions (design principle 5) that define who has rights to withdraw units from the CPR (design principle 1) and that effectively restrict appropriation activities, given local conditions (design principle 2), the commitment and monitoring problem are solved in an interrelated manner. (E. Ostrom 1990, 99)

In other words, in order for the institutions governing the commons to be effective, (1) the actual users of CPR (who were also members of the local community) should be permitted to actively participate in the designing of rules and strategies for operation, monitoring, enforcement, and punishment, and (2) the rules that constitute an institutional arrangement should be compatible with, if not embedded within, the underlying local conditions. Moreover, the conflict resolution mechanisms (design principle 6) adopted across communities revealed how they too should be culturally or locally dependent and can often be quite informal. Her empirical studies exemplified how communities often simply adopted an existing social institution for conflict resolution in CPR problems. For instance, local leaders in some communities already functioned as resolvers of social conflict (e.g., between neighbors) and so functioned as resolvers of conflict in CPR usage and maintenance.

A popular interpretation of results in the literature on social dilemmas (at least among experimental economists) is that group homogeneity tends to mitigate social dilemma problems and that group heterogeneity tends to exacerbate social dilemma problems (see Seabright 1993; Oliveira, Croson, and Eckel 2015; Gangadharan, Nikiforakis, and Villeval 2017; Cox et al. 2020; Klingeren 2020). Yet, Ostrom, along with Vincent Ostrom, foregrounded how it was precisely the heterogeneity and diversity that amplified a community's chances of successful collective action.[10] As Paul Dragos Aligica explained,

> the diversity of perspectives and strategies offers a diversity of ways to imagine solutions and arrangements. Social actors will try different approaches; they will combine and recombine in different configurations and arrangements. It is not just a matter of statistical probabilities. This diversity sets into motion social discovery that increases the changes that poor local optima are identified and replaced with better alternatives. A society, hence, moves via collective process towards better alternatives. (Aligica 2014, 27)

He also added how,

> [t]he mere diversity of situations is enough to create a wide variety of possible [institutional] arrangements [i.e., clusters of rules and human interactions]. If we add to all that the variety of individuals' possible preferences, beliefs, interpretations, and strategies, all leading to possible new rules and situations, we start to grasp the huge range of potential combinations in their evolving dynamism. (Aligica 2014, 1)

For the Ostroms, "diversity, pluralism, [and] heterogeneity are 'social facts,' an inescapable condition of the social world" (ibid., 1), that shape and determine the form of governance a community ultimately implements.

The Ostroms viewed their work to be directly contributing to the Tocquevillian project of examining how citizens in a self-governing, democratic society would have to behave in order to constitute a self-governing, democratic society; they called this the art and science of associations (V. Ostrom 1994, 211). They linked the concept of self-governance and democracy to the concept of polycentrism that presumed general conditions of constitutional liberty (i.e., the liberty to form associations to achieve collective aims). They considered polycentricity as "a nonhierarchical, institutional, and cultural framework that makes possible the coexistence of multiple centers of decision making with different objectives and values, and that sets up the stage for an evolutionary competition between the complementary ideas and methods of those different decision centers" (Aligica and Tarko 2012, 251). While the precise configuration of relationships would depend on details of the local context, the Ostroms believed that governmental units, public agencies, and private businesses can work together to achieve collective goals in a public economy. Such interorganizational arrangements "would manifest market-like characteristics and display both efficiency-inducing and error-correcting behavior. . . . [T]he structure of interorganizational arrangements may create important economic opportunities and evoke self-regulating tendencies" (Ostrom and Ostrom 1965 quoted in Aligica and Tarko 2012, 241). Among other strengths over monocentric systems, they reasoned that a political system with multiple centers of power offers more opportunities for its officials and citizens to innovate and to correct any misallocation of authority and outcomes. "Thus, polycentric systems are more likely than monocentric systems to provide incentives leading to self-organized, self-corrective institutional change" (E. Ostrom 1998 quoted in Aligica and Tarko 2012, 246).

Our discussion of polycentricity above, despite its (incredible) brevity, suggests a sense of dynamism, entrepreneurial spirit, and civically motivated individuals in the Ostroms' work. Indeed, for them, it is the public entrepreneurs, who work closely with citizens, who frequently find innovative and effective ways to provide and maintain essential goods and services to their communities. In *Public Entrepreneurship, Citizenship, and Self-Governance* (2019, 23), Paul Drago Aligica defined public entrepreneurship as "a particular form of leadership [i.e., a group of highly interested and/or highly resourceful individuals who serve essential functions in critical phases of collective action] focused primarily on problem-solving and putting heterogeneous processes together in complementary and effective ways." Public entrepreneurs diverge from market entrepreneurs in that they (1) handle public and commons goods (i.e., goods that can only be acquired when enough people contribute to their acquisition); (2) are granted fundamentally different powers and tools to develop, control, and allocate resources (e.g., powers

of taxation and eminent domain); and (3) operate in fundamentally different conditions (e.g., relative openness to entry and exit across domains and
jurisdictions, room for rivalry, contestation, and voice). But, like market entrepreneurs, public entrepreneurs are the drivers of change and innovation in
a public economy. In junction, citizens are those social actors—the "bearer[s]
of social and political capabilities for collective choice and collective action"
(ibid., 13–14) and "of culture, social norms, and ideology, acting as agents
who operate with rules, values, and strategies in specific contexts and circumstances" (ibid., 95)—who possess the prerequisite civic competence and
knowledge to successfully execute socially beneficial objectives in a public
goods economy.

For the Ostroms, citizenship was a "coherent nexus of attitudes and beliefs
that are beneficial to the cultivation of society" (ibid., 101–2). "In a sense,
in the Ostroms' view," clarified Aligica (ibid., 1), "public entrepreneurship
is a governance ideal and an important political virtue, a feature of citizenship." Aligica explained that civic competence (or civic culture) is relevant
in the theory of self-governance in two ways: first, as "an ingredient in the
functioning of institutional arrangements—a key component in the cultural
and knowledge process mix that supports the management and dynamic
adjustment of governance systems" and second, as the ability of people to
reflect and mentally process their environments in a particular light (ibid.,
105). In short, the Ostroms saw citizenship, civic competence, and political
knowledge as a part of the social learning and collective knowledge process
of a community. Their "citizen-centered governance theory pivot[ed] on the
interrelationship between the institutions of governance and civic and political competencies (i.e., the skills, values, strategies, knowledge, and beliefs
needed by citizens to operate the institutional and procedural apparatus and
to generate and maintain the social relationships necessary for good governance)" (ibid., 5). To the Ostroms, a successful self-governance system
needed to both guide and nurture the ability for civic-minded individuals to
engage in entrepreneurship in collective-action settings (ibid., 10).

Through their studies on social entrepreneurship in community recovery
after natural disasters, multiple mainline political economists also partici-
pated in the same intellectual dialogue on governance. In *Community Revival in the Wake of Disasters* (2015), Virgil Henry Storr, Stefanie Haeffele,
and Laura Grube argued that post-disaster community recovery is in fact a
collective-action problem. Every person (or family) who has had their homes
destroyed by a natural disaster and was subsequently displaced faces the same
decision: whether to stay in their new community/city and start life anew or
to return and rebuild their old home and community/city. Beyond the anticipated costs associated with each action (e.g., cost associated with rebuilding homes, social networks, etc.), there are risks pertaining to decisions of

others who were similarly displaced and to the total number of people who ultimately decide to return to their old community. If less people than what the returnee expected return to their old community or the returnee is the first one to make such a decision, she incurs a high cost; not only does much of the burden of rebuilding a community/city fall onto her (e.g., restoring power and other utilities to communities), she also will not have the community (in terms of social relationships) to which she had hoped to return. Note that, both in this simplified scenario and in reality, it is *her* perceived costs and benefits that matter; it is the people's beliefs—what people *believe* things to be, not what they *actually are*—that guide their decisions.

Focusing on neighborhoods and communities affected by Hurricanes Katrina (New Orleans, LA, in 2005) and Sandy (New York, NY, and surrounding areas in New Jersey in 2012), Storr, Haeffele, and Grube observed how some communities exhibited robust signs of recovery from the start while others were unable to gain momentum and seemed to be caught in a state of suspended animation. They contended that entrepreneurs (i.e., individuals who recognize and act on opportunities to promote social change) play vital roles in determining the success (i.e., swift and robust recovery) of a post-disaster community recovery. Specifically, they offered that entrepreneurs, including social entrepreneurs, perform at least three functions.

First, entrepreneurs provide needed goods and services; social entrepreneurs are community-minded and community-motivated individuals and thus are likely to successfully acquire/provide the necessary goods and services for community recovery. Second, they help to restore or replace disrupted social networks. In fact, they assist other "community members restore, re-purpose and even replace social networks that were disrupted by the disaster" (ibid., 48). Entrepreneurs can discover and create opportunities for displaced community members to connect and share information with one another. (And, in some cases, they have acted as the essential link between displaced portions of a social network that was tightly connected prior to the disaster.) Moreover, they connect demanders and suppliers of disaster aid as well as disaster victims with the donors and volunteers responding to the disaster. Although some details certainly differ, social entrepreneurs in the social economy are just like the public entrepreneurs in the public economy and the market entrepreneurs in the market economy; they are all drivers of change, innovation, and adaptation.

Third, entrepreneurs signal that community rebound is likely and under way. In a world where people's beliefs guide their decisions, social entrepreneurs can act as focal points or points of orientation around whom other displaced residents can formulate their strategies to return to their old communities and rebuild. Serving as signals that specific communities (of which social entrepreneurs are part) will return and rebuild could not only help overcome the collective action problem of community recovery, but it could also attract other resources as the wider city/community, disaster aid suppliers, donors, and others look for opportunities to best provide assistance.

At this point, it is perhaps useful to briefly highlight the roles that social capital and a community's capacity for self-governance play in post-disaster recovery. There is not a specific definition of social capital that is widely accepted by scholars across disciplines. However, they do generally agree that social capital captures (or at least has something to do with) the resources associated with being a member of a particular network that people could employ in the pursuit of their goals (e.g., particular relationships and friendships, parochial trust, social norms, and shared narratives). Having more or stronger social capital can facilitate community return, such as the Vietnamese American community in New Orleans (Chamlee-Wright and Storr 2009, 2011). In less homogenous communities (i.e., loosely connected, culturally, ethnically, and/or socially heterogeneous), social entrepreneurs who, for instance, know people, how to repurpose and reconfigure existing social capital for new objectives, and how to form associations or community-based organizations become even more critical (Storr and Haeffele-Balch 2012).

However, there is no blueprint for overcoming the collective-action problem that is post-disaster community recovery because a successful strategy will be contingent on the specifics of a community. Like what the Ostroms asserted, there is no one-size-fits-all solution here either. Nor does the mere existence of social entrepreneurs guarantee a successful outcome. For instance, many members of the close-knit Vietnamese American community in New Orleans returned and began the recovery process because Father Vien, the respected leader of his church and a social entrepreneur, visited his parishioners who were evacuated to other cities and was able to convince them to return. Had the community been less close-knit or had Father Vien not held the respect that he did (in other words, if the social capital of the community looked different), his strategy of visiting and convincing each individual likely would not have worked. And, when associations are better capable of socially coordinating with one another, a community is better able to leverage shared histories and perspectives and is more socially stable.

As the research mentioned above demonstrates, the approach associated with mainline political economy engages and employs concepts such as that of social capital in a rather versatile way. The notion of social capital has emerged as an important component of the analytical toolbox of the researchers working at the interface between disciplines as diverse as economics, sociology, or political science. As such, there are multiple ways of developing and applying it, and the literature is rich in illustrations in this respect. Some of them are taking advantage of the formal theoretical apparatus assumed and implied by the notion, while others take advantage of the statistical and quantitative analysis made possible by its operationalization. In addition to the analytical value added by the formal apparatus and to the quantitative research potential, the approach advanced by mainline political economists is also emphasizing the important heuristics capability brought to fore by the notion.

The notion of social capital—and other similar notions—are in this view instruments able to illuminate additional factors and phenomena essential for understanding socioeconomic processes. At the same time, they are helping to organize for analytical purposes those factors and variables using the functionalist logic on which the idea of social capital is built. For instance, focusing on social capital from this perspective helps us to better identify the position and role played by moral factors in social and economic life. In this respect, the approach advanced by mainline political economists employs notions such as that of social capital to open up a fresh perspective on the complex reality in which moral factors intertwine with social factors in defining the complexity of economic life.

## ON THE MORAL AND SOCIAL ASPECTS OF ECONOMIC LIFE

Morality and sociality of human beings play no significant roles in neoclassical economics. The quintessential economic man has no attachments (whether it be to people, places, or objects) and cannot be offended by a betrayal or some other (major or minor) transgression, nor be moved by meaningful gestures. Inherently subjective moral codes, which guide people's actions by delineating what is right and wrong, collapse into a cold, objective sense of logic shared by all individuals that populate any social space. For such individuals, social relationships are transactional or hindrances, at best, and meaningless, at worst. Indeed, it would be peculiar for *homo economicus* to not behave in rational and narrowly self-interested manner.

Adam Smith, the father of economics, however, recognized the possibility of strong, deep, and positive social relationships in commercial life. For instance, Smith recognized that "[a]mong well-disposed people, the necessity or conveniency of mutual accommodation, very frequently produces a friendship not unlike that which takes place among those who are born to live in the same family. Colleagues in office, partners in trade, call one another brothers; and frequently feel towards one another as if they really were so" (Smith [1759] 1982, 223–24). In fact, he further added, colleagues are sort of expected to get along and to have a good relationship: "[I]f they are tolerably reasonable people, they are naturally disposed to agree. We expect that they should do so; and their disagreement is a sort of a small scandal" (ibid., 224). Stated another way, Smith believed that the market could be a social space.

Mark Granovetter, an economic sociologist, seemed to agree with Smith. Granovetter recognized how economic action is often affected by social factors. Consequently, the market (or economic life) cannot survive without the communal realm and must coexist and be understood alongside the community. Given the existence of forces that can poison economic life (such as fraud), it seemed obvious to Granovetter that some minimum level of trust must be operating within the market. Rather than some generalized sense of morality, however, he thought the trust that we observe in markets seemed more to do with "concrete personal relations and structures (or 'networks') of such relations" (Granovetter 1985, 490). "[D]eparting from pure economic motives," he wrote, "continuing economic relations often become overlaid with social content that carries strong expectations of trust and abstention from opportunism" (Granovetter 1985, 490) In short, Granovetter believed that social relations and networks played an indispensable role in generating trust and discouraging misbehavior.

This is the thread of the academic conversation on which Virgil Henry Storr picked up and expanded in "The Market as a Social Space." In economics, Storr (2008) lamented, markets are too often portrayed as sterile spaces devoid of souls, sounds, and life. It is too often assumed that only conversations narrowly pertaining to transactions (e.g., on prices, quality, and quantity of goods being exchanged) take place between market participants. In that framework, it is absurd for market actors to be inquiring about each other's family, discussing contemporary politics, inviting each other to barbeques, and going on picnics or vacations with one another. Yet a look at any workplace can debunk (or at least cast considerable doubt on) that view of markets. Colleagues often confide in one another about personal issues, go to happy hour, and have meals with one another. They form a comradery around their shared and common experiences in their workplaces. Their children and spouses sometimes become friends with each other and give each other gifts on special occasions. Some people who meet as a result of the market form deep friendships, sometimes not unlike brother- or sister-like relations and sometimes between competitors. These deep friendships can sometimes develop into romantic relationships. Markets are indeed vibrant social spaces that can foster meaningful relationships, connections that may not have existed or been made without the market. Thus, Storr argued, a complete theory of the market requires an appreciation of the market as a social space where both economic and social relationships are developed and maintained.

An appreciation of the sociality of economic life implies an appreciation for the morality of economic life—a set of "rules" that govern social interactions. In *Discovery, Capitalism, and Distributive Justice* (1989), Israel Kirzner objected to the common moral critique that the market system perpetuates exploitation. In his thoughtful examination of the moral aspects of the market system, he introduced an ethical criterion for economic justice; he called it the finders-keeper rule. As its name implies, the finders-keepers rule applies to situations where "an unowned object becomes the justly-owned private property of the first person who, discovering its availability and its potential value, takes position of it" (ibid., 98). Unlike how it appears at first glance, he argued that the rule actually can be widely applied in the evaluation of the justice of entrepreneurial profits. Of course, the rule applies to instances of first acquisition from nature. But it also (and perhaps more importantly) applies to instances of entrepreneurial discovery.

Suppose the original owner of the resource did not see the true or potential (higher) value of the resource while it was his property and sold it to another who discovered its higher valued use. It is inappropriate and unjust for the original owner then to invalidate the exchange and claim the discoverer's profits. "The additional value now seen by all to have resided in the resource was in fact found by the innovative entrepreneur. . . . Simply to revoke the sale will be to assign to the [original owner] a gain which someone else, not he, discovered" (ibid., 108). Furthermore, the finders-keepers rule applies to instances of market errors and mistakes. While Kirzner recognized that there can be some sense of involuntariness (i.e., the market participants would not have willingly entered transactions had they known they had mistaken facts or operated on flawed logic), eradicating all possibility of market errors erodes what it truly means for market exchanges to be voluntary. These types of errors are what creates the arbitrage, or profit, opportunities on which Kirzner's theory of entrepreneurship relies; after all, discovery, no matter how alert the entrepreneurs, cannot happen if there are no profit opportunities or price discrepancies. If one is convinced by the finders-keepers rule, Kirzner claimed, then one cannot reasonably accuse the market system as an unjust system.

Kirzner seemed to regard the finders-keepers rule as the only moral theory of property rights that is consistent with human agency. He carefully noted how the Nozickian entitlement theory (from which he built his finders-keepers ethic) and other theories of property rights suffer from the underlying assumption that treat inputs and outputs as *already existing*, waiting to be assigned to an individual. This is problematic, as he succinctly explained, because "[t]he morally significant implication of the view that sees resources and output as already 'being there,' is that *this view then commits us to treating the existence of these resources and outputs as being essentially independent of all human decisions,* whether decisions to appropriate resources from nature, or decisions to transform resources into output" (ibid., 148; emphasis in the original). For Kirzner, resources and products were only brought into existence (i.e., become relevant to people) through acts of discovery; they may have physically existed prior to its discovery, but "an undiscovered resource is, for all relevant human and moral purposes, non-existent" (ibid., 149). So long as we accept free choice and people's capacity to be creative and innovate, "a moral philosophy which, in its consideration of property rights and property institutions, treats the world as if the future is an unending series of fully perceived manna-deposits waiting to be assigned and distributed" can never be a satisfactory moral basis for the market system (ibid., 150). Therefore, if we are sufficiently convinced by the ethical legitimacy of the finders-keepers rule, then it is not possible to question the legitimacy of all voluntary and non-fraudulent market exchanges and the distributive justice of economic income (i.e., entrepreneurial profit) on moral grounds (ibid., 100). Kirzner, thus, viewed the market as both a moral system and moral (and social) space.

Although not explicitly in the context of the market and commercial life, James M. Buchanan, one of the founders of the Virginia School of Political Economy, was also concerned about social interactions and the potential social and moral strife that may arise from a heterogeneous society. In "Moral Community, Moral Order, or Moral Anarchy" ([1981] 2001), Buchanan introduced three models of social interactions to guide his discussion on the social stability and governability of heterogeneous societies. He defined a moral community to be a type of social cohesion that occurs when individuals identify with a group or collective unit (e.g., familial or clan-based group, or group identifying with the same ethnicity, religion, political party, social class, or nation). Moral order is described as the mutual respect individuals extend to one another, including to those with whom they do not share moral communities, and the rules of engagement they (implicitly or explicitly) agree to follow. Finally, moral anarchy is said to exist in a society where "individuals do not consider other persons to be within their moral communities and when they do not accept the minimal requirements for behavior in a moral order. In moral anarchy, each person treats other persons exclusively as a means to further his own ends or objectives" (ibid., 190).

Every society is a mix of these three models, although the exact composition may vary. The particular composition, specified Buchanan, would determine the "orderliness" of the society, which in turn would determine the degree of observed government coercion in that society. For instance, a pure moral anarchy would be populated by "[m]en who neither feel a sense of community with others, nor respect others as individuals in their own right, [who] must be ruled" (ibid., 191). These individuals would gladly give up their civil liberties for social order and personal security, but the government itself would also be populated by the same sort of moral anarchists. Consequently, in such societies, social stability will only arise under a coercive state regime, and a repressive government may be required to govern individuals in a moral anarchy. In sharp contrast, many individuals would adhere to precepts and behavioral rules in a moral order; each individual would treat others with mutual respect, even though they do not share moral communities, values, or loyalties. Here, "individual[s] may be secure in their persons and property, social stability may exist, and the needs for governance may be minimized" (ibid., 191). In fact, in a moral order where most, but not all, individuals behave according to the rules, the government would be restricted to only protecting civil liberties and property rights and enforcing contracts among individuals.

In reality, a society is comprised of multiple moral communities (each with their own rules of engagement, values, and loyalties) that may conflict greatly with one another. The degree to which social conflict may occur between moral communities or members of different moral communities will depend on the degree to which everyone in the society can identify with a single moral community. At one end of the spectrum, when a singular moral community is invoked (e.g., say the nation is threatened and its citizens band together), the society would more resemble a moral order. "Since all persons tend to share the same objectives [in this scenario], governance becomes easy" (ibid., 192). On the other end of the spectrum, when a singular moral community is not invoked or such a moral community that can encompass almost all (if not all) individuals does not exist, the society would more resemble a moral anarchy. Because the society would still be comprised of multiple moral communities, social cohesion and mutual respect would likely exist between members of the same moral community but not across moral communities. Because of the prevalent social conflict that would arise between moral communities or members of different moral communities, "there will be a need for governance, and possibly by a coercive sovereign. Without such force, the Hobbesian war of each against all may apply to the separate collectivities rather than to individuals" (ibid., 193). Buchanan emphasized that there are different implications for a society whose source of social cohesion stems from moral communities and for that whose source stems from a moral order:

> The range and scope of governmental action is more extensive in a society that locates its sources of social cohesion in moral community than in adherence to rules of moral order. On the other hand, the society largely held together by moral community is necessarily more vulnerable to shifts in the attitudes and the behavior patterns that might reflect individual departures from the shared purposes of the community. (Buchanan [1981] 2001, 196)

While Buchanan explicitly explained his use of the term moral to be more akin to interpersonal,[11] his exploration of the three models indicated that the exact composition of the society can determine the way in which individuals treat one another, which, at a minimum, was suggestive of the underlying moral values at play. In his paper, Buchanan specifically remarked how his thoughts on moral community, moral order, and moral anarchy were motivated by his observation of the American society. He felt that we were experiencing an erosion of social capital and wished "to identify and to isolate the failures and breakdowns in institutions that are responsible for this erosion" (ibid., 187).

While they were not explicitly engaged in the same intellectual dialogue as Buchanan, Storr and his coauthor Ginny Seung Choi would have strongly opposed Buchanan's diagnosis for the American society. In *Do Markets Corrupt Our Morals?* (2019), Storr and Choi explored whether engaging in market activities was morally corrupting. Using an understanding of how markets function drawn from mainline political economy and the available empirical evidence, they demonstrated that people who live in societies where markets are permitted to thrive (what they called market societies) are wealthier, healthier, happier, and better connected than those of societies where markets are more restricted.[12] For instance, they claimed that the collective empirical evidence on trust (a measure of social capital) showed that while everyone all over the world equally trusted others within a short social distance (i.e., family and neighbors), which deteriorated as the social distance increased (e.g., acquaintances and strangers), trust deteriorated at a significantly faster rate in societies where markets are not allowed to thrive than in market societies (ibid., 177–80). Furthermore, they presented suggestive evidence showing that market societies have stronger social capital than societies where markets are more restricted (ibid., 111–12) and that members of market societies exhibited more altruism (ibid., 164–67) and were more likely to be cosmopolitan (ibid., 172–76) than their counterparts in societies where markets are not permitted to thrive. If trust can be considered as a vital virtue for a well-functioning and healthy commercial society, the evidence they presented would suggest that markets are not morally corrupting.[13]

Perhaps more provocatively, Storr and Choi (2019) argued that markets are not only moral spaces that are populated by virtuous people, but markets also teach people to be more moral. They argued that the way Austrian economists long understood the market process can also apply to moral and social values. Each market exchange, they began, presents an opportunity for opportunism. A buyer could always accept the delivery of a good or service and refuse to pay the agreed sum. Similarly, a seller could always receive payment without delivering the good or deliver a good of poorer quality. So, each successful or unsuccessful consummation of a market deal reveals information about the involved parties. It reveals something about their honesty, ability (or likelihood) to keep promises, and reliability. Moreover, depending on the issues or obstacles that hindered a timely and successful consummation of a deal, the transaction may have revealed something about the seller by the way he treated others in a stressful process, by the way he handled and adapted to sudden changes, and more. And, the next time a market participant needs to repeat a purchase or sale, she would use the information she gleaned from her past transactions to decide whether to return to the same trading partner or to search for a new one. Over time, market participants who lose business will learn how not to behave or will adopt the behaviors of others who are more successful. If the market is truly a process by which market participants learn new information about market prices, quantities, qualities, production methods, and more, Storr and Choi asserted that it must also be the case that they learn something about the people with whom they interact and others who populate their industries and related areas. Through the market's ability to self-regulate, it will reveal the types of virtues that we as a society care about (and the types of vices that we as a society discourage) and teach us to become more virtuous on those margins; in this manner, the market is a moral teacher. Indeed, as we noted earlier, human action is embedded within and inseparable from cultural, social, moral, and historical processes, and a social science that claims to seriously study human behavior simply cannot ignore the meanings that people attach to things. The challenge is not only to recognize this reality—and based on it to outline the broad parameters of a research program recognizing and reflecting it—but also to follow through with its logic and try to apply the logic of this research program to the innumerable social arenas, social processes, cases, and circumstances defining the complex social order that human beings create and occupy.

## CONCLUSION

Many previous studies by those outside the mainline political economy tradition tended to perceive culture, sociality, and morality as determinants of particular outcomes or variables of interest and as factors that impede an individual or a group from achieving optimal or ideal outcomes (see Marmaros and Sacerdote 2002; Calvó-Armengol and Zenou 2005; Wahba and Zenou 2005; Adhikari and Lovett 2006; Ruttan 2008; Alesina and Guiliano 2015). In other words, scholars outside the mainline tradition tended to incorporate culture, sociality, and morality as *inputs* or *complicating factors* to their baseline models and theories. Mainline political economists deal with culture, sociality, and morality quite differently. For them, these concepts are undeniable truths about our real world and are thus already embedded within their phenomena of interest. Their attempts to seriously account for culture, sociality, and morality did not manifest as "throwing in" input variables or confounding factors. Instead, at every step of their argument, they considered how people's beliefs, social norms, relationships, societal rules, expectations around social interactions, and more add to the situational context and analyzed how they shaped the meanings, expectations, and decisions within a context.

In this chapter, we provided an overview of culture, sociality, and morality as understood by the Austrian, Bloomington, and Virginia Schools of Political Economy and focused on three areas of contribution: culture and economy, collective action, and the moral and social aspects of economic life. Scholars of mainline political economy who contributed to these areas, such as F. A. Hayek, James M. Buchanan, and Elinor and Vincent Ostrom, did not assume that people make their decisions in a vacuum devoid of all content and context beyond the directly relevant economic or political information. They did not assume that people were myopic maximizers of utility and profit or selfish cost minimizers. They comprehended that people's beliefs, not the objective facts, shaped their interpretation of their environments and events, as well as others' actions and behaviors. People's beliefs, they recognized, helped expose and distinguish the available and viable profit opportunities and strategies for resolving conflict from the unavailable and unfeasible. Culture, sociality, and morality are not shackles or weights that hold us back from achieving our greatest potentials. Instead, they are precisely what allow us to be creative, innovative, and resourceful and add color to our dreary black-and-white existence.

So long as social science studies human phenomena, depicting culture, sociality, and morality as blemishes in the otherwise perfectly rational human being inhibits our ability to understand how real people live and thrive in societies and overcome conflicts that naturally arise as a result of living in societies. This is a formidable challenge, as the diversity of social life precludes any formulaic approach or universalist methodology. Moreover, an approach sensitive to human action, meaning, subjectivity, context, and heterogeneity has, by its very nature, to be very mindful of the limits of theoretical reason when it comes to the vast realm of practical reason that defines and drives social life.

## NOTES

1. In fact, these meanings were so crucial for Hayek that he believed it would be "no exaggeration to say that every important advance in economic theory during the

last hundred years was a further step in the consistent application of subjectivism" (1952, 31).

2. See Grube and Storr (2015) and Storr and John (2020) for deeper discussions on how Austrian economists view economics as a science of meaning.

3. See Arentz, Sautet, and Storr (2013) for a discussion of how an entrepreneur's prior knowledge and experience impact her ability to identify and exploit entrepreneurial opportunities.

4. Storr and John (2015) defended Kirzner's theory of entrepreneurship against criticisms of it being too simplistic and demonstrated how his theory can account for real world differences in entrepreneurship across cultures.

5. Here, we focused on how the Austrian economic notion of culture shapes and enhances *market* entrepreneurship. The same arguments and implications for the relationship between culture and market entrepreneurship are also applicable to the relationship between culture and *nonmarket* entrepreneurship (e.g., political entrepreneurship). See, for example, Choi and Storr (2019).

6. Tocqueville commented how "often [he] admired the infinite art with which the inhabitants of the United States succeeded in setting a common goal for the efforts of a great number of men, and in making them march freely toward it" ([1840] 2010, 897).

7. While we primarily focus on Elinor Ostrom and her publication here, it should not be forgotten that her research program was also very much Vincent Ostrom's and that they viewed themselves as partners in their research.

8. Ostrom defined common-pool resource (CPR) as "a natural or man-made resource system that is sufficiently large as to make it costly (but not impossible) to exclude potential beneficiaries from obtaining benefits from its use" (1990, 30).

9. Similarly, Chamlee-Wright (2005) and Boettke, Leeson, and Coyne (2008) both argued that institutions (regardless of whether they were introduced by domestic or foreign entities) must fit the local cultural context if they are to "stick" (i.e., take hold and succeed) in the society into which they are being introduced.

10. For clarity, Elinor and Vincent Ostrom defined heterogeneity broadly: for instance, heterogeneity of beliefs, capabilities, preferences, endowments, and even personal experiences, as well as economic, social, cultural, racial, ethnic, gender, technological, and education heterogeneities across individuals and groups/communities.

11. Buchanan wrote,

I am concerned with the ways that persons act and feel towards one another. For this reason, I have inserted the adjective "moral" before each of the nouns in my title. "Community, Order or Anarchy," standing alone, would not convey my desired emphasis on personal interaction. To forestall misunderstanding at the outset, however, I should note that there is no explicitly moral content in the lecture, if the word "moral" is interpreted in some normative sense. ([1981] 2001, 187)

12. See chapters 4 and 5 and the appendix in Storr and Choi (2019) for the statistical analyses and the empirical evidence that they presented to substantiate their main argument. They drew from a wide range of literatures in economics and elsewhere to explore whether market societies were unambiguously morally inferior to societies

where markets were not permitted to thrive. The evidence presented there collectively shed doubt on the popular criticism that markets are morally corrupting.

13. See also Choi and Storr's (2018, 2020) experimental studies on trust and markets.

# REFERENCES

Adhikari, Bhim, and Jon C. Lovett. 2006. "Institutions and Collective Action: Does Heterogeneity Matter in Community-Based Resource Management?" *Journal of Development Studies* 42 (3): 426–45.

Alesina, Alberto, and Paola Giuliano. 2015. "Culture and Institutions." *Journal of Economic Literature* 53 (4): 898–944.

Aligica, Paul Dragos. 2014. *Institutional Diversity and Political Economy: The Ostroms and Beyond.* Oxford: Oxford University Press.

———. 2019. *Public Entrepreneurship, Citizenship, and Self-Governance.* Cambridge, UK: Cambridge University Press.

Aligica, Paul Dragos, and Vlad Tarko. 2012. "Polycentricity: From Polanyi to Ostrom, and Beyond." *Governance: An International Journal of Policy, Administration, and Institutions* 25 (2): 237–62.

Arentz, Jason, Frederic Sautet, and Virgil Henry Storr. 2013. "Prior-Knowledge and Opportunity Identification." *Small Business Economics* 41: 461–78.

Boettke, Peter J. 2004. "Morality as Cooperation." In *Morality of Markets*, edited by Parth J. Shah, 69–82. New Delhi: Academic Foundation.

Boettke, Peter J., Peter T. Leeson, and Christopher J. Coyne. 2008. "Institutional Stickiness and the New Development Economics." *American Journal of Economics and Sociology* 67 (2): 331–58.

Buchanan, James M. [1975] 2000. *The Limits of Liberty: Between Anarchy and Leviathan.* Indianapolis: Liberty Fund.

———. [1981] 2001. "Moral Community, Moral Order, or Moral Anarchy." In *The Collected Works of James M. Buchanan, Volume 17: Moral Science and Moral Order*, 187–201. Indianapolis: Liberty Fund.

Calvó-Armengol, Antoni, and Yves Zenou. 2005. "Job Matching, Social Network and Word-of-Mouth Communication." *Journal of Urban Economics* 57 (3): 500–522.

Chamlee-Wright, Emily. 1997. *The Cultural Foundations of Economic Development.* New York: Routledge.

———. 2005. "Entrepreneurial Responses to 'Bottom-Up' Development Strategies in Zimbabwe." *Review of Austrian Economics* 18 (1): 5–28.

———. 2008. "The Structure of Social Capital: An Austrian Perspective on Its Nature and Development. *Review of Political Economy* 20 (1): 41–58.

———. 2010. *The Cultural and Political Economy of Recovery: Social Learning in a Post- Disaster Environment.* New York: Routledge.

Chamlee-Wright, Emily, and Virgil Henry Storr. 2009. "Club Goods and Post-Disaster Community Return." *Rationality and Society* 21 (4): 429–58.

————. 2011. "Social Capital, Lobbying and Community-Based Interest Groups." *Public Choice* 149 (1–2): 167–85.

Choi, Ginny Seung, and Virgil Henry Storr. 2018. "Market Institutions and the Evolution of Culture." *Evolutionary and Institutional Economics Review* 15 (2): 243–65.

————. 2019. "A Culture of Rent Seeking." *Public Choice* 181 (1–2): 101–26.

————. 2020. "Market Interactions, Trust and Reciprocity." *PLoS ONE* 15 (5): e0232704.

Cox, James C., Vjollca Sadiraj, and Urmimala Sen. 2020. "Cultural Identities and Resolution of Social Dilemmas?" *Economic Inquiry* 58 (1): 49–66.

Gangadharan, Lata, Nikos Nikiforakis, and Marie Claire Villeval. 2017. "Normative Conflict and the Limits of Self-Governance in Heterogeneous Populations." *European Economic Review* 100: 143–56.

Granovetter, Mark. 1985. "Economic Action and Social Structure: The Problem of Embeddedness." *American Journal of Sociology* 91 (3): 481–510.

Grube, Laura E., and Virgil Henry Storr, eds. 2015. *Culture and Economic Action.* Cheltenham, UK: Edward Elgar Publishing.

Hayek, F. A. 1952. *The Counter-Revolution of Science: Studies on the Abuse of Reason.* Glencoe, IL: The Free Press.

————. 1967. *Studies in Philosophy, Politics and Economics.* Chicago: University of Chicago Press.

————. 1973. *Law, Legislation and Liberty, Volume 1: Rules and Order.* Chicago: University of Chicago Press.

————. 1977. *Law, Legislation and Liberty, Volume 2: The Mirage of Social Justice.* Chicago: University of Chicago Press.

John, Arielle, and Virgil Henry Storr. 2018. "Kirznerian and Schumpeterian Entrepreneurship in Trinidad and Tobago." *Journal of Enterprising Communities: People and Places in the Global Economy* 12 (5): 582–610.

Kirzner, Israel M. 1989. *Discovery, Capitalism, and Distributive Justice.* Oxford: Basil Blackwell Limited.

————. 1997. "Entrepreneurial Discovery and the Competitive Market Process: An Austrian Approach." *Journal of Economic Literature* 35 (1): 60–85.

Klingeren, Fijnanda van. 2020. "Playing Nice in the Sandbox: On the Role of Heterogeneity, Trust and Cooperation in Common-Pool Resources." *PLoS ONE,* 15 (8): e0237870.

Lavoie, Don. [1985] 2011. "The Interpretive Dimension of Economics: Science, Hermeneutics, and Praxeology." *Review of Austrian Economics* 24 (2): 91–128.

————. 1986. "The Market as a Procedure for Discovery and Conveyance of Inarticulate Knowledge." *Comparative Economic Studies* 28 (1): 1–19.

————. [1991] 2015. "The Discovery and Interpretation of Profit Opportunities." In *Culture and Economic Action,* edited by Laura E. Grube and Virgil Henry Storr, 48–67. Cheltenham, UK: Edward Elgar Publishing.

Lavoie, Don, and Emily Chamlee-Wright. 2000. *Culture and Enterprise: The Development, Representation and Morality of Business.* New York: Routledge.

Marmaros, David, and Bruce Sacerdote. 2002. "Peer and Social Networks in Job Search." *European Economic Review* 46 (4–5): 870–79.

Mises, Ludwig von. [1949] 1963. *Human Action: A Treatise on Economics.* Auburn, AL: Mises Institute.

Oliveira, Angela C. M. de, Rachel T. A. Croson, and Catherine Eckel. 2015. "One Bad Apple? Heterogeneity and Information in Public Good Provision." *Experimental Economics* 18 (1): 116–35.

Olson, Mancur. [1965] 1971. *The Logic of Collective Action: Public Goods and the Theory of Groups.* Cambridge, MA: Harvard University Press.

Ostrom, Elinor. 1990. *Governing the Commons: The Evolution of Institutions for Collective Action.* Cambridge, UK: Cambridge University Press.

———. 1998. "The Comparative Study of Public Economies." Presented upon acceptance of the Frank E. Seidman Distinguished Award in Political Economy, P. K. Seidman Foundation, Memphis, TN.

Ostrom, Vincent. 1991. *The Meaning of Democracy and the Vulnerabilities of Democracies: A Response to Tocqueville's Challenge.* Ann Arbor: University of Michigan Press.

———. 1994. *The Meaning of American Federalism: Constituting a Self-Governing Society.* San Francisco, CA: ICS Press.

Ostrom, Vincent, and Elinor Ostrom. 1965. "A Behavioral Approach to the Study of Intergovernmental Relations." *Annals of the American Academy of Political and Social Science* 359: 135–46.

Ruttan, L. M. 2008. "Economic Heterogeneity and the Commons: Effects on Collective Action and Collective Goods Provisioning." *World Development* 36 (5): 969–85.

Seabright, P. 1993. "Managing Local Commons: Theoretical Issues in Incentive Design." *Journal of Economic Perspectives* 7 (4): 113–34.

Smith, Adam. [1759] 1982. *The Theory of Moral Sentiments.* Edited by D. D. Raphael and A. L. Macfie. Indianapolis: Liberty Fund.

Storr, Virgil Henry. 2004. *Enterprising Slaves and Master Pirates: Understanding Economic Life in the Bahamas.* New York: Peter Lang Publishing.

———. 2008. "The Market as a Social Space: On the Meaningful Extraeconomic Conversations That Can Occur in Markets." *Review of Austrian Economics* 2 (2–3): 135–50.

———. 2013. *Understanding the Culture of Markets.* New York: Routledge.

Storr, Virgil Henry, and Ginny Seung Choi. 2019. *Do Markets Corrupt Our Morals?* London: Palgrave Macmillan.

Storr, Virgil Henry, and Stefanie Haeffele-Balch. 2012. "Post-Disaster Community Recovery in Heterogeneous, Loosely Connected Communities." *Review of Social Economy* 70 (3): 295–314.

Storr, Virgil Henry, Stefanie Haeffele-Balch, and Laura E. Grube. 2015. *Community Revival in the Wake of Disaster: Lessons in Local Entrepreneurship.* London: Palgrave Macmillan.

Storr, Virgil Henry, and Arielle John. 2015. "The Determinants of Entrepreneurial Alertness and the Characteristics of Successful Entrepreneurs." In *Culture and Economic Action*, edited by Laura E. Grube and Virgil Henry Storr, 68–87. Cheltenham: Edward Elgar Publishing.

———. 2020. *Cultural Considerations within Austrian Economics.* Cambridge, UK: Cambridge University Press.

Tocqueville, Alexis de. ([1835; 1840] 2010). *Democracy in America, Volumes I and II.* Edited by Eduardo Nolla. Translated by James T. Schleifer. Indianapolis: Liberty Fund.

Wahba, Jackline, and Yves Zenou. 2005. "Density, Social Networks and Job Search Methods: Theory and Application to Egypt." *Journal of Development Economics* 78 (2): 443–73.

Weber, Max. [1905] 2011. *The Protestant Ethic and the "Spirit" of Capitalism: The Revised 1920 Edition.* Translated by Stephen Kalberg. New York: Oxford University Press.

## Chapter 2

# Freedom as an Artifact

## *The Cultural Foundations of Ordered Liberty*

### Lewis Hoss

Classical liberalism is commonly accused of bearing an antagonistic relationship toward culture. The normative commitment to private life over public life, and to a government limited to the protection of individual rights and the enforcement of general rules that maintain a market order, is perceived to be destructive, or at best neglectful, of that which is encapsulated in the idea of culture. For generations, some of the most influential political theorists have thus criticized liberal commercial society in terms of its alleged "evisceration of culture" (Deneen 2018, 64; Bloom 1990, 277–94; Adorno and Horkheimer [1944] 1997, 120–67). Whereas culture accounts for the higher and loftier aspects of communal life through which human beings define and pursue a shared sense of meaning, purpose, or value, liberal commercial society is said to disregard these and to lower human horizons by encouraging the pursuit of narrow self-interest, which rarely extends beyond a vulgar concern with money or material comforts. Where the principles of classical liberalism are put into practice, cultural achievements are disregarded, and cultural aspirations are discouraged. Culture is replaced with commerce, and cultured man gives way to economic man who is a sorry, cultureless being animated by self-concern and mechanistic calculations of interest or utility. At best, so the charges run, liberal commercial society can only support a very "thin" conception of culture defined in terms of materialism and consumerism.

In light of such criticisms, those who are sympathetic to liberal aims must ask whether classical liberalism contains within itself the resources to answer these charges. I would suggest that it does, and this can be seen most apparently in the thought of Adam Smith and Friedrich Hayek. These two thinkers, in addition to providing the most robust defenses of liberal commercial society, placed a great deal of emphasis on the importance of culture. Together, they indicate that liberalism can and indeed must support a "thick" conception of culture, but one that is grounded in a very particular understanding of man's fundamental disposition in the world. Liberalism, that is, approaches the idea of culture in a specific manner that may frequently be at odds with common understandings of human culture.

What Smith and Hayek have to teach us about the importance of culture in a free society is worth reflecting on in the present moment, given the growing interest among political economists in the concept of culture. Economics is no longer as dismal a science as its longstanding reputation would suggest. This reputation, which associates the discipline with a doctrine of mathematical formalism wedded to a shallow and sterile conception of the human being as *homo economicus,* has been shed gradually in recent decades as economists and economic historians increasingly have emphasized the importance of culture (Jones 2003; Rose 2019). Leading the way in this trend are scholars working within or adjacent to the classical liberal tradition of political thought, particularly those in the Austrian School of Political Economy (Lavoie 1991; Lavoie and Chamlee-Wright 2000; Boettke 2001; Storr 2013; Grube and Storr 2015; Choi and Storr 2018). This recent outpouring of scholarship reflects a growing awareness that cultural influences cannot be dismissed from scientific analysis or relegated to a static set of fixed "preferences" that are external to the logic of economic processes. Economic activity and outcomes are shaped in no small part by nebulous forces that we struggle to understand, forces that we apprehend in such primordial terms as the "spirit" or "character" of a given community, and which we must courageously grapple with in order to better understand social and economic order. Given the conceptual difficulties involved here, much work remains to be done by those who believe that culture matters. By way of offering a small contribution toward these efforts as a student of the history of political thought, I would suggest that a fruitful step forward might be to look backward, particularly to the seminal thinkers who shaped the classical liberal tradition and who loom large in the background of contemporary Austrian School economics.

I begin in the next two sections by establishing two different ways of thinking about culture. The first conceives of culture as constituting a nebulous middle ground between human nature and human reason, and this is the approach favored by Hayek and the classical liberal tradition more generally. The second conceives of culture as manifesting the powers of the constructive human mind and is perhaps closer to how most of us in the present day think about culture. These differing conceptions of culture point to the tensions that arise from assimilating so many divergent social phenomena under the singular heading of "culture" as we are inclined to do. One benefit of the classical liberal approach is the manner in which it considers different aspects of "culture" in their own right. In the third section, I examine the classical roots of this more nuanced approach to the space between human nature and human reason, focusing especially on the social thought of Aristotle and Adam Smith. Rather than speaking of some monolithic notion of "culture," these thinkers crucially distinguished between cultivated habits and promulgated conventions, or *ethos* and *nomos*. In concluding, the fourth section argues that the free society as Smith and Hayek understood it can readily be conceived of as a cultural phenomenon or "artifact" if culture is understood in terms of *ethos*, or the cultivation of individual habits that sustain the framework of general rules on which a liberal society is built.

## CULTURE AS A MIDDLE
## GROUND BETWEEN NATURE AND REASON

The classical liberal approach to culture is exemplified in the thought of Friedrich Hayek. Throughout his written works, Hayek emphasizes the importance of culture for the study of economics, not so much with a view to understanding how the market process works, but with a view to understanding the foundations of the extended order of cooperation that characterizes a liberal commercial society. The "Great Society" as Hayek conceives it is first and foremost a culturally mediated phenomenon. To begin to unpack Hayek's conception of culture, we can look to the final volume of *Law, Legislation and Liberty* (Hayek 1982). This volume concludes with an epilogue titled "The Three Sources of Human Values," the purpose of which he claims is to convey "more directly the general view of moral and political evolution which has guided me in the whole enterprise" (ibid., xviii). The epilogue thus articulates the first principles that guide Hayek's analysis of social order, particularly the extended order of the Great Society, in both its descriptive and normative dimensions. Those principles resolve into three foundational sources of human social order: nature, culture, and reason. The macro order of human society is a reflection of the simultaneous operation and interaction of these three suborders. Any particular social order is a composite manifestation of moral values that derive from natural instincts, "which are genetically determined and therefore innate"; from dictates of rational thought, or "deliberately chosen rules" that are constructed abstractly and are thus artificial; and from cultural traditions and practices, which are "neither natural nor artificial, neither genetically transmitted nor rationally designed" (Hayek 1979, 153–55).

In assessing the relative importance of these three sources, Hayek indicates that culture is especially important when it comes to the extended order of the liberal commercial society. Indeed, his claims on behalf of culture at times seem to exclude his other two foundational principles entirely. In his account, the liberal commercial society has secured freedom and peaceful cooperation on a scale that is unprecedented in human history, yet these results owe very little to human nature or human reason. That millions of individuals should live together in a large, free, and open society actually seems to run counter to the inclinations of human nature and the dictates of human reason. To the extent that such a way of life has been achieved in numerous societies across the world, Hayek argues that this is the accidental result of certain cultural practices that emerged without deliberate plan or guidance. "Freedom is an artefact" of "culture," convention, or "civilization" (Hayek 1979, 163; cf. Hayek 1988, 11–28). Living in a free society is good for human beings, but "what has made men good is neither nature nor reason but tradition" (Hayek 1979, 160). Thus, although there are three sources of human values that give rise to social order at the macro level, culture is the supreme source of those particular values on which the free society depends.

Hayek has a clear rhetorical purpose in emphasizing the importance of culture to the degree that he does. In his estimation, the foundational importance of culture has been neglected by modern scholars of social order, while nature and reason have been overemphasized. The progress made in the natural sciences, and particularly the life sciences, has resulted in a great deal of scholarly attention given to the natural roots of social and political order as discovered through the study of biology, genetics, and neuroscience. For Hayek, this is exemplified in the rapid emergence of sociobiology and evolutionary psychology in the latter half of the twentieth century (ibid., 153–55). In seeking to make the natural sciences the true foundation and model for the social sciences, these disciplines not only produce erroneous conclusions about social order, but they work to spread deterministic beliefs that undermine notions of freedom and responsibility that are necessary in the Great Society (Hayek 1960, 65, 133–39).

While nature thus has many champions, the excessive emphasis placed on reason as a foundational source of human social order is even more entrenched in the longstanding rationalistic tradition of Cartesian constructivism. This mode of thinking, because it is "so pleasing to human vanity," extends far beyond the confines of any particular discipline or field of study and reinforces the pervasive prejudice that "human institutions will serve human purposes only if they have been deliberately designed for these purposes" (Hayek 1973, 8). The dominance of these two currents of thought has resulted in the general acceptance of a false dichotomy—nature versus reason—in our thinking about social order. It is assumed that all aspects of human social order that cannot be explained as arising from natural instinct must be explained as arising from deliberate rational stipulation. Practices, institutions, or mores that cannot be attributed directly to natural instincts or to deliberate constructions of the human mind are shrugged off as lying beyond the purview of social science. That which is perceived to be arbitrary, epiphenomenal, or superficial in human affairs is easily brushed aside as "merely cultural" and thus unfit for the purposes of explanation or evaluation. Hayek thus indicates his rhetorical purpose in devoting almost exclusive attention to the role of culture:

> That neither what is instinctively recognized as right, nor what is rationally recognized as serving specific purposes, but inherited traditional rules, or that what is neither instinct nor reason but tradition should often be most beneficial to the functioning of society, is a truth which the dominant constructivistic outlook of our times refuses to accept. If modern man finds that his inborn instincts do not always lead him in the right direction, he at least flatters himself that it was his reason which made him recognize that a different kind of conduct will serve his innate values better. The conception that man has, in the service of his innate desires, consciously constructed an order of society is, however, erroneous, because without the cultural evolution which lies between instinct and the capacity of rational design, he would not have possessed the reason which now makes him try to do so. (Hayek 1979, 162)

His project, in other words, is that of charting a distinct middle course between the false dichotomy of nature versus reason that is quite readily accepted in most intellectual circles. Although the rhetorical trajectory of the epilogue is to elevate culture as the sole source of those values on which the liberal commercial society depends while debunking the claims of nature and reason, his aim is not to deny outright the importance of nature and reason. Rather, Hayek seeks to correct for a pervasive underappreciation of culture by demonstrating the crucial role played by the spontaneous order of "grown" conventional arrangements that are neither manifestations of innate natural instincts nor the products of deliberate rational planning.

Nevertheless, the priority that Hayek places on the cultural foundations of the liberal commercial society has elicited a fair share of criticism from political theorists, including many who are otherwise sympathetic to classical liberalism.[1] One such criticism is directed toward the fact that by excessively emphasizing culture, Hayek seems to accept a dismal Freudian view of civilization as entailing the painful repression of man's natural desires and inclinations—a view that renders the free society less attractive than it might otherwise appear. Indeed, Hayek claims in the epilogue that "the morals which maintain the open society do not serve to gratify human emotions" or "innate natural longings," and as a result, "modern man is torn by conflicts which torment him" (ibid., 159–60). Citing these passages, Larry Arnhart asks rhetorically, "Why would human beings want to live in Hayek's 'great society,' if that means repressing all of their natural instincts? If such a life is purely painful, why would anyone desire it?" (Arnhart 2005, 22). A more serious critique is that Hayek's statements on the primacy of culture bring him dangerously close to a kind of cultural relativism that would undermine his case for the superiority of the free society. Thus, political philosopher John Gray argues that because Hayek "allows no limit to the cultural variability" of spontaneously grown traditions, he "cannot avoid a relativist posture which must deprive liberal principles of much of their critical force" (Gray 1980, 130; cf. Arnhart 2005, 23–26; Arnhart 2007).[2] Making a similar point in his review of Hayek's *The Constitution of Liberty*, Jacob Viner remarks, "I do not see how this doctrine can be distinguished from 'social Darwinism,' or from that 'historicism' which Hayek has elsewhere so persuasively warned us against" (Viner 1961, 235). With these difficulties in mind, Peter McNamara argues that Hayek represents a peculiar brand of liberalism that departs from certain core principles of Adam Smith; more precisely, Hayek "studiously" neglects Smith's sentimental liberalism grounded in human nature, opting instead for an "unsentimental liberalism" grounded in human culture (McNamara 2013, 25; cf. Montes 2011).[3]

Many of those who are dissatisfied with Hayek's emphasis on the role of culture appear to be looking for a more robust moral defense of the free society than a "merely cultural" one. If the free society draws no support from the natural order or the rational order and instead it depends upon resisting or overcoming both nature and reason through a blind historical process of cultural evolution, then what are the prospects for the free society maintaining or extending itself? This is a valid concern, and it is one that I believe underlies some of the criticisms directed against Hayek's statements on culture. Yet, I would suggest that Hayek is well attuned to this concern and that his conception of culture is actually intended to grapple with it.

Hayek's understanding of culture is perhaps more nuanced than we are prepared to recognize, as many of us are conditioned to assimilate "culture" to the kind of rational constructivism that Hayek aims to debunk. It is precisely this conception of culture that underlies the assumed antagonism between commerce and culture mentioned at the beginning of this chapter. By contrast, Hayek employs a particular conception of culture that differs in important ways from commonplace understandings of that notion. His way of thinking belongs to the classical liberal tradition, which itself precedes the modern idea of "culture." In this regard, it is useful to contrast Hayek with Adam Smith, who embraces a similar tripartite framework of principles that undergird human social order without speaking explicitly of culture. Such an exercise may help us to shed some of the baggage that accompanies our contemporary understanding of "culture" in order to arrive at something more fundamental to human social order. Before doing so, however, we should first consider the origins of a different conception of culture that stands in opposition to Hayek's and has proven to be especially prevalent in the modern era.

## CULTURE AS A MANIFESTATION OF THE CONSTRUCTIVE MIND

"Culture" is a notoriously tricky idea that can mean all things to all people depending on how it is conceptualized. Its pervasive usage in contemporary discourse can blind us to the fact that culture is a very modern idea—more modern even than the classical liberalism that emerged out of the Age of Enlightenment. Premodern thinkers did not speak explicitly in terms of culture. To be sure, the philosophers and historians of old spoke often of customs; traditions; mores; shared modes of thinking and acting; artistic and intellectual achievements; moral, spiritual, and aesthetic conditions; and the like, but they had no equivalent expression that unifies these disparate phenomena in the way that "culture" apparently does for us today. The first great thinker to use the word "culture" in a manner that would be familiar to us in the present was Immanuel Kant (Bloom 1990, 277–80).[4] The way in which he employed the idea helps to explain the perceived antagonism between commerce and culture that persists in our time, and it is thus worth pausing over briefly.

In articulating this novel concept, Kant ([1786] 1983, 54) actually credits Jean-Jacques Rousseau with being the true inventor of the modern concept of "culture." In his earlier published writings, Rousseau ([1750, 1754] 1965) argued that the fundamental human problem lies in the antagonism between human nature and human society. As a natural being living only for himself, the individual is driven by animal instinct to seek the fulfilment of simple natural desires in complete independence from the will of others. But as a social being forced by circumstance to live among others in a community, and thus to live *for* others to some degree, the individual is subject to countless social constraints that frustrate his natural inclinations and place him in a condition of dependence on others. According to Rousseau, social life as such is a contradiction and the individual living in society is a contradictory creature tortured by a divided and disintegrated psyche, internally torn between his absolute existence as a natural being and his relative existence as a social or communal being. Rousseau's later writings attempted to find a solution that might resolve this contradiction, or at least alleviate the tensions produced by it, and this attempt to reconcile human nature with society or civilization is what Kant considers to be the essence of "culture."[5]

Expanding upon and systematizing Rousseau's ideas, Kant bequeaths to us an understanding of culture that is bound up with notions of progress, enlightenment, and the advance of human reason. According to Kant, culture is manifested in the ongoing historical "transition from the raw state of a merely animal creature to humanity, from the harness of the instincts to the guidance of reason—in a word, from the guardianship of nature to the state of freedom" (Kant [1786] 1983, 53). Inherent in this conception is a sharp dichotomy between nature and freedom, or between instinct and reason, and "culture" is fully assimilated to the latter. Thus, Kant describes culture as the product of "unsociableness that is forced to discipline itself" through the willful exercise of reason, and he claims that it is through the ongoing enlightenment of reason that the human species is led "from barbarism to culture" (Kant [1784] 1983, 32–33). The gradual development of human culture proceeds apace with the gradual perfection of human reason and can thus be interpreted in terms of progress. Culture is portrayed by Kant as a dynamic and unfolding process that is generally linear: the careful examination of culture reveals an underlying historical process that aims toward a natural *telos* or end for the human species, which culminates in the perfection of reason and the realization of "a universal society administered in accord with the right"—a cosmopolitan society in which each will enjoy the greatest amount of freedom that can be guaranteed to all (ibid.).

Understood in this Rousseauean-Kantian sense, the notion of culture is frequently employed as an expression of the desire for freedom, autonomy, and power, especially freedom from or power over nature, where nature is taken to represent the contextual circumstances of human life in their totality. Culture in this sense speaks readily to human aspirations to shape and control the conditions of our existence. It flatters our self-esteem—and perhaps feeds our hubris—with the assurance that there is a godlike element within us, manifested in our capacity for willful agency and even creation. Thus, culture is typically associated with what is high and noble as distinguished from what is low and base, with what is most human as distinguished from what is brutish. It is spoken of as something that somehow partakes of the sublime or the spiritual. When we think of culture in this manner, we tend to think immediately of art, of those extraordinary products of deliberate human creation that distinguish our species from the animals or distinguish one group of us from the rest. Taking this sense of culture seriously and pushing it to its limits, we are led to imagine individuals and communities that are not only capable but responsible for shaping their own destiny and defining the terms of their own existence through a willful and deliberate exercise of the mind. In Hayek's terms, we are led dangerously close to the realm of constructivism, and it is from this conception of culture that Hayek attempts to distinguish his own.[6]

To the extent that Hayek champions the importance of culture, he also challenges the dominant understanding of culture as derived from Rousseau and Kant. We are tipped off to this by the fact that Hayek speaks more often of "cultural traditions" than of "culture" as such. In his view, culture is more frequently something that is received or inherited than deliberately constructed or stipulated through enlightened human reason or creativity. Culture constitutes a broad set of "ideas and skills" that are transmitted over time across generations, "passed on by learning and imitation" (Hayek 1960, 118). These "ideas and skills" are manifested in "explicit knowledge" to some small degree, but they are "to a larger extent embodied in tools and institutions which have proven themselves superior"—repositories of tacit knowledge that include such things as "habits, conventions, language, and moral beliefs" (ibid., 75). Culture in this sense does indeed represent what is artificial as opposed to natural, or what has been superadded to raw nature by human action. But Hayek is keen to teach us that we misunderstand what is artificial when we conceive of it solely in terms of deliberate human creation, or the willful effort to adapt ourselves to nature and thus overcome its limitations. He thus laments the fact that "'merely cultural' has now to many the connotation of changeable at will, arbitrary, superficial, or dispensable" (Hayek 1979, 155). This is unfortunate because "it is only our profound and comprehensive ignorance of the nature of culture that makes it possible for us to believe that we direct and control it" (Hayek 1960, 75).[7] In Hayek's view, the longevity of the free society may ultimately depend on whether we can correct for this misunderstanding.

To a certain extent, the misunderstanding is facilitated by the concept itself, which covers too broad a range of phenomena. What is properly seen as an extraordinarily rich and complex tapestry of human adaptations to the natural world is obscured by subsuming it all within a singular concept of "culture." As the notion of culture is inflated to include the countless disparate artifacts of human activity, qualitative differences and distinctions among them are lost from sight. The monolithic concept of culture then takes on a life of its own as it is appropriated by our more spirited desires and used to flatter the pretensions of human reason and the fatal conceit of human vanity. One of the virtues of the classical liberal tradition is that it resists a monolithic conception of culture in favor of one that allows for gradations and distinctions among particular forms or manifestations of culture. It especially favors distinctions between artifacts of human activity that are the products of deliberate creation as opposed to those that are inherited or learned. Although Hayek does at times follow modern parlance in speaking of "culture" as a singular concept, he generally resists doing so and attempts to awaken his readers to the complex variety of human artifacts that are placed under this label.

## THE CLASSICAL ROOTS
## OF CULTURE AS *ETHOS* AND *NOMOS*

To get a better sense of the classical liberal conception of culture as distinguished from the more commonplace Rousseauean-Kantian one, it is helpful to consider the work of Adam Smith, who wrote before the concept of
"culture" had emerged. Although he does not articulate it as formulaically as
Hayek, in Smith's analysis we can observe the tripartite framework of nature,
culture, and reason as the three sources of social order, even though Smith
speaks of "custom" and "habit" rather than "culture" (e.g., Smith [1759]
1982, 194). It is worth reflecting for a moment on the fact that this tripartite
framework that persists throughout the classical liberal tradition from Smith
to Hayek actually hearkens even further back to the political philosophy of
Aristotle. It is rather fitting that classical liberalism should embrace a method
of social analysis that is itself rooted in a longstanding tradition of thinking
passed down and inherited across so many generations. Moreover, the Aristotelian origins of the Smithian-Hayekian framework help to clarify the role
of culture in that framework.

As James Bernard Murphy (1993, 2002, 2007) has extensively demonstrated, Aristotle appears to be the earliest thinker to realize that the macro
order of human society can be understood as emerging from the simultaneous operation of three micro orders—the natural order, the customary (or
cultural) order, and the rational order—each of which interact with the other
two in complex ways (see Arnhart 1998, 2005). As Murphy (2002, 476; 2007,
55–56) explains, Aristotle rejected the doctrine of the ancient Greek Soph-
ists who explained human society in terms of a sharp dichotomy between
the natural and the artificial—categories that were understood to be mutually
exclusive. Instead, he saw human political communities as manifesting an
ordered triad of nature, custom, and reason, where custom constitutes a tricky
middle ground between those aspects of the social order that arise from innate
natural capacities and those that arise from deliberate human action.[8] Significantly, Aristotle distinguishes between two different components of custom
that tend to be conflated in the present day because they are merged together
within the singular conception of "culture." These are *ethos*, or learned habits,
and *nomos*, or established conventions. Throughout much of the history of
social and political thought, these two separate concepts were held to be quite
distinct, allowing for a more nuanced discussion of the artifacts of human
action than does the monolithic notion of culture.[9] Crucially, the distinction
suggests that not all that is cultural can be assimilated to our capacity for
deliberate creation or construction.

*Ethos*, or learned habit, refers to those behavioral aspects of custom or culture that appear to operate spontaneously, automatically, and tacitly. Yet although habits appear to operate spontaneously and without conscious design, they necessarily presuppose a prior educative process of habituation or learning. To develop a habit first requires deliberate and even painful effort, or "compulsion and force"; only later, once the habit is internalized, might it cease to require a deliberate effort.[10] Thus, although habits must be learned, in becoming automated they transition from a form of explicit knowledge to one of tacit knowledge. For Aristotle, *ethos* is closely bound up with individual character, and the cultivation of a morally virtuous (or *ethical*) character is a matter of training and habituation. In practice, *ethos* closely resembles the operation of nature, and as habits become ingrained and internalized, they come to resemble a kind of second nature that continues to function even when we are not consciously aware of it (Murphy 2007, 60–61).

*Nomos*, or convention, refers to those aspects of custom or culture that are guided by elaborate agreements or protocols that are deliberately stipulated and reflected upon and that entail a greater degree of explicit (as opposed to tacit) knowledge. Whereas *ethos* is the aspect of culture that stands closer to nature, *nomos* bears a much closer resemblance to reason, or to what is deliberately designed and constructed by the human mind. Thus, Aristotle claims that many other animals exhibit *ethos*, or a capacity for social learning and habituation, but only humans exhibit *nomos*. As opposed to established laws, conventions often consist of informal arrangements, or unwritten norms and rules of conduct that individuals must nevertheless be consciously aware of. Aristotle distinguishes between laws or statutes that are rationally designed and subsequently imposed or "laid down" and unwritten conventions that are not legislated or coercively enforced. He indicates that the latter can still carry the weight of authority just like the former.[11]

Thus, *ethos* and *nomos*, habits and conventions, represent two distinct components of custom or culture. Yet habits and conventions are not mutually exclusive; they interact with one another in complex ways that can make it quite difficult to distinguish between them with any degree of precision. Murphy elegantly describes how *ethos* and *nomos* mutually condition one another in a way that refines and embellishes the artifacts of human action:

> Habit gives convention psychological force and performative skill: habitual conventions have spontaneity, speed, and efficiency; they are usually pleasant, familiar, and easy. Conventions give habits cultural sophistication and a social life; they enable us to know what to expect in the behavior of others, enable us to conform to others' expectations, and provide common criteria for evaluating our own and others' conduct. Of course, the marriage of habit and convention is not always a happy one. . . . Nonetheless, as a broad generalization, we might

say that conventions without habits are a burden while habits without conventions are a bore. (Murphy 2007, 66)

The blending together of *ethos* and *nomos* in many social practices often obscures the distinct influence that each has upon the emergent social order. It may be impossible to deconstruct a given social practice and learn with complete certainty whether it is sustained by habit or convention. Moreover, it can be quite difficult to disentangle human customs, whether habits or conventions, from the operations of human nature and human reason. Habits can easily come to resemble natural instincts, while unwritten yet rigid conventions can easily come to resemble the formal laws that have been deliberately stipulated by the dictates of reason. Given the complexity of the countless artificial products of human action and the limitations of human reason, it is likely that complete precision in these matters lies beyond our grasp. Nevertheless, as the passage quoted above indicates, this fact in itself lends a certain beauty to that mysterious realm that lies somewhere between mechanistic nature and deliberate reason. Moreover, as Adam Smith would suggest, the apparent mystery awakens our sense of wonder and impels us to seek out and better understand the foundations of our social order and their various connections (see Smith [1795] 1982, 33–47, 185).

One final point about the tripartite Aristotelian framework that needs mentioning is that nature, custom, and reason fit together in a nested hierarchy, whereby custom is ultimately constrained by nature, and reason is ultimately constrained by both nature and custom (Arnhart 2005, 19; Murphy 2007, 73–75). Nature serves as the ultimate foundation of the social order, representing the material processes of our world that exist prior to and apart from human custom and reason. Social order emerges from the natural order because human beings are naturally social and political animals, driven by propensities that are innate and universal to live and cooperate with others in a community.[12] The precise manner in which human beings act upon these social instincts by associating and cooperating with one another will be reflected in customary social practices. Some of these practices arise unintentionally through a process of trial and error that gradually generates certain habits, while others are deliberately stipulated or agreed upon. While the range of potential customary practices is vast, it is not limitless. Rather, it is constrained by our repertoire of innate propensities and faculties. Custom, in turn, exists prior to and apart from human reason. For Aristotle, "custom presupposes nature, but custom can exist without being the object of rational reflection and stipulation: language existed before grammarians" (Murphy 2007, 74). As reason develops out of human nature and alongside custom, it enables us to reflect on and critically evaluate our natural instincts and customary practices. Yet, the reach of constructive reason is always constrained by the confines of the natural and customary orders. Aristotle advises that deliberately stipulated laws should only be laid down insofar as they take account of human nature and the social customs (both *ethos* and *nomos*) currently in place at any given instance (Aristotle 1957, 1332b8–11). Thus, all three orders are mutually inclusive yet situated in a hierarchical relationship to one another. Each can influence the others, but they only do so with a degree of efficacy that decreases as we move down the hierarchy from nature to custom and from custom to reason.

Moving ahead many centuries to the work of Adam Smith, we can detect this tripartite Aristotelian framework in his analysis of social order.[13] Thus, Smith indicates that the natural order provides the ultimate foundation for the emergent social order as well as the ultimate ground of his defense of the liberal commercial society. A fundamental premise of Smith's thought is that there is a universal human nature that manifests itself in basic psychological structures and patterns that operate across times and places (Fleischacker 2004, 61–70; Griswold 1999, 352). Two such aspects of human nature are especially important for Smith. First, human beings are naturally social animals who universally desire to experience the sympathy and mutual esteem of their fellows (see Smith [1759] 1982, 41). Second, human beings are naturally striving animals who universally desire to better their own condition. As such, they exhibit a natural propensity to engage with one another in commercial exchange (Smith [1776] 1981, 25, 341). Insofar as these natural propensities are generally shared by most individuals, they lend a degree of structure and coherence to the various social arrangements that emerge over the course of history. And ultimately for Smith, the free society is justified as superior to alternative social arrangements because it more reliably advances those ends which our nature compels us to seek (Rasmussen 2008). However, natural instincts alone are of limited use in structuring and guiding social order. Our moral sentiments, innate though they may be, are susceptible to distortions and corruptions that must be corrected for through culture and reason (Smith [1759] 1982, 154, 176).

The customary or cultural order in Smith's view is constrained by, but not reducible to, the natural order. The principles of human custom are amenable to a wide variety of social beliefs and practices, as witnessed in "the many irregular and discordant opinions which prevail in different ages and nations concerning what is blameable or praise-worthy" (ibid., 194). Although they originate from a natural and fixed repertoire of moral sentiments, judgments of propriety and impropriety vary across cultural contexts, and scholars have shown how even Smith's moral standard embodied in the Impartial Spectator turns out to be a culturally conditioned standard (Forman-Barzilai 2010, 166–75; Rasmussen 2014, 48–53). Yet, the power and influence of custom are not boundless but eventually run up against the hard limits of human nature. While certain "principles of the imagination" that are susceptible to the influence of custom or culture "may easily be altered by habit and education," our "sentiments of moral approbation and disapprobation, are founded on the strongest and most vigorous passions of human nature; and though they may be somewhat warpt, cannot be entirely perverted" (Smith [1759] 1982, 200). Thus, custom cannot radically restructure "the *general* style of character and behavior," but it is more than capable of drastically altering beliefs and opinions as to "the propriety or impropriety of *particular* usages" (ibid., 209, emphases added).[14] The notion of social order as such presupposes a certain degree of uniformity or universality in "the general style and character of conduct and behavior," which lies beyond the vagaries of custom and can only be understood to reflect the natural order (ibid., 211).

Smith does leave room for the deliberate exercise of human reason in his analysis, although he seeks to limit the influence of reason to within the boundaries of the natural and customary orders. Because Smith believes that most of the important social arrangements of the free society have emerged unintentionally out of a long and gradual process involving countless discrete individuals pursuing their natural desires (e.g., Smith [1776] 1981, 26, 454), he frequently draws attention to the unforeseen negative consequences that often result from even the most well-intentioned applications of constructive human reason at the social level (Muller 1993, 84–92; Wolf 2017). When it comes to the question of constructing and enforcing deliberately stipulated laws that are intended to alter the social order, Smith famously counsels moderation against unbounded idealism. He castigates the "man of system" who is "very wise in his own conceit," is "enamoured with the supposed beauty of his own ideal plan of government," and aspires "to erect his own judgment into the supreme standard of right and wrong," believing that "his fellow-citizens should accommodate themselves to him and not he to them" (Smith [1776] 1981, 234). On the contrary, he maintains that the legislator should "content himself with moderating" that which cannot be reconstructed without force, should "accommodate, as well as he can, his public arrangements to the confirmed habits and prejudices of the people," and should humbly acknowledge that "in the great chess-board of human society, every single piece has a principle of motion of its own, altogether different from that which the legislature might chuse to impress upon it" (Smith [1759] 1982, 233–34).[15] Part of the task of human reason, then, is to understand its limited causal role in the broader social order.

We can see now that Smith employs a triadic framework of nature, custom, and reason in his analysis of social order that is inherited from Aristotle and that anticipates Hayek. How then might we begin to characterize Smith's understanding of "culture," given that he never uses this term? This is a difficult question to ponder, given that Smith provides a nuanced and variegated account of the space between nature and reason that defies categorization beneath any singular heading. Refusing to treat culture as a monolithic entity and instead taking its discrete components on their own terms allows for a richer understanding of the human social order; yet, the way in which we think about custom or culture and its relationship to social order will still depend on which of those components we prioritize as most important. Throughout his surviving writings and lectures, Smith considers separately much of what gets lumped together under the heading of "culture" today. For instance, he frequently pays homage to artistic and intellectual achievements and the extraordinary creations of human genius that occupy a crucial place in the social life of our species.[16] Yet, such extraordinary achievements bear little direct relationship to ordinary social life, and they provide us with little guidance in regard to the structuring of our social order; they cannot be taken to suggest possibilities for the application of creative genius at the social or political level in the way that they can in the aesthetic or philosophical realm. To consider another component of "culture," Smith, particularly in his *Wealth of Nations* and *Lectures on Jurisprudence*, provides numerous examples of *nomos* throughout human history—those conventional arrangements that are to some degree stipulated and agreed upon and that seem to blur the distinction between formal and informal law (Smith [1776] 1981). Yet, we have also noted above the degree to which Smith thinks that rational stipulation is quite limited in its applications to the broader social order. It would seem then that Smith resists drifting toward a Rousseauean-Kantian conception of culture.

I would suggest that the conception of culture that can be gleaned from Smith—a conception that is embraced by Hayek and indeed the classical liberal tradition in general—is one that prioritizes *ethos*, or learned habit, above other cultural considerations. Indeed, *ethos* can be seen as the pervasive theme of Smith's social and political thought, as he deems it to be an especially crucial support for the social order of a free society, which is not sufficiently supported by natural instinct or human reason. If a social order that was largely unintended is to sustain itself and to continue evolving and developing in unintended ways, it requires a population of individuals who are habituated to social practices and arrangements such that their beliefs and actions are not guided solely by natural instinct or the conceits of unbounded reason. Instinct and reason must be harnessed through a training that internalizes the modes of thinking and acting that are appropriate to social practices, such that those practices operate as a kind of second nature. In the free society, individuals are always prone to the delusions suggested by the voices of nature and reason, and it is the task of *ethos* to guard against this danger.

The necessity for some kind of learning or habituation to social practices comes to light most apparently in Smith's educative proposals near the end of *Wealth of Nations* (Smith [1776] 1981, 784–86). Smith indicates that in a free society, individuals are especially prone "to the delusions of enthusiasm and superstition" and that learning is necessary to render individuals "more disposed to examine, and more capable of seeing through, the interested complaints of faction and sedition" (ibid., 788). Indeed, cultivating within individuals a proper disposition toward political enthusiasm and contending political factions is "the most essential circumstance in the publick morals of a free people" (ibid., 775). Smith's statements on political enthusiasm bring to mind his characterization of the "man of system" described above, who embodies the dangers of excessive political rationalism and excessive political passion alike. In a social order that allows for a large degree of freedom, what is to keep individuals from being carried away by their natural passions or their rationalistic ideals, from falling prey to the dangers of enthusiasm and thus jeopardizing the social order itself? For Smith, the answer can only lie in education and habituation.

In *Wealth of Nations*, Smith famously calls for a publicly subsidized program of scientific education that aims to cultivate reason and proliferate enlightened thinking throughout the society. The improvement of reason is an important first step, yet only a first step, in guarding against the passionate and rationalistic delusions of enthusiasm. In *The Theory of Moral Sentiments*, Smith indicates that something more is needed, namely a moral education that aims to habituate individuals to the modes of action and belief that are appropriate to the social practices and arrangements of a free society (Smith [1759] 1982). The theory of virtue that he describes with broad strokes in part VI of that book points to the general qualities and beliefs that must be made into habits if the free society is to succeed (Hanley 2009). At the core of Smith's virtue ethical theory is the quality of self-command, or the kind of habitual discipline over one's heart and mind that would enable one to embrace social practices and arrangements that do not necessarily appeal to instinct or reason. To the extent that *ethos* is the dominant theme of Smith's moral, social, and political thought, it can properly be considered as the defining feature of his conception of human "culture."

## LIBERAL CULTURE AS LIBERAL *ETHOS*

If we return to view Hayek's account of the three sources of human values in light of the tradition extending back through Adam Smith to Aristotle, certain perplexities might seem to be clarified. The most obvious difference between

Hayek's and Smith's accounts, which I alluded to above, is that Hayek affords much less of a role to human nature; unlike Smith, Hayek does not seek "to ground his explanation and defense of liberty in a full account of human nature or, for that matter, any other kind of foundationalism" (McNamara 2013, 20). Two points are worth noting on this matter. First, to the extent that Hayek sees the extended order of a free society as conflicting with human nature, it conflicts specifically with our social and moral emotions that evolved under radically different conditions within a close-knit tribal society (Hayek 1976, 133–34). Following Aristotle and Smith as opposed to Rousseau and Kant, Hayek sees human beings as naturally social animals, animated by moral emotions like solidarity, altruism, and compassion, and by a desire for shared purposes and aims. While these innate qualities contribute little to the maintenance of an extended order, they need not be brutally repressed; a free society leaves room for the pursuit of the natural instincts within the many smaller sub-orders that exist locally (see Hayek 1988, 37). Second, Hayek has a rhetorical aim in de-emphasizing the role of human nature insofar as contemporary scientism, as manifested in sociobiology, has tended to monopolize naturalistic explanations of social order (Hayek 1979, 153–55). On the whole, Hayek's fundamental point is that the free society is not natural to us. It is quite far removed from the natural conditions in which our innate instincts evolved, and it is thus something that we must secure to ourselves through artifice and custom (Hayek 1960, 107).

This is where culture comes crucially into play, and on the issue of culture Hayek can be interpreted as standing much closer to Smith in his emphasis upon *ethos*. Of the many disparate "tools and institutions" which constitute culture, Hayek maintains that "moral rules are the most important"; and where moral rules draw little support from nature or reason, they depend almost entirely on "the force of habit" (ibid., 123; see Hayek 1988, 6). Thus,

> it is indeed a truth, which all the great apostles of freedom outside the rational-istic school have never tired of emphasizing, that freedom has never worked without deeply ingrained moral beliefs and that coercion can be reduced to a minimum only where individuals can be expected as a rule to conform voluntarily to certain principles. (Hayek 1988, 123)

The free society requires a culture, understood in terms of *ethos*, that can foster an appreciation for and a commitment to the abstract, undesigned, and artifactual social processes that animate it. Instinct and reason will not do the heavy lifting for us; we must choose to impose upon ourselves the "discipline" of freedom (ibid., 68).

In this way, Hayek illustrates how the free society that classical liberalism aims at is predicated on an intimate relationship between sociality, morality, and culture. "Culture" in this sense, from the perspective of maintaining a particular kind of social order, is laden with normative significance. Liberal society requires a liberal culture that entails the cultivation of liberal habits, such that individuals learn to internalize the tacit knowledge and develop the psychological predispositions that will enable them to willingly embrace and adhere to the general rules of a market order. In this sense, liberal culture is not something that is created in the sense that many other human artifacts are said to be created; rather, it is something that is acquired through prudent cultivation. Unlike a poem, painting, or song that is the product of the inspired mind, the habits that constitute a liberal culture are more akin to plants or crops that come into being through the diligent care of a knowing farmer, one whose efforts and intentions are always constrained by a broader order outside of his control. In the final analysis, the necessity of a liberal *ethos* points beyond the confines of this chapter and toward the central importance of a liberal education that prepares individuals to live and flourish in the free society through a training in culture.

We have seen above how some have criticized Hayek for presenting the free society as an entirely cultural—and therefore accidental—phenomenon. Dissatisfied with Hayek's defense of liberty, John Gray complains that "when the natural selection of forms of life and their associated rules and practices occurs in the form of competition between political orders, it seems wildly unrealistic to suppose that liberal societies always have the advantage" (Gray 1980, 128). I would suggest that this is precisely Hayek's point, and it is why his conception of culture relies so heavily upon *ethos*. The free society may indeed have emerged without intention, but it cannot be expected to survive—let alone flourish—without intention. The kind of intention that is required is properly directed toward the cultivation of liberal habits and commitments. In Hayek's view, we have accidentally stumbled upon this kind of social order, discovered some of the rules that uphold it, and gotten a taste of the benefits it has to offer. Having come this far, it is now up to us to seek out those rules and sustain them, not through the rational construction of new conventions, but through a process of individual habituation. Admittedly, this is no small task, but it is nonetheless the paramount challenge that liberalism faces. To borrow a statement that Hayek employs in a slightly different context: "On that question may rest the survival of our civilization" (1988, 140).

## NOTES

1. I leave aside here the intense scholarly debates surrounding the mechanics of cultural evolution, especially group selection, in Hayek's account; on this matter, see Caldwell (2000) and those cited therein at 19n1.

2. For a thorough critique of John Gray's reading of Hayek, see Klein (1999).

3. McNamara goes on to claim that Hayek had good rhetorical reasons for making this move. As I have already indicated above, I agree that Hayek's elevation of culture and simultaneous demotion of nature and reason can be justified as part and parcel of a particular rhetorical strategy—a point to which I will return below; I disagree that Hayek's final position is radically different from Smith's when it comes to the three sources of human values.

4. Prior to the modern era, "culture" was spoken of in relation to the practices and arts associated with agriculture or the cultivation of the earth. Thus, for instance, the ancient poet Virgil describes the first human beings as nomadic hunter-gatherers who possessed no culture (*cultus*) prior to the emergence of such primitive agricultural practices as allowed for a sedentary way of life (Virgil, *Aeneid* VIII 370–85).

5. Rousseau explored two potential solutions to what he believed to be the fundamental human problem: in his *Emile* ([1762] 1979) and *Reveries of a Solitary Walker* ([1782] 1992) he articulates an individualistic solution that allows for man to fully embrace his nature by withdrawing from society or at least living on its fringes; in his *Social Contract* ([1762] 1978) he articulates a political solution that de-natures man by forcefully transforming him from an individual into a citizen who is thoroughly subordinated to yet integrated within the political community. The best introduction to Rousseau's philosophical project is Melzer (1990).

6. Rousseau and Kant did not themselves go quite so far, even if their rhetoric would encourage others to do so. Moreover, it should be kept in mind that Kant's primary interest was in demonstrating that human beings are moral agents capable of bearing moral responsibility; his statements on "culture" should thus be considered in the context of this intention.

7. Hayek quotes this statement from an article by the anthropologist Leslie Alvin White as containing a truth that we need frequently to be reminded of.

8. For the clearest articulation of this ordered triad, see Aristotle's *Politics*, 1332a38.

9. See Polybius, *Histories* VI 47: "In my opinion there are two fundamental things in every state, by virtue of which its principle and constitution is either desirable or the reverse. I mean customs and laws (*ethē* and *nomoi*). What is desirable in these makes men's private lives righteous and well-ordered and the general character of the state gentle and just." A similar distinction is found in the Latin of ancient Roman thinkers; see Cicero (1999, *On the Commonwealth* I 2), who declares that a society comes to be well-ordered through the combined effect of "custom" (*moribus*, related to our usage of "mores") or "law" (*legibus*).

10. Aristotle (2007, *Rhetoric* 1369b34).

11. Aristotle (*Politics* 1287b5, 1319b40; 2007, 1368b7, 1375a16); see Murphy (2007, 62–65).

12. See Aristotle (*Politics* 1253a1–5); Adam Smith ([1759] 1982, 85, 87–88, 116).

13. Smith was well versed in the political philosophy of Aristotle, and likely influenced by it (see [1759] 1982, 270–72; [1795] 1982, 122); for the intellectual affinities between Smith and Aristotle, see Hanley (2009, 86–91) and Vivenza (2001).

14. The paradigmatic example that Smith grapples with is the custom of infanticide—a custom of the "greatest barbarity"—that prevailed in the ancient Greek city-states and "even among the polite and civilized Athenians." The practice of killing infant children was "thoroughly authorized" by an "uninterrupted custom" transmitted across generations from "the earliest period of society." Smith goes on to point out that this custom was so entrenched that even such enlightened philosophers as Plato and Aristotle did not venture to criticize it ([1759] 1982, 209–211). This passage serves as a useful illustration of the limits of human reason vis-à-vis custom in Smith's view and supports Hayek's (1979, 156–58) contention that mind is better understood as the product of culture than the cause of it.

15. On Smith's "science of the legislator," see Hanley (2008) and Griswold (1999, 305), who both suggest the continuity between Aristotle and Smith on this matter; see Haakonssen (1981, 83–98).

16. In this regard, consider Smith's *Lectures on Rhetoric and Belles Lettres*, as well as his essays "On the History of Astronomy" ([1795] 1982, 33–105) and "Of the Imitative Arts" ([1795] 1982, 176–213).

# REFERENCES

Adorno, Theodor W., and Max Horkheimer. [1944] 1997. *Dialectic of Enlightenment.* Translated by John Cumming. New York: Verso.
Aristotle. 1957. *Oxford Classical Texts: Aristotelis: Politica.* Edited by William David Ross. Oxford: Clarendon Press.
———. 2007. *On Rhetoric: A Theory of Civil Discourse.* Translated by George A. Kennedy. Oxford: Oxford University Press.
———. 2011. *Nicomachean Ethics.* Translated by Robert C. Bartlett and Susan D. Collins Chicago: University of Chicago Press.
Arnhart, Larry. 1998. *Darwinian Natural Right: The Biological Ethics of Human Nature.* Albany, NY: State University of New York Press.
———. 2005. *Darwinian Conservatism.* Charlottesville, VA: Imprint Academic.
———. 2007. "Friedrich Hayek's Darwinian Conservatism." In *Liberalism, Conservatism, and Hayek's Idea of Spontaneous Order*, edited by Louis Hunt and Peter McNamara, 127–48. New York: Palgrave Macmillan.
Bloom, Allan. 1990. *Giants and Dwarfs: Essays 1960–1990.* New York: Simon and Schuster.
Boettke, Peter J. 2001. *Calculation and Coordination: Essays on Socialism and Transitional Political Economy.* New York: Routledge.
Caldwell, Bruce. 2000. "The Emergence of Hayek's Ideas on Cultural Evolution." *The Review of Austrian Economics* 13: 5–22.
Choi, Seung Ginny, and Virgil Henry Storr. 2018. "A Culture of Rent Seeking." *Public Choice* 181 (1–2): 101–26.
Cicero. 1999. *On the Commonwealth and On the Laws.* Edited by James E. G. Zetzel. Cambridge, UK: Cambridge University Press.

Deneen, Patrick J. 2018. *Why Liberalism Failed*. New Haven, CT: Yale University Press.

Fleischacker, Samuel. 2004. *On Adam Smith's "Wealth of Nations": A Philosophical Companion*. Princeton, NJ: Princeton University Press.

Forman-Barzilai, Fonna. 2010. *Adam Smith and the Circles of Sympathy: Cosmopolitanism and Moral Theory*. Cambridge, UK: Cambridge University Press.

Gray, John N. 1980. "F.A. Hayek on Liberty and Tradition." *The Journal of Libertarian Studies* 4 (2): 119–37.

Griswold, Charles L., Jr. 1999. *Adam Smith and the Virtues of Enlightenment*. Cambridge, UK: Cambridge University Press.

Grube, Laura E., and Virgil Henry Storr, eds. 2015. *Culture and Economic Action*. Cheltenham, UK: Edward Elgar Publishing.

Haakonssen, Knud. 1981. *The Science of a Legislator: The Natural Jurisprudence of David Hume and Adam Smith*. Cambridge, UK: Cambridge University Press.

Hanley, Ryan Patrick. 2008. "Enlightened Nation Building: The 'Science of the Legislator' in Adam Smith and Rousseau." *American Journal of Political Science* 52 (2): 219–34.

Hanley, Ryan Patrick. 2009. *Adam Smith and the Character of Virtue*. Cambridge, UK: Cambridge University Press.

Hayek, F. A. 1960. *The Constitution of Liberty*. Chicago: University of Chicago Press.

——. 1973. *Law, Legislation and Liberty, Volume 1: Rules and Order*. Chicago: University of Chicago Press.

——. 1976. *Law, Legislation and Liberty, Volume 2: The Mirage of Social Justice*. Chicago: University of Chicago Press.

——. 1979. *Law, Legislation and Liberty, Volume 3: The Political Order of a Free People*. Chicago: University of Chicago Press.

——. 1982. *Law, Legislation and Liberty: A New Statement of the Liberal Principles of Justice and Political Economy*. London: Routledge.

——. 1988. *The Fatal Conceit: The Errors of Socialism*. Edited by W. W. Bartley III. Chicago: University of Chicago Press.

Jones, Eric. 2003. *The European Miracle: Environments, Economies, and Geopolitics in the History of Europe and Asia*. 3rd ed. Cambridge, UK: Cambridge University Press.

Kant, Immanuel. [1784] 1983. "Idea for a Universal History with a Cosmopolitan Intent." In *Perpetual Peace and Other Essays*. Translated by Ted Humphrey. Indianapolis: Hackett.

——. [1786] 1983. "Speculative Beginning of Human History." In *Perpetual Peace and Other Essays*. Translated by Ted Humphrey. Indianapolis: Hackett.

Klein, Daniel B. 1999. "The Ways of John Gray: A Libertarian Commentary." *The Independent Review* 4 (1): 63–89.

Lavoie, Don. 1991. "The Discovery and Interpretation of Profit Opportunities: Culture and the Kirznerian Entrepreneur." In *The Culture of Entrepreneurship*, edited by Brigitte Berger, 33–52. San Francisco: Institute for Contemporary Studies.

Lavoie, Don, and Emily Chamlee-Wright. 2000. *Culture and Enterprise: The Development, Representation, and Morality of Business*. New York: Routledge.

McNamara, Peter. 2013. "Hayek's Unsentimental Liberalism." In *F.A. Hayek and the Modern Economy: Economic Organization and Activity*, edited by Sandra J. Peart and David M. Levy, 11–28. New York: Palgrave Macmillan.

Melzer, Arthur M. 1990. *The Natural Goodness of Man: On the System of Rousseau's Thought*. Chicago: University of Chicago Press.

Montes, Leonidas. 2011. "Is Friedrich Hayek Rowing Adam Smith's Boat?" In *Hayek, Mill, and the Liberal Tradition*, edited by Andrew Farrant, 7–38. London: Routledge.

Muller, Jerry Z. 1993. *Adam Smith in His Time and Ours: Designing the Decent Society*. Princeton, NJ: Princeton University Press.

Murphy, James Bernard. 1993. *The Moral Economy of Labor: Aristotelian Themes in Economic Theory*. New Haven, CT: Yale University Press.

———. 2002. "Nature, Custom, and Reason as the Explanatory and Practical Principles of Aristotelian Political Science." *The Review of Politics* 64 (3): 469–95.

———. 2007. "Habit and Convention at the Foundation of Custom." In *The Nature of Customary Law: Legal, Historical, and Philosophical Perspectives*, edited by Amanda Perreau-Saussine and James Bernard Murphy, 53–78. Cambridge, UK: Cambridge University Press.

Polybius. 1922. *The Histories*. Translated by W. R. Paton. Cambridge, MA: Harvard University Press.

Rasmussen, Dennis C. 2008. *The Problems and Promise of Commercial Society: Adam Smith's Response to Rousseau*. University Park, PA: Pennsylvania State University Press.

———. 2014. *The Pragmatic Enlightenment*. New York: Cambridge University Press.

Rose, David C. 2019. *Why Culture Matters Most*. New York: Oxford University Press.

Rousseau, Jean-Jacques. [1750, 1754] 1965. *The First and Second Discourses*. Translated by Roger D. Masters and Judith R. Masters. Boston and New York: Bedford/St. Martin's.

———. [1762] 1978. *On the Social Contract, with Geneva Manuscript and Political Economy*. Translated by Roger D. Masters and Judith R. Masters. Boston and New York: Bedford/St. Martin's.

———. [1762] 1979. *Emile, or On Education*. Translated by Allan Bloom. New York: Basic Books.

———. [1782] 1992. *The Reveries of the Solitary Walker*. Translated by Charles E. Butterworth. Indianapolis: Hackett.

Smith, Adam. [1759] 1982. *The Theory of Moral Sentiments*. Edited by D. D. Raphael and A. L. Macfie. Indianapolis: Liberty Fund.

———. [1776] 1981. *An Inquiry into the Nature and Causes of the Wealth of Nations, Volumes I and II*. Edited by R. H. Campbell, A. S. Skinner, and W. B. Todd. Indianapolis: Liberty Fund.

———. [1795] 1982. *Essays on Philosophical Subjects*. Edited by W. P .D. Wightman and J.C. Bryce. Indianapolis: Liberty Fund.

Storr, Virgil Henry. 2013. *Understanding the Culture of Markets*. New York: Rout-ledge.

Viner, Jacob. 1961. "Hayek on Freedom and Coercion." *Southern Economic Journal* 27 (3): 230–36.

Virgil. 2006. *The Aeneid*. Translated by Robert Fagles. New York: Viking Penguin.

Vivenza, Gloria. 2001. *Adam Smith and the Classics: The Classical Heritage in Adam Smith's Thought*. Oxford: Oxford University Press.

Wolf, Brianne. 2017. "Beyond the Efficiency of the Market: Adam Smith on Sym-pathy and the Poor Law." In *Interdisciplinary Studies of the Market Order: New Applications of Market Process Theory*, edited by Peter J. Boettke, Christopher J. Coyne, and Virgil Henry Storr, 39–62. Lanham, MD: Rowman and Littlefield.

## Chapter 3

# Do We Own Our Data?

## The Finders-Keepers Ethics of the Cyber Commons

### James Goodrich

Amazon, Facebook, Google, and other companies collect information about us and our online activity. Using this information and data mining techniques, these companies are able to make good probabilistic inferences about what sorts of ads would be most effective in getting each of us to purchase particular goods. These companies are then able to sell ad space on their websites to other companies with the promise of maximizing the effectiveness of those other companies' ads. The collection of our personal data with the aforementioned business model has become a billion-dollar industry.

There is increasing concern, however, about whether this business model is morally acceptable. Some contest that it violates our rights to privacy, while others worry that it is unfair because it allows companies to internalize profits while externalizing their costs (Cheneval 2018). Still others believe that the model is exploitative or perhaps even constitutes theft (Arrieta-Ibarra et al. 2018). Whether using our data as a means of profit is exploitative or constitutes theft, however, surely turns on the question of whether we are entitled to the products of our data. In turn, this issue resolves itself into the question of whether we, in some sense, own our data in the first place (Ritter and Mayer 2018).

Much of our useful data is generated from our actions. In this sense, data looks to be the result of our labor. Thus, any account of property rights that closely links labor and our ownership entitlements will entail that we have rights to our personal digital data. This, in turn, would entail by the usual logic of property that so long as some consent mechanism is in place, companies would owe compensation to individuals for using their data. Failure to pay compensation would thus be constitutive of exploitation. (And if no consent mechanism was in place, this would constitute theft.) However, whether this rough line of thought is cogent hinges crucially upon the theory of property rights we adopt and what we mean by capacious phrases like "the product of our labor."[1]

In particular, this chapter concerns itself with the specifics of the theory of property rights we might adopt. Which theory of property rights we adopt, after all, may well have implications about whether or not we have property rights in our personal digital data (Nolin 2019). We cannot, of course, do justice to all theories of property rights within a single chapter. We will need to focus more narrowly. My interest is in which implications the Kirznerian theory of property rights has for the debate over property rights in personal digital data. The results of this inquiry, however, should nevertheless prove instructive for teasing out the implications of other theories of property rights in the context of personal digital data.

To foreshadow my conclusions, the Kirznerian theory of property rights *itself* does not have the tools to claim that each of us as individuals have rights to our personal digital data (or rights to the profits generated by the use of that data). However, the larger Kirznerian view of distributive justice may give us reasons to prefer a set of institutions that would recognize conventional versions of such property rights. Roughly, the thought is this: data should be considered a common pool resource. Rights to access a commons (in order to acquire property rights over some resource in that commons) differ from rights to acquire private property in the first place (Schlager and Ostrom 1992). The Kirznerian's wider views of distributive justice may give us reasons to adopt institutions that constrain access to the cyber commons of personal digital data. Respecting such constraints imposes at least *some* duties on Amazon et al. that are owed directly to the individuals who could make use of that commons. These duties, in turn, imply some correlative rights for these individuals to their digital data (or profits from that data).

Here is how I will proceed. First, I will consider the question of whether we can own our data really makes good conceptual sense. Some have expressed skepticism on this point. Next, I will briefly introduce the Kirznerian theory of property rights and raise some worries about one attempt to bring the Kirznerian theory into conversation with disputes over our data. This will lead to an examination of each part of the Kirznerian theory, which I will argue provides no help to justifying claims about natural property rights in our digital data. Finally, I will argue that Kirznerians have available to themselves a conventional account of property rights that would have interesting implications for the debates surrounding ownership and our data.

## CONCEPTUAL PRELIMINARIES

I have assumed that it made sense to ask, "Do we have property rights over our personal digital data?" But does it? Some have contested that, due to some apparent conceptual or metaphysical difficulties, personal digital data is just not the kind of thing that could, even in principle, be owned. Our inquiry is thus a nonstarter if these worries are on mark. As such, it behooves us to discuss them here at the outset before we turn to the questions of moral theories that presuppose their answers. (However, if you find yourself antecedently convinced that data could in principle be owned, then you may wish to skip this section.)

Let's start simply. Some kinds of things clearly *can* be owned. I own the laptop I'm typing on, the chair I'm sitting on, and the coffee mug out of which I'm drinking. Other kinds of things clearly cannot be owned. I could not, even in principle, own the number nine, the color green, or the second law of thermodynamics. But what distinguishes the kinds of things that can be owned from the things that cannot? And on which side of this line does our personal digital data fall? The first set of objects I named—the laptop, the chair, and the coffee mug—are concrete particulars. They are among the physical stuff we can bump into in the world. The second set of objects I named—the number nine, the color green, and the second law of thermodynamics—are abstract universals. We cannot bump into these things. And more importantly, we cannot do a lot of other things with abstract universals. We cannot sell them, earn profits from them, or exclude others from using them. All of these characteristics are hallmarks of the kinds of things we are capable of owning. Thus, the fact that abstract universals seem to lack these features gives us reason to doubt that they could be the proper objects of ownership.[2] One might look at our personal digital data and think, "Well, I can't bump into that either." So perhaps our data is more like the aforementioned abstract universals than it is like the laptop, chair, or coffee mug. And if so, perhaps our personal digital data is also not the kind of thing that can be owned, even in principle.

Of course, we can in principle sell our data, earn profits from it, and exclude it from being used by others. Suppose there was no monitoring of our online activity. But instead, I simply wrote down on a piece of paper some demographic information about myself, all the Google searches I made in a day, and all of the links that I clicked on. I could, at least in principle, sell this piece of paper or prevent you from looking at it. This may not mean that I have the right to do so. But that is a moral point, not a conceptual or metaphysical one. In other words, all our personal digital data is just a kind of information, and we're all familiar with ways to sell and exclude people from

information. Entire businesses are founded on the very idea that we can exclude information from those who do not pay for it—bookstores and universi-
ties are clear examples. But this might extend to any sector of the economy in
which one pays for the advice of experts on some question or another since
such a service involves an exchange of information to the buyer. Insofar as
our data is information, it seems reasonable that despite any conceptual or
metaphysical worries regarding our data as property, it is not that such data is,
in principle, incapable of being sold or that we cannot, in principle, exclude
others from using it.

Here is a different worry.[3] The worry is that our personal digital data cannot be the object of a property right because information about one individual
is often also information about another individual. For example, my mother's
birthday is data about my mother at least as much as it is data about myself.
It is *her* birthday, but it is also *my* mother's birthday. And it's also my sister-
in-law's mother-in-law's birthday, her mother's daughter's mother-in-law's
birthday, and so on. Who has a right to this data? What principle could possibly tell us?

These questions may appear intractable. However, they are not. As a pre-
liminary conceptual matter, "Ellen Goodrich's birthday" and "my mother's
birthday" refer to the same date. But they are nevertheless not identical pieces
of information. After all, some facts could be true of a person whose mother's
birthday was $X$ that are not true of the mother who is having the birthday.
Here is a relevant example. My consumption habits approaching my mother's
birthday are likely to be quite different than my mother's consumption habits.
I will want to buy a present for my mother, and my mother might hold off
on buying something because she believes that I might give it to her for her
birthday. Thus, all we need to see is that the referent—namely, the birth date
in question—does not exhaust the content of the data or the uses to which it
could be put.[4] Therefore, we should opt for a relatively fine-grained notion
of "personal digital data" and a fine-grained understanding of our rights over
that data. If I own my data, I thus own the data that "my mother's birthday
is $X$." My mother owns the data that "her birthday is $X$." There is at least no
conceptual conflict here.

But perhaps a more practical problem remains. The problem is this: suppose I sign a contract with Facebook to give them all of my personal digital
data. Among the data they will receive is "my mother's birthday is $X$" and
"my mother is Ellen Goodrich." From this data, they can infer that "Ellen
Goodrich's birthday is $X$." Thus, it's difficult for me to sign away my data in
a contract to Facebook while preserving my mother's ability to successfully
exclude Facebook from using her data. Put somewhat differently, they may
not need to use my mother's data if they can use mine to target ads toward

her anyway. Thus, the objection goes, the fine-grained information response I provided above does not avoid the practical problem of what to do when two individuals' data is connected.

However, this practical problem is not the hurdle it may first appear to be. What it means is that one of the entitlements associated with my property right to my data—my ability to consent to others using my data—is limited by the rights of other individuals. This is hardly surprising. In general, I have a right to bodily autonomy. I can move and use my body as I like. Perhaps I like to shadow box. However, if someone stands in front of me in a public place where I usually shadow box, I may not intentionally shadow box there at that moment. Why? Because what would usually be an exercise of my right to control the movements of my own body now involves violating the rights of others, and I clearly am not allowed to do so. Thus, I'm simply not allowed to sign a contract that would give some of the data I usually have rights over to Facebook if this would violate my mother's rights. In practice, this might mean that I could contract out either the data that "my mother's birthday is *X*" or "my mother is Ellen Goodrich" but not both. Perhaps in practice this would also mean that someone would need to create an app that could check for logical or probabilistic entailments of one's data to ensure no such violation occurs.

An alternative solution would be to only recognize moral rights to certain predefined bundles of data so that no such conflict would occur. This might mean, in practice, that some natural moral rights to data may not be recognized, but this may be an acceptable consequence if it provides a better overall solution to the practical problem. What would these predefined bundles look like? I couldn't tell you. They'd have to be determined via a political process. The bundles would thus, in some sense, be socially constructed. This need not bother us, however, since we have property rights over socially constructed objects already (e.g., currency, shares of funds, and so on). I thus conclude that my guiding question—Do we own our personal digital data?—makes conceptual sense. I can make sense of it, and I suspect you can too.

## KIRZNER'S THEORY OF PROPERTY RIGHTS

Most of us believe that what is just or fair depends upon, *inter alia*, individual moral rights. A subset of these moral rights are ownership rights—a bundle of entitlements to (1) use an owned good, (2) exclude use of the owned good by others, (3) rent or sell the use of the owned good to others, and (4) gain profits from the use of the owned good. Thus, if you own a car, *ceteris paribus*, I owe you a *pro tanto* moral duty to not use your car without your permission.[5]

If I did use your car without your permission, then I would, *ceteris paribus*, be violating your rights and thereby wronging you. And wronging you, in turn, would be unfair or unjust. (Though to be clear, the dimension of justice associated with property rights may not exhaust all dimensions of justice nor morality as a whole.)

Most theories of the content, scope, and grounds of ownership rights have been developed with tangible goods in mind. Given the historical context in which such theories were developed, this made perfectly good sense. In recent decades, however, questions concerning ownership over non-tangible goods have become increasingly important politically, socially, and economically. Perhaps the most well-attended to example of putative ownership rights in non-tangible goods is intellectual property. Of course, what we should say about intellectual property, especially from the perspective of moral theory, is far from settled. But questions concerning intellectual property only make up a small subset of potential ownership rights in non-tangible goods. There are less well-attended to moral and political questions concerning potential ownership rights in other kinds of non-tangible goods. This chapter focuses on one such family of questions: What are the contents, scope, and grounds of ownership rights in digital data—if there are any at all?

As I said in my introductory remarks, our focus will be on what the Kirznerian theory of property rights should say about digital data. To a first approximation, the Kirznerian theory of property rights is a version of the Lockean theory of property rights.[6] We can state the Lockean theory, roughly, as follows:

**The Lockean View**: An agent S possesses an ownership right over a good G if and only if (i) G is a part of S's person OR (ii) G is the result of S's legitimate appropriation AND (iii) enough and as good of G is left for others.

There are two ways appropriation of a good might be legitimate. Either S receives a good G from someone who owns G or S does not. If someone owns G, then G must be given to S by contract or consent of its owner. However, if G is unowned, then S owns G if S meets *an original appropriation condition*. What exactly constitutes the original appropriation condition in Locke's original view is debated, for it turns on what exactly Locke meant by "mixing one's labor." As Robert Nozick famously made the point, one does not own the ocean merely by mixing orange juice one has made with it (Nozick 1974).

Contemporary neo-Lockeans agree with much of Locke's picture, but they often disagree about how we should best understand the original appropriation condition. (They also often disagree with how to understand clause (iii), which is sometimes called "The Lockean Proviso." More on this in due course.) This is where Kirzner comes in. Israel Kirzner offers a novel *suffi-*

*cient*, but not necessary condition for what it takes to originally appropriate a good. His thought is as follows (Kirzner 2016). Most of us would agree that if one causes there to exist some new good G in excess of the good G* required to create G, then, *ceteris paribus*, one is entitled to at least the difference in value of G and G*. Let's call this "the Creation-Entitlement Premise." The Creation-Entitlement Premise is itself a sufficient condition for legitimate original appropriation of some good. Kirzner exploits the Creation-Entitlement Premise by offering a novel interpretation of the "causes there to exist some new good" locution. His key insight is that *discovery* of a new good is itself a form of causing a new good to exist, *practically speaking*. That is, there are epistemic constraints on what we should consider the total set of *status quo* owned or unowned goods to be. Put roughly, if no one is aware of a good, then no one can make use of it. If no one can make use of it, it does not exist, practically speaking, and therefore no one is entitled to it.[7] Thus, when someone discovers a valuable item, they are in fact causing the total set of owned or unowned goods to increase. They are "enlarging the pie," as it were. Discovery, thus, is an act of creation according to what we might call Kirzner's "Finders-Keepers" version of the Creation-Entitlement Premise, or "the Finders-Keepers Premise" for short. Our question for now becomes: What, if anything, does the Finders-Keepers Premise imply about our personal digital data?

## AN INSTRUCTIVE MISUNDERSTANDING

It will be instructive for our purposes to consider a misunderstanding of the Finders-Keepers Premise already present in the literature. Marijn Sax has argued that (1) something akin to Kirzner's Finders-Keepers Premise indeed underlies much of the rationale for the potential moral entitlement of companies like Amazon, Facebook, and Google to use our data and (2) Kirzner's Finders-Keepers Premise can be shown to possess problematic assumptions in the case of our personal digital data (Sax 2016).

With respect to (1), Sax argues that the aforementioned companies are best understood as discovering a valuable product of our data because our data is not itself so valuable until one exploits data-mining techniques to extract further information from it. And in this sense, he believes Kirzner's Finders-Keepers Premise applies. This is an interesting point. Notice that any version of the Creation-Entitlement Premise that was non-epistemic—to wit, that required the capital "E" Existence of a new valuable item—likely would not apply to the case of Amazon et al. Why? Well, new information is plausibly not created by the act of data mining since that information is entailed by the underlying data. Or it would be, at any rate, highly controversial to say that new, valuable objects were *created* as opposed to *discovered*. The resulting information collected from data mining our personal digital data is, in other words, already out there to be discovered. And on Kirzner's discovery interpretation of creation, this is good enough to create an entitlement.

Now, I would like to note a minor, passing objection to (1). No one to my knowledge actually employs Kirzner's thinking in the way described by Sax, so Sax risks strawmanning both the defenders of current data practices and Kirzner by presenting them as allies.

Let's now consider (2). Sax deploys a combination of objections to the Kirznerian Finders-Keepers Premise approach to current data practices, but the heart of his objection seems to rest on the idea that the Finders-Keepers Premise, if it's applied, leads us astray in the case of personal digital data. Why? Here he appeals to the idea that our personal digital data is somehow closely connected to our person: "the idea that your identity as a person is always necessarily constituted—at least partly—by your information" (Sax 2016, 29). Sax seems to be implicitly invoking clause (i) of the Lockean View. Just as we own our bodies, so too do we own our information. Thus, according to Sax, just as a company cannot use our bodies without consent to derive entitlements to profits, so too they cannot use our information.

Sax makes a rather bold metaphysical claim in saying that our information is necessarily constitutive of us. To see the falsity of Sax's claim, it's sufficient to see that not all of our information is necessarily constitutive of us. Indeed, likely very little of it is. Whether I used Google to search the terms "Sax," "Kirzner," and "big data" is hardly necessarily constitutive of me. I would have been the exact same person typing this chapter had I never performed that action. Moreover, whether I was born in Generation Y or Generation Z may be relevant data. However, such a difference could hardly be constitutive of me. After all, which of the two generations I was born into comes down to whether I was born a minute before or a minute after midnight on December 31, 1994. But a mere difference of two minutes could hardly make me a different person. It would likely indicate more about the procedures of the given hospital at which I was born than it would about me.

There are, of course, moves Sax could make in response. But the further we wade into such metaphysical waters, the more controversial and therefore less compelling Sax's objection is liable to become. If Sax must rely on a much more complicated story about how quite a lot of our data that does not seem essential to us in fact is essential, we should begin to wonder whether we are adopting a less plausible metaphysical picture to gerrymander the result we want about data. And surely, that is not the direction in which we should go.

For the sake of argument, however, suppose Sax is right that our personal digital data is necessarily constitutive of us. Sax's objection nevertheless fails to be compelling. Kirzner's Finders-Keepers Premise is just a sufficient condition for legitimate original appropriation of some good. Thus, it tells us nothing about what should be said in cases that involve the use of already-owned property. In other words, Kirzner's view is neo-Lockean. Therefore, it matters to him a great deal whether a given good is already owned. Kirzner would not think, for example, that if Jack stole a bunch of apples from Jill's orchard and made apple juice out of them, then Jack owns the resulting apple juice even if no one had previously discovered the concept of apple juice. Therefore, whether Kirzner's Finders-Keepers premise is even implicated in the case at hand depends on the prior question of whether or not individuals own their data. And thus, Sax's point about (1), while interesting in its own right, is only relevant if Kirzner's view is antecedently committed to the view that individuals do not own their own personal digital data.

Sax might respond by saying that he was never attacking the Kirznerian view, and he was just attacking its application to personal digital data. He could certainly be clearer on this point. Again, framing the issue as he has creates at least the specter of a strawman. In any case, the Kirznerian should be interested in the question, "Do individuals own their personal digital data?" If they do, then Amazon et al. are wronging individuals. If they do not, then perhaps Amazon et al. are not simply failing to wrong individuals; perhaps they are entitled by the Kirznerian's lights to the profits of the products of everyone's personal digital data.

## THE LOCKEAN PROVISO

The Kirznerian is working within a neo-Lockean framework. One way to understand Sax—once we have clarified that his objection is not actually to the Kirznerian *per se*—is that Sax was suggesting that we do own our personal digital data because of clause (i) of the Lockean View. For reasons that I previously discussed, I rather doubt that this is a successful move. A different move one might make is to argue on the basis of clause (iii) of the Lockean View—also known as "the Lockean Proviso"—that individuals own their own personal digital data. Notice, however, that the Lockean Proviso is a constraint on the Creation-Entitlement Premise. Thus, it could only be invoked to rule out the acquisition of some kinds of property. (In other words, it's a necessary condition of a sufficient condition of property acquisition.) It cannot be invoked to actually ground a property right itself. It is thus of no use if what we want is a theoretical story about how people possess a legitimate property right; it can only tell us who does not have such a right. Because it could become relevant, however, it's worth pausing to consider whether the Lockean Proviso might rule out the putative ownership right by Amazon et al. over our personal digital data.

Kirzner himself makes some interesting remarks on how we should best understand his Finders-Keepers Premise in relation to the Lockean Proviso. For Kirzner, insofar as the Finders-Keepers version of the Creation-Entitlement Premise is in play, the Lockean Proviso may not apply (Kirzner 2016, 149–55). Why? In Kirzner's interpretation, the argument for the Lockean Proviso assumes that there is a fixed amount of resources. When individuals make a useful good, they have to use up other resources to make it. Given that resources are scarce, this means that for a system of property rights not to lead to horrible consequences for many, it has to be that individuals have an equal opportunity to make use of the scarce resources. If the system lacks this, the argument goes, then those individuals without an equal opportunity to make good use of a scarce resource will be harmed by being deprived of various resources. Individuals have a right to their bodies and against being harmed. Kirzner, however, argues that the kind of entrepreneurial discovery at work in the Finders-Keepers Premise invalidates this argument. The reason is that entrepreneurial discoveries are, in a certain sense, creations *ex nihilo*. They are discoveries of more value than we previously knew were there. Thus, discovery in Kirzner's view increases the size of the value pie. And if that is right, then no one can be said to be harmed by the discoverer's acquisition of that value (or perhaps means to it). This is because it does not impose the potential harms of deprivation on anyone for the discoverer to acquire that extra value. Thus, the thought goes, the Lockean Proviso does not apply if the Finders-Keepers Premise does.[8]

Whatever one thinks of this argument on Kirzner's behalf, it must be admitted that the Lockean Proviso applied to Amazon et al. would conflict with the heart of the Kirznerian position on discovery. And if that is so, then any invocation of the Finders-Keepers Premise could not also invoke the Lockean Proviso in defense of ownership rights (in anything). In other words, a Kirznerian can only invoke the Lockean Proviso by not invoking what is distinctive of the Kirznerian position. And if they cannot invoke what is distinctive of the Kirznerian position, then there is no way the Kirznerian position could rule out the possibility that Amazon et al. have a given property right. Indeed, as I mentioned in the previous section, the Finders-Keepers Premise can be used—if we agree with Sax's point (1) —to defend Amazon et al.'s property right in our data (or to the use of our data to make a profit).

## THE FINDERS-KEEPERS PREMISE

At this point, I have argued that neither clause (i) nor (iii) aids us in explaining why or how individuals could have property rights over their personal digital data. This leaves clause (ii), which, interestingly, is what the Kirznerian version of the Lockean View is about. Put more precisely, it is about original appropriation. Because consensual appropriation of good G presupposes ownership of G, only original appropriation is relevant to the issue of whether each of us owns our personal digital data. This invites an interesting question: Could the Finders-Keepers Premise itself underlie our initial ownership rights to personal digital data, thereby undermining the unrestricted rights of Amazon et al. to profit from our data?

Notice, of course, that other versions of the Creation-Entitlement Premise might be able to play the aforementioned right-grounding role as well. And it is certainly open to the Kirznerian to invoke such a premise. However, all such versions of the premise are controversial, so considering such positions would take us far afield of what the Kirznerian is entitled to by their own lights.

One candidate proposal is that our data-generating actions constitute discoveries of our own preferences. What we are disposed to prefer may in one sense be "out there," but it's not until we perform data-generating actions that we discover what our own preferences are. I have three worries about this view.

My first worry is that some of my personal digital data would not be covered by this view, even in principle. For example, it may well be useful for a business to know when my birthday is without knowing anything else about me. And yet, just having a birthday is in no way a discovery. Or take another example. Suppose I become friends on Facebook with someone I have known for a very long time outside of the internet. It is difficult to see how I have learned anything about my preferences by agreeing to be their Facebook friend. And yet, this is potentially the kind of data at stake in our larger discussions about property rights and personal digital data. Of course, this might mean we have to simply restrict the scope of the Kirznerian response.

The second worry about this proposal is that in performing many of our data-generating activities, we do not recognize the results of those activities as teaching us about our preferences. This is a slightly different worry from the first. When I used Google to look for Sax's article, I did not learn anything about my preferences. Or perhaps I did. But what I learned surely is not apparent to me. And yet, this was a data-generating action. Again, it's open for the Kirznerian, of course, to claim that we only have a right to the data resulting from activities that do teach us about our preferences. This may be right as far as morality goes. However, it is worth noting that it would be a difficult distinction to codify into law, thus creating potential problems downstream from this discussion for how to handle Amazon et al. in practice.

The third worry is that this view would overgenerate data ownership if the concept of a "data-generating" activity is sufficiently wide. Do I have ownership over the contents of my perceptual experiences or the visual contents of a photograph if I find that I enjoy looking at sunsets? After all, such contents are plausibly just information. Perhaps we do have such ownership rights, but this is surely taking us in a direction one would not have thought we would end up going in when we started with the Finders-Keepers Premise.

However, even if we grant that these three worries can be abated, it is unclear whether a discovery of my own preferences counts as the kind of discovery that is at the heart of Kirzner's theory. Kirzner was interested in entrepreneurial discoveries. These are discoveries of new valuable uses for token resources, services, or assets. Thus, even if I learn something about my preferences via my data-generating activities, it is far from clear that what I am discovering is a new, valuable use for my data. For example, suppose I learn that I enjoy chickpea vindaloo. This might be valuable information in one sense. There are now more entrée options I enjoy than I previously thought. But it is unclear that this particular discovery generates new value by itself. If I learn I can make chickpea vindaloo at a lower cost than any other dish that I equally enjoy, then this might generate some new value (for me at least). If I instead discover that chickpea vindaloo is always more expensive than dishes I equally enjoy, then this is not a value-increasing discovery. Thus, there are at least some differences between discovering I have a preference and discovering a piece of information with value. They can, of course, be related in important ways. But such information is insufficient without the right mean-ends relationship in place.

The Kirznerian does not seem to have resources to claim, by the light of their neo-Lockean commitments at least, that we have ownership rights in our digital data. Despite this seeming skepticism, I will now shift gears to argue that there are limits to the ownership rights of companies like Amazon, Facebook, and Google in our digital data. Properly understood, these limits imply duties on the part of Amazon et al. to the rest of us. We can claim that such duties do correlate to rights possessed by individuals. However, these rights are not exactly to their personal digital data per se. And all of this rests, with some exegetical liberties taken, on a wider understanding of Kirzner's Finders-Keepers ethics.

## NATURAL VERSUS CONVENTIONAL RIGHTS

Notice that Lockean commitments, as they are typically understood, are only commitments to so-called "natural" or "nonconventional" rights. This leaves it open for the Kirznerian to argue that recognizing a conventional property right to personal digital property could be morally justified on consequentialist grounds. This involves two steps. The first step is identifying a good consequence that a society could legitimately promote. This requires attending to the usual squabbles of mainstream liberal political philosophy. But it could be done. The second step would be to show empirically that enforcing a conventional right to personal digital data would promote the aforementioned good. Again, this could be done. And if it could, the Kirznerian could defend the position that personal digital data should be recognized as owned by those who produced the data even if this is not a matter of natural justice. Moreover, this would be in keeping with a Kirznerian view insofar as the thing to be promoted looks valuable by Kirzner's lights. For example, if one of two schemes of property rights looked to better promote entrepreneurial discovery, one could see how Kirzner's wider conception of Finders-Keepers ethics might entail that the property rights regime that better promoted entrepreneurial discovery is preferable.

But there is really a third step as well. If we think that the heart of Sax's point (1) is correct, then by the Kirznerian's lights, Amazon et al. satisfy the Finders-Keepers Premise. Insofar as that is true, Amazon et al. have an entitlement to the products of our data assuming we do not naturally own them. Furthermore, the good consequences of recognizing conventional ownership rights in personal data would need to be sufficiently weighty to outweigh Amazon et al.'s natural entitlement to the profits from our personal digital data. Thus, the Kirznerian must find a sufficiently weighty good to be achieved, lest they allow for natural ownership rights to be frequently outweighed by lesser, conventional consequentialist considerations. And this may not be in keeping with Kirzner's distinctive claim that pure profits in capitalism are, in fact, just.[9]

However, there may be a different strategy. This would be to show that Sax's point (1) is wrong or that insofar as it's right, it's limited in scope. In other words, Amazon et al. may have some moral entitlement to profiting from our data, but they are currently profiting more than they are entitled to by the Kirznerian's lights. If that is so, one could explain why some have the intuition that there is something morally problematic about Amazon et al.'s business model while still making essential appeals to some claims about the Kirznerian view of property rights. In the next two sections, I will sketch one promising way this could be accomplished.

## DISCOVERY IN THE CYBER COMMONS

The Kirznerian should distinguish between the discovery of valuable uses of some asset and the discovery of a commons producing those assets. It is plausibly the former and not the latter that generates a property right. To see why, think of our data-generating activity as a kind of commons. Our continual acts of searching, posting pictures, and so on should thus be thought of similarly to more familiar self-sustaining natural resource commons such as fisheries. Just as a local environment will create a self-sustaining system in which new fish will continually be produced, cyber commons also continually produce new data, which can then be put to various valuable purposes. This intuition can be extended by recognizing a layer of separation between us and what is useful about our data: it is useful in aggregate to spot trends. It is the emerging patterns to which we contribute that allow for serious companies like Amazon et al. to flourish.

Let's note a few further things about the cyber commons and its relationship to the Kirznerian's more general Finders-Keepers ethics. First, the Kirznerian view of property rights can easily explain why the discovery of new valuable uses of data can entitle the discoverer to profits from those *token* uses. But Kirzner would never hold that the discovery of the uses of data could entitle an individual to the profits generated by *types* of valuable uses. For example, if I discover that you can make juice out of apples, this entitles me to profit from the juice I make. However, *ceteris paribus*, I am not thereby entitled to profits from the juice that others might make from the apples in their orchards.[10] It's thus the discovery of token uses of resources that deliver entitlements, not types of uses. If this is right, it in turn explains why many different companies can act justly (or at least not unjustly) when they use our personal digital data. No one company can have the entitlement to the big data business model itself.

Second, the question of who is entitled to access the cyber commons in the first place differs from the question of whether those who discover valuable uses of data in the cyber commons are entitled to the profits of their discovery. Again, let's return to a natural resource commons like a fishery. Individuals who catch fish in these fisheries may well be entitled to the profits generated by selling those fish. However, there are often mechanisms in place to ensure that no one individual gets complete, unfettered access to the commons (Ostrom 1990). Like Kirzner's view, nothing in the logic of a neo-Lockean view of property rights entails that an individual has a right to (or a duty against) accessing a commons. This creates a kind of elbow room for the more general Kirznerian Finders-Keepers ethics. While nothing in the neo-Lockean Finders-Keepers Premise entails that each of us presently possesses a property right in our data that Amazon et al. are violating, it is unclear whether Amazon et al. have an initial right to access the cyber commons constituted by our data. Perhaps it is in keeping with Kirznerian Finders-Keepers ethics more generally that such access rights to the just acquisition of property can or should be withheld from Amazon et al. We will probe this possibility further in the next section.

Third, the cyber commons clearly differs from a natural resource commons in a variety of ways. Perhaps the most fundamental difference is that the cyber commons is thoroughly socially constructed. This is true in the simple sense that, without human beings engaging in social interactions, we would not have this cyber commons.[11] But the cyber commons is also socially constructed in the further sense that data-generating activities are both constituted by and constitute cultural activities. In other words, many of our data-generating activities are only economically valuable insofar as they are enmeshed within various cultural institutions. I am engaging in social activity when I search for concert tickets or "like" a post about my friend's new job. I am performing actions that reflect my tastes in cultural activities (e.g., I have bought concert tickets and not theater tickets) and signal some facts about who is within my social circles. Moreover, insofar as market activities are cultural and social activities, there is a credible claim to be made that Amazon purchases are themselves a kind of social and cultural activity.[12] The data generated from these activities is thus about me, my social relations with others, and my preferences. And it is the continual dynamic updates to this kind of information—often within a larger data set, of course—that have economic value. Natural resource commons, like fisheries, are occasionally sites for social exchange, but they do not possess these features by necessity and perhaps rarely possess them saliently.

Moreover, such data-generating activities spawn new cultural artifacts and thereby support new social constructions. That is, "internet culture" is itself a kind of social product of our data-generating activities. People create and share "memes" more efficiently than they once did. And these memes then get turned into products. One only needs to type "grumpy cat" into Amazon. com to find many pages of products inspired by an internet joke. Buying and wearing a Grumpy Cat T-shirt would do more social signaling than my selling of a fish to a cafe would. My point here is simply that there is a kind of social feedback loop to our data-generating activities. We are simultaneously engaging in and creating widespread cultural artifacts by engaging as we do in online activities.

This point about the social construction of the cyber commons may seem like little more than a digression. However, it is emphatically not. One obstacle to appreciating the idea that our data-generating activities could constitute a kind of commons is that we are used to thinking about particular commons in terms of asocial natural resources. But there is no conceptual reason we must think this way. And if the thought that our data-generating activities are a kind of commons is correct, then we must ask the question of who has rights of access to this commons. Our answer to this question is important if we are to consider the wider question: What, if anything, does the Kirznerian have to say about whether we should recognize individual data-generators as having property rights in their personal digital data?

We can make this point about the relevance of the social construction of the cyber commons to the Kirznerian's Finders Keepers ethics clearest by considering a worry about the direction in which I am heading. One might say,

> These are all fine points. However, I cannot see how they could become relevant. Clearly Amazon et al. have rights of access to the cyber commons. After all, this cyber commons was *created* for us by various companies. It's not as if they simply came upon it like a new body of water in which they began fishing. Amazon, Facebook, and Google spent a great deal of time and capital to construct their website and make them user-friendly. So how could any of this make a difference? It's clear how the aforementioned rights to access fall.

Not so fast. It's unclear whether the assumption that Amazon et al. created the cyber commons is in fact true. Here is a different interpretation: Amazon et al. improved the cyber commons. After all, our data and our data-generating activities are nothing new in one important sense. Our data—or our most valuable data—is about and generated by our social or cultural exchanges. But we've always had such exchanges. And there has always been information about such exchanges. What Amazon et al. have allowed us to do (among many other things, of course) is engage in cultural and social exchanges at lower costs to ourselves. To be clear, the improvements made by Amazon et al. may well be moral entitlement-generating improvements. That is, we may owe Amazon et al. something for reducing the costs of some of our cultural and social activities. However, this does not imply that they have the unfettered and unrestricted property rights in the cyber commons that would be generated if they had created something new as opposed to improving something that was already there.

Consider an analogy. Suppose there is an unowned fishery that a given community makes use of. Someone comes along and improves this fishery, and it thus produces more fish. *Ceteris paribus*, the community that uses this fishery benefits from this improvement. All the fishers can acquire more fish to sell. Intuitively, the person who improved the fishery is morally entitled to some nontrivial compensation for their actions. Perhaps they're even owed some percentage of the improved output of the fishery. Suppose, however, that they are unwilling or unable to do some of the labor of fishing itself. If that is right, there is some percentage of the improved output of the fishery that would not (intuitively) be owed to this person. Moreover, this person would not be owed a percentage of the output of the fish that were already being produced by this fishery.

In other words, as I mentioned when outlining the basics of a neo-Lockean theory of property rights, most of us would agree that if one causes there to exist some new good G in excess of the good G* required to create G, then, *ceteris paribus*, one is entitled to at least the difference in value of G and G*. There are therefore intuitive limits to what one is entitled to by virtue of improving a commons. If this analogy is apt, we might say the same of Amazon et al. and the cyber commons. There are limits to that which they are entitled to. And perhaps they are not entitled to all of their profits.[13]

Let me now put my larger point more succinctly. The discoveries of valuable uses for data made by companies like Amazon et al. entitle them to at least some of the resulting profits. However, whether this entitles them to the present distribution of profits acquired from the collection of our data is a separate matter. Insofar as their collection of our data based off of our activity online is a way for them to capitalize on what was already there—our larger cultural and social exchanges—the cyber commons should be seen as an improvement on the already-existing cultural and social commons. If that is right, then they do not morally possess the entitlements to all of the profits they now have.

I have argued that if it's best to construe Amazon et al. as having improved the cyber commons and not created it, they *might* be entitled to less than the status quo legal situation would suggest. Thus, Sax's point (1) is, strictly speaking, true, but it is more limited in scope than we might have previously thought. However, just because Amazon et al. lack this entitlement does not mean that they have done anything morally wrong. Some moral reason for them to not act as they have would need to be shown. Or alternatively, there would need to be a moral reason to institute a different set of restrictions on Amazon et al.'s use of the cyber commons. In the next section, I will take up this question.

## GOVERNING THE CYBER COMMONS

I argued in the previous section that in some interpretations of what Amazon et al. did for the cyber commons, they are not entitled to all of the profits of using our data. This does not mean they have done anything wrong. And for the sake of argument, I will set aside the question of whether they have. What I am interested in now is that, given that Amazon et al. lack an entitlement to at least some of their profits, are we entitled to limit their access to the rest of the remaining profits? This will depend upon what else is at stake. If nothing else of moral relevance is at stake, then it would constitute little more than spite to deny Amazon et al. the additional profits. As I said before, the Kirznerian could claim here that, so long as it does not run afoul of other morally important principles, we could seek to promote entrepreneurial discovery. In the Kirznerian picture of the world, this is important; for it is the entrepreneur at rock bottom who explains the success of the market process. It's the entrepreneur who grows the value pie. Our question thus becomes this: Can we give to Amazon et al. what they are owed for their improvements to the cyber commons while also better promoting entrepreneurship within the cyber commons?

Any set of institutions that attempts to do so would be wise, other things being equal, to avoid top-down control by a bureaucracy. Such control would allow bureaucratic forces to shape who has access to the cyber commons. This, in turn, may lead to corruption due to political capture, a deficit of entrepreneurship, or an objectionable distribution of access to entrepreneurial opportunities. And, of course, which form the best bottom-up scheme should take is largely an empirical matter that cannot be adjudicated here (see Ostrom 1990). Moreover, there may not be just one. It could be that different kinds of competing institutions would be preferable to a single type of institution. Again, this is an empirical issue that cannot be decided here.

Note that some institutions that would limit access to the cyber commons by Amazon et al. and have bottom-up organization would not so clearly be entrepreneurship-promoting. For example, some have proposed a "data labor union" (Imanol et al. 2018). This would limit access by Amazon et al. in the sense that such companies must engage in negotiations with a data labor union. This proposal is interesting in its own right, but it is unclear that the Kirznerian should be interested in such a union if it is not primarily focused on promoting entrepreneurial uses of that data.

Here is one way to attempt to increase entrepreneurship while giving to Amazon et al. what they are owed. We treat the cyber commons like other commons—it is either not owned or it is owned by all of us collectively, depending on one's theoretical predilections. In particular, we open up the anonymized data sets and/or metadata acquired by such companies for public use. However, to access this data, one must pay a fee. Part of this fee goes to Amazon et al. This fee allows Amazon et al. to make profits from their improvements to the cyber commons while enhancing opportunities for others to make valuable discoveries with the data that is collected and mined from Amazon et al.

How does the fee to gain access to the cyber commons get set? In a perfectly moral world, such companies would set the fee in proportion to the value they have added to the cyber commons so that they can gain a profit, but not more than they are entitled to. Figuring out this fee exactly would be quite a tall order. It would likely require some further institution—perhaps a data entrepreneurship union. Or perhaps we simply allow different companies to set their own prices for access to their data sets. Under the right conditions, this could create fair competition and therefore a market price mechanism for access to the cyber commons. Thus, even if one of two search engines is considered inferior, it could price its fee for access to its data lower than its competitor. This creates, in turn, an incentive for individuals to find creative uses for such data.

To be clear, I am instead making a moral point, not an economic one. The thought is this. By having monopoly control of the cyber commons, Amazon et al. prevent individuals from discovering new valuable uses for their data sets. If Amazon et al. are best understood as only having improved the cyber commons, they are not entitled to prevent this entrepreneurship. Given that we can further promote entrepreneurship (at least in principle) without violating the rights of Amazon et al., the Kirznerian is morally justified, *ceteris paribus*, to move toward institutions that would.

If some such institution is feasible, then the Kirznerian can say something rather nuanced and interesting about the intuition that many seem to have that we have a right to our personal digital data. While we do not have the usual property rights to our own personal digital data, we have at least some rights to our data. It is a commons. Neither Amazon nor Facebook nor Google has the right to exclude us from its use. Indeed, they have a moral duty to make it available to all of us in some form. And as a consequence, we thus have rights that it be made available to us. We are not to be excluded from the use of that data. We are not to be denied opportunities to profit from its use. Whether this view ultimately satisfies us, it provides an interesting avenue for further inquiry for the Kirznerian. It also presents an interesting lacuna in the debates over private property in our personal digital data.

## NOTES

1. Of course, not all of our personal digital data is generated by anything that looks like our labor. For example, it is often useful for companies to have demographic data about us. If I fit certain demographic descriptions, I may be more likely to buy things if I am presented with certain ads. However, much of this is complicated by the fact that a lot of our demographic data is not very useful unless companies can make educated guesses about how various parts of our demographic data interact with

ever-evolving market behavior. Therefore, our demographic data is often used alongside our other data to generate predictions for ad effectiveness. The larger point here is that the real-world details about which data is being used and how matter quite a lot. The scope of my conclusions is thereby limited by the extent to which any given company is making at least some use of "labor-generated" data as opposed to some other kind.

2. We can, of course, exclude individuals from using particular instances of them. For example, in a peculiar legal scheme, someone might copyright a certain color. And every time someone uses this color, they must pay some fee back to whomever owns the copyright on that color. This could imply, of course, that the individual in question owns all instances of the abstract, universal color. According to a rather simplistic nominalist view of abstract universals, an abstract universal is just the set of all its particular concrete instances. If one holds this view, then it is perhaps possible to own an abstract universal. Because I am arguing that digital data is the kind of thing that we could own in principle, it does not bother me if, upon careful metaphysical reflection, the category of objects that cannot be owned is tinier than we would have pre-theoretically thought.

3. This worry, as far as I know, has been introduced by Glenn Weyl in a talk in 2019 for the "Future of Work" conference at the Mercatus Center at George Mason University. To my knowledge it is not yet published.

4. This is not surprising in a certain sense. It is an increasingly unpopular view among linguists and philosophers of language that the referent of a lexical item exhausts its informational content. Thus, insofar as data is just a kind of information, the problem at hand misleads us by focusing our attention on the referent.

5. By "pro tanto moral duty," I mean that there is a moral reason to not use my car without permission. But this reason could be outweighed or defeated by other moral factors. I thus reject the implausible and out-of-fashion view that those moral duties that flow from our rights are inalienable trumps across all possible contexts.

6. The interpretation of Kirzner on this count is actually a bit complicated. He sometimes appears to use Locke and neo-Lockeans like Nozick for merely expository purposes. He certainly disagrees with and finds criticisms for both. However, I think these can all be understood as in-house disputes among neo-Lockeans as opposed to criticisms from the outside. After all, Locke and Nozick, though widely discussed, did not have a monopoly on the theory of private property at the time they were writing.

7. Perhaps think about this practical-epistemic constraint on analogy with a cure for cancer. Perhaps there is presently a chemical formula that a doctor is capable of writing down and understanding that would cure cancer. We can then ask if that doctor is obligated in virtue of other individuals' entitlements to write that formula down. One reason to say that the doctor is not failing an obligation if they do not write the formula down is that the doctor does not know what the formula is. As such, we might think, for the purposes of practice, there is no obligation-inducing formula to write down.

8. It is unclear whether Kirzner would accept that, if there were other valid forms of the Creation-Entitlement Premise, the Lockean Proviso would apply to those. However, these would not, in Kirzner's view, be cases of entrepreneurial discovery.

Therefore, they may not be relevant to his defense of the justness of capitalist profits. And in any case, this exegetical point does not much matter to the inquiry at hand.

9. It might be contested that Kirzner's understanding of the relationship between justice and morality more generally is sufficiently nuanced to countenance this point. For helpful commentary, see Kirzner (2016, 124–26). However, such a move would have costs. If Kirzner availed himself of it, he might be accused of not taking justice as seriously as does his hypothetical interlocutor who wants to be convinced of the claim that pure profits in a capitalist system can be just.

10. There may, of course, be complications that arise when one considers intellectual property rights since such rights might appear, *prima facie* at least, to be property rights to types of assets. I do not mean to prejudge that issue. I do, however, suspect that if we are to believe that it's just to recognize such rights, it will not be for Kirznerian reasons. Thus, neither fans nor foes of intellectual property rights are entitled to infer much from what I say here in this chapter.

11. Perhaps there could be a limited range of data-generating search engine activities that are not themselves social or cultural, but social network websites clearly constitute social activity.

12. There are many ways one could go about emphasizing this point. Some have to do with the intrinsically social nature of economic exchange itself, the social and cultural opportunities that are provided for by market contexts, or the social nature of entrepreneurship. For various approaches to this issue, see Grube and Storr (2015). Unfortunately, it would take a whole essay to fully defend the claim that some of these features remain in an online marketplace like Amazon, so I am unable to provide this defense here. Part of my thesis thus relies on this further argument being cogent.

13. One might point out that Amazon et al. have, in a sense, already paid us back for the profits they receive in excess of what they are entitled by providing us with free services. Amazon gives impressively low-cost, fast shipping. And the use of both Google and Facebook are completely free. Some have argued that what we are owed still exceeds what we have been given in these free services (see Arrieta-Ibarra et al. 2018). This argument, of course, deserves more attention than I can give it here. One reason this argument is not entirely convincing, however, is that some data (e.g., produced by celebrities) is more valuable than others. And yet, they often enough receive the same "payment" in terms of the same free service. This suggests at the very least that the business model is not set up in order to properly compensate others. Thus, the objection must rely on the idea that it is a happy accident that we are all getting compensated to the right degree.

## REFERENCES

Arrieta-Ibarra, Imanol, Leonard Goff, Diego Jiménez-Hernández, Jaron Lanier, and E. Glen Weyl. 2018. "Should We Treat Data as Labor? Moving beyond 'Free.'"*American Economic Association Papers and Proceedings* 108: 38–42.

Cheneval, Francis. 2018. "Property Rights of Personal Data and the Financing of Pensions." *Critical Review of International Social and Political Philosophy* 1–23.

Grube, Laura E., and Virgil Henry Storr, eds. 2015. *Culture and Economic Action.* Cheltenham, UK: Edward Elgar Publishing.

Kirzner, Israel M. 2016. *The Collected Works of Israel M. Kirzner: Discovery, Capitalism, and Distributive Justice.* Edited by Peter J. Boettke and Frédéric Sautet. Indianapolis: Liberty Fund.

Nolin, Jan Michael. 2019. "Data as Oil, Infrastructure or Asset? Three Metaphors of Data as Economic Value." *Journal of Information, Communication and Ethics in Society* 18 (1): 28–43.

Nozick, Robert. 1974. *Anarchy, State, and Utopia.* New York: Basic Books.

Ostrom, Elinor. 1990. *Governing the Commons.* Cambridge, UK: Cambridge University Press.

Ritter, Jeffrey, and Anna Mayer. 2018. "Regulating Data as Property: A New Construct for Moving Forward," *Duke Law and Technology Review* 16 (1): 220–27.

Sax, Marijn. 2016. "Big Data: Finders Keepers, Losers Weepers?" *Ethics and Information Technology* 18 (1): 25–31.

Schlager, Edella, and Elinor Ostrom. 1992. "Property-Rights Regimes and Natural Resources: A Conceptual Analysis." *Land Economics* 68 (3): 249–62.

# Chapter 4

# Artisanship, Artifact, and Aesthetic Fact

## Jaime L. Carini

> Maximizing utility without attention to the way that ideas shape deeds leads people to trample civilization underfoot.
>
> —Elinor Ostrom and Vincent Ostrom, "The Quest for Meaning in Public Choice" ([2004] 2014)

The political economy project shaped by the Austrian, Virginia, and Bloomington Schools heavily relies upon epistemology (Aligica 2018; Aligica, Lewis, and Storr 2017; Dekker 2016; Tarko 2015).[1] Austrian, Virginia, and Bloomington scholars, including Nobel laureates Friedrich Hayek, James Buchanan, and Elinor Ostrom (along with her husband Vincent Ostrom), assert that there are multiple types of fact and knowledge (Buchanan [1979] 1999, 2003; Hayek 1989, 2014; E. Ostrom 2005; V. Ostrom [1976] 2012, 1980a, 1997), such as "artifact," brute fact, historical fact, institutional fact, natural fact, scientific fact, and social fact.[2] Epistemology is intertwined with ontology and artisanship. In his discussions of artisanship, Vincent Ostrom hints at an additional type of fact, aesthetic fact, by using the terms "aesthetic satisfaction," "aesthetic purpose," and "aesthetic quality" (V. Ostrom 1975, [1976] 2012, 1980a, 1980b, 1997). These scholars offer explanations and, in some cases, examples for most of these facts, centering them in discussions of knowledge, personal change, social rules, and institutional development.

The Ostrom Workshop hosts a podcast titled "Governance Roundtable of the Ostrom Workshop (GROW)" in which interviewers ask guests this question: "What work did the Ostroms leave undone?" (Ostrom Workshop n.d.). In this chapter, I answer this question two ways. I first posit that an exposition of the role that aesthetic fact plays in the Bloomington School is one facet of the Ostroms' work that remains undone. Second, I suggest that an Ostromian approach to the science of culture remains underdeveloped. Thus, the task at hand includes providing these explications, extending them to the Virginia and Austrian Schools, and demonstrating how thinking about aesthetics and the cultural sciences challenges us to consider political economy through fresh lenses. Furthermore, aesthetic knowledge and a science of culture prompt us to consider how we today can answer the greater questions of preserving and cultivating civilization with which all three schools of political economy historically have been and presently are engaged.

Accomplishing these aims is a threefold endeavor. First is engaging deeply with the development of the concepts of artisanship and fact in political economy, focusing on the ongoing conversation between the Bloomington and Virginia Schools. Second is extending this conversation by recognizing that the Bloomington School offers further insights into the concept of fact and connecting this conversation to the Austrian School through discussing various types of knowledge. Last is reiterating that the quest to develop a science of culture is still very much underway. It is a quest we must pursue if we are to continue the Ostroms' work by considering how to solve complex problems that concern human society.

## THE DEVELOPMENT OF
## ARTISANSHIP AND FACT IN POLITICAL ECONOMY

The Bloomington and Virginia Schools of Political Economy both trace their genealogy back to the Austrian School, specifically early Viennese scholars like Menger and Mises (Aligica, Lewis, and Storr 2017; Dekker 2016). These scholars, considered students of civilization rather than pure economists, engaged with multiple types of knowledge and fact (in addition to economic knowledge and fact) throughout their careers. The Ostroms, Buchanan, and Hayek similarly engaged with many types of knowledge, among them culture, history, the physical and natural sciences, and the social sciences.

We see a clear line of epistemological and ontological influence centered around the concepts of artisanship and fact, which Vincent Ostrom initially formulated in his paper "David Hume as a Political Analyst" ([1976] 2012), given at the Conference on the Scottish Contributions to Social and Political Philosophy (Allen 2012, 3). Ostrom weaves together ideas about facts drawn from John R. Searle and David Hume—"brute and institutional facts" (Searle 1969, 50) and "natural facts" and "artifacts" (V. Ostrom [1976] 2012, 14)—to posit that humans are artisans who create artifacts, including institutional artifacts. Buchanan ([1979] 1999) extends these ideas by applying Ostrom's theory of artisanship to people themselves, considering the concepts of "natural man" and "artifactual man" (247). Ostrom (1980a) then applies artisan-ship to organizations and argues that organizations are artifacts containing the artisans who build these organizations. There is thus an epistemological and ontological genealogy that one can trace directly from Searle (1969) and Hume ([1742] 1948) through V. Ostrom ([1976] 2012) and Buchanan ([1979] 1999) to V. Ostrom (1980a).[3]

In this section, I trace this genealogy, demonstrating that there are many different types of artisans, facts, and artifacts produced through the process of artisanship. Aligica and Boettke (2009), Lewis and Dold (2020), and Aligica (2018) have each worked out the implications of each link in this chain of influence. Presenting here each link in its sequential context yields additional insights. Rather than commencing with Searle (1969) and Hume ([1742] 1948), I begin with V. Ostrom ([1976] 2012), using this essay as a hub from which we look backward to Searle (1969) and Hume ([1742] 1948) and for-ward to Buchanan ([1979] 1999) and V. Ostrom (1980a).

## Ostromian Artisanship

Both Vincent and Elinor Ostrom believe that people are artisans who shape their own lives. Vincent Ostrom (1997) asserts that people's efforts to cul-tivate their world could be better understood by using what he deems "the artisanship-artifact relationship" (220), which is based on the concepts of "artisan" and "artifact." As he describes it, "Artisans create artifacts," and artifacts are created for "human purposes" (V. Ostrom 1980a, 310). In *Under-standing Institutional Diversity*, Elinor Ostrom instructs her readers "to learn the artisanship of working with rules" (E. Ostrom 2005, 132). Elsewhere, she uses the term "craft" to describe both the rule-making process and the need to develop analytical tools (E. Ostrom and Basurto 2011). Artisanship, then, has an infinite number of applications.

A grasp of epistemology, or (1) how people use facts and knowledge and (2) the types of facts and knowledge available for their use, is critical to un-derstanding the Ostromian theory of artisanship. Artisanship first appears in Vincent Ostrom's "David Hume as a Political Analyst" ([1976] 2012), where Ostrom engages with Searle's "brute and institutional facts" (Searle 1969, 50). Brute facts, as Searle simply puts it, are "essentially physical" (ibid., 50). Such brute facts form certain "paradigms of knowledge," the model for which is "the natural sciences, and the basis for all knowledge of this kind is generally supposed to be simple empirical observations recording sense expe-riences" (ibid., 50). Institutional fact is less obvious. It contains physical fact, but it additionally requires and "presupposes the existence of certain human institutions" that contain "constitutive rules" (ibid., 51). An institutional fact is thus a type of symbol that contains institutional knowledge and "constitutive rules."

Searle (1969) provides an example of an institutional fact: that portion of a football game known as "the huddle." To show us how much knowledge one institutional fact like "the huddle" communicates to us, Searle first describes certain aspects of playing football (like huddling or lining up) in terms of brute fact. The huddle, for example, is depicted as occurring "at statistically regular intervals," during which "organisms in like colored shirts cluster together in a roughly circular fashion" (ibid., 52). Searle (and later Ostrom) argues that such a description paints an incomplete picture of the action on the football field. As an institutional fact, "the huddle" functions as an easily communicable symbol of a concept that completes our knowledge about the game. Searle posits that society is constructed from similar institutional facts.

Aligica and Boettke (2009) note that "Vincent Ostrom used Searle's argument to make the point that the observed 'facts' do not speak for themselves and that they are in some sense 'artifacts'" (79). By "observed facts," Aligica and Boettke (2009) refer to Searle's "brute facts." These "observed" or "brute" facts are much like what Hume deemed "nature" or "natural" in the context of his discussion of virtue. Similarly, what Searle deemed "institutional facts" are similar to Hume's "artifice" or "artificial." Ostrom reinterprets Hume, arguing for the existence of "natural fact" and "artifact," then draws comparisons between "natural fact" and "brute fact" as well as "artifact" and "institutional fact" (V. Ostrom [1976] 2012, 13–16).[4]

Vincent Ostrom utilizes these two types of facts, natural fact and artifact, to underpin his theory of the artisanal process. He perhaps most thoroughly describes this process of artisanship in Ostrom ([1976] 2012), which contains a passage so thoughtfully worked out that it merits restating in full. Here, Ostrom distinguishes between the raw materials of nature—the things that are turned into artifacts ("natural facts")—and the artifacts themselves:

> Nature and the realm of natural facts can . . . be distinguished from culture and the realm of artifacts. Artifacts are created by reference to *human knowledge and action*. They are a combination of natural events organized in relation to conceptions held by an *artisan* and used to create some *new artificial event*. As such, they reflect *natural elements, elements of human understanding and elements of human passions, feelings or sentiments*. Natural elements are selected and combined by relying upon a knowledge of cause-and-effect relationships. But the *process* of selecting and combining natural elements is always informed by some objective or purpose where *the intention is to produce some desired effect*. The criteria or standards used in selecting from alternative possibilities may be viewed as having reference to *purposes or values* that are grounded in human passions, desires, wants, or feelings. *The nature of artifacts always entails*

*consideration of values.* In this sense, all artifacts represent *a union of both fact and value.* Discourses about the design and performance of artifacts necessarily include reference to propositions that are joined by "ought" and "ought not" as well as "is" and "is not." (V. Ostrom [1976] 2012, 14; emphasis added)

Artisanship requires an artisan and natural materials. The artisan shapes the natural materials, using "human knowledge and action" to "create some new artificial event," or, as the Ostroms often assert, "relating ideas to deeds" (E. Ostrom and V. Ostrom [2004] 2014, 65). Artifacts, taken as natural materials turned cultural artifacts, thus exhibit several "elements" related to the natural and artifactual realms: (1) natural materials, (2) human understanding, and (3) human passions, feelings, or sentiments. The artifact reflects not only these elements but also the process of creating that artifact, which manifests "the intention to produce some desired effect" according to human "purposes or values." Thus, artifacts unite "fact and value."

Vincent Ostrom crafted his theory of artisanship and artifactuality to describe how people first create artifacts and then imbue these artifacts with meaning and value through the creative process. His theory is applicable to any object that a person could craft, from a physical coffee table to an abstract political system of self-governance. Elinor Ostrom (1990, 2005) also emphasized the importance of artisanship and craftsmanship, applying these concepts to institutional development and rules. Buchanan ([1979] 1999), as we see next, considers man himself as an artifact.

## Buchanan's Artifactual Man

Buchanan's essay, "Natural and Artifactual Man" ([1979] 1999), extends Ostromian thinking on artisanship and artifacts. Artisanship in Buchanan's treatment becomes the human propensity for self-fashioning, and artifacts are people themselves rather than (im)material objects. He articulates it this way: "man . . . conceived in the image of an artifact . . . constructs himself through his own choices" (Buchanan [1979] 1999, 258). This propensity is grounded in thinking "of man as an imagining being," who first perceives of himself as becoming a different person from the person he presently is and then acts upon this perception to achieve his goal (ibid., 250).

Lewis and Dold (2020) credit the ideas of Frank H. Knight and G. L. S. Shackle for exerting primary influence upon Buchanan's conception of the artifactual man (2020, 6; see Dold 2018). Vincent Ostrom's influence may also be substantial. For instance, just as Ostrom differentiates between natural fact and artifact as well as brute fact and institutional fact, so Buchanan makes a distinction between "natural man" and "artifactual man," noting that he borrows the term "artifactual" from Ostrom (Buchanan [1979] 1999, 255; Ostrom [1976] 2012).

Describing natural man, Buchanan ([1979] 1999) explains, "For my purposes, to the extent that individuals are rigidly bound by culturally evolved rules of conduct or modes of behavior, these elements would make up part of 'natural man,' or, better stated, 'nonartifactual man'" (247). He continues by describing natural man as one whose behavior is "'programmed,' and hence 'predictable scientifically'" (247). By contrast, those who are artifactual people possess "some recognition of the basic constraints of human nature while, at the same time, allowing for wide areas of choice within these constraints, areas within which we can, and do, construct ourselves as individuals, from the base largely constructed for us by our forebears" (ibid., 252). The differentiating factor between natural man and artifactual man is the element of choice. Natural man lets himself be programmed by "culturally evolved" rules and behaviors while artifactual man engages with these human and cultural institutions by choosing how he will fashion himself. To put it another way, artifactual man engages in artisanship.

There are other similarities between Vincent Ostrom's and Buchanan's theories of artisanship, outlined in table 4.1.

**Table 4.1.  Comparison of Artisanship**

|   | *Ostrom* | *Buchanan* |
|---|---|---|
| 1 | human knowledge and action | takes action |
| 2 | conception | imagination |
| 3 | some desired effect | imagined states of being |
| 4 | process | becoming |
| 5 | value | value |

Ostrom's artisan uses (1) "human knowledge and action" to transform (2) a "conception" into (3) "some desired effect" by working through (4) a "process" that produces (5) "value" ([1976] 2012, 15). Correspondingly, Buchanan's artifactual man (1) "takes action" prompted by his (2) "imagination" to achieve (3) "imagined states of being" through a process of (4) "becoming" that yields (5) "value" ([1979] 1999, 250–55). In both cases, man uses his intelligence to activate a preconceived mental image by transforming raw materials, either natural materials or himself, into a new artifact that bears the cultural and aesthetic markings of meaning and value with which this transformative process imbues the artifact.

The similarities between Vincent Ostrom's and Buchanan's scholarship are striking. The simple explanation is that they result from a long intellectual conversation between the two men (Aligica 2018; Aligica, Lewis, and Storr

2017). Though each scholar refers to different intellectual materials—Ostrom ([1976] 2012) cites Searle (1969) and Hume ([1742] 1948), and Buchanan ([1979] 1999) cites Knight (1967) and Shackle (1972, 1976)—both discuss similar ontological and epistemological questions. Human knowledge and imagination, the belief that people can choose to change their situations or themselves by activating their ideas, and the understanding that a process of *becoming* can produce a desired effect that contains and communicates value are assertions that one sees in the scholarship of the two men. Buchanan's ([1979] 1999) process of self-realization is an extension of Ostrom's ([1976] 2012) process of artisanship, but with an additional layer of complexity. A person is both the artisan and the artifact. Artisanship, as we have seen, can be applied to (im)material objects and self-fashioning. We will now see how artisanship can be applied to organizations.

## Ostromian Artisanship and Artifactuality

Vincent Ostrom responds to Buchanan ([1979] 1999), particularly the latter's assertion that people themselves can be considered artifacts, by treating organizations as artifacts. Ostrom returns to his original idea of "natural fact" and "artifact" (V. Ostrom [1976] 2012), modifying them in the context of organizations. He initially acknowledges that his "earlier perspective had been shaped by the presumption that the methods of the natural sciences applied to the study of public administration" (V. Ostrom 1980a, 309). Ostrom then exhorts us "to look upon administrative tasks and administrative arrangements as works of art or as artifacts" because doing so "may require somewhat different perspectives than understanding natural phenomena" (ibid., 309).

Aligica and Boettke (2009) observe that Vincent Ostrom's "view subtly, but profoundly, challenges the way one sees the relation between theory and practice, between ideas and action" (71). To explain the change in his perspective, Ostrom begins with the idea of "simple artisanship" and "the example of a potter who is making a pot" (1980a, 309). Ostrom presents many of the same core ideas on artisanship that he developed earlier ([1976] 2012), including natural materials, a transformative process, a mental conception, a desired outcome, and "value" elements derived from "the artisan's expression of preference, standards of choice, and sense of proportion" (V. Ostrom 1980a, 309–10). Ostrom then juxtaposes this simple artisanship with the more complex concept of "organizations as artifacts." Such complexity arises from the fact that organizations are not only artifacts constructed by people but also "artifacts that contain their own artisans" (ibid., 310). Rather than shying away from complexity, Ostromian thought embraces it as a natural part of the biophysical and socioeconomic world (E. Ostrom 2005, 242–43).

We see throughout the academic conversation between Vincent Ostrom and Buchanan a progression in complexity, presented in table 4.2, as both men develop the idea of artisanship as well as the nature of fact.

**Table 4.2.  Development of Artisanship and Fact**

| Author | Artisanship | Fact |
|---|---|---|
| Searle (1969) | | "institutional fact" = "brute fact" + human institutions |
| V. Ostrom ([1976] 2012) | the process of artisanship | "artifact" = natural fact + institutional fact |
| Buchanan ([1979] 1999) | artisanship applied to people | "natural man" versus "artifactual man" |
| V. Ostrom (1980a) | artisanship applied to organizations | organizations as "natural phenomena" versus organizations as "artifacts" |

Ostrom first presents his conception of the process of artisanship, weaving Searle's (1969) "brute fact" and "institutional fact" with Ostrom's own reinterpretation of Hume ([1742] 1948) as "natural fact" and "artifact" ([1976] 2012). Buchanan ([1979] 1999) takes up these points by applying the process of artisanship to people themselves, which adds complexity, as a person is now considered to be both the artisan and the artifact. Ostrom (1980a) layers yet another level of complexity. He changes Buchanan's ([1979] 1999) idea that an entity can simultaneously be the artisan and the artifact by recognizing that an artifact (the organization) can contain its own artisans.

The nature of "fact" is also transformed throughout the conversation. Searle (1969) presents the idea of "brute fact," arguing that once brute facts are combined with a human institution, such as "Mr. Smith," "Miss Jones," and "marriage," an institutional fact is formed: "Mr. Smith married Miss Jones" (51). An "artifact" (akin to Searle's "brute fact") comes into existence when a person uses their "knowledge and action" to integrate "natural fact" and "institutional fact" (V. Ostrom [1976] 2012, 14–16). Buchanan ([1979] 1999) takes up Ostrom's "natural fact" and "artifact," modifying them to "natural man" and "artifactual man." Finally, Ostrom (1980a) recognizes that he and other scholars previously treated organizations as "natural phenomena" and advances the notion that these organizations themselves could instead be considered artifacts.

## EXTENDING THE CONVERSATION:
## FACT AND KNOWLEDGE IN POLITICAL ECONOMY

Circumscribing our initial investigation around a limited conversation—Searle (1969), then Vincent Ostrom ([1976] 2012), then Buchanan ([1979] 1999), and finally Ostrom (1980a)—allows us to make new observations about patterns of human experience pertaining to artisanship and fact. We can extend this conversation by first examining a type of fact that Ostrom ([1976] 2012) hints at, aesthetic fact, and then exploring how aesthetic fact, artifact, brute fact, institutional fact, and natural fact belong to various categories of knowledge that the Bloomington, Virginia, and Austrian Schools collectively advance. Before doing so, it will be helpful to explore briefly what aesthetics is.

### What Is Aesthetics?

Aesthetics is the study of beauty. Nicholas Wolterstorff (2015) explains that there have been two historical approaches to aesthetics since the early modern period: a "construction model" and a "contemplation model." In the construction model, one evaluates the technique and materials that are used to construct the artwork and the purpose for which that object is created. In the contemplation model, one evaluates the artwork itself with "disinterested contemplation" (Wolterstorff 2015, 7–8). There was a shift from the construction model to the contemplation model—a movement that was reflected by those who wrote about art and accompanied by a subsidiary "split between art and craft, between artist and craftsperson, and between aesthetic and practical concerns" (ibid., 17). Beauty was then associated with fine art and the practice of contemplation rather than craftsmanship: "it's the *beauty* of the object that makes the act of attending to it intrinsically worthwhile" (ibid., 311). Furthermore, in the eighteenth and nineteenth centuries, the new term "aesthetic" yielded two frameworks for evaluating aesthetic merit: the beautiful and the sublime. The value of art thus became dependent upon the beauty or sublimity of the finished artifact and was divorced from the artisanal process.

However, certain philosophers who today write about beauty and aesthetics point us toward more holistic evaluations of the role of human creativity in the artisanal process as well as the completed artifact, whether a piece of fine art or the product of a craft. Wolterstorff (1980) exhorts us to consider how "works of art are objects and instruments of action," particularly *"responsible* action" (78; emphasis in the original). Roger Scruton (2011) evaluates the role of personal and social experiences as we interact with beauty. Our personal aesthetic choices help us to develop self-knowledge in relation to society, or as Scruton (2011) puts it, "in coming to understand how you yourself fit in to the world of human meanings" (77). Such aesthetic choices are grounded in human interactions and human meaning.

Ultimately, experiencing, evaluating, and engaging with beauty is a cognitive activity. Scruton (2011) writes, "[T]he experience of beauty implies that it is rationally founded. It challenges us to find meaning in its object, to make critical comparisons, and to examine our own lives and emotions in the light of what we find. Art, nature and the human form all invite us to place this experience in the centre of our lives" (163). By asserting that there is a rationality to the experience of beauty, Scruton brings us back to the idea that beauty is something that we can know intellectually. If we can have a knowledge of beauty, then we can also have aesthetic facts that comprise this knowledge.

## Aesthetic Fact

The Bloomington School observes that human knowledge and action are critical to producing artifacts that are useful. Vincent Ostrom writes that a sense of beauty is just one aspect of usefulness: "Artifacts are created to be used and enjoyed by human beings. Their use and employment in some cases may be purely consumptive in the sense of deriving aesthetic satisfaction from viewing an object of beauty. Many artifacts are also used as tools or instruments for the realization of still other possibilities" (V. Ostrom [1976] 2012, 15). Artisanship in Ostrom's theory thus culminates in artifacts that contain both aesthetic and utilitarian qualities, which Ostrom links to human intention and purpose. We might call any element that could alter the end product an "aesthetic fact," whether raw materials, human labor, or artist's license. This proposition can be corroborated by referring to Searle, whose reference to "statements in ethics and esthetics" also suggests the idea of aesthetic fact (1969, 50).

Elinor Ostrom describes how an artisan contemplates aesthetic fact during the process of creating an artifact by relating how she and Vincent Ostrom engaged in the real-world experience of artisanship. They wanted to learn the art of woodworking, so they undertook an apprenticeship with master woodworker Paul Goodman at his workshop, crafting various pieces of furniture. This experience influenced the name of their initiative at Indiana University Bloomington: Workshop in Political Theory and Policy Analysis. Elinor Ostrom explains:

> One of the reasons we called this place a workshop instead of a center was because of working with Paul [Goodman] and understanding what artisanship was. You might be working on something like a cabinet and thinking about the design of it, and thinking this idea versus that idea, and then Paul could pick up

a board and say, oh, you shouldn't use this one because it will split. He could see things in wood that we couldn't. So the whole idea of artisans and apprentices and the structure of a good workshop really made an impression on us. (Leonard 2009)

Artisanship involves design, thought, ideas, and the act of making comparisons ("this idea versus that idea"). Expertise is also critical because an expert has perception and knowledge that a nonexpert lacks, such as when Goodman could evaluate a piece of wood using woodworking knowledge that the Ostroms did not possess. The quality of the materials is important. A piece of wood that will split is not the best material to use for making a cabinet or a coffee table. And finally, there must be a synthesis of design and materials. To craft an artifact, the materials that one uses must support the design and the intended purpose of the artifact, and the design of the artifact must account for the nature of the materials at hand. Aspects of the mental processes in this list—design, thought, idea, comparison, expertise—are just as much aesthetic fact as the characters of the materials and physical labor used to fashion the cabinet.

One aesthetic fact can be exchanged for another. Vincent Ostrom, referring to the two Ostroms' apprenticeship with Goodman, writes how he constructed a coffee table that fulfills "both utilitarian [useful] and aesthetic purposes in the ecology and economy of a household" (V. Ostrom 1997, 206). He depicts the artisanal process, writing that he used "two odd boards cut from black walnut trees. The cut edge of one, a piece of slab wood, became the surface of the table. A konky knot had to be removed and filled with a wedged replacement. Another gnarled and splintered board was used to construct a set of legs" with "curves" (ibid., 206). To achieve the dual purposes of usefulness and bringing beauty to the Ostroms' home, Ostrom had to address an imperfection in the material, "a konky knot." Though the board itself is considered a natural fact, the "konky knot" as a characteristic of the board is an aesthetic fact. This "konky knot" can be replaced with a different aesthetic fact, "wedged replacement," to alter the outcome of the artifact.

Certain characteristics or aspects of the mental processes, physical materials, and manual labor used to create an artifact can all be considered types of aesthetic fact that influence the final outcome of the artifact. Value can be considered an aesthetic fact, as well, because it refers to an artisan's "sense of meaning" and "criteria of choice," as Vincent Ostrom explains,

All artifacts entail both material elements and spiritual elements. Tangible artifacts or "material values" as Thayer uses the term, may not only be appreciated for their practical utility as tools but for their beauty and aesthetic qualities as well. A simple pot can be both a thing of beauty and a useful tool. All artifacts,

thus, represent a union of fact and value where value has reference to the sense
of meaning and the criteria of choice used by artisans in their creations. (V.
Ostrom 1980b, 15)

Just as Ostrom's ([1976] 2012) artifact unites natural fact and institutional
fact, so an aesthetic fact unites natural fact and value. An artifact acquires an
aesthetic quality, or that thing that causes us to deem the object beautiful, precisely because it contains and communicates an artisan's intention and purpose, which is constructed from a seemingly infinite array of aesthetic facts.

An aesthetic fact can be comprised of a variety of things, from the characteristics of the physical materials (e.g., wedged replacement) used to
construct the artifact to the choice of manual labor (e.g., cutting or sanding)
exerted upon these materials to the mental process (e.g., considering various
ideas) that one follows when shaping the artifact. Vincent Ostrom's scholarship hints at the idea of aesthetic fact through the terms "aesthetic satisfaction," "aesthetic purpose," and "aesthetic quality" (V. Ostrom 1975, [1976]
2012, 1980a, 1997). By recognizing that Ostrom uses aesthetic terms in reference to human meaning and patterns of human experience, we can assert that
aesthetic fact can communicate any number of ideas about human intention,
purpose, meaning, and experience.

## Fact and Knowledge

In addressing or hinting at various facts—brute fact, natural fact, institutional
fact, natural fact, artifact, and now aesthetic fact—Searle, Vincent Ostrom,
and Buchanan refer to the various types of knowledge and science that organize these facts. Brute fact and natural fact belong to the realm of systematic
knowledge, that of the natural sciences with its emphasis on "simple empirical observations recording sense experiences" (Searle 1969, 50). Similarly,
institutional fact, artifact, and aesthetic are governed by the cultural and
social sciences, with their focus on communication, language, patterns of
meaning, union of fact and value, and so forth.

Searle (1969) recognizes that the model of the natural sciences is "taken to
form the model for all knowledge," which then excludes "statements in ethics and esthetics" for being "not readily assimilable" as brute or natural facts
because they are "mere expressions of emotions, or . . . simply autobiographi-
cal statements of a psychological kind" (50). Aligica and Boettke (2009)
observe, "Searle's distinction between 'institutional facts' and 'brute facts'
restores, on solid epistemological grounds, the role of ideas in social science
and explains why even positivists have to rely on the understanding of rules,
common knowledge and language" (80). Institutional fact and "statements in

ethics and esthetics," or what we might call "ethical fact" and "aesthetic fact," thus all fall under the domain of the social sciences.

Vincent Ostrom ([1976] 2012) extends Searle's critique of the natural sciences and advocacy for the social sciences by deeming scientific methods as "not fully appropriate to the cultural sciences" and thus not fully appropriate to evaluations of the artifactual realm (18). Elsewhere Ostrom writes that "the methods of the natural sciences" are "concerned with the development of theory as basic knowledge" (1980a, 309). He asserts that an alternative discourse is used in the realm of artifacts from that used in the realm of natural facts—distinctions in discourse that result from the simple fact that natural facts and artifacts are different types of knowledge.

We should instead treat products of human intelligence as "works of art or artifacts"—whether pots, organizations, or constitutions—using methods appropriate to "a science of culture" (V. Ostrom 1980a, 309; 1997, 206). Artifacts (and works of art) contain aesthetic fact and can thus be treated with the science of culture, which in this case is aesthetic knowledge. Aesthetic knowledge utilizes both "tacit knowledge" (Polanyi 1958) and "objective knowledge" (Popper 1972). Furthermore, aesthetic knowledge does not remain firmly within the boundaries of art studies but can be vital to organizations (Strati 2003), international relations (Bleiker 2001, 2017, 2018), and political economy (Griswold 1999; Hanley 2009; Smith [1759] 1982).

Artifacts created for either the private or the public spheres can thus possess aesthetic fact. For instance, Vincent Ostrom's coffee table brings "aesthetic purpose" to the Ostrom household, and a public good can also be beautiful, as in the "aesthetic quality of an urban landscape" (V. Ostrom 1975, 846). Ostrom perceives the relationship between beauty and utility, or value and fact, as emanating from spiritual and material elements. These elements come from the artisan. Finally, an artifact is not a value-free object. The artisan infuses their own "meaning" and "criteria of choice" into the artifact. Thus, the artifact's value is neither purely intrinsic nor extrinsic, objective nor subjective. The artifact thus possesses intrinsic, objective value comprised of aesthetic facts derived from the materials, the artist's labor, and processes of choice that go into its creation. The artifact also maintains extrinsic, subjective value that results from external valuation or what Elinor Ostrom calls the "valuation patterns held by the participants" (E. Ostrom 2005, 33). Both types of value—intrinsic, objective and extrinsic, subjective—can only be perceived with the proper knowledge in mind.

Knowledge is thus critical to the process of artisanship. As Vincent Ostrom has argued, artisanship utilizes and blends many forms of knowledge: material knowledge (natural fact), execution (labor studies), design (aesthetic knowledge), and expertise (institutional knowledge). Elinor Ostrom also advances similar propositions, that (1) there are different types of knowledge and (2) these can often be effective when used in consort. She writes, for instance, of the "skillful pooling and blending of scientific knowledge and local time-and-place knowledge" (E. Ostrom 1990, 34). Elsewhere, Charlotte Hess and Elinor Ostrom observe,

> The traditional study of knowledge is subdivided into epistemic areas of interests. . . . The focus here is to explore the puzzles and issues that all forms of knowledge share, particularly in the digital age. The intention is to illustrate the analytical benefits of applying a multitiered approach that burrows deeply into the knowledge-commons ecosystem, *drawing from several different disciplines.* (Hess and Ostrom 2007, 3; emphasis added)

In this excerpt, the authors address knowledge as its own form of commons, but the principle that several different disciplines can be used to understand puzzles shared by "all forms of knowledge" remains true in any circumstance.

By advocating for thoughtful craftsmanship and design throughout her oeuvre, Elinor Ostrom advances the roles of human agency and cognitive choice in the use of knowledge. She explains that people have "the capacity . . . to use complex cognitive systems to order their own behavior" (E. Ostrom 2005, 19). In other words, people use systems and institutions to make decisions. According to Vincent Ostrom (1997), artisanship can be a means through which people build relationships with each other as they use social capital: "Human relationships are integrally bound together through artisanship and the artifactual character of human creations that are constitutive of cultures, societies, and civilizations as aggregate patterns of order" (202). Knowledge (or the lack of knowledge) can thus transform communities (E. Ostrom 1990, 209–10). The creative process of artisanship thus yields discernible order that scholars can evaluate from cultural, social, and civic perspectives.

Human relationships, formed as one moves between personal and social knowledge and chooses between alternatives and preferences, are critical to Buchanan's contribution to the development of artisanship (Buchanan [1979] 1999, 252; see V. Ostrom 1980a, 311). So are the concepts of limited imagination and imperfect knowledge, the latter of which Vincent Ostrom terms "fallibility" (Buchanan [1979] 1999, 250; V. Ostrom 1980a, 311; Aligica and Boettke 2009, 59–60). One of the markers of an artifactual man is his willingness to pursue choices that seem antithetical to utility maximization, as Buchanan expresses in the concluding paragraph to his essay:

> *Man wants liberty to become the man he wants to become.* He does so precisely because he does not know what man he will want to become in time. Let us remove once and for all the instrumental defense of liberty, the only one that can

possibly be derived directly from orthodox economic analysis. Man does not want liberty in order to maximize his utility, or that of the society of which he is a part. *He wants liberty to become the man he wants to become.* (Buchanan [1979] 1999, 259; emphasis in the original)

Another necessary component of artifactuality is liberty. An artisan who creates an object or transforms himself must have the institutional structures to be able to actualize his own choices through this process at will. An artifactual man must also possess the ability to think in terms of bettering himself, which can then lead him "to envisage changing the basic rules of social order in the direction of imagined good societies" (Buchanan [1979] 1999, 258). He is thus oriented toward the future (see V. Ostrom 1980a, 311; Aligica and Boettke 2009, 59). Not only does artifactual man resist becoming programmed by social rules through making choices within societal constraints, but he also eventually transforms those rules. Finally, artifactual man must be comfortable with operating in a world in which his knowledge is incomplete. This is the world of institutional fact and imperfect knowledge, a world in which man constructs aesthetic meaning through rules and institutional structures.

## Hayek and Knowledge

Aligica and Boettke (2009) write, "The vision behind the Bloomington School is built around a series of concepts such as adaptability, choice, learning, knowledge, ideas and rules" (60). These same concepts characterize the Virginia and Austrian Schools. This sharing of concepts between the Ostroms and Buchanan as they worked together on common intellectual projects, including the Public Choice Society and a unified school of political economy (Aligica 2018), naturally led to similarities in the kinds of topics they wrote about. The series of concepts that Aligica and Boettke (2009) identify also typify the Austrian School, resulting in part from the interactions of the Ostroms and Buchanan with Hayek.

Hayek tackles problems of knowledge, order, and social process throughout his oeuvre, including "The Use of Knowledge in Society" ([1945] 2014), "The Facts of the Social Sciences" (Hayek [1943] 2014), and *The Sensory Order* (Hayek 1952). Hayek's "The Use of Knowledge in Society" is often cited for its emphasis on the localized knowledge of time and place. However, the article also takes the stance that there are many kinds of knowledge, not just "one kind of knowledge, namely, scientific knowledge, [which] occupies now so prominent a place in public imagination that we tend to forget that it is not the only kind that is relevant" ([1945] 2014, 95–96). Hayek critiques the public's sole reliance upon scientific, statistical knowledge to the exclusion of other knowledge that "by its nature cannot enter into statistics" (ibid., 98), including knowledge that is concerned with the social process. This latter type of knowledge, subject to "the unavoidable imperfection of man's knowledge," requires us to develop a process by which we continuously revise and update what we know and to communicate our new knowledge most efficiently (ibid., 104). We do this in two ways, either with "formulas, symbols, and rules" or by "building upon habits and institutions which have proved successful in their own sphere and which have in turn become the foundation of the civilization we have built up" (ibid., 101; see V. Ostrom [1976] 2012, 15). Hayek thus encourages us to embrace the idea that the umbrella concept of "aggregate knowledge" is a dynamic entity made up of multiple types of knowledge, each with its own rules and institutions. Accepting the contributions of these various bodies of knowledge allows us to solve knowledge problems and advance our civilization (Hess and Ostrom 2007), despite the "unavoidable imperfection" in our knowledge that threatens to hinder our efforts.

Hayek ([1943] 2014) addresses various types of facts. Hayek first acknowledges that physical fact, by which we know the "external world" through our "sense perception," precedes all other types of facts. He then takes his reasoning one step further by posing this critical question: "But does this mean that all our knowledge is of physical facts only? This depends on what we mean by 'a kind of facts'" ([1943] 2014, 79). Hayek answers his question by challenging "the belief that social phenomena are ever given to us as the facts of nature are given to us" (ibid., 92) and concluding that the concepts we call "social fact" and "historical fact" are not facts at all but rather theories. Hayek arrives at this position after first exploring what people mean by the terms "social fact" and "historical fact."

Social fact, Hayek acknowledges, addresses two key concepts: (1) human behavior "towards their environment" and (2) human action (ibid., 80–81). At the time, historical fact and methods were considered the most empirical of the social sciences, so social scientists were encouraged to utilize historical techniques. However, historical fact is not all that it is portrayed to be. Hayek concludes, "To put it paradoxically: what we call historical facts are really theories which, in a methodological sense, are of precisely the same character as the more abstract or general models which the theoretical sciences of society construct" (ibid., 89). What people call "social" or "historical" facts are not really facts at all, but rather should be more accurately described as theories of human intention and action.

The goal of the social sciences, Hayek asserts, is to classify human behavior and action "to provide an orderly arrangement of the material which we have to use in our further task" (ibid., 86). In other words, the task of social scientists, including economists, is to discern and organize meaningful patterns of human behavior (Caldwell 2004, 248–50). This arranging and classifying allows social scientists "to provide schemes of structural relationships which the historian can use when he has to attempt to fit together into a meaningful whole the elements which he actually finds" (Hayek [1943] 2014, 90). Here, Hayek touches upon concepts that remain important to political economy: (1) structural relationships, (2) human intention, and (3) meaning. Structural relationships are tools used by historians to organize knowledge. Political economists recognize that these structural relationships, or what we might call institutions, are used to organize additional things, among which are social and political systems.

Human intention and meaning both permeate the historian's task of discernment. This is because of the human element with which these models are infused, as Hayek ([1943] 2014) writes, "These models can never possess any properties which we have not given to them or which do not derive deductively from the assumptions on which we have built them" (91). The historian intentionally looks for patterns in the knowledge at hand and determines what these patterns mean when examining the human experience.

The historian, therefore, uses theory and reasoning to weave together individual facts, drawn from our observations about how humans behave, into an intelligible whole. Hayek writes that this process yields a "common structure of thought" that facilitates two things: (1) communication and (2) institutions. He writes, "Just as the existence of a common structure of thought is the condition of the possibility of our communicating with one another, of your understanding what I say, so it is also the basis on which we all interpret such complicated social structures as those which we find in economic life or law, in language, and in customs" (Hayek 2014, 92). We see, therefore, that our theories provide us with rules for establishing thoughts that we can hold in common because they become institutionalized facts, to use Searle's term.

Throughout both articles, Hayek maintains a dichotomy between scientific and nonscientific knowledge, which is also expressed as a juxtaposition between natural fact and social or historical fact. Bruce Caldwell (2004) explains that this dichotomy between the natural sciences and the social sciences was a hallmark of Hayek's writings from the 1940s, including the two articles that we touched upon here. By 1952, when Hayek's psychological work *The Sensory Order* was published, Hayek no longer subscribed to that dichotomy, instead opting for one between simple and complex phenomena (Caldwell 2004, 248–49; Hayek 1952). However, as we have seen, the Ostroms and Buchanan recognize the continued presence of this dichotomy between scientific fact and nonscientific fact in academic scholarship.

Not only is it important that we consider the types of facts, knowledges, and theories that enable us to infuse the social sciences with a meaningful understanding of the world, but it is also valuable for us to understand (1) how we acquire this knowledge and (2) the nature of this knowledge. Hayek (1952) offers us both in his book *The Sensory Order*.

On the first point, the acquisition of knowledge, Caldwell (2004) briefly explains that when Hayek became interested in psychology, he spent a few weeks in a brain anatomy laboratory, learning and observing neural networks in actual brains. Hayek later used this experience when he wrote that people build neural networks in their brains through a "physiological response" caused by an "external stimulus" that acts upon a person's senses (Caldwell 2004, 240–41). We thus acquire knowledge, particularly scientific fact, by engaging with the external world through our sensory experiences, which causes a physical response as neural pathways form in our minds. Paul Lewis (2017) recognizes that if this external stimulus is a social rule, it can also become acquired knowledge. He writes,

> Repeated action in conformity with a social rule can—via social psychological processes of habituation, imitation, conformism, etc.—cause neurological changes that lead to the formation of new cognitive (neural) structures and, therefore, to people having new dispositions to conceptualise and respond to their circumstances in certain ways. In this way, *social rules can become physically embodied in people*. (Lewis 2017, 20; emphasis added)

Similarly, structures and rules can affect people's conduct by activating the mental processes that people use to engage these social institutions (V. Ostrom [1976] 2012, 6–20; E. Ostrom 2005, 15–22).

Second, Hayek notices that knowledge by its nature is a type of spontaneous order. Caldwell (2004) observes that Hayek makes a direct correlation between the development of the mind and the development of society: "When Hayek turned to write *The Sensory Order*, he soon began to see the mind as another example of a spontaneously forming order, analogous to the social orders that formed as the result of the unintended consequences of human action" (248). This correlation between mind and society, as a network of relationships formed by human intentionality, suggests that there is not a correlation between the mind and the natural sciences. Lewis (2017) thus claims that Hayek aimed "to explain why the phenomenal (subjective, mental) picture of the world provided by our senses differs from the physical order revealed to us by the natural sciences" (7).

Hayek's approach to fact and knowledge differs slightly from that of the Ostroms and Buchanan. Earlier in his career, he embraced the dichotomy between scientific and nonscientific knowledge, later rejecting this for a dichotomy between simple and complex phenomena. The Ostroms and Buchanan retain and engage both dichotomies. Hayek maintains throughout his career the premise that knowledge and social order form spontaneously, an idea that we see in Ostromian thought. However, both the Ostroms and Buchanan also acknowledge that humans have agency. As people are shaped by the social order to which they belong, they also shape the rules that determine how this social order will evolve.

## THE QUEST TO DEVELOP A SCIENCE OF CULTURE

The concepts of knowledge and artisanship yield several themes common to the scholarship produced by the Ostroms, Buchanan, and Hayek. They all address epistemological questions, sparring with the notion that natural facts and scientific knowledge form the model for all types of knowledge and advancing an alternative position, which is that there are many different ways to know about the human experience. This position leads these scholars to integrate such concepts as "institutional fact" into their epistemology. They also address issues of artisanship, particularly how ideas shape deeds to form artifacts, acknowledging that man interacts with his world by observing and categorizing social rules and by physically transforming himself in response to these institutions by forming neurological maps of the relationships between these rules and institutions. Such activity operates on the premise that abstract knowledge can be more useful than concrete knowledge for interpreting human action.

If it is true that man can, in part, construct an order that only exists first in his imagination, then any institution that seems to have been spontaneously ordered, to use Hayek's term, has an element of human intentionality in it. There is a process that consists of making rules, contesting ideas, and developing consensuses and coalitions that lies behind emergent conventions. Finally, the Ostroms, Buchanan, and Hayek recognize the critical role that language plays in communicating human intentionality throughout the nonscientific, artifactual realm that lies outside the scientific, natural realm. If people are to collate individual facts into meaningful structures, their concepts of the world must overlap on some level and so must the symbols of language and meaning that they use to communicate these common thoughts. Vincent Ostrom (1997) calls these habits of using language "concurrent patterns of communication in associated relationships" (161). These patterns result from human intentionality as people make value judgments through the process of artisanship, judgments that produce various mixes of fact and value in the resulting artifacts. This is true for material objects like Ostrom's coffee table or more abstract creations, such as private and public constitutions.

Hayek, Buchanan, and the Ostroms also reject the notion of perfectibility on several fronts. Hayek (1989), in his 1974 Nobel Memorial Lecture "The Pretence of Knowledge," asserts, "I prefer true but imperfect knowledge, even if it leaves much indetermined and unpredictable, to a pretence of exact knowledge that is likely to be false" (5). He drew attention to this position throughout his career. He also offered a potential remedy for this imperfection, which is that people should craft systems by which to collect, organize, and communicate new knowledge with great efficiency. Buchanan ([1979] 1999) addressed imperfection on a more individual level, observing that people do not always know what their preferences are: "I am here advancing the more radical notion that *not even* individuals have well-defined and well-articulated objectives that exist independently of choices themselves" (258; emphasis in the original). Loss is another form of imperfection, as when society lost the wisdom that people use to navigate incomplete knowledge and to cultivate self-awareness about their preferences: "The essential wisdom of the 18th century, of Adam Smith and classical political economy and of the American Founders, was lost through two centuries of intellectual folly" (Buchanan 2003, 11). Finally, both Ostroms acknowledge that people are fallible and capable of spoiling institutions with deception, oppression, and tyranny, among other ills (E. Ostrom and V. Ostrom [2004] 2014, 63–64).

There is an antidote to excessive imperfection and folly. Vincent Ostrom, like Buchanan, points us back to the wisdom of eighteenth-century political economy, suggesting that we can recover some of our incomplete knowledge by returning to foundational thinkers. He writes,

> Hobbes, Hume, Smith, and others give us foundations for dealing with language, learning, knowledge, communication, artisanship, and moral judgment in the exercise of choice. Languages are the vehicles for creating bodies of common knowledge, mutual understanding, social accountability, and patterns of trust that are themselves the most fundamental sources of capital upon which peoples can draw in realizing productive potentials. These are the conventional foundations upon which all forms of choice are fashioned. (V. Ostrom 1993, 164)

The wisdom is essential to artisanship. These eighteenth-century scholars recognized that "the exercise of choice" requires many supporting institutions, such as "language, education, knowledge, communication, artisanship, and moral judgment," concepts that the Austrian, Bloomington, and Virginia Schools developed in the twentieth and twenty-first centuries. The eighteenth-century engagement with artisanship to which Ostrom refers most certainly includes the element of aesthetic discernment through considerations of beauty and taste, which formed an important theoretical and practical piece of nearly every significant moral and political philosophy.

Political economists from the eighteenth century who wrote about aesthetics—for instance, Francis Hutcheson, David Hume, and Adam Smith—described many of the same concepts with which we have just engaged in our discussion of the Ostroms, Buchanan, and Hayek (Hutcheson [1726] 2004; Smith [1759] 1982; Hume [1777] 1987). These overlapping ideas include, first and foremost, artisanship, artifact, knowledge, and fact as well as the elements that comprise knowledge and artisanship, such as sensation, perception, the mind, ideas, categories, value, taste, and utility. Eighteenth-century political economists were not merely concerned with the physical appearance of an artifact—to refer to Vincent Ostrom's and Buchanan's use of the word for an object, a person, or an organization—or with a person's subjective evaluation of that object. They were also concerned about human processes: artisanship, education, valuation, and culture. Thus, Hutcheson, Hume, and Smith, among others, used the term "beauty" (the term "aesthetics" did not yet exist) in both a theoretical and a practical sense throughout their scholarship to describe human ideas, human action, and human artifacts.

Ostromian theories of artisanship and artifact, with its hint of aesthetics, thus bear many similarities to those of the historical authors whom Vincent and Elinor Ostrom study and cite. Eighteenth-century political economic concepts of beauty and Ostromian aesthetics both emphasize human processes and human qualities: action, becoming, choice, culture, deeds, knowledge, ideas, imagination, (im)perfection, perception, social rules, taste, and utility. By rooting aesthetics in the meaning and choice of an artisan and by articulating that an artifact unites "fact and value," Vincent Ostrom bridges the historical division between aesthetics and utility. The cultural sciences, as Ostrom interprets them, can encompass both artisans and the artifacts they create (V. Ostrom [1976] 2012, 15).

Knowledge is vital to artisanship, and it is vital to a science of culture. Vincent Ostrom (1997) wanted to develop the concept and practice of the cultural sciences, hypothesizing that such a science would be inclusive of other sciences: "A science of culture would then have reference to all of the sciences as they manifest themselves as intellectual creations in semiautonomous cognitive systems" (204). Advancing and developing a science of culture prompts us to engage all the various types of facts, knowledges, and sciences that exist, including aesthetic knowledge.

Scholars in other fields make similar claims about how aesthetic knowledge furthers academic engagement in their particular disciplines. Strati (2003), who contributes to the field of organizational learning, writes, "As the act of perceiving and judging sensorially, *aesthetics is that form of organizational knowledge which is personal and collectively socially constructed at once.* To have a good eye or a refined taste is a personal sensorial faculty acting in—and shaped by—interpersonal relationships in organizational settings and in society" (55; emphasis in the original). Similarly, Bleiker's (2001) piece, which introduced aesthetic knowledge to the discipline of international relations, asserts, "[aesthetics] allows for productive interactions across different faculties, including sensibility, imagination and reason" (511). Scholars who incorporate aesthetic knowledge into their work use it to bridge personal knowledge, social knowledge (imagination, sensorial experience, social rules, and thought), and physical knowledge. This operationalization of aesthetic knowledge demonstrates the pressing need for a more robust science of culture that properly accounts for such knowledge.

Aesthetic knowledge and a cultural science would be useful for studies that grapple with culture. Culture influences institutions and the social rules that people create (Boettke 2001, 254). Institutional stickiness depends upon cultural contexts (Boettke, Coyne, and Leeson 2015). Cultural heterogeneity complicates such constructs as nationalism (Aligica and Matei 2015). The norms of a culture shape morality and conduct (Smith [1759] 1982; Storr and Choi 2019; Smith and Wilson 2019). Finally, some have argued that certain academic disciplines like economics are cultural sciences (Storr 2015, 32). Thus, a rigorous cultural science would promote the use of "thick" descriptions to analyze complicated cultural contexts (Boettke 2001, 249).

Furthermore, a science of culture would continue to build upon, to use Elinor Ostrom's words, the "essential foundation of a more eclectic (and classical) view of human behavior" (2005, 110). A culture is shared and communicated through mental models, as Ostrom writes, "When we indicate that people share a culture, it is a shorthand way of indicating that the wide diversity of mental models that individuals have invented has been reduced to a smaller set within those sharing the culture" (ibid., 106). Ostrom refers to our intellectual comprehension of the world around us as consisting of multiple mental models. A science of culture should likewise be expansive enough that there is an abundance of models with which we examine and describe the research at hand.

The quest to develop a science of culture that uses diverse forms of knowledge, such as aesthetic knowledge, would take the Ostroms' work in a direction that they had hoped to follow. This chapter began with an epigraph that expresses the Ostromian concern for preserving and advancing civilization: "Maximizing utility without attention to the way that ideas shape deeds leads people to trample civilization underfoot" (E. Ostrom and V. Ostrom [2004] 2014, 65). The Ostroms believed, as the Viennese students did, that civilizations could both regress and progress. If we are to advance civilization, we must follow the lead of the Austrian, Virginia, and Bloomington Schools by continuing to develop a science of culture that accounts for the ideas that lie at the heart of human action.

# NOTES

1. I gratefully acknowledge the Mercatus Center, the American Institute for Economic Research (AIER), and The Vincent and Elinor Ostrom Workshop in Political Theory and Policy Analysis at Indiana University Bloomington for the manifold ways they supported this project. Special recognition is due to two librarians, in particular, who assisted me with my many requests for research materials: Emily Castle at the Ostrom Workshop and Suzanne Hermann at AIER. Scholars who shaped my thinking through dialoguing with me or reviewing various drafts of my paper include Bill Blomquist and Angie Raymond of the Ostrom Workshop; Art Carden, Max Gucker, Thomas Hogan, Phil Magness, Ed Stringham, and Jeffrey Tucker of AIER; and of course my editors and colleagues at the Mercatus Center who initiated and contributed to the intellectual conversation that has culminated in this volume. *Mille grazie, tutti.* Any portions of this chapter that need further improvement are my responsibility.

2. Like others before me, I use the term "Ostromian" to refer to the combined corpus of scholarship produced by Vincent and Elinor Ostrom (Boettke and Candela 2015).

3. On this very topic, Bill Blomquist warned me about the temptation of tracing an idea in hopes of finding its source. This advice has proven wise as Searle (1969) cites Anscombe's (1958) article, "On Brute Facts," which beckons one further down this path. However, to start with Searle (1969) makes sense because Vincent Ostrom and McGinnis (1999) included Searle (1969), "The Distinction Between Brute Facts and Institutional Facts," in the first week of the graduate seminar they co-taught at Indiana University Bloomington.

4. Elinor Ostrom (2005) reiterates these ideas of "natural fact" and "institutional fact" with the term "physical and institutional factors" (17).

# REFERENCES

Aligica, Paul Dragos. 2018. "Artefactual and Artisanship: James M. Buchanan and Vincent Ostrom at the Core and Beyond the Boundaries of Public Choice." In *James M. Buchanan: A Theorist of Political Economy and Social Philosophy*, edited by Richard E. Wagner, 1105–29. Cham, CH: Palgrave Macmillan.

Aligica, Paul Dragos, and Peter J. Boettke. 2009. *Challenging Institutional Analysis and Development: The Bloomington School*. Abingdon, UK: Routledge.

Aligica, Paul Dragos, Paul Lewis, and Virgil Henry Storr. 2017. *The Austrian and Bloomington Schools of Political Economy*. Bingley, UK: Emerald Publishing.

Aligica, Paul Dragos, and Aura Matei. 2015. "National Cultures, Economic Action and the Homogeneity Problem: Insights from the Case of Romania." In *Culture and Economic Action*, edited by Laura E. Grube and Virgil Henry Storr, 295–317. Cheltenham, UK: Edward Elgar Publishing.

Allen, Barbara, ed. 2012. *The Quest to Understand Human Affairs: Essays on Collective, Constitutional, and Epistemic Choice, Volume 2*. Lanham, MD: Lexington Books.

Anscombe, G. E. M. 1958. "On Brute Facts." *Analysis* 18 (3): 69–72.

Bleiker, Roland. 2001. "The Aesthetic Turn in International Political Theory." *Millennium: Journal of International Studies* 30 (3): 509–33.

———. 2017. "In Search of Thinking Space: Reflections on the Aesthetic Turn in International Political Theory." *Millennium: Journal of International Studies* 45 (2): 258–64.

———. 2018. "Aesthetic Turn in International Relations." *Oxford Bibliographies*. Last Modified June 27, 2018. https://www.oxfordbibliographies.com/view/document/obo-9780199743292/obo-9780199743292-0236.xml.

Boettke, Peter J. 2001. "Why Culture Matters: Economics, Politics, and the Imprint of History." In *Calculation and Coordination: Essays on Socialism and Transitional Political Economy*, 248–65. New York: Routledge.

Boettke, Peter J., and Rosolino Candela. 2015. "Rivalry, Polycentrism, and Institutional Evolution." In *New Thinking in Austrian Political Economy*, edited by Christopher J. Coyne and Virgil Henry Storr, 1–20. Bingley, UK: Emerald Group Publishing.

Boettke, Peter J., Christopher J. Coyne, and Peter T. Leeson. 2015. "Institutional Stickiness and the New Development Economics." In *Culture and Economic Action*, edited by Laura E. Grube and Virgil Henry Storr, 123–46. Cheltenham, UK: Edward Elgar Publishing.

Buchanan, James. [1979] 1999. "Natural and Artifactual Man." In *The Collected Works of James M. Buchanan, Volume 1: The Logical Foundations of Constitutional Liberty*, 246–59. Indianapolis: Liberty Fund.

———. 2003. *Public Choice: The Origins and Development of a Research Program*. Fairfax, VA: Center for Study of Public Choice, George Mason University.

Caldwell, Bruce. 2004. "Some Reflections on F. A. Hayek's *The Sensory Order*." *Journal of Bioeconomics* 6 (3): 239–54.

Dekker, Erwin. 2016. *The Viennese Students of Civilization: The Meaning and Context of Austrian Economics Reconsidered*. Cambridge, UK: Cambridge University Press.

Dold, Malte F. 2018. "Back to Buchanan? Explorations of Welfare and Subjectivism in Behavioral Economics." *Journal of Economic Methodology* 25 (2): 160–78.

Griswold, Charles. 1999. *Adam Smith and the Virtues of Enlightenment*. Cambridge, UK: Cambridge University Press.

Hanley, Ryan. 2009. *Adam Smith and the Character of Virtue*. Cambridge, UK: Cambridge University Press.

Hayek, F. A. [1943] 2014. "The Facts of the Social Sciences." In *The Collected Works of F. A. Hayek, Volume 15: The Market and Other Orders*, edited by Bruce Caldwell, 78–92. Chicago: University of Chicago Press.

———. [1945] 2014. "The Use of Knowledge in Society." In *The Collected Works of F. A. Hayek, Volume 15: The Market and Other Orders*, edited by Bruce Caldwell, 93–104. Chicago: University of Chicago Press.

———. 1952. *The Sensory Order: An Inquiry into the Foundations of Theoretical Psychology*. London, UK: Routledge and Kegan Paul.

———. 1989. "The Pretence of Knowledge." *The American Economic Review* 79 (6): 3–7.

———. 2014. *The Collected Works of F. A. Hayek, Volume 15: The Market and Other Orders.* Edited by Bruce Caldwell. Chicago: University of Chicago Press.

Hess, Charlotte, and Elinor Ostrom. 2007. "Introduction: An Overview of the Knowledge Commons." In *Understanding Knowledge as a Commons: From Theory to Practice,* edited by Charlotte Hess and Elinor Ostrom, 3–26. Cambridge, MA: MIT Press.

Hume, David. [1742] 1948. "Idea of a Perfect Commonwealth." In *Hume's Moral and Political Philosophy,* edited by Henry D. Aiken, 384–85. New York: Hafner.

———. [1777] 1987. "Of the Standard of Taste." In *Essays: Moral, Political, and Literary,* edited by Eugene F. Miller, 226–249. Indianapolis: Liberty Fund.

Hutcheson, Francis. [1726] 2004. *An Inquiry into the Original of Our Ideas of Beauty and Virtue.* Edited by Wolfgang Leidhold. Indianapolis: Liberty Fund.

Knight, Frank H. 1967. "Ethics and the Economic Interpretation." In *The Ethics of Competition,* 19–40. Chicago: Midway Reprint.

Leonard, Mike. 2009. "What a Prize." *Hoosier Times,* December 5. https://www.hoosiertimes.com/tmnews/uncategorized/what-a-prize/article_32921e46-8a8f-5579-bbd3-8db6de0b8975.html.

Lewis, Paul. 2017. "Shackle on Choice, Imagination and Creativity: Hayekian Foundations." *Cambridge Journal of Economics* 41 (1): 1–24.

Lewis, Paul, and Malte Dold. 2020. "James Buchanan on the Nature of Choice: Ontology, Artifactual Man and the Constitutional Moment in Political Economy." *Cambridge Journal of Economics* 44 (5): 1159–79.

Ostrom, Elinor. 1990. *Governing the Commons: The Evolution of Institutions for Collective Action.* Cambridge, UK: Cambridge University Press.

———. 2005. *Understanding Institutional Diversity.* Princeton, NJ: Princeton University Press.

Ostrom, Elinor, and Xavier Basurto. 2011. "Crafting Analytical Tools to Study Institutional Change." *Journal of Institutional Economics* 7 (3): 317–43.

Ostrom, Elinor, and Vincent Ostrom. [2004] 2014. "The Quest for Meaning in Public Choice." In *Choice, Rules and Collective Action: The Ostroms on the Study of Institutions and Governance,* edited by Filippo Sabetti and Paul Dragos Aligica, 61–93. Colchester, UK: ECPR Press.

Ostrom, Vincent. 1975. "Public Choice Theory: A New Approach to Institutional Economics." *American Journal of Agricultural Economics* 57 (5): 844–50.

———. [1976] 2012. "David Hume as a Political Analyst." In *The Quest to Understand Human Affairs: Essays on Collective, Constitutional, and Epistemic Choice, Volume 2,* edited by Barbara Allen, 3–30. Lanham, MD: Lexington Books.

———. 1980a. "Artisanship and Artifact." *Public Administration Review* 40 (4): 309–17.

———. 1980b. "Some Reflections on Methodological Individualism in Light of Comments by Vickers, Catron and Harmon, and Thayer." *Dialogue* 2 (3): 14–19.

———. 1993. "Epistemic Choice and Public Choice." *Public Choice* 77 (1): 163–76.

———. 1997. *The Meaning of Democracy and the Vulnerability of Democracies: A Response to Tocqueville's Challenge*. Ann Arbor: University of Michigan Press.

———. 2012. *The Quest to Understand Human Affairs: Essays on Collective, Constitutional, and Epistemic Choice, Volume 2*, edited by Barbara Allen. Lanham, MD: Lexington Books.

Ostrom, Vincent, and Michael McGinnis. 1999. "Graduate Level Seminar in Empirical Theory and Methodology: Democracy, Civilization, and World Order." *The Good Society* 9 (2): 87–89.

Ostrom Workshop. n.d. "Podcast." Indiana University Bloomington. Accessed October 31, 2020. https://ostromworkshop.indiana.edu/library/podcast/index.html.

Polanyi, Michael. 1958. *Personal Knowledge: Towards a Post-Critical Philosophy*. Chicago: University of Chicago Press.

Popper, Karl R. 1972. *Objective Knowledge: An Evolutionary Approach*. Oxford: Clarendon Press.

Scruton, Roger. 2011. *Beauty: A Very Short Introduction*. Oxford: Oxford University Press.

Searle, John R. 1969. *Speech Acts: An Essay in the Philosophy of Language*. Cambridge, UK: Cambridge University Press.

Shackle, G. L. S. 1972. *Epistemics and Economics*. Cambridge, UK: Cambridge University Press.

———. 1976. "Time and Choice." *Proceedings of the British Academy* 67: 306–29.

Smith, Adam. [1759] 1982. *The Theory of Moral Sentiments*. Edited by D. D. Raphael and A. L. Macfie. Indianapolis: Liberty Fund.

Smith, Vernon L., and Bart J. Wilson. 2019. *Humanomics: Moral Sentiments and the Wealth of Nations for the Twenty-First Century*. Cambridge, UK: Cambridge University Press.

Storr, Virgil Henry. 2015. "Economists Should Study Culture." In *Culture and Economic Action*, edited by Laura E. Grube and Virgil Henry Storr, 11–47. Cheltenham, UK: Edward Elgar Publishing.

Storr, Virgil Henry, and Ginny Seung Choi. 2019. *Do Markets Corrupt Our Morals?* London: Palgrave Macmillan.

Strati, Antonio. 2003. "Knowing in Practice: Aesthetic Understanding and Tacit Knowledge." In *Knowing in Organizations: A Practice-Based Approach*, edited by Davide Nicolini, Silvia Gherardi, and Dvora Yanow, 53–75. Armonk, NY: M.E. Sharpe.

Tarko, Vlad. 2015. "The Role of Ideas in Political Economy." *The Review of Austrian Economics* 28 (1): 17–39.

Wolterstorff, Nicholas. 1980. *Art in Action*. Grand Rapids, MI: William B. Eerdmans.

———. 2015. *Art Rethought: The Social Practices of Art*. Oxford: Oxford University Press.

*Chapter 5*

# Sculptures of Stolen Marble

## *Applying Austrian Insights to Cultural Analyses of the Social, Political, and Economic Systems of Indigenous Peoples of the Pacific Northwest Coast*

### Rosaleen McAfee

In this chapter, I couple insights from the Austrian School of Economics with qualitative examples from the field of cultural anthropology. In doing so, I highlight the entanglement of politics, culture, and economics in Indigenous Pacific Northwest Coast cultural systems from the United States and Canada. The interpretive framework I employ involves an exploration of cultural systems that are traditionally analyzed within the realm of anthropology and historically disregarded in neoclassical economic theory. Through the application of this framework, I expose some of the underlying epistemological issues embedded in Enlightenment-era philosophy and neoclassical economic theory. I argue that this level of analysis enriches both sociocultural and economic studies.

Economists in the Austrian School advocate for the injection of cultural considerations into economic analyses (Grube and Storr 2015; Lavoie and Chamlee-Wright 2000; Chamlee-Wright 1997). Austrian economist Virgil Henry Storr argues, "Since culture plays a significant role in determining who can legitimately engage in market transactions, what constitutes an acceptable exchange, which items and services can be traded and what counts as money, it would seem to make sense for economists to concern themselves with how culture affects economic behavior" (Storr 2015, 34). Like Austrian economists, many contemporary anthropologists also critique the limitations of neoclassical economic studies. Anthropologist Stephen Gudeman argues specifically for a culturally situated understanding of economic systems, noting,

> Economy has two sides. One is the high-relationship economy that is rooted in the house. Neglected by economic theory, it is prominent in small-scale economies, and hidden and mystified yet salient in capitalism. The other side consists

of competitive trading. Anthropologists know one side of economy and economists know the other, but the two are intertwined. (Gudeman 2016, 2)

In this chapter, I aim to bridge the gap explicated by Gudeman above by
coupling Austrian economic insights with empirically grounded anthropological examples. Specifically, I draw from examples of social, political, and
economic systems of three Indigenous communities from the Pacific Northwest Coast of the United States and Canada. Two of these communities live
in the northern ranges of the Northwest Coast—the first being the Tlingit,
whose traditional territory covers the Southeastern Alaska panhandle; the
second being the Tsimshian, whose communities range from coastal British
Columbia to southern Alaska. The third cultural group, the Nuu-chah-nulth,
lives on the western coast of Vancouver Island, British Columbia.

I begin my analysis with a brief explanation of epistemology as it applies to Indigenous-specific epistemic discrimination, which I argue is
implicit in the foundations of classical economic theory. I then provide a
review of relevant concepts in early economic and anthropological theory,
highlighting some crucial areas where, I argue, these theorists misrecog-
nize Indigenous social, political, and economic systems. Following this,
I elucidate the Austrian School's reframing of *property rights, wealth,
production, market,* and *entrepreneurship*, applying these concepts to an
analysis of nineteenth- and early twentieth-century Indigenous Pacific
Northwest Coast people's cultural systems. I draw on relevant theories
from the Austrian School, including Virgil Henry Storr (2010, 2015), Paul
Dragos Aligica and Aura Matei (2015), Emily Chamlee-Wright (1997),
and Peter J. Boettke's (2001, 2004) discussions on culture and the market, Boettke (2004) and Don Lavoie and Emily Chamlee-Wright's (2000)
framings of wealth, and entrepreneurship theories developed by Lavoie
(2015) and Chamlee-Wright (1997). I then provide specific examples of
precolonial-contact Indigenous political, economic, and cultural systems
along the Northwest Coast, such as "salmon ranching" and the potlatch, as
well as postcolonial contact engagement with the market economy, exemplified by Tlingit women's participation in the tourism industry through
the production and sale of handwoven baskets. The Austrian School's
insights on culture and economic activity, I argue, enhance my critique
of early economists' and social theorists' misunderstanding of Indigenous
social, political, and economic systems. Finally, I advocate for the further
application of cultural studies within economics, arguing that the Austrian
School offers unique avenues for doing so.

## EPISTEMIC ISSUES UNDERPINNING CLASSICAL THEORY

Epistemology is broadly concerned with "who can be a knower, what can be known, what constitutes knowledge, sources of evidence for constructing knowledge, what constitutes truth, how truth can be verified, how evidence becomes truth, how valid inferences are to be drawn, the role of belief in evidence, and related issues" (Gegeo and Watson-Gegeo 2001, 57). Indigenous epistemology focuses on a "theory of knowledge that is based on Indigenous perspectives, such as relationality, the interconnection of sacred and secular, and holism" (Antoine et al. 2018, 72). Indigenous Yaqui legal scholar Rebecca Tsosie states that, due to their spiritual and thus inherently "nonsecular" nature, Indigenous epistemologies are continuously marginalized within Western academia. As Tsosie writes, "the legal and policy structures that determine [Indigenous peoples'] contemporary rights . . . are built upon a model that disregards Indigenous values and excludes them from full participation in the social and epistemic practices of the dominant culture" (Tsosie 2017, 359). Tsosie argues that Indigenous peoples suffer from epistemic discrimination as they are "foreclosed from participating in the creation of epistemic practices and excluded from institutions where meaning is made" (ibid., 358–59). I argue here that the dismissal of Indigenous knowledge in Western institutions also ignores the origins of Anglo-European knowledge, erroneously reinforcing the idea that Anglo-European knowledge and the subsequent scientific advances developed from it are *objective* and *value-free*. In this framing, Indigenous epistemologies, due to their interconnection with emotional and spiritual dimensions (Antoine et al. 2018), are considered *subjective* and *value-laden.*

Economists in the Austrian School critique epistemological shortcomings embedded within Enlightenment-era philosophy and economic studies. For example, Austrian economist Don Lavoie notes, "The procedure of starting with the individual mind, which is presumed to be a self-contained, unproblematic entity, and then moving on to address the problem of 'Other Minds' has been the mainstream approach in philosophy ever since Descartes" (Lavoie 2015, 61); Lavoie draws here from Hans-Georg Gadamer, who, in critiquing Cartesian philosophy, argued that "the mind is already social before it is rational" (ibid., 61). Lavoie further extends this analysis writing, "All understanding of the natural world is already social understanding, embedded in and meaningful only in relation to culture. The methodological priority given to the rational choice of individual minds implicitly treats them as if they could exist in isolated, cultureless, languageless brains" (ibid., 62).

In line with this critique, Peter J. Boettke and David L. Prychitko quote an early Austrian economist, Ludwig von Mises, as follows:

> Because the classical economists were able to explain only the action of businessmen and were helpless in the face of everything that went beyond it, their thinking was oriented toward bookkeeping, the supreme expression of the rationality of the businessman. . . . This explains several of their ideas—for example, their position in regard to personal services. The performance of a service which caused no increase in value that could be explained in the ledger of the businessman had to appear to them as unproductive. Only thus can it be explained why they regarded the attainment of the greatest monetary profit possible as the goal of economic action. Because of the difficulties occasioned by the paradox of value, they were unable to find a bridge from the realization, which they owed to utilitarianism, that the goal of action is an increase of pleasure and a decrease of pain, to the theory of value and price. Therefore, they were unable to comprehend any change in well-being that cannot be valued in money in the account books of the businessman. (Mises 1981 quoted in Boettke and Prychitko 2004, 19–20)

Here, Mises points to some of the key critiques employed by Austrian economists in their analyses of classical and neoclassical economic theory. The Austrian approach does not treat people as purely materialistic, nor their behaviors as motivated by purely rational or irrational economic choices. I argue that this approach demonstrates a shift away from traditional Anglo-European epistemologies that prioritize objective and value-free ideals and supports a move toward incorporating traditionally designated "value-laden" concepts into economic analysis.

In pursuit of a richer application of cultural theory in economic studies, I will provide some additional context into the epistemological underpinnings of early cultural theories that, I argue, continue to limit our understanding of Indigenous cultures. Of interest here is the work of the Scottish moralist Henry Home, Lord Kames, who provides an early reference to unilinear cultural evolution, stating, "I venture to suggest, that as, with respect to individuals, there is a progress from infancy to maturity; so there is a similar progress in every nation, from its savage state to its maturity in arts and sciences" (Kames [1813] 1967, lxxi). Building upon the insights of Scottish moralists and inspired by Charles Darwin's theory of biological evolution, social theorists of the late nineteenth and early twentieth centuries sought to trace the development of humanity through unilinear stages of cultural progression, beginning with "primitive peoples," whose behavior they modeled after living nomadic hunter-gatherers, and peaking with "civilized peoples," modeled after Europeans of the Victorian era. Building from their philosophical contemporaries, theorists in the nascent field of anthropology developed models of cultural evolution specifically referencing living Indigenous peoples of North America. Lewis Henry Morgan was a key thinker here, and Morgan's comparative studies of kinship among the Haudenosaunee (Iroquois) peoples of New York in the mid-nineteenth century developed into a theory of social evolution that influenced scholars like Friedrich Engels and Karl Marx (Cattelino 2018, 279). The theory of unilinear cultural evolution led to concepts of racialized hierarchy that placed living Indigenous peoples at the bottom of an evolutionary scale. As I argue below, Indigenous peoples also served as the "other" upon which Enlightenment-era framings of natural law and property rights were built.

Dutch humanist Hugo Grotius was a foundational thinker on theories of natural rights—theories forwarded by John Locke in his construction of private property rights. Grotius, as political scientist Barbara Arneil argues, used the lifeways of Indigenous peoples in North America to describe his "natural man," living in a state of "primitive simplicity." Grotius describes "This primitive state . . . exemplified in the community of property arising from extreme simplicity, [which] may be seen among certain tribes in America [who] have lived for many generations in such a condition" (Grotius quoted in Arneil 1992, 590–91). This narrative is echoed by Robert Cushman, organizer of the Mayflower journey to the northeastern coast of what is now the United States, who describes the aboriginal land of the New World as follows: "The country is yet raw; the land untilled; the cities not builded; the cattle not settled. We are compassed about with a helpless and idle people, the natives of the country, which cannot . . . help themselves, much less us" (Cushman quoted in Arneil 1996, 63).

John Locke also looked to the New World to stage his framework for the "state of nature," which he describes as "temporally located in a past time before humans had advanced to higher stages of development and thereby situated at the theoretical limits of the social and the civilizational. . . . Thus in the beginning all the world was America, and more so than that is now; for no such thing as money was any where known" (Locke [1690] 1988 quoted in Cattelino 2018, 277). By characterizing his "state of nature" as the America he saw before him at present, Locke placed contemporary Indigenous peoples squarely in the past and rejected the political and social systems they employed to govern their societies and control their property.

Arneil argues that Locke's theorizing was heavily influenced by colonial expansion into North America and that his conceptualization of agrarian labor was influenced by the need to differentiate Indigenous people's property rights and criteria for ownership from those of Europeans. The key to Locke's framing of property ownership rights was that the land in question must be enclosed and cultivated, and the resulting "products" must not be allowed to go to waste. In Locke's words,

> As much Land as a Man Tills, Plants, Improves, Cultivates and can use the Product of, so much is his Property. He by his Labour does, as it were, inclose [*sic*] it from the Common. (Locke [1690] 1988, II, para. 32)

> God gave the World to Men in Common; but . . . it cannot be supposed that he meant it should always remain common and uncultivated. He gave it to the use of the Industrious and Rational, (and Labour was to be his Title to it). (Locke [1690] 1988, II, para. 34)

Locke's framework for the possession of property was put to use by English colonial interests in the New World to justify colonial expansion into large swaths of North America. In framing the land of interest as "common" and "uncultivated," rights of occupancy, which Indigenous people may have otherwise claimed, could now be denied under the terms of natural law. In the framings of Grotius, Locke, and Cushman, people who cultivated the land were "industrious" and "rational," and people who benefited from the land's natural resources without exerting any apparent effort upon it were thus "idle" and "irrational." These thinkers, and the colonial forces that internalized and mobilized their philosophical models, were unable—or unwilling—to recognize Indigenous ownership of and labor expended upon the land that colonial forces came to occupy. I provide specific examples of such acts of misrecognition in following section.


## WHAT THE AUSTRIAN SCHOOL OFFERS

The Austrian School's critique of traditional economic theories and their attention to the role of culture in shaping economic systems creates space for the analysis of Indigenous economic systems along the Pacific Northwest Coast of North America both prior to colonial contact and thereafter. I argue that, by applying Austrian insights to cultural examples, we can further critique the epistemological framings of early thinkers and their misinterpretations of Indigenous Northwest Coast social, political, and economic systems.

Israel Kirzner, a prolific thinker in the Austrian School, provides a critique of John Locke's moral framing of labor and property rights as follows:

> [C]ritics have severely questioned the simple assumption that joining one's labor to an unowned object constitutes a morally acceptable final annexation of it, even under circumstances in which the Lockean proviso has been satisfied.

. . . Who says that without the consent of the rest of the world I have the *right* to perform labor upon that which is not mine? (Kirzner 2016, 137; emphasis in the original)

Kirzner touches upon a critical failing of Locke's theory of property as it was applied by colonial forces. The land usurped through colonization was Indigenous-occupied territory that sustained Indigenous cultures for over ten thousand years—cultures that maintained complex systems of titles and land use rights. On the Northwest Coast specifically, by 1861 "the Legislative Assembly of Vancouver Island petitioned to extinguish Aboriginal title," and land on lower Vancouver Island was opened for colonization (Anderson and Halpin 2000, 198–99). Simultaneously, homesteading laws in America allowed men, women, previously enslaved peoples, and European settlers to "obtain federal land virtually free if they met certain requirements, including living on the land and cultivating a portion of it" (U.S. Department of the Interior 2016). The land allotted to homesteaders, however, belonged to Indigenous people whose cultivation and ownership rights were not recognized by the colonial government and who were subsequently dispossessed of their territories.

Further questioning the moral underpinnings of the Lockean proviso, Kirzner states that "[i]f initially acquired original inputs were *unjustly plundered from others*, or from the human race in general, all the subsequently discovered valuable uses that can be made out of these inputs (or out of products made out of those inputs, and so on, and so on) *are sculptures created out of stolen marble*" (Kirzner 2016, 148; emphasis added). While Kirzner was not intentionally describing the unjust acquisition of Indigenous land and resources by colonial forces in North America, he has provided a very clear parallel for these exploits.

Having briefly outlined the historical and epistemological context within which Enlightenment-era philosophy was developed, I now provide five definitions given by Austrian economists that, I argue, are applicable to Northwest Coast cultural, political, and economic systems in the nineteenth and twentieth centuries. The concepts engaged here are *property rights, wealth, production,* the *market,* and *entrepreneurship.* I argue that economists can extend their definitions of each of these concepts beyond Western capitalist systems to include intangible and tangible property rights and exchanges that traditionally fall under the analytical scope of nonmarket economies.

Austrian economists Matthew D. Mitchell and Peter J. Boettke, in their text *Applied Mainline Economics: Bridging the Gap between Theory and Public Policy,* discuss the cultural significance of *property rights* as follows:

Economists studying how different property rights regimes work in practice have found that the right to hold property also appears to be a fundamental prerequisite for human flourishing. A system of well-defined private property rights helps us live together peacefully, use our resources wisely, and plan for the future effectively. (Mitchell and Boettke 2017, 25)

Peter J. Boettke and David L. Prychitko, in a paper titled "Is an Independent Nonprofit Sector Prone to Failure? Toward an Austrian School Interpretation of Nonprofit and Voluntary Action," describe *production* as "the creation of anything we value . . . production is not to be limited to the production of new things. Simple acts of trading already-produced items (as in barter, for example) are productive because they increase the wealth of both trading parties" (Boettke and Prychitko 2004, 19). Boettke and Prychitko provide a subjective theory of value that defines *wealth* as "whatever a person strives for: it consists not only of material things (from food, water, and shelter to fast cars, video games, and money), but also of nonmaterial goods (such as love, respect, intelligence, historic preservation, beauty, and so forth)" (2004, 19). This is in line with the Austrian School's economic methodology of radical subjectivism, which economist Emily Chamlee-Wright argues allows for the introduction of cultural analysis into the interpretation of the market process (Chamlee-Wright 1997, 50).

In discussing the *market*, Virgil Henry Storr writes,

> The Austrian school has always argued that the market is a product of human activity. "The market," Mises (1963: 312) has stated, "is a social body; it is the foremost social body. The market phenomena are social phenomena. They are the resultant of each individual's active contribution." . . . For Austrians, then, the market is "produced by man in the course of his ongoing externalization" (Mises 1963) within the economic realm. (Storr 2010, 201)

Don Lavoie shares this framing of the market, writing, "Markets can be viewed as offshoots of, and complements to, the process of cultural dynamics" (Lavoie 2015, 64). Finally, Austrian economists argue that entrepreneurs hold a place outside of the traditionally defined market economy, explaining *entrepreneurship* as "the achievement not so much of the isolated maverick who finds objective profits others overlooked as of the culturally embedded participant who picks up the gist of a conversation" (Lavoie 2015, 51). Like Lavoie, Emily Chamlee-Wright recognizes the role that culture plays in economic activity. In her 1997 book *The Cultural Foundations of Economic Development: Urban Female Entrepreneurship in Ghana*, Chamlee-Wright argues that "culture guides and directs the attention of entrepreneurs by placing them in a specific position within the social order and providing them with an interpretive framework to piece together profit opportunities creatively" (131). Further, Chamlee-Wright notes the Austrians' recognition that entrepreneurial activity is carried out by "real human beings operating with a specific context, not the cultureless and institutionless *homoeconomicus* of neoclassicism" (ibid., 48; italics in the original). This shift away from the "narrow Robbinsian notion of economizing" (ibid., 44) and toward a recognition of the role of culture in economic choice enriches our understanding of Nuu-chah-nulth, Tsimshian, and Tlingit cultural, political, and economic systems in place in the nineteenth and early twentieth century. I exemplify this shift in the following section.

## EXAMPLES FROM THE PACIFIC NORTHWEST COAST

### Property Rights, "Goodness," and Wealth

Aboriginal forestry scholar Ronald Trosper has identified six key ideas that define property, exchange, and leadership rules in the Pacific Northwest. I provide these points in full, as they effectively describe the key components of Indigenous Northwest Coast social, political, and economic systems with which I engage:

1. Rights of access and use of valuable lands and fishing sites were recognized as something similar to the European idea of property, meaning that individuals or groups could exclude others from using the valuable lands. To distinguish the idea from that of property, I shall call their territorial system one of proprietorship. The distinction is necessary because the person with the rights of proprietorship was not able to sell the land. He was also obligated to share some of the land's products. Neither of these conditions is typical of "property" in the European sense.
2. Proprietorship over territory was contingent on proper management of the territory. Not only did the chief of a house holding territory need to demonstrate he had been trained successfully for the job; he had to perform well as chief.
3. A system of ethics defined proper use; the ethical beliefs defined abuse of land in terms of reduction of its productivity for future generations.
4. Systems of reciprocity defined economic exchange relationships among people, both individually and in groups. Reciprocity provided incentives that supported proper use of lands both by providing insurance against misfortune and by reducing the incentives to harvest too much.
5. Enhancement of reciprocity rules was totally public.
6. Rules about the behavior of chiefs provided a system of governance that could maintain the other five elements and allow modifications as needed. (Trosper 2009, 15)

The complex economic and political systems maintained by Indigenous peoples living along the Pacific Northwest Coast perplexed early social theorists, who attempted to organize these groups into the preestablished categories of unilinear cultural evolution. In the twentieth century, Indigenous social organization across the Northwest Coast centered around corporate groups, linked by kinship and divided by rank (Trosper 2009, 15). Northern communities, such as the Tsimshian and Tlingit, were matrilineal and divided into "clans," while southern communities such as the Nuu-chah-nulth were organized ambilaterally into "houses" or nations (Wolf 1982, 186). Houses, comprising extended families, controlled geographical territories containing "fishing sites, berry-picking sites, gardens, and other sites that produced food or plant material for use of the house" (Trosper 2009, 16). For the Alaskan Tlingit, land rights were tied to ancestral ownership. For example, anthropologist Viola Garfield documented in 1947 that Tlingit legal theory accorded bays, streams, and other productive areas as the private property of certain house groups or local divisions of clans. Further, once use and occupancy were established, these properties became inalienable (Garfield 1947, 451).[1] Garfield provides an example of the deeply entrenched nature of these land rights writing,

> When asked how his clan came into possession of a certain stream one man angrily stated that his ancestors had always owned it; they had settled on its banks after the Flood. He then proceeded to relate the migrations of his ancestors from the Stikine River, designating the villages they had located and the new areas they had acquired during their wanderings. (Garfield 1947, 452)

This principle of *property* is further demonstrated by the Alaskan Tlingit, who, through complex systems of hierarchy, controlled tangible and intangible rights across their territories. United States Navy Lieutenant George T. Emmons, who was stationed among the Tlingit in the nineteenth century, observes that "they had formulated and were following a code of exact laws which regulated in detail their relations with each other and which were generally accepted by the neighboring coastal tribes. Property rights were strictly observed, and compensations were made for injuries or killings according to the rank of the victim" (Emmons quoted in Austin 1999, 9). In addition to controlling fishing, hunting, and cultivation sites, chiefs within Northwest Coast societies owned specific knowledge that was passed down through generations via secret ceremonies; ownership of this knowledge was said to aid in successful leadership.

Austrian economic insight provides some helpful concepts for understanding the systems exemplified here as performing economic, rather than purely social, functions. In their 2000 book *Culture and Enterprise: The Devel-*

*opment, Representation and Morality of Business*, Don Lavoie and Emily Chamlee-Wright, for example, stress that wealth can mean radically different things to different people, based on their cultural backgrounds (Lavoie and Chamlee-Wright 2000, 55). Looking outside the traditional definitions of "wealth," Peter J. Boettke describes the power of "goodness" in a contractual society as such:

> [W]ith clearly defined and strictly enforced property rules, all are required to honor contracts, abstain from using force, be truthful in deals, etc. Being "good" does not necessarily translate into doing "well" more often than not, but in a truly contractual society one cannot do well unless by doing good. In other words, individuals can only acquire material wealth by satisfying the demands of others. (Boettke 2004, 47)

For the Nuu-chah-nulth, the *law of generosity* exemplifies the concept of "being good" as presented by Boettke. Nuu-chah-nulth chief Umeek speaks of the law of generosity as follows: "It is necessary to give in order to receive. According to this law, it is not better to give than to receive because both giving and receiving are equivalent and interactive values. Consequently, generosity can be viewed as a natural law of reciprocity" (Atleo 2004, 129, quoted in Trosper 2009, 13–14). Like the Nuu-chah-nulth values described by Chief Umeek, for the Tsimshian, basic social principles included "hierarchy, reciprocity, and an expansive notion of corporate ownership of tangible and intangible properties" (Hosmer 1999, 112). For the Tsimshian, links to the chiefly class by broader clan and lineage relationships "carried reciprocal responsibilities where, for instance, chiefs 'exchanged' protection and material aid for goods, labor, and assistance that not only enhanced a chief's wealth but also elevated the prestige of all members of a house, lineage, clan, and village" (ibid., 118). Extending the concept of property beyond material goods, the Tsimshian counted "ceremonial prerogatives, names, songs, and sacred histories . . . as the exclusive property of corporate groups but held in trust by the highest-ranking individuals" (ibid., 112). Thus, for both the Tsimshian and the Nuu-chah-nulth, the chief's responsibilities included managing material and immaterial property as well as wealth.

As highlighted by the Nuu-chah-nulth and Tsimshian examples here, private property rights, including ownership of territories used for hunting, collecting, and fishing, existed across the Northwest Coast. Although resembling the European idea of property, these rights of access were disregarded by Anglo-Europeans in their formulations of property rights in North America. Contemporary conceptualizations of goodness and wealth, such as those outlined by the Austrian School, I argue, help to move away from the epistemological shortcomings of colonial models and present more holistic economic theories that better describe these noncapitalist structures.

## Sustainability and Production

Indigenous Northwest Coast societies developed complex social-ecological systems "based on the tending and care of plants, fisheries, and other resources" (Trosper 2009, x). When Europeans arrived on the Northwest Coast, they observed a highly productive environment rich with natural resources. Colonizers were confused by Indigenous Northwest Coast people's "complex societies, with fixed winter villages, large houses, dense populations, and a highly developed art" (Trosper 2009, ix); and they could not understand how all of these traits were developed and sustained without traditionally defined agricultural practices. When Captain James Cook arrived on Vancouver Island in 1778, he noted that, although the Indigenous peoples were "indolent," "wild and uncouth," and "incapable of the most basic civilized pursuits," they were "blessed by tremendous natural wealth in the form of fish and other marine animals" (Cook and King 1784 quoted in Deur and Turner 2005, 2). Erroneously labeling Indigenous peoples of the Northwest Coast as hunter-gatherers, colonizers misrecognized their active management of environmental resources and failed to connect this to the high level of resource productivity observed.

Indigenous peoples have been sustainably harvesting their physical environment for thousands of years. Specifically, Indigenous peoples along the Northwest Coast practiced harvesting methods whereby portions of material were harvested from a living plant, such as the bark from a cedar tree, without harming the source, allowing it instead to further produce harvestable materials (Deur and Turner 2005, 17). Cedar trees were a critical resource along the Northwest Coast, and the controlled stripping of bark from the trees provided continuous access to a raw material used in innumerable ways, primarily for clothing, bedding, containers, and basketry. This form of harvesting continues to be practiced by Indigenous peoples of the Northwest Coast contemporarily.

The regional transplanting of plants and the act of selective harvesting were also widespread cultivation practices in the nineteenth and twentieth centuries. These actions improved plant productivity and resulted in increased accessibility to harvestable sources (ibid., 17). Specifically, root vegetables were selectively harvested by size so that younger roots would continue growing, while "routine digging and cultivation of the soil, both during the harvesting process or as a separate management activity . . . [enhanced] the growth of root vegetables" (Beckwith 2004 quoted in Deur and Turner 2005, 17). The tending of salmon for fishing serves as a further example of intentional management of resources along the Northwest Coast. Law scholar D. Bruce Johnsen notes this practice as extending back three thousand years. Johnsen refers to the "purposeful husbandry and active management of [relevant] resources" (2004, 5) as "salmon ranching," stating that "conditional on their strong attachment to place and their inability to harvest large numbers of salmon in the open sea, [Indigenous Northwest Coast communities] effectively owned the salmon stocks that spawned in their streams and harvested them largely in terminal fisheries during their upstream migration" (Johnsen 2009, 43). These river-based fisheries, Johnsen states, were "subject to exclusive tribal property rights enforced through long-term reciprocity relations," with chiefs managing these resources as stewards for the tribe (Johnsen 2009, 42). Other examples of sustainable harvesting include the tending of clam beds and the transporting of salmon smolts or eggs for harvesting.

Following Boettke and Prychitko's definition of production—which recognizes production as the creation of anything valued within a culture—we can see how Indigenous cultivation practices sustained successful agricultural systems over millennia while also encouraging sustainability in consumption, which Indigenous peoples of the Northwest Coast valued beyond any material returns. Further, the successful maintenance of property rights along the Northwest Coast exemplifies Mitchell and Boettke's insight that "well-defined private property rights helps us live together peacefully, use our resources wisely, and plan for the future effectively" (2017, 25). Taken together, these reformulations of traditional economic concepts allow us to better represent the cultural and political values held within Indigenous Northwest Coast societies while recognizing the economic components supporting these systems.

## Potlatch and The Market

Indigenous Northwest Coast peoples maintained organized political structures encompassing control of both tangible and intangible property, as described above. Hierarchy within these structures was continuously endorsed within and across communities in events called "potlatches." While there are many variations on potlatching or feasting across the Northwest Coast differing between cultural groups and in the types of occasions marked by their occurrence, they all share the primary function of being ceremonial events. By the late nineteenth century, the Canadian and United States governments criminalized the practice of potlatching across the Northwest Coast. Policymakers believed that potlatches were wasteful—harking back to Locke's spoilage limitation and the European condescension for what they perceived as "wastefulness." Despite this ban, potlatching—sometimes done in secret and other times done publicly, resulting in fines or arrests of Indigenous participants and the destruction (or collection for sale to museums) of their property—continued to play a major role in Indigenous cultural, political, and economic systems and persisted after the introduction of market capitalism. Potlatches are still held in communities across the Northwest Coast and infuse contemporary elements with traditional components, such as the giving away of objects like pencils, cotton bandanas, puzzles, and money, as well as the gifting of intangible property, such as names, dances, and other prerogatives.

Alaskan Native Alexis C. Bunten defines the potlatch as "a gathering at which key clan or group business is publicly conducted, and at which marriages, transfers of leadership or ownership, memorials, or other markers of life-status change are celebrated and guests are paid to witness the proceedings" (Bunten and Graburn 2018, 189, footnote 2). These distributions were "witnessed" by guests of a potlatch, who were in turn given payment for the act of witnessing. Claims to territory, including rivers and coastal ocean areas, were also affirmed during potlatches. Potlatches further served to demonstrate a chief's power to the invited guests of the event. Speaking about Tsimshian potlatches, anthropologists Marjorie Halpin and Margaret Seguin write, "[T]he prestige accorded to the potlatch-giver . . . depended upon the amount of wealth he displayed and gave away" (Halpin and Seguin 1990, 278). Potlatches were also held to settle conflicts between competing groups or to erase shame from a house, village, or individual. For the Tsimshian specifically, historian Brian C. Hosmer states that potlatches,

> constituted a powerful statement of one's social position and, by extension, of his or her right to the prerogatives in question. Conversely, it was unthinkable for an individual to lay claim to an important name, and its associated prerogatives, without demonstrating publicly his or her "fitness" to lay claim to that honor. To circumvent established conventions opened that person to ridicule and brought shame and dishonor in lineage, house, and perhaps village. (Hosmer 1999, 121)

The potlatch, like land management and property rights, was misunderstood by nineteenth- and twentieth-century anthropologists and government officials, who failed to grasp the economic, social, and spiritual functions embedded in these ceremonies. Anthropologist Jessica Cattelino describes this struggle as follows:

> They [anthropologists and government officials] could not decide whether [the potlatch] was an exemplary case of competitive quasi-capitalist accumulation of goods and exchange for interest that showed Native people to share settlers' own economic principles and promise, or an elaborate system of gift-giving

that showed Native peoples to be of a different time and type than settlers, or an even-more-radical spectacle of wanton destruction and waste of property that sealed the argument for indigenous irrationality. (Cattelino 2018, 296)

The potlatch continuously appears as a model for interpreting reciprocity and gift giving in economic and anthropological studies. However, contemporary anthropologists argue that these occasions involved far more than the simple exchange of material goods. Although potlatches placed an emphasis on collecting and redistributing accumulated goods across houses, many intangible belongings were gifted and exchanged as well. Connections formed through the exchange of intangible goods helped maintain positive relationships between groups and continuously endorsed family histories and stories while subsequently reaffirming connections between people and the territories they held rights to.

The market, Austrian economists contend, is not a space of pure economic exchange but a social setting within which people exchange material goods while establishing and upholding systems of values for those exchanges. As Emily Chamlee-Wright states, "[M]arkets are an extension of culture because it is culture that shapes the rules necessary for a market to function" (1997, 41). Following Austrian economists' lead, I broaden the scope of the market to include the exchange of immaterial goods, such as titles and prerogatives, and the exchange of social goods, such as songs and dances. Further, I argue that social integration and cultural continuity, as they pertain to potlatching, can be read as market functions. I do not argue that the potlatch be interpreted only as a venue for economic exchange, nor do I contend that economic transaction be removed from our interpretation of the potlatch. Rather, I propose a middle ground whereby the potlatch may be read as a market space that encompasses material and immaterial transactions that are economically, politically, and socially motivated.

## Weaving and Entrepreneurship

Emily Chamlee-Wright argues that the role of women in the market system has been largely ignored by mainstream economists, with the male bias of the field and Western notions of women's role in economic activity contributing to this oversight (ibid., 22). Forwarding Chamlee-Wright's critique, as I will elucidate below, Tlingit women's interactions with the tourist market of early twentieth-century Alaska should be read as entrepreneurship functioning within a dual economy.

Paul Dragos Aligica and Aura Matei frame the concept of a "dual economy" as the relationship between a capitalist economy (with its values and culture) accommodating and/or overcoming a traditional economy, stating that "the two, while in contact with each other, are not fully integrated" (Aligica and Matei 2015, 304). Aligica and Matei outline the necessary considerations for realizing the dynamics of a dual system as "first, understanding the traditional sector; second, understanding the modern sector; and, third, understanding the interrelationship—interaction and symbiosis—between the traditional sector and the modern one" (ibid., 305). I argue that a dual economy existed along the Northwest Coast for a period of time spanning the nineteenth and twentieth centuries, and it involved Indigenous people's resistance to—and necessary participation in—market capitalism introduced by colonization.

Specifically, as a response to the introduction of market capitalism in the Americas, Indigenous people coproduced ideas of "authentic Indian-ness" to "access the social, political, and economic means necessary for survival under colonialism" (Raibmon 2005, 3). Tourism on the Northwest Coast presented opportunities for engaging the market economy introduced by co-lonialization—specifically for Indigenous women who sold handcrafted ob-jects to tourists seeking collectables made by "authentic" Indigenous peoples. Anglo-European travelers to the Americas brought with them a new interest in the "disappearing" native peoples, leading tourists to seek "authentic" ex-periences among these communities and to collect their cultural belongings before they "disappeared entirely." While Indigenous engagement in tourism occurred across North America, I focus here on Tlingit women's involvement in the tourist market.

The Tlingit saw large waves of outsiders on their lands, beginning with military presence resulting from the purchase of Alaska by the United States in 1867; shifting to waves of missionaries, wage laborers, and gold miners[2] in the late nineteenth century; and turning to tourists from cruise ships trav-eling along the Alaskan coastline in the early twentieth century. The city of Sitka, Alaska, became a popular stopping point for these steam ships, and the Sitka Tlingit capitalized on the economic possibilities of this influx. Tlingit women, specifically, responded to new economic opportunities by weaving baskets made exclusively for sale and by selling these goods near cruise ship ports. Baskets were especially popular among the Victorian tourist crowd, who sought "exotic" items for their curio corners. Tlingit women, who had been weaving basketry items for practical uses for millennia, saw and seized upon the opportunity to market these items to tourists. Not only did they craft brightly colored baskets and mats—which were similar in form to the tradi-tional ones woven for everyday use—they designed and wove new shapes purely for tourist consumption. For example, a miniature woven teacup and saucer, measuring five centimeters wide and four centimeters high, was pur-chased from the Tlingit and donated to the American Museum of Natural His-tory in 1905. Tlingit women wove other basketry shapes as well, including miniature non-functional baskets with ornate Victorian motifs and doll-sized hats and boots (American Museum of Natural History n.d.).

Tlingit women who sold their goods to tourists may have uniformly set prices for these items. While there is no written record demonstrating Tlingit women doing so, travelers remarked on the uniformity of their prices across communities. For example, one tourist wrote, "We came to the conclusion that there must be a Trades Union here, for the uniformity of prices was remarkable, and there was a positive firmness about the market" (Lukens 1889, 54; Smetzer 2014, 68 quoted in Bunten and Graburn 2018, 174).

Tlingit women also designed a system to ensure payment was given for photographs taken of them; if payment was not received up front, the women would turn their faces away from the camera or find other ways to block their faces from the shot.[3] By creating opportunities for economic success within the new capitalist market, Indigenous people experiencing the dissolution of their traditional economies were able to gain "funds to reinforce hereditary positions or increase status within Indigenous social systems without regard for—and even in contradiction to—colonial policies interdicting those systems" (Bunten and Graburn 2018, 166).

Entrepreneurship, as described by Lavoie, "should include genuine novelty and creativity and should not be rendered as a mechanical search for pre-existing conditions" (Lavoie 2015, 51). Two properties of entrepreneurship highlighted in the Austrian School, "discovery" and "interpretation," are both captured in the Tlingit example given here. "Discovery," as described by Lavoie, "suggests an element of radical change, a surprising find, an unanticipated break with past patterns" (ibid., 51). "Interpretation" describes the idea that "the profit opportunities entrepreneurs discover are not a matter of objective observation of quantities, but a matter of perspectival interpretation, a discerning of the intersubjective meaning of a qualitative situation" (ibid., 51). The Tlingit women who wove basketry for sale, I argue, can be seen as entrepreneurs as defined by the Austrian School, in that they were attuned to opportunities for income in a shifting economic and cultural terrain and were simultaneously able to maintain their cultural values by collectively setting prices for the sale of their goods and acting in unison when not paid for the goods they provided.

## CONCLUSION

For many generations we Indigenous people have been in a life and death struggle for survival, for respect of our humanity, restoration of our nationhood, and recognition of our rights. This whole time, a constant surge of ancestral memory running through our veins has empowered and enlivened us and given us the gifts of tenacity, anger, patience and love, so that the people may continue and so that the generations that are yet to rise from the earth may know themselves as the real people of their land. (Alfred 2017)

By utilizing culture as a lens through which to understand economic processes and moving beyond the epistemological shortcomings of traditional economic and anthropological analyses, I argue that we can better recognize the breadth of economic activities maintained by Indigenous peoples along the Pacific Northwest Coast. Further, I argue that we are better suited to appreciate the scope of these activities as situated within a broader cultural discourse. Throughout this chapter, I have guided readers through a series of examples to demonstrate that the Indigenous peoples of the Northwest Coast—specifically the Tlingit, Nuu-chah-nulth, and Tsimshian—maintained complex social, political, and economic systems that were misrecognized by early philosophers, economists, and anthropologists. Early economists and the schools that built upon their theories failed to recognize alternative economic institutions and cultural practices outside of capitalism, leading to a lacuna in the hermeneutical resources developed by these schools.

The Austrian School has productively criticized the limited application of cultural studies in neoclassical economic theory. As Emily Chamlee-Wright states, "Economists usually recognize only two functions of culture within the economy—determining preferences and constraining optimizing behavior" (1997, 25). The Austrian School pushes against the narrowed lens of neoclassical economic theory, recognizing instead the "*enabling* role culture plays in economic processes" (Lavoie 2015, 91; italics in the original). Scholars in the Austrian School have provided novel framings of traditional economic concepts such as *property rights*, *wealth*, *production*, the *market*, and *entrepreneurship* that, I argue, leave room for cultural meaning within economic analyses. Further, I contend that the application of Austrian theory in cultural studies provides novel opportunities for the incorporation of Indigenous epistemological framings into empirical economic models.

As Indigenous Kwakwa̱ka̱'wakw scholar Sarah Hunt contends, "The situatedness and place-specific nature of Indigenous knowledge calls for the validation of new kinds of theorizing and new epistemologies that can account for situated, relational Indigenous knowledge and yet remain engaged with broader theoretical debates" (Hunt 2014, 31). Guided by Taiaiake Alfred's quote above and following Hunt's call, I argue for an economic discourse that creates space for Indigenous epistemologies and believe that the fruitful connections made by the Austrian School of economic theory provide a novel framework for this work.

## NOTES

1. Garfield notes, however, that territories did occasionally change hands, including transfers of title property in order to satisfy a debt, or the extension of fishing, hunting, and home-site rights (Garfield 1947, 452).

2. The Klondyke gold rush was responsible for the homestead laws that extended to Alaska in 1898, as settlers sought the ownership of land for settlement and economic development (Raibmon 2005, 143).

3. Photographic evidence and oral histories show that this became a widespread practice along the Northwest Coast (Campbell 2007, 165–66; Collis 1890, 99–100; Raibmon 2005, 145–46; Scidmore 1885, 28 quoted in Bunten 2015, 174).

## REFERENCES

Alfred, Taiaiake. 2017. "It's All About the Land." In *The Decolonization and Reconciliation Handbook*, edited by Peter McFarlane and Nicole Schabus, 10–13. Vancouver, BC: Federation of Post-Secondary Educators of BC.

Aligica, Paul Dragos, and Aura Matei. 2015. "National Cultures, Economic Action and the Homogeneity Problem: Insights from the Case of Romania." In *Culture and Economic Action,* edited by Laura E. Grube and Virgil Henry Storr, 295–317. Cheltenham, UK: Edward Elgar Publishing.

American Museum of Natural History. n.d. "Division of Anthropology Online Database." Accessed March 29, 2019. https://anthro.amnh.org/collections.

Anderson, Margaret, and Majorie Halpin, eds. 2000. *Potlatch at Gitsegukla: William Beynon's 1945 Field Notebooks.* Vancouver, BC: University of British Columbia Press.

Antoine, Asma-na-hi, Rachel Mason, Roberta Mason, Sophia Palahicky, and Carmen Rodriquez de France. 2018. *Pulling Together: A Guide for Curriculum Developers.* Victoria, BC: BC campus.

Arneil, Barbara. 1992. "John Locke, Natural Law and Colonialism." *History of Political Thought* 13 (4): 587–603.

———. 1996. "The Wild Indian's Venison: Locke's Theory of Property and English Colonialism in America." *Political Studies* 44 (1): 60–74.

Atleo, Umeek, E. Richard. 2004. *Tsawalk: A Nuu-chah-nulth Worldview.* Vancouver, BC: University of British Columbia Press.

Austin, Kenneth Frank. 1999. *The Changing Vista of the Northern Northwest Coast Indian Deer Ritual.* PhD diss., University of Alaska Fairbanks.

Boettke, Peter J. 2001. "Why Culture Matters: Economics, Politics, and the Imprint of History." In *Calculation and Coordination: Essays on Socialism and Transitional Political Economy*, 248–65. New York: Routledge.

———. 2004. "Morality as Cooperation." In *Morality of Markets*, edited by Parth J. Shah, 43–50. New Delhi: Academic Foundation.

Boettke, Peter J., and David L. Prychitko. 2004. "Is an Independent Nonprofit Sector Prone to Failure? Toward an Austrian School Interpretation of Nonprofit and Voluntary Action." In *Conversations on Philanthropy Volume I: Conceptual Foundations*, edited by Lenore T. Ealy, 1–40. Alexandria, VA: DonorsTrust.

Bunten, Alexis C. 2015. *So, How Long Have You Been Native?: Life as an Alaska Native Tour Guide.* Lincoln: University of Nebraska Press.

Bunten, Alexis C., and Nelson Graburn. 2018. *Indigenous Tourism Movements.* Toronto: University of Toronto Press.

Campbell, Robert. 2007. *In Darkest Alaska: Travel and Empire along the Inside Passage.* Philadelphia: University of Pennsylvania Press.

Cattelino, Jessica R. 2018. "From Locke to Slots: Money and the Politics of Indigeneity." *Comparative Studies in Society and History* 60 (2): 274–307.

Chamlee-Wright, Emily. 1997. The *Cultural Foundations of Economic Development: Urban Female Entrepreneurship in Ghana.* New York: Routledge.

Collis, Septima M. 1890. *A Woman's Trip to Alaska: Being an Account of a Voyage through the Inland Seas of the Sitkan Archipelago in 1890.* New York: Cassell Publishing Company.

Deur, Douglas, and Nancy Turner. 2005. *Keeping It Living.* Seattle, WA: University of Washington Press.

Garfield, Viola E. 1947. "Historical Aspects of Tlingit Clans in Angoon, Alaska." *American Anthropologist* 49 (3): 438–52.

Gegeo, David Welchman, and Karen Ann Watson-Gegeo. 2001. "'How We Know': Kwara'ae Rural Villagers Doing Indigenous Epistemology." *The Contemporary Pacific* 13 (1): 55–88.

Grube, Laura E. and Virgil Henry Storr, eds. 2015. *Culture and Economic Action.* Cheltenham, UK: Edward Elgar Publishing.

Gudeman, Stephen. 2016. *Anthropology and Economy.* Cambridge, UK: Cambridge University Press.

Halpin, Marjorie M., and Margaret Seguin. 1990. "Tsimshian Peoples: Southern Tsimshian, Coast Tsimshian, Nishga, and Gitksan." In *Handbook of North American Indians, Volume 7: Northwest Coast*, edited by Wayne Suttles and William Sturtevant, 267–97. Washington, DC: Smithsonian Institution Scholarly Press.

Hosmer, Brian C. 1999. *American Indians in the Marketplace: Persistence and Innovation among the Menominees and Metlakatlans, 1870–1920.* Lawrence, KS: University of Kansas Press.

Hunt, Sarah. 2014. "Ontologies of Indigeneity: The Politics of Embodying a Concept." *Cultural Geographies* 2 (1): 27–32.

Johnsen, D. Bruce. 2004. "A Culturally Correct Proposal to Privatize the British Columbia Salmon Fishery." Working Paper, George Mason University Antonin Scalia Law School.

———. 2009. "Salmon, Science, and Reciprocity on the Northwest Coast." *Ecology and Society* 14 (2): 43.

Kames, Henry Home, Lord. [1813] 1967. "Sketches of the History of Man." In *The Scottish Moralists: On Human Nature and Society*, edited by Louis Scheneider, 255–70. Chicago: University of Chicago Press.

Kirzner, Israel M. 2016. *The Collected Works of Israel M. Kirzner: Discovery, Capitalism, and Distributive Justice.* Edited by Peter J. Boettke and Frédéric Sautet. Indianapolis: Liberty Fund.

Lavoie, Don. 2015. "The Discovery and Interpretation of Profit Opportunities: Culture and the Kirznerian Entrepreneur." In *Culture and Economic Action,* edited by Laura E. Grube and Virgil Henry Storr, 48–67. Cheltenham, UK: Edward Elgar Publishing.

Lavoie, Don, and Emily Chamlee-Wright. 2000. *Culture and Enterprise: The Development, Representation and Morality of Business.* New York: Routledge.

Locke, John. [1690] 1988. *Two Treatises of Government.* Student ed. Edited by Peter Laslett. Cambridge, UK: Cambridge University Press.

Lukens, Matilda B. 1889. *The Inland Passage: A Journal of a Trip to Alaska.* San Francisco: s.n.

Mitchell, Matthew D., and Peter J. Boettke. 2017. *Applied Mainline Economics: Bridging the Gap between Theory and Public Policy.* Arlington, VA: Mercatus Center at George Mason University.

Northern Plains Reservation Aid. "History and Culture." *Partnership with Native Americans.* Accessed March 20, 2020. http://www.nativepartnership.org/site/PageServer?pagename=airc_hist_boardingschools.

Raibmon, Paige. 2005. *Authentic Indians: Episodes of Encounter from the Late-Nineteenth- Century Northwest Coast.* Durham, NC: Duke University Press.

Smetzer, Megan A. 2014. "From Bolts to Bags: Transforming Cloth in 19th Century Tlingit Alaska." *Journal of Material Culture* 19 (1): 59–73.

Storr, Virgil Henry. 2010. "The Social Construction of the Market." *Society* 47: 200–206.

———. 2015. "Economists Should Study Culture." In *Culture and Economic Action,* edited by Laura E. Grube and Virgil Henry Storr, 11–47. Cheltenham, UK: Edward Elgar Publishing.

Trosper, Ronald. 2009. *Resilience, Reciprocity and Ecological Economics: Northwest Coast Sustainability.* New York: Routledge.

Tsosie, Rebecca. 2017. "Indigenous Peoples, Anthropology and the Legacy of Epistemic Injustice." In *The Routledge Handbook of Epistemic Injustice,* edited by Ian James Kidd, José Medina, and Gaile Pohlhaus, Jr., 356–69. New York: Routledge.

U.S. Department of the Interior. 2016. *History of Alaska Homesteading: The Last Chapter in America's Homestead Experience.* Anchorage, AK: Bureau of Land Management.

Wolf, Eric R. 1982. *Europe and the People Without History.* Berkeley, CA: University of California Press.

*Chapter 6*

# Internet, Culture, and the New Feminist Phase

## *De-Westernizing Hashtags for Global Social Movements*

### Ololade Afolabi

When Arjun Appadurai (1990) wrote about global cultural flows, he mentioned the need not to get excessively confident and comfortable with the terms "cultural imperialism" or "global homogeneity" perpetrated through the flow of media from Western nations. Instead, he argued that culture assumes indigenized forms when transposed into new societies. More importantly, he noted that to explain the flow, there is a need to theorize the disjuncture between culture, economy, and politics. Only after this explanation is achieved can we see that the global cultural process has moved beyond Americanization or Euro-colonial ideology. Instead, we have entered a world where people construct identities from the way that different global images are represented and filtered through different landscapes that shape people's perspectives across the world. These landscapes, thus, create a nuanced and dialectical way of understanding global cultural flows.

In global feminist studies, there is a tension concerning division that fissures around Western hegemony, colonialism, and race. That is how Western feminist practices enmesh all women into a notion of universalism that sees the oppression of all women as similar, if not the same. This tension underscores the seeming simplicity that Western feminists associate with the struggles of all women across the world without paying attention to a specific society's cultural, social, economic, and political landscapes. For example, how do you capture the lives of women in Northern Nigeria, whose identities are divided between Northern Christian/Northern Muslim, veiled/unveiled, educated/non-educated, and adult-marriage/child-marriage, to mention a few, in just the simple word "women"? The biggest concern of transnational feminists is that the term "women" has created an idealism of global sisterhood that tries to mash every woman into the fight for freedom. That the term has become politicized to mean Western/white and the struggles of non-white women have been less represented in the Western category of woman. Freedom in this Western model is described as freedom of choosing sexuality, freedom of economic independence, and freedom from male hegemony. But what about women whose identities, in addition to all these, are still locked within the web of interconnection between nationalism, postcolonial life, race, and historical specificities? Western feminism has become inadequate in capturing the oppression of these women. Therefore, transnational feminism/Black feminism becomes the alternative intellectual site of struggle.

Therefore, this chapter proceeds with the aim of understanding feminist struggles from a transnational perspective by paying attention to the cultural, political, and historical networks that shape how these struggles succeed or fail. The chapter argues that feminist hashtags do not have an inherent ability to affect people across the world in the same way. While the internet might be a universalizing space where social boundaries are melted for marginalized and elites all together to commune, this space is not all the way determinist. In other words, digital feminists' social actors need to be sensitive to indigenous cultural constraints, the interaction between power, state, and race in how global messages are received and how they are denied agency or allowed to flourish in international markets. This cultural specificity allows the feminists to produce hashtags or other online social movements strategy that can be productive in the different communities around the world.

This chapter takes off on some guiding questions: What is the role of culture in the new phase of digital feminism? How can digital feminists' actions become more successful in the transnational arena? How do culture and other forces such as state, power, and race determine how feminists' global messages flourish or fail in communities across the world? This chapter treats the internet and hashtags as the market space of digital feminists where communicative practices on how to demolish the socio-psychological border of masculinity and misogyny are exchanged. This chapter also reacts against the construction of the internet and the hashtag movements as a universal instrument of social change that is embedded in Western ideologies. For hashtag feminism to be successful globally, it needs to operate by the principle of "cultural alertness" and become critically subjective rather than objective.

The chapter is contextualized within the framework of culture and entrepreneurship, Lavoie (2015) as well as social entrepreneurship (Storr, Haeffele-Balch, and Grube 2018). Lavoie and Chamlee-Wright (2015) argue that the entrepreneurial process is not independent of the cultural process of the society where such economic actions takes place. Put more clearly, culture is the spine of a successful economic action. It has "everything" to do with how an entrepreneur acts in a society and how he reads and maximizes profit. Lavoie and Chamlee-Wright highlight two elements that are fundamental to a theory of culture and entrepreneurship, which are "the notion of discovery and interpretation" (2015, 50). Discovery denotes the spontaneous identification of new opportunities that have not been previously discovered by other entrepreneurs. This discovery is a result of innovative exploration of the entrepreneur to discover new opportunities and create a kind of market that previous entrepreneurs have not been able to find. It is through this innovative market adventure that the entrepreneur discovers new opportunities. Interpretation, on the other hand, suggests that profit maximization is not an objective phenomenon that can be represented in a natural scientific form. Rather, it is culturally perspectival; that is, it involves an interaction of the entrepreneur with the culture of the society where he is operating. In other words, a profit in Society $X$ might not mean a profit in Society $Y$. Profit opportunity is, therefore, a thing of social discourse that is influenced by the way each society constructs success and failure and how such terms are socially interpreted.

This cultural sensitiveness to the entrepreneurial process makes the concept of "market as a social space" important where the noneconomic activities have become mechanisms that allow the entrepreneurs to understand the social settings in different markets (Storr 2008). Storr argues that the market is not merely a space of economic activities where only price discussions occur, as according to the neoclassical economists, but it is also a social space that allows extra-economic activities to take place (Storr 2008). Thus, it is not just about the economic conversations that go on in the market space, but it is also about how social bonds are formed through social interactions and other types of conversations that inform our broader understanding of the market as a bigger social structure. These kinds of activities are underlying social factors that inadvertently influences the market space and make markets differ across cultures. Grube and Storr (2015) accentuates this point that culture is a strong predictor of the success of the entrepreneur. Culture does not just help to understand economic action, but it helps to "predict economic behavior" (Grube and Storr 2015, 26). The concepts of understanding and prediction shift the comprehension of an economic action from just knowing the result to a more involved process of answering the "how" question in which an economic action takes place. Culture is therefore a process to an end.

The theory of social entrepreneurship developed by Storr, Haeffele-Balch, and Grube (2018) complements these arguments on culture and extra-economic activities and provides a more useful theoretical base to conceptualize the works of digital feminists as activities that have a "social change agenda." Storr, Haeffele-Balch, and Grube describe social entrepreneurs as individuals whose "chief aim is social transformation, not monetary profits or political power" (Storr, Haeffele-Balch, and Grube 2018, 21). The social entrepreneur focuses on bringing changes to his community through actions such as advocacy, protests, campaign, lobbying, and many others. However, their argument extends the concept of social entrepreneurship beyond the dichotomization of market/nonmarket or social/commercial entrepreneurs. Social entrepreneurs do not necessarily have to operate independent of other types of entrepreneurs. Rather, the coalition between the commercial, ideological, and social entrepreneur can allow for maximization of the full social identity of the entrepreneur. For instance, a small not-for-profit organization campaigning for women's education in a rural community is not only changing the social status of rural women from being uneducated, but the organization is simultaneously championing an institutional reform, or ideological shift, in the community whereby women's education becomes prioritized and deemed relevant. At the same time, the organization is improving the worth of women in the society whereby their education can benefit the market sector of the society, especially in societies where acquiring more education leads to upward social mobility.

Therefore, the understanding of how market and nonmarket forces cooperate to determine the success of the entrepreneur is the overarching argument that the scholars above emphasize. The need to contextualize an entrepreneur's work within specific socio-cultural perspective is even more important. Thus, the success of digital feminists lies in their ability to understand the different social spaces in which their activism takes place. It is in the process of this understanding that discovery happens, and innovation is birthed, ultimately leading to success. Thus, considering the above, this chapter seeks to understand the work of digital feminists as social entrepreneurs whose actions are focused on bringing about social change in their respective communities. It extends the argument of Storr, Haeffele-Balch, and Grube (2018) on the overlapping identity of the social entrepreneur as they concurrently change social orders, ideologies, and markets while also alerting to the distinctiveness of each society's culture to carry out these actions. Hence, this chapter challenges the utopianism attributed to the online space and instead emphasizes that digital activism functions disparately across borders. As social entrepreneurs who are attuned to new opportunities, digital feminists will need to understand this disparity and customize their activism in a way that speaks to these differences to produce maximum social change.

To concretize this argument, I examine the #MeToo movement that started in the United States and discuss how the movement is being implemented elsewhere by acknowledging the cultural specificities of the society and tapping into opportunities that have not been explored. I also discuss how a social movement crosses the border of only being social by allowing for interactions between the people, social institutions, and other structures of the society to produce pragmatic social change.

## DIGITAL FEMINISTS AS SOCIAL ENTREPRENEURS

It is clear that we have entered a new phase in global communications. This phase, according to Marshall McLuhan, has made the world a "global village" where electronic communications have formed a massive interconnectedness of the world (McLuhan 1964). This phase is characterized by the rise in new global social actors in almost all aspects of human life. This is because the internet has created new affordances where people demolish the boundaries of nation-states that deny them access into a common public sphere and allows conversations outside of the normal, and somewhat inaccessible, space created by governments (Castells 2008). While this new development is not totally liberating for all people, as there are still societies that are outside of the mainstream democratic population, the internet raises some hope for the forgotten and marginalized. It provides access to people who do not hold the political and economic power to discuss within mainstream media.

Noam (2010), for example, explains how the internet and globalization can be transformative agents of world economy, specifically the economy of developing countries. He explains the need to see beyond the digital divide caused by the internet and focus instead on the economic transformation that comes with it. This economic opportunity means that ordinary citizens can become producers rather than always being the consumers. That is, they can participate in the income-generating process for their societies, become better managers of their labors, and generally contribute to the social and economic development process of their communities. Among the new social actors who have mounted the digital stage for social development are the digital feminists.

Digital feminists are defined as feminists who use the online space to create feminist messages in the fight against women's oppression in their societies. This includes online social communities such as Facebook, Twitter, chat rooms, blogs, and websites. This form of feminism is the use of digital technology to promote feminist activism. At the center of feminists' activities are social developments. That is, the overall betterment of the social experiences of women in every aspect of a society including health, family, work, and so forth. The digital space has allowed feminist activities to flourish by providing a universal platform where women of similar beliefs can commune to increase their social well-being. Baer (2016) mentions that "digital platforms" are transformative spaces that allow feminists to produce new discourses about feminism, connect these discourses to "different constituencies," and allow social change protests to be more "creative." This highlights the dynamism of feminism online; it should not be unidirectional. Rather, it should adapt to the cultures of the targeted audiences and create content that can be subjectively read as successful in forging social change within such disparate societies. The term "subjective" here denotes that it should appeal to the specific cultural schemata of the target audiences, and such audiences should be able to recognize whether a feminist process is resulting in a positive social change within their societies. Jouët (2018) also argues that the digital space has led to a new form of leadership for women mediated through the affordances of online platforms. This allows the women to produce "unconventional repertoires" whereby they challenge hegemonic beliefs. But it has also equally led to an increase in "cyber-sexism," thereby questioning the effectiveness of the platform. Likewise, Lopez, Muldoon, and McKeown explain that #feminism is used in different ways online. This can include providing pro-feminists the platform to defend the "ideas and ideals of feminism" but also giving anti-feminists a stage to proliferate their beliefs (Lopez, Muldoon, and McKeown 2019, 213).

As social entrepreneurs, feminists' core message is bridging the inequality gap between men and women in different domains of their societies by campaigning against social structures and systems that perpetuate this inequality. However, digital feminists extend this work beyond the physical space and, in addition, employ online resources such as technology, virality, and the fluidity of the techno-space to chisel out the discourse in a way that complements the activism in physical gatherings. They also tap into the relatively democratic online space as an opportunity to confront hegemonic attitudes that are usually impossible in offline settings. In what Jennifer Motter describes as the "feminist virtual world," online spaces for feminists "offer transitional spaces for challenging dominant culture . . . by providing options for anonymity and identity projections" (Motter 2011, 109).

It is also a space where "tactical interventions" are employed to create messages that are apt and address the multiple areas of protest. What this means for the digital feminist is that the discovery of anonymity embraced by women online is one of the factors that allow feminist practices to flourish online. This anonymity is usually impossible in offline settings. This might discourage many women from participating in social movement activities that they think may threaten their safety in their communities. Therefore, discovering this safety (relatively used) that comes with online gatherings creates an enterprising opportunity for digital feminists to explore options that have been previously impossible. Being tactical also means being strategic to create content that can push feminist discourse forward toward women's social development.

However, anonymity is not a universal element in digital feminist practices. While some women want to be "hidden" and talk, others really want a space where they can be "live," but safely. In fact, scholars have noted that online activism for women might even be a place where the women become more divided by finding the feminist group to which they belong. It may also be more profitable, because it allows these different categories of women to explore choices that might not be presented offline. For example, Herring et al. (2002) discuss two categories of digital feminist groups that capture the reactions of women online. First, there is the libertarian group, where the women feel extremely free to air their opinion to the public. In this group, individual freedom is of paramount importance and the women want to be completely responsible for their comments, actions, and participation. The second category is the communitarian group, where the women feel more secure when speaking as a group instead of speaking individually. This second category is usually more encouraging for "less empowered women [who] may require a community where they feel safe creating their own identities" (Dixon 2014, 39).

While both categories have a social change agenda in mind, their practices require customized approaches that allow the members to navigate any social threat in a more effective way. Therefore, as social entrepreneurs, digital feminists must create a space that is most appropriate and helpful in the society in which their activism is being targeted. This emphasizes the notion of cultural alertness mentioned above. For example, a Muslim woman fighting sexual abuse may find it more secure to engage in communal online practice like online community than starting a hashtag on her own. While the former shields her within a body of other similar women, the latter exposes her identity and may open her to threats from institutions that oppose her views. By understanding the disparity between these two groups of women, digital feminists can be culturally sensitive to the specificity of each society to which the women belong and customize their approach in a way that would be locally profitable to the women.

Aside from understanding the social structure and opportunities that are available in driving social change, the digital feminist must also be aware of the discouraging factors that are fighting against this change in the community being targeted. These include government policies, social institutions, and religious organizations that detest feminist activities so that they are unable to yield any concrete results. In discussing how social media activism can help publicize feminist activities against violence in South Africa, Kangere, Kemitare, and Michau emphasize the need to "re-center women and feminist analysis" within projects that work to oppose violence against women (2017, 1). Kangere, Kemitare, and Michau (2017) mentioned that although protesting women subjugation is gaining momentum in Africa, activists are still hindered by factors such as poor funding, absence of "civil society space," and "predominance" of transnational not-for-profit organizations in the movement. Therefore, by creating their own original hashtags, African feminists can spread their activities more broadly to diverse audiences through cheap social media campaigns. They can also "build solidarity" with one another because "social change movements grow from communities of like-minded individuals and groups" (Kangere, Kemitare, and Michau 2017, 2). It can also promote "new ideas" and "current thinking" that have not been previously accessed.

Clearly, the feminist as an entrepreneur occupies a central role in shaping feminist discourse in a way that produces maximum social change that can be socially interpreted and meaningful in the society where the activism takes place. The examples discussed above further contextualize Lavoie and Chamlee-Wright (2015) and Storr, Haeffele-Balch, and Grube (2018) on how the entrepreneurial process should burrow into specific social conditions and "discover" opportunities that have been previously nonexistent. They also show that the digital feminist may have more opportunity than the traditional offline feminist because the former has access to a space that is more accessible and easily proliferated. Feminist tweets can go viral within minutes, while the same issue can take much longer to spread when it is raised in an offline gathering. Also, as a driver of social change, the digital feminist social entrepreneur must be able to link the social aspect of activism to the ideological aspect. Kangere, Kemitare, and Michau (2017) describe this in the case of Africa as promoting "new ideas" and "current thinking."

This means that the end goal of all feminists is to bring about ideological change such that women's issues are thought of differently and in a way that brings progress and identity transformation to women. Therefore, as digital feminist activism continues to increase across the world, it is important to understand how the cyberspace brings additional resources to feminists so that their movements can become easily accessible. But it is equally important to recognize that such added opportunities should be explored in ways that allow feminist struggles to be more socially constructed and interpreted.

## LOCALIZING GLOBAL HASHTAGS FOR SOCIAL CHANGE

Hashtags may have emanated from the West, but they do not remain in the West. Because of increased access to the internet globally, hashtag activism moves within borders quickly and begins to shape discourse in those new societies. The purpose of this section is to discuss how the #MeToo movement moves across borders and theorize why hashtags need to be culturally sensitive for them to flourish and be effective for women's development. First, I examine the discourse emanating from the movement in the United States, and then, I consider the #ArewaMeToo movement which was later adopted in Nigeria.

## The Discourse of Intersectionality in the #MeToo Movement

Intersectionality is a term coined by Kimberlé Crenshaw in a paper she wrote for the University of Chicago Legal Forum (Crenshaw 1989). The term later began to appear in feminist social science research after Patricia Hill Collins broadened its use in 2000. Crenshaw (1989) attacks the marginality and insensitivity of legal procedures to take into consideration the multiple identities of Black women in court proceedings. She critiques the one-sided framework that is used to describe the experiences of Black women as problematic because it treats sex and race as mutually exclusive categories, thereby bypassing the intersectionality of the two. That is, Black women are either treated as Black or as women but not both. She examines five court proceedings of Black women who were discriminated against in their employment and discusses how the court hearings did not consider the racial identity of the women.

In one of the cases where there was an allegation against a company that more white females were promoted during the period observed and reported, the court dismissed the allegations against the company because, as far as the court was concerned, all women were just women. The women could not prove that they were discriminated against based on race because their claim did not include Black women. Similarly, they could not prove that they were discriminated against based on sex because their claim did not include white women. Crenshaw also examines how the discourse of rape often misrepresents Black women and is indicative of white hegemonic attitudes. She argues that early rape laws were not set up to protect women from forced sexual relationships. Rather, they were established to maintain the purity of women as "property-like interest" to their male owners (Crenshaw 1989, 157). She questions legal procedures that tend to correct discrimination against women because they are inherently sexist and racist. Her framework of intersectionality promotes a multifaceted analysis of the oppression of Black women by taking racism, sexism, and patriarchy as interconnected practices.

Collins's (2000) concept of intersectionality is even more encompassing because she writes from a sociological perspective. She develops a critical social theory whereby Black women can address questions of race, class, and gender that they face. Her work closes the gap between Black women in the academe and those in other "institutional locations" by creating a means for collecting on their experiences. Collins (2000) also attempts to reconceptualize existing works on Black feminism that have been marginalized or barely survived because they did not "qualify" for academic scholarship. She argues that to create a truly unifying Black feminist movement, the line between intellectual and non-intellectual Black women must be erased because Black women who do not belong to institutions but also have lived experiences of Black women oppression are also intellectuals.

One of the main discourses in the #MeToo movement is the exclusion of Black women's voices and their unique experiences from the movement. The "Me Too" phrase was first coined by Tarana Burke in 2006 to help women who have experienced sexual violence find healing (Garcia 2017). However, the phrase became ignited on social media in 2017 after Alyssa Milano made a call on social media to all women who have been sexually abused to write "Me Too" on their timeline so that people could understand the severity of the problem. This was also during a time when Hollywood film producer Harvey Weinstein was accused of abusing women in several allegations. Shortly after Milano's call, #MeToo began trending on social media as women began to pour out their personal stories, and in less than a day there were more than 12 million posts on Facebook from women around the world (Khomami 2017). Gradually, "Me Too" became a catchphrase for women globally. However, the question of race or intersectionality is what many scholars have problematized about the #MeToo movement. That is, the fact that the movement has not yet recognized the voices of non-white women even though the phrase was initially coined by an African American.

For example, Onwuachi-Willig (2018) questions the production of the #MeToo practice in the United States and argues that the movement presents "racial biases" against women of color by not articulating their "contributions and experiences." Writing from a legal perspective, Onwuachi-Willig (2018) mentions that the erasure of Black women's voices like Tarana Burke's, who coined the phrase in 2006, by the #MeToo movement is why legal procedures against sexual harassment must adopt a more critical and intersectional approach. This is because these women do not only face sexual harassment, but they also face racial injustice. For these women to experience justice, their multiple oppressions will need to be simultaneously considered. Thus, Onwuachi-Willig raises the question "What About #Us-Too?" This question demonstrates that many Black women's sexual abuse stories have been coalesced under the bigger Feminism movement without capturing their unique struggles. Similarly, Valdivia (2019) questions the marginalization of Black women in the #MeToo movement and the feminist movement generally in the United States. She examines, like Onwuachi-Willig (2018), how Burke has been denied agency in the overall movement and argues that this denial further emphasizes the marginalization of Black women in the feminist society.

According to Valdivia (2019), identity plays a major role in how the #MeToo movement has played out. Burke is a "Black woman who struggled to bring justice to women and girls of color," while Milano, who coined the hashtag, is a well-known actress who also enjoys the privilege of being white (Valdivia 2019, 162). This identity difference between the two actors privileged Milano and gave her tweet more publicity than Burke. Although, Milano has been mentioned to have given the credit back to Burke (Ohlheiser 2017). Even so, Burke still occupies a very tiny position in the overall movement and most of the praise goes to Milano. Ceron (2018) argues similarly to Valdivia (2019) and Onwuachi-Willig (2018) about the exclusion of women of color from the online feminist movement. In her analysis of two feminist hashtags, #MeToo and #TimesUp on Twitter, she argues that the term "women" has been technically employed by white feminists and does not necessarily present the opinions and struggles of women of color (Ceron 2018). According to Ceron, the term "women" in its organic sense does not well articulate the different positionalities that all women occupy in terms of sexual abuse or gender wage gap. Thus, the term has been politicized to strategically exclude other women whose identities do not represent normative white women.

Battaglia, Edley, and Newsom (2019) extend this argument by contending that the exclusion of the voices of minority women or women of color from the #MeToo movement is a form of violence against such women. Their essay advocates for the use of inclusive language that reflects intersectionality in the #MeToo movement and that the coverage and analysis of the movement should not be completely determined by mainstream media. This is because mainstream media tend to background the salient actors, as has been the case of Burke, and the focus is usually on telling the story of rape and other sexual abuse that white women experience instead of focusing on the healing that was the original motive of the movement. Thus, the challenge to feminists, and particularly white feminists, is to produce works that employ "multi-linguistic narratives; . . . feminist (auto)ethnographies; and community-based participant action research to keep mainstream media from systemically redefining a movement founded and led by a black woman and created specifically for black girls' healing" (Battaglia, Edley, and Newsom 2019, 164). Battaglia, Edley, and Newsom also mention that academic scholars have a huge role in rewriting the history of the movement by producing research that would put the experiences of the marginalized at the center.

The ongoing discourse of intersectionality in the #MeToo movement shows that the movement might have gained popularity, but it is still far behind its promise of capturing all women's oppression. The studies examined above are testimonies of the many ways in which Black women's agency has been threatened and why Black feminists continue to explore alternative sites to contest their social identities. As a response to this marginalization, Tynes, Schuschke, and Noble (2016) mention that there is a need to examine digital activism from an intersectional perspective, which allows for a multiplicative analysis. They argue that Black online movements have long excluded the presence of female social actors both as front-liners in the movement and as victims for which the movement is made. Specifically, they discuss how the #BlackLivesMatter movement displays "an almost complete erasure of Black women" (Tynes, Schuschke, and Noble 2016, 22). According to Tynes, Schuschke, and Noble, the term "women" is vaguely expressed by white feminists and does not reflect the different ways that race and other identity markers influence the lives of women. Thus, cyberfeminism should not be reduced to the audiences of white, wealthy, and educated women. Instead, it should challenge academic scholars to push the scholarship of digital intersectionality toward discussing how Black women can seize the new space of online activism as a form of counterpower to the hegemonic control of Black men and white women dominance in online movements and mainstream media.

Although existing literature on the #MeToo movement has largely examined the way Black women have been ignored in the protest, race is only one of the many indices that shape how the protest affects women of color. What about other women who, in addition to gender and race, have other identities that need to be challenged? This is where the concept of intersectionality becomes even more useful. For women in non-Western countries, localizing the hashtag involves understanding the social and political landscapes of their countries and producing protest that is realistic in such environments. Therefore, to underscore the importance of this point, I will now discuss a new breed of the #MeToo protest that has been adopted in Northern Nigeria and discuss how the feminist entrepreneurs in the region work with local forces to produce social change.

## #ArewaMeToo Movement in Nigeria

In Northern Nigeria, the #ArewaMeToo movement began in February 2019 after a young pharmacist tweeted about her horrifying sexual abuse experience committed by her boyfriend whom she claimed almost killed her. After Khadija Adamu posted her tweet, another lady, Fakhrriyah Hashim, coined the #ArewaMeToo to contextualize the global #MeToo movement into Northern Nigerian society. Arewa is the Hausa word for "northern," and so the new coinage translates to "Northern Me Too" (Unah 2019). #ArewaMeToo has appeared almost ten thousand times on Twitter since it was first coined, and the protest continues to grow more in offline gatherings. Northern

Nigeria is a place predominantly occupied by Muslims. Therefore, in starting a social movement against sexual abuse, the women did not only have to fight abuse, they also had to tear the border of religion that many of the women dare not cross because of the conservativeness of the Islamic practices. Thus, when Adamu and Hashim started what would later become Northern Me Too, they were risking their safety for other fellow Muslim women to speak out against injustice.

In an article Hashim wrote for Quartz Africa, she recounts the story of how #ArewaMeToo began and how the culture of rape and silence has been systematically engrained into the Northern Nigerian social system (Hashim 2019). According to her "Northern Nigeria . . . is an ultraconservative region. . . . Islam, the dominant religion . . . is interwoven into the cultures of a diverse populace. This cultural and religious syncretism has resulted in an interpretation of Islamic thought that makes it difficult for victims of sexual violence to come forward for fear of ostracism." (Hashim 2019). The peculiarity of the social structure of the Northern Nigerian region makes the invention of "Arewa" necessary. However, including "Arewa" in the protest is not enough to contextualize it within the social realities of the Northern Nigerian women.

In an interview Hauwa Shaffi and I conducted with three of the pioneer members of the #ArewaMeToo, we understood that the fight against women subjugation in Northern Nigeria is not just a fight against domestic violence. It is a fight against religious molestation, poor education among the women, and a weakened social structure that makes activism more difficult but more necessary. Many of the women share identities that are networked between rural/urban life, educated/uneducated, religious/non-religious, and more. These complex identity networks make #ArewaMeToo more than just a fight against domestic violence. The movement is much more a fight against inequality in almost all areas of the women's social life. For example, the United Nations Children's Fund (UNICEF) reports that one girl to two boys or one girl to three boys go to school in the northern part of Nigeria (UNICEF 2018). This is not only due to poverty and illiteracy levels among parents, but it is also because of sociocultural and religious factors like early girl child marriage, where girl children are married off as early as thirteen years of age and where Islamic belief treats women as a domestic part of the home and society.

Therefore, when we asked the pioneer members if they thought that women's social problems in Northern Nigeria were the same as those in the West, the consensus was no. The women believe that there are peculiarities and areas of overlap. Culture and tradition in Northern Nigeria are more rigid and regulated than in the West because of the strong Islamic presence. One of our interviewees mentioned that she "believes every region's struggle is defined by the implication of its culture and tradition and most importantly, the level of development. What the average Northern Nigerian woman is fighting against is quite distinct from the Western woman, but one common thread is all these women are fighting for human dignity." Others mentioned that the level of underdevelopment and poor policy application makes the struggle of Northern Nigerian women more complex to address.

Therefore, a lot must be done outside of the social media space. The women have split the movement into regions to make offline changes more realistic. Some of the strategies they have adopted include organizing rallies and workshops in schools and communities on gender-based violence and working with local officials on how to enforce the Violence Against Persons Prohibition (VAPP) Act (Nuhu 2020). The effort being put into domesticating the movement also shows the corruption that is entrenched in the Nigerian public offices. For example, when Nuhu went to the police station last year to get a permit to organize a rally for the movement, the chief police officer she met tried to downplay the intensity of the movement. He asked her and her team to "adopt a milder approach" because he believed the issue was not as demanding as the women were taking it. Also, many of the rally organizers have been beaten by police, like in the case of Sadiya Taheer, who was the head of a state branch of the movement. Idris Abbas was arrested and made to forcefully delete a recording of the "assault" on his phone (Nuhu 2020).

These multiple layers of oppression faced by Northern Nigerian women make social change a process that cannot be done only online. For the #ArewaMeToo pioneers and branch leaders, tackling the problem of sexual abuse involves a complex and systematic process that would recognize the way Northern Nigeria functions between religion and culture. This is not something that Western women usually have to deal with. In the literature on #MeToo in the United States, most of the concern raised is about the exclusion of Black women's voices. For the Northern Nigerian women, it is more about contesting social change from multiple areas of the society including injustice in public offices and combatting illiteracy among women.

So then, as social entrepreneurs, Northern Nigerian women cannot just adopt the #MeToo movement without adapting it. The specificity of the Nigerian social landscape, and especially the ultra-conservativeness of the northern region of the country, makes online activism more of an offline project that requires many parts for it to prosper. It also shows that feminism as a body cannot produce the necessary changes that are needed in communities worldwide if it does not decentralize itself such that it recognizes that there are many parts to the struggles of women in distinct places. While the #ArewaMeToo movement has not yet peaked, the pioneers are continuously finding ways to penetrate both the political and social spheres of such a closed society. The movement has birthed similar movements such as #northnormal, which focuses on policy change for women's empowerment at the grassroots level. By adopting a strong offline strategy to reach the interiors of the society and perhaps people who do not have access to online spaces, the movement continues to exemplify the notion of discovery and interpretation found in Lavoie and Chamlee-Wright (2015). That is, in a region with high levels of poverty and illiteracy, the need to go beyond online activism is very important, and in order to have maximum success, the organizers need to discover ways in which the movement can be heard beyond the online medium.

Returning to the question posed earlier about how digital feminists can be successful in transnational arena, the main points would be to decentralize and localize. I will return to this issue of decentralization shortly. But it is important to say that digital feminism cannot be successful without paying attention to indigenous cultures in disparate communities and adapting global activism to such communities. Culture and society are interwoven; therefore, it is nearly impossible to have an effective movement that does not allude to these local ways of life. Digital feminists should also pay attention to how state, power, and race function in transnational communities. In many of the Third World nations, racial prejudice is not as big of an issue as it is in the United States. This is mainly because many of these nations are more or less racially homogenous but extremely ethnically diverse. Therefore, feminist movements in these societies largely address ethnic problems rather than racial problems.

For example, in the #ArewaMeToo movement, the goal is to speak to the peculiarity of women in the northern part of Nigeria. Although race is rarely talked about in Nigerian politics, the wide cultural gap among the three main ethnic groups—Igbo, Yoruba, and Hausa (which is the north)—is a major issue in every sector of the society. Thus, digital activism between women in the southern and northern parts of the country will emphasize different issues that are central to both regions. The role of the state is also very important in determining whether digital feminist activism flourishes or fails in these communities. For example, in societies where women do not enjoy the right to speak in public or have access to online communication, how do these women become a part of these global online social movements? In the #ArewaMe-Too movement, the women are risking their lives to fight a social structure that has been largely sponsored by the state. Most of the northern part of Nigeria is dominated by Islam, which is also the religion largely endorsed by the government. Therefore, the movement is simultaneously addressing state and social structures that have helped perpetuate abuse of women. The main point here is to emphasize that digital feminism is a powerful platform to set a tone of urgency and importance for women struggles globally, but for such activism to be successful, it will need to adapt to practical ways within each local community.

## DECENTRALIZATION

As I begin to bring this chapter to a close, I would like to return to the issue of decentralization mentioned above and how this can help digital feminism to be more successful transnationally by discussing the #ArewaMeToo. I focus on how a polycentric system can help digital feminists understand that as social entrepreneurs, they are working toward the public good of reconstructing women's identities on a global platform. Although I do not intend to delve deep into the Ostroms, understanding the rudiments of public entrepreneurial spirit might provide a unique perspective for digital feminist workers on how to dehegemonize hashtag feminism as a Western concept and instead adopt a more decentralized approach for the utmost success.

According to Ostrom (1965), a successful public entrepreneurial process will operate in two dimensions. First, it will need to adopt a collectivist model whereby what constitutes a public good is defined by many people rather than one person or institution. Second, public entrepreneurship should not be too closed up to repel any form of changes. Instead, individuals should be able to freely think, choose, and act in embarking on any new task. These two dimensions underscore what Smith (2008) describes as "ecological rationality," or the logic of the environment. This refers to the flexibility of any social process or public enterprise to recognize the imbuing way in which non-market forces such as culture, people, social institutions, and environment shape the actions of people. Ostrom's emphasis on institutional approach to market/nonmarket entrepreneurship also contends that the rules of certain institutions can either facilitate a public good or deter it. In other words, institutions have the responsibility of creating formal codes for the working of any public enterprise. However, the kind of opportunities and incentives that are made available, both socially and economically, can determine how people are able to collectively carry out an initiative. In this view, if the rules offer opportunities to collaborate at both the individual and communal levels, such initiatives have a higher tendency to attract more people and would likely yield greater success.

From this standpoint, we can articulate a few lessons that digital feminist can adopt in facilitating better protests globally. The first lesson is that feminism requires collaboration, flexibility, and individual freedom. Although it could be argued that many feminist protests have always adopted the "many voices" stance, we see from the literature on the #MeToo movement that intersectionality is a missing link that would have nested different types of women together in telling their sexual abuse stories and ultimately healing together. The grievances of Black women and women of color generally about their exclusion from the movement, which is even accentuated in how Burke's voice became marginalized in her own initiative, is already a threat to the success of the movement within the United States and transnationally.

Taking Ostrom's approach to feminist practices means seeing feminism as an institution with many parts. These many parts range from the individual, to the group, to the various societies, and perhaps back to the individual woman who, at the end of the struggle, wants to be completely free of her burden of abuse. Looking at the #MeToo protest again, the goal of the women is to heal together, but their ultimate goal is to be individually healed. This means that if there is no collaboration between the personal, which is the woman at her individual and intersectional level of multiple identities, and the public, which is the women at their group level of being feminists, the goal of healing would end up being unfulfilled or at least experienced by just a certain group of people. Therefore, as Paul Dragos Aligica stated, "some goods can only be supplied if many people align their contribution" (Aligica 2019, 22). Likewise, the goal of helping all women speak out and heal will never be actualized if a transnational attitude that recognizes the different experiences and peculiarities of several women's realities is not embraced.

The second point in de-Westernizing digital feminism through the Ostromian lens is adopting the polycentric approach initiated by Vincent Ostrom. Ostrom, Tiebout, and Warren (1961) lay out the components for a polycentric system, which include having many separate parts that are not dependent on one another. While not dependent on one another, they should still consider one another in the way they carry out their operations. This means that they can freely compete and conflict with one another and resolve the conflict in a decentralized way (Ostrom and Ostrom 2014). In articulating Ostrom's view, Aligica posits that the kind of competition and freedom of "entry and exit" that exists in a polycentric system can induce a "better calibration and public services to the demand" (2019, 25). This allows suppliers to become more responsive and efficient in providing the best conditions for workers to produce the best attitude for public good.

In addition to the institutional structure that the Ostroms emphasize in public entrepreneurship, the adoption of a polycentric system also makes the institutions more effective and produce their best output. Recognizing several independent parts of the institution leads to increased competition with the opportunity for workers to enter and exit any part of the institution freely. Thus, the several independent units would be more proactive in giving

their best ability to the system. This ultimately produces better public entrepreneurial spirit and strengthens the production of public good. For the
digital feminists, the point here is clear. Although Feminism as a body operates transnationally to accommodate [all] women oppression, it still needs
to be polycentric to generate the best result. Even though feminists separate
themselves into groups such as white, Black, transnational, Third World, and
so on, they do not seem to operate as overlapping institutions that have a
central agenda. Instead, they tend to question the capability of one another in
representing those who are outside their groups and how one group is more
useful in pursuing social change.

While competition is necessary according to the Ostroms, it must be done
within the overall social structure and not outside of it. This means that
competition is no longer useful if the aim is to silence one group instead
of encouraging a more challenging and productive environment. Therefore,
feminist struggle as a body must operate a transnational, multiplicity stance
that is independent but operates as a whole structure to foster equal chance for
all women. In the #MeToo movement, it was obvious that what was happening was a division in the movement and not a competition or even a necessary
conflict that happens in the process of competing. It is largely argued that the
protests have taken a complete U-turn and made white women's struggles the
dominant focus while completely ignoring other women. When other Black
feminists began to react against white women's dominance, the intention was
largely to voice Black women's struggles and "defeat" white women.

The #ArewaMeToo movement may have been closer to the Ostroms'
perspectives. The adaptation of the global #MeToo movement to the local
situation of the Northern Nigerian women shows how a polycentric system
of activism can lead to success in different communities. For example, the
#ArewaMeToo movement recognized the global #MeToo movement from
the United States as an umbrella under which it functions. However, rather
than taking a universalizing approach where it could function under just one
or two names like Burke and Milano, it has several leaders who interpret the
movement in their local communities. Adamu and Hashim may have been
the two women initially associated with the movement, but the movement
has since progressed to include more people who act as facilitators across the
region. For the #ArewaMeToo movement, it feels that the best way to appeal
and be successful to the local audience is not to say it is an extension of the
#MeToo movement in United States but to say that it has taken cues from
sisters abroad to see how it can reproduce similar movements in the Northern
Nigerian community. However, the #ArewaMeToo movement is still growing, and therefore, we cannot completely say it has fulfilled all the Ostromian
paradigms for a successful movement. Nevertheless, what is obvious is that
the way the movement has been structured from its inception, with individual

voices, local chapters, and rural rallies, shows that it gives agency to a multiplicity of ideas and innovations that can make the many types of Northern Nigerian women (elite, illiterate, urban, rural, poor, and rich) find expression within the institutional body of the #ArewaMeToo movement.

This ability of the movement to localize without losing the center gave it the necessary component to survive the harsh conservativeness of the Muslim north. Also, the Nigerian movement might not have been successful if the #MeToo phrase was missing from their own coinage. Therefore, to practice "feminism without borders"—to borrow the phrase of the great scholar and feminist, Mohanty (2003)—feminists would have to operate as an institution bound by a common goal of achieving public good (which should be culturally determined). The specific units' goals should align with the overall interest of all women, irrespective of their gender, class, or color, but these goals should still allow for flexibility. This is where feminism can truly cross borders and bring the utmost social change.

## CONCLUSION

It is imperative to emphasize the work of digital feminists as social entrepreneurs who are seeking social revolution. Practicing feminism within this framework creates the public spirit atmosphere whereby the intention is not to speak for one person or group but for all women. As social entrepreneurs, digital feminists are more attuned to specific cultures because they understand that feminist processes can only be successful if they are read as such in different communities. Interpretation must be at the center of every feminist movement and a successful protest can only be determined by how the protests influences social change among people of different cultures. Thus, culture is a major coefficient of success in the social process of feminist online movements. Although the internet provides a universal space for all women to converge, it does not provide a uniform experience for all women. If feminist hashtag movements continue to treat the online space as a determinist platform, they risk the alienation of many women (especially women of color) and make the feminist experience unrealistic to contest new identities that can bring about social change.

## ACKNOWLEDGMENTS

I want to thank Hauwa Shaffi Nuhu for her support in reaching out to pioneers of the #ArewaMeToo movement and being very helpful throughout the interview process.

# REFERENCES

Aligica, Paul Dragos. 2019. *Public Entrepreneurship, Citizenship and Self-Governance*. Cambridge, UK: Cambridge University Press.

Appadurai, Arjun. 1990. "Disjuncture and Difference in the Global Cultural Economy." *Theory, Culture & Society* 7: 295–310.

Baer, Hester. 2016. "Redoing Feminism: Digital Activism, Body Politics, and Neoliberalism." *Feminist Media Studies* 16 (1): 17–34.

Battaglia, Judy E., Paige P. Edley, and Victoria Ann Newsom. 2019. "Intersectional Feminisms and Sexual Violence in the Era of Me Too, Trump, and Kavanaugh." *Women and Language* 42 (1): 159–71.

Castells, Manuel. 2008. "The New Public Sphere: Global Civil Societies, Communication Networks, and Global Governance." *The ANNALS of the American Academy of Political and Social Science* 616 (1): 78–93.

Ceron, Daniela. 2018. "How Women of Color Are Discussed in Hashtag Feminist Movements." *Elon Journal of Undergraduate Research in Communications* 9 (2): 76–86.

Collins, Patricia Hill. 2000. *Black Feminist Thought: Knowledge, Consciousness, and the Politics of Empowerment*. New York: Routledge.

Crenshaw, Kimberlé. 1989. "Demarginalizing the Intersection of Race and Sex: A Black Feminist Critique of Antidiscrimination Doctrine, Feminist Theory and Antiracist Politics." *University of Chicago Legal Forum* 1 (8): 139–67.

Dixon, Kitsy. 2014. "Feminist Online Identity: Analyzing the Presence of Hashtag Feminism." *Journal of Arts and Humanities* 3 (7): 34–40.

Garcia, Sandra E. 2017. "The Woman Who Created #MeToo Long before Hashtags." *New York Times*, October 20. https://www.nytimes.com/2017/10/20/us/me-too-movement-tarana-burke.html.

Grube, Laura E. and Virgil Henry Storr, eds. 2015. *Culture and Economic Action*. Cheltenham, UK: Edward Elgar Publishing.

Hashim, Fakhrriyyah. 2019. "How Nigeria's Conservative Northern Region Came to Terms with Its MeToo Movement." *Quartz Africa*, July 22. https://qz.com/af rica/1671204/nigeria-metoo-movement-shook-up-north-with-arewametoo/.

Herring, Susan, Kirk Job-Sluder, Rebecca Scheckler, and Sasha Barab. 2002. "Searching for Safety Online: Managing 'Trolling' in a Feminist Forum." *The Information Society* 18 (2): 371–84.

Jouët, Josiane. 2018. "Digital Feminism: Questioning the Renewal of Feminism." *Journal of Research in Gender Studies* 8 (1): 133–57.

Kangere, Maureen, Jean Kemitare, and Lori Michau. 2017. "Hashtag Activism: Popularizing Feminist Analysis of Violence against Women in the Horn, East and Southern Africa." *Feminist Media Studies* 17 (5): 899–902.

Khomami, Nadia. 2017. "#Me Too: How a Hashtag Became a Rallying Cry against Sexual Harassment." *The Guardian*, March 29. https://www.theguardian.com/world/2017/oct/20/women-worldwide-use-hashtag-metoo-against-sexual-harass ment.

Lavoie, Don, and Emily Chamlee-Wright. 2015. *Culture and Enterprise: The Development, Representation and Morality of Business*. London: Routledge.

Lopez, Kimberly J., Meghan L. Muldoon, and Janet K. L. McKeown. 2019. "One Day Of #Feminism: Twitter as a Complex Digital Arena for Wielding, Shielding, and Trolling Talk on Feminism." *Leisure Sciences* 41 (3): 203–20.

McLuhan, Marshall. 1964. *Understanding Media: The Extensions of Man*. New York: McGraw-Hill.

Mohanty, Chandra Talpade. 2003. *Feminism without Borders: Decolonizing Theory, Practicing Solidarity*. Durham, NC: Duke University Press.

Motter, Jennifer L. 2011. "Feminist Virtual World Activism: 16 Days of Activism against Gender Violence Campaign, Guerrilla Girls BroadBand and subRosa." *Visual Culture and Gender* 6: 109–19.

Noam, Eli. 2010. "Overcoming the Three Digital Divides." In *International Communication: A Reader*, edited by Daya Kishan Thussu, 48–55. London: Routledge.

Nuhu, Hauwa Shaffii. 2020. "What Happens When We Protest: #MeToo in Northern Nigeria." *African Arguments*, March 11. https://africanarguments.org/2020/03/are-wametoo-what-happens-when-we-protest-against-sexual-violence/?fbclid=IwAR0pH35KSonrZvVtbGVe9T8AI-qDkhYeVnX0M4u2NMk3iMSgGlO4wmXYoKI.

Ohlheiser, Abby. 2017. "The Woman behind 'Me Too' Knew the Power of the Phrase When She Created It—10 Years Ago." *The Washington Post*, October 19. https://www.washingtonpost.com/news/the-intersect/wp/2017/10/19/the-woman-behind-me-too-knew-the-power-of-the-phrase-when-she-created-it-10-years-ago/.

Onwuachi-Willig, Angela. 2018. "What About #UsToo?: The Invisibility of Race in the #MeToo Movement." *The Yale Law Journal Forum* 128: 105–20.

Ostrom, Elinor. 1965. "Public Entrepreneurship: A Case Study in Ground Water Basin Management." PhD diss., University of California, Los Angeles.

Ostrom, Elinor and Vincent Ostrom. 2014. *Choice, Rules and Collective Action: The Ostroms on the Study of Institutions and Governance*. Colchester, UK: ECPR Press.

Ostrom, Vincent, Charles M. Tiebout, Robert Warren. 1961. "The Organization of Government in Metropolitan Areas: A Theoretical Inquiry." *American Political Science Review* 55 (4): 831–42.

Smith, Vernon L. 2008. *Rationality in Economics: Constructivist and Ecological Forms*. Cambridge, UK: Cambridge University Press.

Storr, Virgil Henry, Stefanie Haeffele-Balch, and Laura E. Grube. 2018. *Community Revival in the Wake of Disaster: Lessons in Local Entrepreneurship*. London: Palgrave Macmillan.

Tynes, Brendesha M., Joshua Schuschke, and Safiya Umoja Noble. 2016. "Digital Intersectionality Theory and the #BlackLivesMatter Movement." In *The Intersectional Internet: Race, Class, and Culture Online*, edited by Safiya Umoja Noble and Brendesha M. Tynes, 21–40. New York: Peter Lang.

Unah, Linus. 2019. "The #MeToo Movement Has Reached Muslim-Majority Northern Nigeria." *Al Jazeera*, March 31. https://www.aljazeera.com/indepth/features/metoo-movement-reached-muslim-majority-northern-nigeria-190330231518587.html.

UNICEF. 2018. "Education." *UNICEF Nigeria.* https://www.unicef.org/nigeria/ education.

Valdivia, Angharad N. 2019. "#IntersectionalActivism: Tales of Origin and Intersectional Negotiations." *Interactions: Studies in Communication & Culture* 10 (3): 159–68.

## Chapter 7

# Automation, Not Immigration?

## *A Case Study of Japan*

### Nicole Wu

When faced with a scarcity of workers, industrialized economies generally use one or a combination of several standard strategies to ease supply issues caused by gaps in the labor market. The conventional framework in international political economy states that governments could open up borders to foreign workers, lower trade barriers, and/or allow domestic firms to relocate production to countries with abundant labor (Peters 2015). In other words, states could respond to labor scarcity by adjusting and varying the movement of people, capital, and goods. This tradition, which aptly emphasizes critical aspects of contemporary economic globalization, fails to acknowledge the important technological changes of late. Robots and machines are now performing a wide variety of tasks that were traditionally completed by humans. In the past, technology had mostly threatened routine workers who performed repetitive tasks with well-defined rules and procedures. Today, rapid advancements in robotics and artificial intelligence mean that even nonroutine jobs (e.g., drivers, journalists) could now be at risk of automation (Frey and Osborne 2017).

Decades of economic scholarship shows that technology has led to lower levels of wages and employment (Acemoglu and Restrepo 2019), the disappearance of middle-income jobs (Goos, Manning, and Salomons 2009), rising income inequality (Michaels, Natraj, and Reenen 2014; Goos and Manning 2007), and even worse health outcomes (Patel et al. 2018). Technology overall plays a much more important role than globalization in disrupting the labor market (Tella and Rodrik 2019). However, there is little resistance to labor-replacing technology, and political opposition to globalization looms large. Many believe that technology will raise the competitiveness of their firms and facilitate human progress (Milkman 1997; Thelen 1991), but outgroups like immigrants and foreign workers are often viewed in zero-sum terms

(Blumer 1958; Krosch and Amodio 2014). Research suggests that outgroup blaming helps individuals restore a sense of personal control (Bukowski et al. 2017)—some politicians are quick to otherize and vilify immigrants and foreign workers, but job automation does not fit as neatly into the "us-versus-them" narrative (Wu 2021).

In this chapter, I argue that popular and elite reluctance to accept immigrants may in turn motivate governments to promote workplace automation more aggressively. Deciding on how to fill jobs is often not a straightforward economic calculus whereby marginal costs solely determine outcomes. Resolving problems of economic nature often involves much more than "objective forces" or "allocation mechanisms" of the market (Lavoie and Chamlee-Wright 2000). Cultural influences and historical legacies help people recognize and understand available opportunities (Choi and Storr 2019) and offer them the framework within which to interpret their best course of action (Chamlee-Wright 2002). Moreover, culture shapes people's concerns and beliefs (including that of the political leadership) and thus plays a critical role in determining the agenda and nature of the national conversation (Lavoie 1991; Chamlee-Wright 2002). It is also often these culturally influenced opinions and beliefs—even though they might not be grounded in reason or rational calculation—that guide people's actions (Storr 2013). While close-mindedness about outsiders and perhaps prejudice might deter elites from pursing immigration reform as a solution to labor shortages, it could have the unintended effect of incentivizing private innovation and faster technological adoption.

This chapter presents a case study of Japan to illustrate how noneconomic factors of culture and history influence what people believe to be the preferred solution to a problem. In response to labor scarcity, Japanese political elites emphasize automation, as opposed to the common strategy of importing workers via opening up immigration, as a solution to the labor market problem. Due to the country's positive experience with and acceptance of technology (Robertson 2018) on one hand and its long history of restrictive immigration controls (Strausz 2019) on the other, automation is a path of lesser resistance. It helps the government avoid or delay thorny public discussions about reforming Japan's conservative immigration system. The Japanese government called for a "Robot Revolution" (*robotto kakumei*; Ministry of Economy, Trade, and Industry 2015). While most governments downplay the labor-displacing effects of technology, Prime Minister Shinzo Abe's government's plan explicitly described automation as a means to reduce the demand of labor. Citing concerns about a shrinking productive-age population and increased competition from abroad, the Ministry of Economy, Trade, and Industry (METI) proposed initiatives and funding to promote Japan's robot building capabilities, popularize the use of robots to "every corner of the country," and make Japanese robots and technologies a global standard (Headquarters for Japan's Economic Revitalization 2015).

However, this robot–immigrant substitution strategy has real limits too. Prime Minister Abe's "Robot Revolution" is slow to arrive. Japan's small- and medium-sized enterprises (SMEs) remain relatively backward and unproductive. On the other hand, some early adopters are finding out the hard way that humans still have an upper hand in performing many tasks. In addition, the strategy would also likely leave many firms behind. Although it is estimated that 49 percent of jobs in Japan can—in theory—be automated (Nitto, Taniyama, and Inagaki 2017; Frey and Osborne 2017), not all firms can afford to purchase state-of-the-art equipment. While large firms stand to benefit from automation, robots are not realistic alternatives to low-wage labor for firms with limited capital. The persistently low levels of low-wage immigration would disproportionately harm SMEs. Government interventions, especially those that limit firms' options (in this case, the option to employ foreign labor), could have important distributional effects, affecting day-to-day operation, profits, and even corporate survival.

The chapter proceeds as follows. The next section gives the necessary background to understand Japan's labor market challenges. Then, the chapter moves on to discuss Japan's history with immigration and technology. Finally, the penultimate section discusses the limitations of the strategy of robot–immigrant substitution. The final section concludes.

## BACKGROUND: JAPAN'S LABOR MARKET PROBLEMS

Japan has a well-documented demographic problem. Less than 10 percent of its population is between fifteen to twenty-four years old, and more than a quarter are aged sixty-five or above (Koudela 2019). The dependency ratio, defined as the ratio of the number of dependents aged sixty-five or above compared to the total population aged between twenty to sixty-four, is projected to reach 60 percent by 2030 and will exceed 80 percent by 2080 (Kitao 2018). In numeric terms, roughly 38.5 million working-age workers will exit the workforce between 2005 and 2055, and Japan would need 770,000 more workers every year during that period to replenish the labor market (Shinkawa 2012). However, the birth rate in Japan is well below the replacement rate, and the fertility rate has been falling since as early as the 1970s (Koudela 2019).

Japan also fails to rejuvenate the labor force by immigration. Due to its restrictive immigration policies, the net migration rate was merely 0.56 per

1,000 population in 2018. Although immigration has increased in the past decades, foreign residents only make up less than 2 percent of the Japanese population today (Japanese Government Statistics 2018). Japan has far fewer immigrants than other industrialized economies. Many foreigners who live there are on temporary training visas or student visas. In November 2018, Prime Minister Shinzo Abe successfully passed an immigration bill, amid strong protests from opposition parties, to allow low- and semi-skilled foreign workers to work in designated sectors on limited five-year visas, which can be renewed once only for laborers with specific occupations. Considering that the scheme provides no pathway for most to settle permanently, the new law does little to address the labor shortage or contribute to labor upskilling issues in the long run. Other schemes, such as the guest worker program for descendants of Japanese emigrants (e.g., *Nikkeijin* from Latin America), are likewise aimed to meet immediate labor demands but not designed to tackle the root of the problem. Aside from these stringent restrictions, naturalization is also relatively rare, partly because of the government's insistence on assimilation—migrants are required to give up their current citizenship as well as adopt Japanese legal names in Japanese characters.

With an ever-shrinking labor force, the ratio of job openings to applicants has increased to about 1.61 in 2018, the highest since 1974, while the unemployment rate stood at only 2.4 percent (Japanese Government Staistics 2019). The Bank of Japan's Short-Term Economic Survey of Enterprises shows that Japanese employers are facing the worst labor shortage since the early 1990s (Morikawa 2018). There is a critical shortage of labor in fourteen sectors, including restaurants, construction, agriculture, and particularly caretaking. The relatively educated and affluent native workforce actively rejects unskilled "3K" jobs that are dangerous *(kiken),* dirty *(kitanai)*, and physically difficult *(kitsui)* (Tsuda and Cornelius 2004). Japan's persistent and growing labor shortfall has caused immediate and long-term concerns among the business community, including staffing problems, declining quality of service, increasing wages, and the sustainability of the Japanese economy.

In a stylized scenario, states facing a shortage of workers may (1) open up immigration to bring in foreign workers, (2) facilitate production by offshoring, (3) liberalize trade, and/or (4) promote the adoption of labor-replacing machinery. In tradable sectors, all four strategies are logically possible, whereas in nontradable sectors, only immigration and automation are viable options. While multiple strategies may be pursued simultaneously, governments are likely to be especially motivated to facilitate automation when globalization (i.e., immigration, trade, and offshoring) is politically unpopular, inexpedient, or unfeasible. In this chapter, I argue that the higher acceptance and prevalence of robots and machines in Japan, compared to that of immigrants and foreign workers, prompts bold governmental initiatives to promote labor-saving technologies.

## RESISTANCE TO OPEN BORDERS

Thus far, despite the glaring need for labor, no political leadership has supported reforms to liberalize permanent immigration to Japan (Tsuda and Cornelius 2004; Koudela 2019). Japan is one of the least diverse societies in the developed world. Although scholars have written extensively about the existence and suppressed histories of ethnic minorities like the Ainu, Buraku, and Zainichi Koreans (Weiner 2009; Chapman 2008), there is no denying that these groups still represent only a very small fraction of the Japanese population. Despite Japan's chronic labor shortfall, the government has not tapped into the international labor market as much as other advanced economies. For instance, about 13 percent of the population in the United States and Germany are born outside of the country, whereas foreign residents make up less than 2 percent of the Japanese population (Japanese Government Staistics 2019). Given the higher wages in Japan, many in the developing world would be eager to resettle there for better economic and job opportunities. However, immigration reform remains a politically sensitive topic in Japan.

### Popular Opposition

Scholars have attributed Japan's persistent immigration restrictions to the people's desire to preserve the country's cultural uniqueness and ethnic homogeneity. The popular postwar narrative of *Nihonjinron* is said to be used to delimit the parameters of Japan's national identity. It portrays Japan as a racially unified nation (*tanitsu minzoku kokka),* constituted of people of the same blood (*tanitui minzoku*) (Howell 1996; Dale 1986; Hein 2012; Sugimoto 1999). This conception of Japan implies that there is no place for foreign workers and immigrants in the country. According to this logic, opening up borders for immigrants would fundamentally destroy what it means to be Japanese. In their widely cited work, Kazufumi and Befu (1993) claim to have empirically "established the extent of the popularity of Nihonjinron" (90). However, a careful read of their survey results reveals the limitations of *Nihonjinron* as a be-all and end-all explanation for the country's hostility to open immigration as it is commonly asserted. Surprisingly, only 36 and 38 percent of the survey respondents agree that Japan is a homogenous society and a homogenous people, respectively (ibid.). Merely 26 percent of respondents believe that "blood" is essential for one to become a part of the society, and just around 20 percent think that it enables an understanding of Japanese culture and language (ibid.).[1]

To the extent that the Japanese public is hesitant about open borders, they may not be nearly as concerned about immigrants' negative impact on Japan's monocultural identity as scholars had previously assumed. A recent Pew Research Center (2018) poll also shows that 75 percent of respondents believe that immigrants want to adopt Japanese customs and way of life, and about 60 percent of them believe that immigrants will make the country stronger because of their work and talents. The Japanese public today is also likely to be different from that of decades ago. There are now far more opportunities for the Japanese to come into contact with a foreigner, including tourists, guest workers, international students, or immigrants.

That being said, it would also be hugely inaccurate to characterize the Japanese people as welcoming to foreigners. They have expressed concerns over the societal implications of immigration. The World Values Survey finds that roughly two out of five Japanese respondents would not want immigrants or foreign workers as their neighbors, compared to just about one out of ten Americans in the United States (Inglehart et al. 2014). Even though most believe the impact of immigrants on society to be positive, sizable minorities think otherwise. A Pew survey finds that 40 percent think that immigrants are more to blame for crimes, 33 percent believe immigrants increase the risks of future terrorist attacks, and 31 percent see immigrants as burdens who take jobs and social benefits (Stokes and Devlin 2018). In all, over 70 percent of respondents would like to see either no changes or even tighter controls on Japan's already very restrictive immigration system (ibid.). In other words, there is little bottom-up demand for immigration reform.

## Ambivalence from Political Elites

Japan's illiberal immigration policies can also be partly explained by the political elites' own preferences and electoral calculations. Immigration reform incurs high political risks but has a very low immediate payoff. As benefits of immigration are generally diffuse (perhaps except for business owners), individual supporters of reform have little incentive to organize collective action or reward politicians for successfully implementing reform. On the other hand, the radical right and some interest groups (e.g., labor unions) have a strong disdain for immigrants due to xenophobia or economic self-interest and are thus very vocal about their objections.

A case in point: Masaharu Nakagawa, a Democratic Party lawmaker and former Minister of Education, Culture, Sports, Science and Technology, faced massive public backlash after openly expressing his support for expanding immigration. His office was flooded by "a deluge of angry calls and a pile of faxes protesting the move," even to the extent that his ministry "was temporarily paralyzed" (Osaki 2017). Likewise, another Democratic Party politician felt that he could not express his pro-immigration stance publicly because of "strong opposition from the radical right" (Strausz 2019).[2] Even within the long-time leading party, the Liberal Democratic Party, "there are some right-wing elements who oppose any foreigners" (ibid., 127).

Some politicians, like their constituents, are averse to immigration reform due to unfamiliarity. Yoichi Kaneko, a former OECD economist and an upper house member of the Democratic Party of Japan, was quoted saying that he "can't imagine how Japan will be" if the country accepted more immigrants, adding that it had not done this aggressively to date and that there was a lack of knowledge on how to make the country livable for both Japanese and foreign residents simultaneously (Murai 2016). He also worried that accepting more immigrants would drastically increase the financial and social burden on Japan, even when the preponderance of evidence in the economics literature suggests that immigrants, on average, contribute more in taxes than the benefits they receive from the government.

Given the restrictiveness of the current regime, most updates to the immigration system would be seen as substantively significant and controversial, making any push for reform appear even more politically risky. For example, Prime Minister Shinzo Abe's latest revision of the Immigration Control and Refugee Recognition Act allows foreigners to work *temporarily* in fourteen designated sectors with manpower shortage. Most of them would be granted a work visa of a maximum of five years, with the exception of those working in construction and shipping industries, whose visas are eligible for renewal. A majority of these workers would also *not* be allowed to change jobs or bring family members along. The scheme offers most of these workers no pathway to attaining permanent residency or citizenship. After the "training" ends, they must return to their home countries. Even though the amendment shuns permanent immigration and thus does very little to change the long-term social fabric of the country,[3] Prime Minister Abe's bill was nonetheless described as "controversial" (Denyer and Kashiwagi 2018), "a break from historical stance" (Gale 2018), and "dramatic" (Suzuki 2018).

There is no consensus as to whether postwar governing elites had intended to keep Japan largely "immigrant free" (Tsuda and Cornelius 2004). However, Japanese immigration policy development has shown path dependence. Throughout most of the twentieth century, Japan was not welcoming of foreigners (Kondo 2002). During the American Occupation after World War II, the government promulgated a series of restrictive decrees and laws that govern former colonial citizens and ethnic minorities (Yamanaka 2004). Zainichi

Koreans (literally Koreans in Japan), the Ainu, and other groups faced institutional and everyday discrimination. Zainichi Koreans, for example, were barred from public and private sector employment—many had to work in the informal sector or engage in illegal work.

Unlike Euro-American corporations, the Japanese business sector has not been very successful in lobbying for immigration liberalization. In Japan, there are a few visa statuses that allow foreigners to engage in paid employment, most of them for only a specified amount of time. Some of these categories are people with specialized knowledge and skills (e.g., university professors and lawyers), spouses of Japanese citizens, trainees from developing countries, people visiting Japan under working holiday agreements, and students (who are allowed to work part-time). When the business sector faced low-skilled labor scarcity, the government has only offered "side doors" from which foreigners could work in Japan temporarily, bringing in ethnic repatriates (e.g., Japanese Brazilians)[4] and "technical interns." However, these programs have not afforded Japanese businesses access to foreign workers in numbers that they actually need to meaningfully address the labor shortfall they confront (Strausz 2019).

Overall, there is evidence of Japanese ambivalence, if not outright resistance, to immigration among the population and the elites. Previous research has emphasized the perceived importance of preserving ethnic homogeneity and cultural uniqueness as key explanations of Japan's harsh immigration regime (Koudela 2019). Survey results suggest that Japanese citizens are less fixated on ideas about purity and blood espoused in *Nihonjinron*. Today, it still remains a very popular explanation of Japan's strict immigration policies. Instead, these polls show that the Japanese share very similar concerns with their counterparts in industrialized economies about the social and economic effects of immigration. Political elites may have also inaccurately assumed the general public to be more anti-foreigners than they actually are in reality (Strausz 2019). This assumption may be a result of vocal opposition from the radical right and risk aversion on the part of politicians themselves. Immigration reform has long-term economic benefits but little immediate political payoff. Japan's many decades of restrictive immigration controls—the status quo—also make initiating meaningful reforms more politically challenging.

## ACCEPTANCE OF TECHNOLOGY

While there are relatively few labor migrants, machines and robots are omnipresent in Japan. One of the most primitive but common forms of automation is vending machines. Japan boasts the highest vending machine density in the world, some of which feature color LCD screens and sell large varieties of beverages, noodles, eggs, takoyaki, and even (ten-kilogram bags of) rice all year round. Washizu (2003) argues that the prevalence of vending machines—one per twenty-three people—can be attributed in part to the Japanese people's obsession with technology and automated systems.

## The Public's Cultural and Social Acceptance

The Japanese public's penchant for technology is not new. For nearly a century in Japan, robots have predominately been portrayed as helpful to human beings in the media and entertainment industries (Robertson 2018). Japanese popular culture is also known to characterize robots as benign, fun, and human friendly (ibid.). Popular Japanese manga and animated films have frequently showed possible future scenarios wherein humans and robots coexist, such as *Astro Boy* (1951–1968) and *Doraemon* (1970–present).

*Astro Boy*, written and illustrated by Osamu Tezuka, features a friendly humanoid who has human friends and even a robot family of his own (Robertson 2014). Astro behaves like an everyday human boy, but the series also features his heroic side—standing up for human beings while fighting crime, injustice, and evil (Hornyak 2006).

Doraemon is a bipedal, blue, chubby robotic cat from the twenty-second century. He traveled two hundred years back in time to change the circumstances of the Nobi family in hopes that they will live an easier life. He helps the young son of the family, Nobita, on a day-to-day basis—from passing tests to escaping bullying and helping him impress his crush—using novel gadgets from the future. Doraemon, albeit a robotic cat, is given humanlike emotions (e.g., he wears a big smile), traits (e.g., being in love with the cat next door), and interests (e.g., afternoon dorayaki snacking). The popular series is still in production today. Doraemon has his own museum in Kawasaki-city, in the outskirts of Tokyo. The famous character was also chosen to be the mascot of the 2018 World Robot Summit in Tokyo.

This contrasts with American and European early portrayals of robots. *R.U.R.*, the successful science fiction play by Karel Capek, helped shape Euro-American skepticism and fear about robots (Robertson 2014). The robots in *R.U.R.* are made up of artificial blood and flesh. They appear to be happy to work for humans at the onset, but they are in fact plotting a robot revolution, which ultimately leads to the extinction of the human race. In the award-winning Blade Runner series, the human protagonist is tasked to kill replicants that are a result of "advanced robot evolution" and engineering. Replicants are very similar to humans, except that they are stronger, more intelligent, and more resilient. Some have malicious intents and aim to destabilize the world. While the Japanese entertainment industry frequently depicts robot protagonists working alongside humans, many popular Western films portray robots as more complex and sometimes menacing.

The idea that some Japanese people treat robots as a part of their family is seemingly bizarre outside the country. In the early 2000s, the Japanese firm Honda ran a print ad in an American magazine featuring its new humanoid, ASIMO, which was advertised to have "unprecedented human-like abilities." ASIMO was pictured in a typical American family portrait alongside a father, mother, two siblings, and a golden retriever. A majority of readers who responded to the ad were alarmed that robots could replace human workers (Robertson 2014). Honda, recognizing the negative reception, quickly pulled the advertisement from the magazine (ibid.). On the other hand, in Japan, Robertson (2014) finds that humanoids are being introduced into the society "in the spirit of adopted members of a household." Robots are also talked about as though they are living objects. In the Japanese language, the verb *aru/arimasu* is used to describe the existence of a thing, while the verb *iru/imasu* is used to refer to the existence of a person or an animal. *Iru/imasu* is frequently used in reference to robots (ibid.), suggesting a personification of or emotional attachment to machines.

The warm reception of robots among Japanese people is perhaps not surprising, given that a majority of them have been exposed to positive portrayals of robots not only through the popular media but also in real life. As mentioned earlier, Japan's millions of vending machines represent a form of primitive automation. In some sushi restaurants, food is delivered using a conveyor belt after orders are placed on a tablet. After finishing the meal, customers put dirty dishes into a slot that feeds directly into an automated washing station. Softbank's popular humanoid Pepper can be found in many places, including retail stores, government offices, health care facilities, and airports. Pepper can converse in fifteen languages and roam around freely on its own. One can also pay ASIMO, the famous Honda robot, a visit at Tokyo's National Museum of Emerging Science and Innovation (*Miraikan*). ASIMO performs for the public four times a day. It is also sometimes featured in the news as it played soccer with United States President Barack Obama, greeted the Queen of Denmark with flowers, and danced for German Chancellor Angela Merkel. Familiarity with technology may increase liking. Research in psychology suggests that repeated exposure to a stimulus increases one's preference for it, given an absence of a preexisting negative attitude (Bornstein and D'agostino 1992).

Furthermore, most of the previously identified concerns related to liberalizing immigration generally do not apply to job automation. Robots and machines, as they currently stand, have no mind of their own. They thus could

**Figure 7.1.   Humanoid Pepper.**
*Source:* Author's own photograph taken in Tokyo, Japan

not initiate terrorist attacks, commit crimes, or get government benefits.[5] Instead of threatening Japan's unique culture, robots have even been taught or programmed to preserve them. Some robots perform traditional Japanese dance, read sermons, and can even conduct Buddhist funerals. Furthermore, it could also be easier for native Japanese to communicate with a robot than a human. Not all immigrants can speak Japanese, but most machines can be programmed to communicate in the language, rendering the latter a "culturally odorless" alternative to immigration (Wright 2019).

## Elites' Preference for Technology

While initiating immigration reform is politically risky, technology promotion is almost always universally applauded. Few would like to be called a luddite. Additionally, if technological promotion is successful and automation does address at least part of Japan's labor shortfall, it will lessen the urgency for thorny political discussions and decisions related to low-skilled immigration. Japan does already have one of the highest robot densities in the world,[6] indicating ready acceptance by various stakeholders. Ranking fourth, the country boasts 327 installed industrial robots per 10,000 employees in manufacturing (International Federation of Robotics 2019). Robot installations in Japan had also increased by over 20 percent in 2018; the annual robot installation growth rate stands at around 17 percent since 2013 (ibid.). In terms of market share, Japan delivered over 50 percent of the world's supply of industrial robots in 2016 (International Federation of Robotics 2017).

Since the 1990s, robotics development has been jointly funded by the government and private firms. The Ministry of Economy, Trade, and Industry (METI); the New Energy and Industrial Technology Development Organization; research institutes; and the business sector jointly launched the five-year (1998–2002) Humanoid Robotics Project (HRP), aiming to develop general domestic helper robots. The HRP was followed by the Next Generation Intelligent Robots Project and, more recently, the Living Assist Robots Project (Robertson 2018).

During Shinzo Abe's first term as prime minister (2006–2007), he "actively and relentlessly promoted a robot-dependent society and lifestyle" and published a visionary blueprint called *Innovation 25* (Robertson 2014, 578). *Innovation 25* was described as a plan to pave the way to "a life that will become so much more convenient (*benri*), safe (*anzen*) and comfortable (*anshin*)" (Robertson 2007, 386). *Innovation 25*, written almost twenty years ago, included a visual presentation of what the government envisioned to be the future of the typical Japanese household in 2025. The family consists of a married couple, their two children, the husband's parents, and a robot,

Inobe-kun. Inobe takes charge of caretaking and housekeeping and is capable of conversing with members of the family. Fast forward to today, in 2020, it is safe to say that this vision has not (yet) been realized as the Japanese norm. However, the blueprint is indicative of the government's penchant for technology as a solution to chronic labor shortages. The idea implied is that robots could free up time of the married woman in the household, such that she could pursue a career of her own (i.e., become a part of the workforce) or become a "birthing machine" (i.e., to contribute to the labor force)—as infamously described by Yanagisawa, the then Health and Welfare Minister (Robertson 2007).

As a part of *Innovation 25,* the government allocated JPY 3 trillion (equivalent to about USD 26 billion) over a period of ten years to promote robotics. In addition, the METI had also earmarked over JPY 2 billion (or about USD 17.4 million) in its 2007 budget to support the development of workplace robots capable of decision making (ibid.). The framework was retained between the two Abe administrations. The Robot Revolution Realization Council (Robotto Kakumei Jitsugen Kaigi), which was a part of the vision laid out in *Innovation 25*, was formed in 2014.

When Prime Minister Shinzo Abe was reelected for his second term in 2012, he had not abandoned his vision for a Japan wherein robots would play increasingly important roles. Robotics development has become a part of the government's long-term strategy (Ministry of Economy, Trade, and Industry 2015). The METI pledged funding to promote Japan's robot production capabilities, popularize the use of robots, and make Japanese robotics a global standard (Headquarters for Japan's Economic Revitalization 2015). The Robot Revolution Initiative (RRI) formulates concrete steps to accelerate robot development, including the removal of bureaucratic barriers to innovation and streamlining the approval of new technologies in conventionally heavily regulated sectors (e.g., nursing, road use, and aviation).

Much unlike its passivity on immigration-related issues, the Japanese government actively promotes automation in areas that most people would least expect it. For example, nursing and elderly care are often considered to be at low risks of automation, as these occupations require social intelligence, perception, immediate interpersonal communication, and other skills in which humans have a comparative advantage (Frey and Osborne 2017). Despite this, the Japanese government identified automated or robot-assisted elderly care as one of its goals in its action plan (Ministry of Economy, Trade, and Industry 2015). The government has laid out its policy goals across multiple dimensions in hopes to make their vision of robot–immigrant substitution in old-age care more plausible to the public. It has a three-prong strategy: first, to increase the market for and the variety of nursing care robots (for bed transfers, walking support, bathing support, excretion support, and watching over dementia patients); second, to encourage the use of lifting robots to lower the risk of injury for existing workers; third, to increase awareness and acceptance of nursing care robots among the general population (Ministry of Economy, Trade, and Industry 2015).[7] While the leadership might lack imagination in immigration policies or picturing how a multicultural Japan would look (2016), they are ahead of the world in promoting the vision of machine-heavy nursing care.

## THE LIMITS OF ROBOT–IMMIGRANT SUBSTITUTION

Despite Japan's overall acceptance of robots and other such technology, the strategy to fill jobs using robots instead of immigrants has apparent limits. First, the Japanese labor shortage problem has already persisted for decades, but Prime Minster Abe's "Robot Revolution" would take many years to be realized. While Japan is home to multiple innovation giants and highly productive multinational corporations, many of its companies are surprisingly backward and inefficient (OECD 2017). For instance, most supermarkets have not implemented automated checkout counters and many airlines do not use self-service check-ins (*Economist* 2018). On the other hand, some early adopters now find their decisions rash or premature. The Henn-na Hotel (the Weird Hotel) in Nagasaki, the first robot-staffed hotel in the world, "laid off" over half of its robot staff as they increased overtime for human staff and created more problems than they could solve (Gale and Mochizuki 2019). The president of the parent company, Hideo Sawada, was quoted saying, "When you actually use robots you realize there are places where they aren't needed—or just annoy people" (ibid.). Despite the many wonders of technology, it is not a reliable substitute for humans in many settings. For many understaffed firms, it is impractical to wait for autonomous technologies to become broadly reliable and commercially viable.

Second, the simultaneous push for automation and rejection of immigration may inadvertently leave many behind. Not all firms can afford to purchase state-of-the-art equipment. While large, capital-rich firms stand to benefit from automation, robots are not realistic substitutes for low-wage labor for capital-poor firms. SMEs will have to rely on immigrant labor absent a domestic labor supply boom. The half-hearted measures to increase supply of foreign workers through guest visa programs fall short of fulfilling the manpower needs of enterprises.[8] Therefore, the abysmal level of low-skilled immigration would disproportionately harm SMEs. Government interventions, especially those that limit firms' options (e.g., to hire foreign labor), could thus have important distributional effects, affecting firms' day-to-day operation, profits, and even corporate survival.

Third, while there is evidence that shows Japanese people's penchant for robots and general-purpose technology, given the novelty of the issue, it is unclear how opinions might change if human workers feel threatened by their robotic counterparts at work. Job automation has sparked discussions regarding employment in the United States, Europe, and elsewhere. Although Japan has a labor shortage problem, automation may still displace existing workers from their current jobs. While technology creates new jobs (mostly high-paying, high-skilled jobs), displaced workers are not necessarily qualified for these new positions. Despite the well-known labor shortage problem, the Japanese do not have a particularly positive outlook on their jobs, even at present. According to the World Values Survey, 75.5 percent of respondents say that they worry "very much" or "a great deal" about losing their jobs (Inglehart et al. 2014). An OECD report (2015) finds that about half of laid-off workers in Japan could not find re-employment within a year after displacement. The economic data imply that there is a mismatch between available jobs and the skills of jobseekers.

There is simultaneously a surplus of jobs in the labor market and a high level of job insecurity among the population. The Japanese people could be nervous about technological displacement despite the official rhetoric. When directly asked about their views on automation, the Japanese people are concerned about technology's impact on the future of work. Almost 90 percent of Japanese respondents think that robots and computers will "probably" or "definitely" do much of the work currently done by humans in the next fifty years. If that happens, 74 percent of respondents believe that people would have a hard time finding jobs, 83 percent think that inequality would worsen, and only 35 percent envision there to be better-paying jobs (Stokes and Devlin 2018). It would be worthwhile for government agencies as well as researchers to better understand the public's opinion of labor-replacing technology. Sudden, large-scale labor market disruptions may lead to a backlash against technology, as is evident from the Industrial Revolution.

## CONCLUSION

In this chapter, I argue that popular and elite reluctance to accept immigrants may motivate governments to instead promote workplace automation. Outgroups tend to be vilified, but technological progress is often lionized. Deciding on how jobs are filled is frequently not a straightforward economic calculus whereby marginal costs determine outcomes. The processes of problem solving—even for a problem of economic nature—are rarely just "objective forces" or "allocation mechanisms" (Lavoie and Chamlee-Wright 2000). Culture and history provide the lens through which people recognize and understand available opportunities and remedies (Choi and Storr 2019). They shape the public's—as well as elites'—beliefs and concerns. These opinions play important roles in determining the agenda, nature, and outcome of the national discourse, even though such beliefs could be wrong, irrational, or based on prejudice (Storr 2013). Political actors' longstanding opposition to open immigration, despite Japan's labor shortage problem, reveals calculations that go beyond rational accounts in mainstream economics. The country's seeming close-mindedness about multiculturalism and perhaps even anti-foreigner bias might suffocate the prospects of open immigration, but it could have also incentivized private innovation and swifter technology adoption, as Japan could not count on migrants to fill gaps in the labor market.

I seek to demonstrate this dynamic using a case study of Japan. Japan has a shrinking and aging population. The dwindling of working-age cohorts, combined with a low birth rate, has raised a multitude of short-term and long-term concerns, including staffing problems, rising labor costs, declining quality of service, and the vitality of Japan's future economy. To address the country's labor shortage problem, the Japanese government pursues automation over replacement migration.

This strategy can be attributable to the country's predilection for technology and ambivalence toward foreigners. For decades, the Japanese media, manga, and films have portrayed robots as friends and companions of human beings. New technology and autonomous systems are also ubiquitous in Japan, breeding familiarity and preference. On the other hand, foreign residents only make up less than 2 percent of the Japanese population. Throughout most of the twentieth century and even through today, Japan is one of the most ethnically homogenous societies in the industrialized world and has not been particularly welcoming of foreigners. Given the restrictive regime and low numbers of migrants, any proposal to change Japan's immigration system might be perceived as more controversial and impactful than it actually is, making any push for change appear even more politically explosive.

In response to labor scarcity, the Japanese government chooses a path of lesser resistance and emphasizes automation promotion, as opposed to opening up thorny public discussions about reforming the country's conservative immigration system. Prime Minister Shinzo Abe called 2015 the year of "Robot Revolution" (*robotto kakumei*) (Ministry of Economy, Trade, and Industry 2015).

The *New Strategy for Robots* proposal aims "to make Japan the world's most advanced robot showcase and achieve a society in which robots are utilized more than anywhere in the world, from nursing care and agriculture to small- and medium-sized enterprises." (Robertson 2007, 44). The government pledges to provide funding, reform the regulatory regime, and make Japan the world's foremost innovation country.

Although Japan boasts one of the highest robot densities in the world, the strategy to substitute immigrant labor with robots has apparent limits. First, "robot revolution" is slow to arrive. While robots excel at jobs that can be specified, there are research and anecdotal examples that suggest that automated systems are not yet suited to tasks that require social intelligence, creativity, persuasion, perception, and manipulation (Frey and Osborne 2017).

Second, the simultaneous shunning of immigrants and promotion of robots would likely leave many smaller firms behind. While large firms stand to benefit from automation, robots are not financially realistic alternatives to low-wage labor for small firms. The consistently low levels of low-skilled immigration would disproportionately harm SMEs. Continued government restrictions on immigration could have important distributional effects, affecting operation, profits, and even corporate survival. Last, the adoption of technology has historically been ridden with conflict and resistance across the world (Frey 2019). Even though the Japanese people have developed a liking for machines and robots, both policy practitioners and researchers should further investigate potential differences between mass attitudes toward general-purpose and labor-replacing technology.

## NOTES

1. A sizable share of respondents also chose "Don't Know." There is no way of knowing if these respondents chose "Don't Know" to reflect their indecision or that they did so out of a concern of social desirability. (And if so, in which direction?) If we take these individuals' responses at their face value, it casts doubts on the prevalence of *Nihonjinron*.

2. Although some lawmakers see anti-foreign sentiments as a hurdle to reform, survey results show that the Japanese public actually do not hold consistently more negative views toward immigration than political elites (Strausz 2019). While immigration reform is no doubt a controversial issue, political elites may have underestimated the public's openness to change.

3. While the Abe government had expected the new visa policy to attract up to 345,150 workers to Japan in the first five years of the framework, there were only 2,258 applications (and 616 approvals for "specific skilled" status) at the half-year mark of the policy's implementation (Murakami and Kaneko 2019). Documentation, skill tests, and language examinations are said to be blamed for the scheme's sluggish start.

4. In the aftermath of the 2008 Financial Crisis, the Japanese government had offered to pay thousands of foreign workers with Japanese ancestry to go home (JPY 300,000 for the unemployed Nikkeijin and JPY 200,000 to each family member), mostly to Brazil and Peru, on the condition that they would not return to Japan again.

5. These are concerns about immigration identified in a Pew Research Center survey (Stokes and Devlin 2018).

6. Japan's restrictive immigration regime could have also incentivized the private sector to automate so as to lessen their staffing problems.

7. Currently, about 60 percent of people wish to use nursing care robots to provide care and 65 percent wish to be cared for by robots (Ministry of Economy, Trade, and Industry 2015). The RRI aims to increase acceptance to 80 percent.

8. While the government is resistant to expanding immigration, it has enacted a new *guest visa* policy that came into effect in April 2019. It was expected to attract up to 345,150 workers to Japan. These laborers are supposed to backfill SMEs in industries such as agriculture, nursing, and construction. However, by October 2019, there were only 2,258 applications and 616 approvals for "specific skilled" status (Murakami and Kaneko 2019). Its unpopularity may be due to a few reasons: applicants are generally unable to bring their families with them to Japan, bureaucracy, complex verification process, and a lack of a viable pathway to permanent residency.

## REFERENCES

Acemoglu, Daron, and Pascual Restrepo. 2019. "Automation and New Tasks: How Technology Displaces and Reinstates Labor." *Journal of Economic Perspectives* 33 (2): 3–30.

Blumer, Herbert. 1958. "Race Prejudice as a Sense of Group Position." *Pacific Sociological Review* 1 (1): 3–7.

Bornstein, Robert F., and Paul R. D'agostino. 1992. "Stimulus Recognition and the Mere Exposure Effect." *Journal of Personality and Social Psychology* 63 (4): 545–52.

Bukowski, Marcin, Soledad de Lemus, Rosa Rodriguez-Bailón, and Guillermo B. Willis. 2017. "Who's to Blame? Causal Attributions of the Economic Crisis and Personal Control." *Group Processes & Intergroup Relations* 20 (6): 909–23.

Chamlee-Wright, Emily. 2002. *The Cultural Foundations of Economic Development: Urban Female Entrepreneurship in Ghana.* New York: Routledge.

Chapman, David. 2008. "Tama–Chan and Sealing Japanese Identity." *Critical Asian Studies* 40 (3): 423–43.

Choi, Seung Ginny, and Virgil Henry Storr. 2019. "A Culture of Rent Seeking." *Public Choice* 181 (1–2): 101–26.

Dale, Peter N. 1986. *The Myth of Japanese Uniqueness.* New York: Routledge.

Denyer, Simon, and Akiko Kashiwagi. 2018. "Japan Passes Controversial New Immigration Bill to Attract Foreign Workers." *The Washington Post*, December 8. https://www.washingtonpost.com/world/japan-passes-controversial-new-im

migration-bill-to-attract-foreign-workers/2018/12/07/a76d8420-f9f3-11e8-863a
-8972120646e0_story.html.

Frey, Carl Benedikt. 2019. *The Technology Trap: Capital, Labor, and Power in the Age of Automation.* Princeton, NJ: Princeton University Press.

Frey, Carl Benedikt, and Michael A. Osborne. 2017. "The Future of Employment: How Susceptible Are Jobs to Computerisation?" *Technological Forecasting and Social Change* 114: 254–80.

Gale, Alastair. 2018. "Japan to Accept More Foreign Workers in a Break from Its Historical Stance." *The Wall Street Journal*, December 7. https://www.wsj .com/articles/japan-to-accept-more-foreign-workers-in-a-break-from-its-historical -stance-1544215014.

Gale, Alastair, and Takashi Mochizuki. 2019. "Robot Hotel Loses Love for Robots." *The Wall Street Journal*, January 14. https://www.wsj.com/articles/robot-hotel -loses-love-for-robots-11547484628.

Goos, Maarten, and Alan Manning. 2007. "Lousy and Lovely Jobs: The Rising Polarization of Work in Britain." *The Review of Economics and Statistics* 89 (1): 118–33.

Goos, Maarten, Alan Manning, and Anna Salomons. 2009. "Job Polarization in Europe." *The American Economic Review* 99 (2): 58–63.

Headquarters for Japan's Economic Revitalization. 2015. *New Robot Strategy: Vision, Strategy, Action Plan.* Accessed March 15, 2020. https://www.meti.go.jp/ english/press/2015/pdf/0123_01b.pdf.

Hein, Patrick. 2012. "Does Ethnic Origin Determine Integration Success? A Comparison of Immigration Policies in Germany and Japan." *Asian Ethnicity* 13 (2): 161–85.

Hornyak, Timothy N. 2006. *Loving the Machine: The Art and Science of Japanese Robots.* Tokyo: Kodansha International.

Howell, David L. 1996. "Ethnicity and Culture in Contemporary Japan." *Journal of Contemporary History* 31 (1): 171–90.

Inglehart, Ron, Christian Haerpfer, Alejandro Moreno, Christian Welzel, Kseniya Kizilova, Jaime Diez-Medrano, Marta Lagos, Pippa Norris, Eduard Ponarin, and Bi Puranen. 2014. *World Values Survey: Round Six-Country-Pooled.* Madrid: JD Systems Institute.

International Federation of Robotics. 2017. "Robots: Japan Delivers 52 Percent of Global Supply: Japan Is the World's Predominant Industrial Robot Manufacturer." https://ifr.org/ifr-press-releases/news/robots-japan-delivers-52-percent-of-global -supply.

———. 2019. "World Robotics 2019."

Japanese Government Statistics. 2018. Accessed March 20, 2020. https://www.e -stat.go.jp/stat-search/files?page=1&layout=datalist&toukei=00250012&tstat=000 001018034&cycle=1&year=20170&month=24101212&tclass1=000001060399& stat_infid=000031669224.

———. 2019. *Statistical Handbook of Japan.* Accessed March 20, 2020. https://www .stat.go.jp/english/data/handbook/pdf/2019all.pdf.

Kazufumi, Manabe, and Harumi Befu. 1993. "Japanese Cultural Identity: An Empirical
Investigation of Nihonjinron." *Japanstudien* 4 (1): 89–102.

Kitao, Sagiri. 2018. "Policy Uncertainty and Cost of Delaying Reform: The Case of
Aging Japan." *Review of Economic Dynamics* 27: 81–100.

Kondo, Atsushi. 2002. "The Development of Immigration Policy in Japan." *Asian
and Pacific Migration Journal* 11 (4): 415–36.

Koudela, Pál. 2019. "Robots Instead of Immigrants: The Positive Feedback of Japanese Migration Policy on Social Isolation and Communication Problems." *Asia-
Pacific Social Science Review* 19 (1): 90–104.

Krosch, Amy R., and David M. Amodio. 2014. "Economic Scarcity Alters the Perception of Race." *Proceedings of the National Academy of Sciences* 111 (25):
9079–84.

Lavoie, Don. 1991. "The Discovery and Interpretation of Profit Opportunities." In
*The Culture of Entrepreneurship*, edited by Brigitte Berger, 33–51. Ithaca, NY:
ICS Press.

Lavoie, Don, and Emily Chamlee-Wright. 2000. *Culture and Enterprise: The Development, Representation and Morality of Business.* New York: Routledge.

Michaels, Guy, Ashwini Natraj, and John Van Reenen. 2014. "Has ICT Polarized
Skill Demand? Evidence from Eleven Countries over Twenty-Five Years." *Review
of Economics and Statistics* 96 (1): 60–77.

Milkman, Ruth. 1997. *Farewell to the Factory: Auto Workers in the Late Twentieth
Century.* Berkeley, CA: University of California Press.

Ministry of Economy, Trade, and Industry. 2015. *Japan's Robot Strategy Was Compiled: Action Plan toward a New Industrial Revolution Driven by Robots.* Accessed
March 15, 2020. https://www.meti.go.jp/english/press/2015/0123_01.html.

Morikawa, Masayuki. 2018. "Labor Shortage Beginning to Erode the Quality of
Services: Hidden Inflation." *Research Institute of Economy, Trade, and Industry*,
January 4. https://www.rieti.go.jp/en/columns/s18_0012.html.

Murai, Shusuke. 2016. "Government Weighs Immigration to Maintain Population,
Boost Workforce." *The Japan Times*, January 6. https://www.japantimes.co.jp/
news/2016/01/06/national/social-issues/government-weighs-immigration-maintain-population-boost-workforce/.

Murakami, Takakazu, and Jun Kaneko. 2019. "Japan's New Skilled Foreign Labor
Acceptance System off to Sluggish Start." *The Mainichi*, October 29. https://
mainichi.jp/english/articles/20191029/p2a/00m/0na/018000c.

Nitto, Hiroyuki, Daisuke Taniyama, and Hitomi Inagaki. 2017. "Social Acceptance
and Impact of Robots and Artificial Intelligence: Findings of Survey in Japan, the
U.S. and Germany." NRI Papers No. 211, Nomura Research Institute.

OECD. 2015. *Back to Work: Japan Improving the Re-Employment Prospects of Displaced Workers: Improving the Re-Employment Prospects of Displaced Workers.*
Paris: OECD Publishing.

———. 2017. "Japan Policy Brief: Innovation." OECD Better Policies Series. https://
www.oecd.org/japan/japan-strenghtening-innovation-for-productivity-and-greater
-wellbeing.pdf.

Osaki, Tomohiro. 2017. "In a Break from LDP, Kono Calls for Japan to Open Doors to Blue-Collar Foreign Workers." *The Japan Times,* March 3. https://www.japan times.co.jp/news/2017/03/03/national/social-issues/break-ldp-kono-calls-japan -open-doors-blue-collar-foreign-workers/.

Patel, Pankaj C., Srikant Devaraj, Michael J. Hicks, and Emily J. Wornell. 2018. "County-Level Job Automation Risk and Health: Evidence from the United States." *Social Science & Medicine* 202: 54–60.

Peters, Margaret E. 2015. "Open Trade, Closed Borders Immigration in the Era of Globalization." *World Politics* 67 (1): 114–54.

Robertson, Jennifer. 2007. "Robo Sapiens Japanicus: Humanoid Robots and the Post-human Family." *Critical Asian Studies* 39 (3): 369–98.

———. 2014. "Human Rights vs. Robot Rights: Forecasts from Japan." *Critical Asian Studies* 46 (4): 571–98.

———. 2018. *Robo Sapiens Japanicus: Robots, Gender, Family, and the Japanese Nation.* Berkeley, CA: University of California Press.

Shinkawa, Toshimitsu. 2012. "Substitutes for Immigrants? Social Policy Responses to Population Decreases in Japan." *American Behavioral Scientist* 56 (8): 1123–38.

Stokes, Bruce, and Kat Devlin. 2018. "Despite Rising Economic Confidence, Japanese See Best Days behind Them and Say Children Face a Bleak Future." *Pew Research Center*, November 12. https://www.pewresearch.org/global/2018/11/12/ despite-rising-economic-confidence-japanese-see-best-days-behind-them-and-say -children-face-a-bleak-future/.

Storr, Virgil Henry. 2013. *Understanding the Culture of Markets.* New York: Routledge.

Strausz, Michael. 2019. *Help (Not) Wanted: Immigration Politics in Japan.* Albany, NY: SUNY Press.

Sugimoto, Yoshio. 1999. "Making Sense of Nihonjinron." *Thesis Eleven* 57 (1): 81–96.

Suzuki, Wataru. 2018. "Abe Bets Big on Adding Foreign Workers." *Nikkei Asian Review*, November 3. https://asia.nikkei.com/Spotlight/Japan-immigration/Abe-bets-big-on-adding-foreign-workers.

Tella, Rafael Di, and Dani Rodrik. 2019. "Labor Market Shocks and the Demand for Trade Protection: Evidence from Online Surveys." Working Paper, National Bureau of Economic Research.

*The Economist.* 2018. "Human Endurance: Japan Is Both Obsessed with and Resistant to Robots." *The Economist*, November 8. https://www.economist.com/ asia/2018/11/08/japan-is-both-obsessed-with-and-resistant-to-robots.

Thelen, Kathleen Ann. 1991. *Union of Parts: Labor Politics in Postwar Germany.* Ithaca, NY: Cornell University Press.

Tsuda, Takeyuki, and Wayne A. Cornelius. 2004. "Japan: Government Policy, Immigrant Reality." In *Controlling Immigration: A Global Perspective.* 2nd ed. Edited by Wayne A. Cornelius, Takeyuki Tsuda, Philip L. Martin, and James F. Hollifield, 439–76. Stanford, CA: Stanford University Press.

Washizu, Tsutomu. 2003. *Jido Hanbaiki No Bunkashi.* Tokyo: Shūeisha.

Weiner, Michael, ed. 2009. *Japan's Minorities: The Illusion of Homogeneity.* New York: Routledge.

Wright, James. 2019. "Robots vs Migrants? Reconfiguring the Future of Japanese Institutional Eldercare." *Critical Asian Studies* 51 (3): 331–54.

Wu, Nicole. 2021. "Misattributed Blame? Attitudes toward Globalization in the Age of Automation." *Political Science Research and Methods:* 1–18.

Yamanaka, Keiko. 2004. "Commentary." In *Controlling Immigration: A Global Perspective.* 2nd ed. Edited by Wayne A. Cornelius, Takeyuki Tsuda, Philip L. Martin, and James F. Hollifield, 477–78. Stanford, CA: Stanford University Press.

## Chapter 8

# Might at the Museum

## *Moral Communities, Moral Orders, and Museum Narratives*

### Lee Moore

In the past decade, museums have come to play an important role in the society of the People's Republic of China (PRC) and in Taiwan (or the Republic of China, ROC). China has built approximately a museum a day for the past ten years, most of these built by the national government. Likewise, Taiwan has also built and reimagined many of its museums in a bid to remake its society.

This chapter will argue that the reason the Chinese state has built so many museums is because it intends to utilize museums to construct what Buchanan calls a "moral community." This chapter will demonstrate that museums have played an important role in (re)constructing the PRC into a nationalistic[1] society organized around the moral community of China and Han Chineseness.[2] That moral community around which the country's identity is constructed is a narrow one, an identity that excludes many of the citizens of the PRC. Taiwan, too, has utilized museums for a starkly different purpose: to construct a moral order. By comparing these two countries, which are derived from a shared Chinese cultural tradition, this chapter will demonstrate the role that museums play in the construction of the ideological elements of a society and demonstrate how museums function as metaphors for the societies that build them.

In his paper titled "A Two Country Parable," James Buchanan imagines a natural experiment that a social scientist might do if they had the power to construct countries (Buchanan 2001, 211). Two countries, identical in social structure and economic capacity, are separated by an unbridgeable chasm, existing in autarky. He uses this imagined natural experiment to think through how specific policies might affect an economy. Of course, Buchanan's experiment is imaginary, and no social scientist has ever been able to run such an experiment. However, there are at least two countries that do form a kind of natural experiment: China and Taiwan. Both countries share similar cultures, and, to a certain degree, they also have a shared political history. However, after 1949, both countries cut off all intercourse with each other for more than half a century. In 2003, the two countries began by restoring postal services and other lines of communication, but, by that time, China had set itself up as a moral community. Taiwan had set itself up as a moral order. Because the situation of these two countries functions so much like Buchanan's two-country parable, this chapter will use these two countries to explore the ways that museums are connected with moral communities and moral orders.

Buchanan defines moral communities as single, cohesive units that offer moral recognition to in-group individuals but do not offer the same moral recognition to those outside the group. Moral communities, as Buchanan defines them, are formed when "individual members of the group identify with a collective unit, a community rather than conceiving of themselves to be independent, isolated individuals." (ibid., 188). Fellow feeling in moral communities can be organized around a variety of identities: race, religion, lineage, or ethnicity. Whatever the organizing principle of the moral community, those deemed outside are not treated as moral equals. The individuals within the moral community are not conceptualized as individuals per se, but rather they are conceptualized as components of groups. In other words, they are understood to derive their personal meaning from their membership within the moral community. Those outside the moral community are deemed to lack this necessary meaning, resulting in what Buchanan refers to as "moral anarchy" (ibid., 190).

In Buchanan's conceptualization, a moral order is the opposite of a moral community. In the moral order, fellow feeling is not organized along in-group status, but rather it is organized along the lines of amoral laws that substitute for the personal ties of the moral community (ibid., 208). Within the moral order, participants do not need religion, race, ethnicity, or any other sense of shared loyalties to the in-group in order to maintain social order. If the moral community is grounded on each member viewing themselves as a component of a group, the moral order is grounded on each member viewing themselves as an individual (ibid., 194).

Buchanan is not the only philosopher of the liberal tradition to think along similar lines. Hayek conceptualizes the world as divided into two kinds of communities: those communities he calls "micro-cosmos" and "macro-cosmos" (Hayek 1988, 18). Micro-cosmoses resemble the kinds of societies that primitive bands of humans lived in before cities began to emerge. These micro-cosmoses are constituted by members who identify not as individuals but rather only as parts of groups, whose allegiance is to what Hayek calls the "micro-ethic of the small band" (ibid., 80). They conceive of themselves not as individuals, but rather as members of a solidarity. Hayek suggests that the other kind of community is that of the macro-cosmos, and it fits well within the realm of civilized man. The macro-cosmos is part of what Hayek calls "the extended order." Those communities that are macro-cosmoses are ones in which members define themselves not by the micro-ethic of the band, but rather conceive of themselves as individuals and do not show solidarity along the lines of a particular ethnic, national, religious, or other community.

The concept of Hayek's micro-cosmos significantly overlaps with Buchanan's moral community, and the macro-cosmos overlaps with Buchanan's moral order. Both concepts understand human communities as divided along lines of primitive versus advanced or solidarity versus individualism. They are also both clear on the violence that awaits those who do not identify with the moral community/micro-cosmos. Hayek notes that calls for solidarity lead to a general rule where "one's natural reactions of hostility to strangers and solidarity with those who are like oneself" become "an ever more severe threat to political liberty" (ibid., 65)—a situation similar to Buchanan's "moral anarchy."

Since the 1989 Tiananmen Square Massacre, the inflection point at which China's socialist ideology largely lost its relevance in legitimizing the state, the PRC has attempted to construct an ideology based on Han Chinese nationalism (Varutti 2011, 306; Zha 1998, 20; Langfitt 2019, 157). Much of the ideological labor involved in the reconstruction of the PRC's legitimacy has been done using museums. The country has constructed museums at a pace more rapid than any other museum-building spree in history, building approximately a museum a day for the past decade. In 1991, the PRC had only approximately five hundred museums (Zhou 2005, 77). By 2018, the country had 5,354 (Xinhua News Agency 2019). The focus of these museums has largely been on constructing China into a moral community, based on the idea that China is a national Han Chinese community. At the same time, starting in the 1980s, Taiwan was transitioning from a nationalistic dictatorship into a democracy—from a moral community to a moral order. This transition involved a reconceptualization of the state's legitimacy, and museums were one of the main channels for propagating this reconceptualization.

To demonstrate this, this chapter will first examine the history of China in relation to Xinjiang (still a part of China today) and Taiwan (a de facto separate country). The next section will theorize about the nexus between museum studies and Buchananian philosophy, particularly how museums articulate whether the society that builds them is a moral community or a moral order. After that, the chapter will look at two different museums, one museum in China, the Kashgar Urban Planning Exhibition Hall (KUPEH), and one in Taiwan, the Ketagalan Cultural Center. These two museums are both concerned with how ethnic minorities function in Chinese and Taiwanese society and are emblematic of the kinds of museums that China, as a moral community, and Taiwan, as a moral order, create. As we examine these two museums, the tension between moral communities and moral orders will articulate itself in the way that these two different museums conceptualize the relationship between the state and a community outside of the social mainstream.

## HISTORICAL BACKGROUND

A brief political history of the spaces that this chapter will discuss is necessary in order to contextualize the situation of China and Taiwan.

Today, Mandarin is the official language in both China and Taiwan. The two countries share confusingly similar names. China is officially known as the People's Republic of China, whereas Taiwan is officially known as the Republic of China. Despite the claims today from Chinese nationalists in both China and Taiwan, except for the period between 1945 and 1949, Taiwan and China have operated as separate polities for more than a century. Taiwan has a convoluted political history. Before the fifteenth and sixteenth centuries, the island of Taiwan was largely populated by groups of Austronesian speakers, completely unrelated to the Chinese speakers who make up the majority of the island's population today (Roy 2003, 11). During the Ming Dynasty (1368–1644), Han Chinese migrants traveled from southern China to the island of Taiwan and began establishing outposts on the island (ibid., 12). Slowly, the Han Chinese colonized the island, pushing the indigenous groups onto increasingly less desirable land. During this period, Taiwan was not a part of the Chinese state (Teng 2006, 45).

But in the seventeenth century, Taiwan became the site of political competition between empires; the Spaniards, the Japanese, the Dutch, and the Portuguese all briefly occupied parts of the island. At the same time, the Ming state lost control of China. In 1644, a new dynasty was established in China, the Qing Dynasty, while a rump of the Ming fled to Taiwan and chased out all the powers that still occupied the island. The new dynasty ruling over China, the Qing Dynasty, established control over Taiwan in the 1680s, expelling the rump Ming government and, after some debate as to whether it was necessary, semi-incorporated Taiwan into the Qing imperial realm.

Simultaneously, the Qing Dynasty was also expanding westward. The region today known as Xinjiang (literally meaning "New Territories") was conquered by the Qing state in the 1750s after a massive genocidal campaign (Moses 2010, 188). Xinjiang had largely been outside Chinese political control for centuries. After the Qing conquest of the region, the Uighurs, who allied with the Qing state against the ruling Zunghar Mongols, were largely left to operate autonomously under the Qing imperial state.

The Qing maintained control over the island of Taiwan until 1895, when the expanding Japanese empire took Taiwan from the Qing. From 1895 to 1945, Taiwan was Japan's first and most well-ruled colony. In China, the Qing collapsed in 1912, with a party known as the KMT[3] establishing control over all of the state that it called the Republic of China. In 1945, the United States, fresh off its victory in World War II, declared that Taiwan should be returned to its rightful owner: China.[4] However, the United States never stated who should represent China—the KMT or the Chinese Communist Party (CCP). By this time, the KMT's rule over China was challenged by the CCP. The two parties fought a bitter civil war for control of China, and, in 1949, the CCP won. The KMT retreated to Taiwan but still claimed to be the only rightful sovereign of all of China (and Mongolia). The CCP proclaimed the People's Republic of China, while the KMT took the government of the Republic of China with them to Taiwan, imagining that they would be reclaiming China for themselves in a few years.

Unlike Taiwan, Xinjiang largely remained within the political sphere of the various Chinese regimes that emerged after the collapse of the Qing state. There were brief periods where Xinjiang operated autonomously. On several occasions, independence was declared, though Xinjiang has never been consistently independent of the main Chinese polity. Still, political control over Xinjiang was hotly contested from the 1840s to 1949, and there were several instances where Xinjiang, with the help of a colonial power, could possibly have become independent (Newby 1996, 71).

It is important to note that the PRC leaders express an interest in imagining that Chinese control over the region is unbroken (Millward 2009, 63). In discussions of Xinjiang in the PRC, the state often emphasizes the fact that, from 150 BCE–900 CE, various Chinese states exercised sporadic control over the region of Xinjiang—though probably not for more than four hundred to five hundred years of this millennium-long period. Still, in discussions of Xinjiang, the PRC narrative generally emphasizes these periods of control, rarely acknowledging that this control was always tenuous, nor acknowledging that, for approximately eight hundred years, the Chinese state was largely absent from the region.

For the first three decades of their existence, from 1949 to 1979, the PRC and the KMT-ruled regime on Taiwan maintained mirror versions of each other in China and Taiwan. At this time, both states were illiberal states ruled by authoritarian leaders. Of course, the PRC was run by a communist party and the KMT aligned itself with the United States in the Cold War, allowing for the development of a managed capitalist economy while simultaneously brooking no political dissent. In some ways, Taiwan during this period under the Leninist KMT party–state was more a moral community than the PRC was.

Starting in the late 1980s, the PRC and the ROC switched roles. Particularly after the 1989 massacre around Tiananmen Square, communism was no longer viewed as an ideology with any practical valence. Though the CCP remained in power, communism was replaced by nationalism as the legitimizing force in the PRC; the Chinese became a communist state without any communists. This nationalism that they conceived of as the new legitimizing force in the Chinese polity was a nationalism that was predicated on the nation belonging to the Han Chinese. Under socialist ideals, ancient Chinese culture was regarded as "backward" and "feudal" by the CCP. Since 1989, the CCP has reversed itself, promoting Han Chinese nationalism and exalting Han Chinese heritage.

This post-1989 nationalism is the exclusive nationalism of a moral community, one that promoted the Han Chinese ethnic identity and increasingly rendered all other identities as unauthorized, if not officially illegal. Increasingly, all non–Han Chinese identities became suspect. Whereas, when the PRC was a moral order under socialism, all ethnic identities were authorized to participate in the business of state and all ancient, "feudal" identities were attacked by the state, and the PRC came increasingly to legitimize itself on the promotion of ancient Han Chinese identities and to exclude all ancient non–Han Chinese identities from state-sanctioned discussion.

Increasingly, this advocacy for the Han Chinese moral community has taken a violent form. In Xinjiang, in the far western part of China where the KUPEH is located, the state has established a campaign of cultural genocide in which the Uighurs and other Muslim ethnic groups indigenous to the region have been imprisoned by the millions in reeducation camps. The goals of these camps are to rid them of their culture and identity—to convert them into Han Chinese members of society in terms of their culture. The PRC is imprisoning Uighurs for practicing Islam and for speaking Uighur, Kazakh, or other non-Mandarin languages. In place of these Islamic identities and Central Asian languages, a Chinese identity is promoted alongside the use of Mandarin Chinese in order to create a moral community centered on the identity of Han Chineseness. The state has begun to try to erase all non-Chinese identities out of existence, trying to force Uighurs and others to fit within the Han Chinese moral community.

In the 1980s, Taiwan also reoriented itself politically. The state went from being a moral community, built around a sense of Chineseness that prioritized a Mainland Chinese identity, to promoting itself as a multiethnic state with many Han ethnic groups. Suddenly, the state went from making it almost illegal to speak any language other than Mandarin to sponsoring projects that instantiated numerous forms of Taiwanese identities: museums were built to honor Hoklo speakers and Hakka speakers (the two most important Chinese languages on the island before 1945). The National Museum of Taiwanese Literature was built to acknowledge the many different languages that Taiwanese authors have used (before the KMT had limited discussion of literature in Taiwan to those writing in Mandarin). Many museums were also built to honor the non–Han Chinese indigenous groups. Within a few decades, Taiwan had become a moral order, built around the rule of law, in which all ethnic and subethnic groups on the island could have their identity recognized, not repressed. Now, in Taiwan, solidarity is not conceived of as allegiance to a specific ethnic group, but rather as allegiance to what Buchanan called "the law." Today, identity is connected to the ideal of the state and largely stripped of a nationalistic understanding.

## MUSEOLOGICAL THEORY AND BUCHANAN

Though few scholarly works have focused on the connection between democracy, autocracy, and museums, what little work has been done on the topic in museological studies supports my connection of Buchanan's differentiation between museums and the tension between moral orders and moral communities. Museums can be conceived of as narratives, similar to books. Museums tell stories. The kind of story that they tell and the way that they tell that story is inexorably related to the effect that they want to produce in the reader. All stories are meant to change readers. The different stories that museums in China and Taiwan tell reveal a great deal about the state and society that created these museums, and those stories are directly related to the difference between the moral community and the moral order.

Though no book-length studies have been done on the topic, scholars of museum studies have long noticed a connection between the type of government under which a museum is built and the kind of narrative that the museum produces. Peter Aronsson noted how the Italian Fascists used museums to attempt to construct a line of continuity directly from the Roman empire to Mussolini's own state, and Aronsson hypothesized that there must be some connection between democracy, authoritarianism, and the way that museums constructed their narratives. Aronsson theorized that the more a state lacked other legitimizing factors, like democracy, the more that state would rely on museum narratives connecting the modern state with the glories of an ancient past (Aronsson 2011, 48). These imagined continuities that museums propagated became one of the legitimizing forces bolstering the autocratic state.

Eileen Hooper-Greenhill has noted that, unlike museums in illiberal states, museums in democracies tend to be polysemous, that is they tend to allow their narratives to be infused by multiple voices (Hooper-Greenhill 1995, 8). She suggests that museums in a liberal state tend to be more reflective of the multiple individual voices that exist within all societies. I would add the corollary to this: museums in illiberal states tend to attempt to cover over the polysemy inherent in all societies. Museums in illiberal states tend to prioritize a single voice's discussion of a single narrative, replicating the way that the state itself tends to direct all voices into a single goal.

Buchanan points out that the moral order allows for individuals to exist in a variety of forms. Rather than being required to show solidarity in the form of the "micro-ethic of small bands" (Hayek 1988, 80), moral orders allow for what Hayek calls the "freedom to be different" (ibid., 79). On the other hand, the moral community demands that members prioritize the goals of the community over their own goals. As Hayek suggests, for a moral community to function, the members of the moral community have to not only work toward the ends of the moral community, but they also have to believe that the ends of the moral community are their own ends. "To make a totalitarian system function efficiently, it is not enough that everybody should be forced to work for the same ends. It is essential that the people should come to regard them as their own ends" (Hayek [1944] 2008, 171).

In China, as this chapter will demonstrate, the museum becomes the space where the ends of the authoritarian state can be inculcated into the populace. The PRC uses museums as a place to imagine a continuity that prioritizes the Han Chinese narration of history while simultaneously erasing the Uighurs out of history. Just like Aronnson (2011) suggests, the imagined continuity of the PRC is meant to legitimize the modern state's imagined continuous rule over the region because it has little else, other than this imagined continuity, to legitimize its rule over Xinjiang. In the sections below, we will discuss in-depth how this imagined continuity works, but, like Aronnson points out in the case of Fascist Italy, China today uses the museum as a space to narrate an imagined continuity of Chinese nationalism because it has little else to legitimize its rule in Xinjiang.

On the other hand, Taiwanese museums no longer need to resort to an imagined continuity. The narrative that the Taiwanese have is already self-sufficiently legitimate. That narrative is grounded in the democratic ideals of a moral order. Rather than promoting a singular, monovocal narrative where a single ethnic group is deemed the only authorized ethnic group to be recognized as moral beings, the Taiwanese museums offer a narrative that is polysemous, where history can be narrated from multiple perspectives. As we turn to the two museums, we will see how these differences between the monovocal Chinese museum and the polysemous Taiwanese museum articulate the different understandings that moral communities and moral orders have of themselves.

## THE KASHGAR URBAN PLANNING EXHIBITION HALL

The KUPEH was built in 2011 on an island sitting in an artificial lake in a historical desert oasis city in the western corner of the PRC. A large section of the city's traditional architecture was torn down to build the lake and the museum. Thus, the museum, built ostensibly to preserve the memory of Kashgar's urban past, is itself an agent of Kashgar's destruction.

In many ways, the construction of the museum epitomizes the relationship that the museum has to the city that it represents. Kashgar is a city with a population that is 83.5 percent Uighur,[5] but the museum mentions Uighurs only once in the entire narrative it offers on Kashgar's history and future. According to news reports, the museum's architecture, an odd-looking saddle parabola, architecturally quotes the Sydney Opera House (Kashgar City Network 2015), rejecting indigenous Central Asian architectural styles. According to interviews and media reports, the museum, built in 2011, functions as a full museum with exhibits ready and a staff reporting to work daily. However, strangely, the museum has never been opened to the public and is only occasionally opened to visitors from government delegations, military units, and cadres.

As discussed in the historical background section, Chinese imperial power in the region of Xinjiang has been an object of contestation. What is interesting about the museum is that contestation is a core concern of the museum, but that contestation is only expressed by the museum narratives eliding any discussion of that contestation. Even though the region is 83.5 percent Uighur, the museum is trying to build the case for the region to be included as a space for a Han Chinese oriented moral community. The only way to do that is to erase this history of contestation and to present history as a series of events that unambiguously demonstrate the region's Han Chinese character and implicitly erase the Uighurness of this region.

The first part of the museum text we will examine will do just that. This text is taken from the history section of the museum, though what it represents is a discussion of Chinese mythology narrated as if it were history. This short text is titled "Mythical City," and it reads as follows:

According to Records: "King Mu of Zhou left Haojin (today's Xi'an) going west all the way to Kunlun." "He traveled to the north of the Red River (today's

Kizil River)," reaching "Caonu" (today's Kashgar). This is the earliest historical record of Kashgar.[6]

Already in this short text, anyone familiar with the history of the region and its role in Chinese history can recognize how this text is excising any discussion of the non-Chinese groups out of the region's history. King Mu is a real historical personage (reign 976–922 BCE or 956–918 BCE), an actual king of the Zhou Dynasty who, many generations after his death, was elevated to mythological status. As a mythological figure, King Mu has generally been understood as a symbol of the early Chinese state's westward expansion in the regions today occupied by the Uighurs, and he clearly embodies the Chinese state.[7]

By presenting King Mu as the discoverer of Kashgar, the text makes an interesting epistemological claim. It claims that the "earliest historical record of Kashgar" is not something that is written by Kashgaris but rather was written by Chinese speakers.[8] The records of local Kashgaris, in the museum text, are not legitimate because non-Chinese-language texts are not authorized to speak. This is because, in order to fit the region into Beijing's schema where all the PRC's territory is understood to be a Han Chinese moral community, all regions in the PRC, including those occupied by non–Han Chinese ethnic groups, must have the historical memory of their non–Han Chinese history erased. With this first exhibit, the passage on King Mu of Zhou begins the process of erasing non–Han Chinese elements from the collective memory of Kashgar. Implicit in King Mu's visually seeing Kashgar is symbolic of an act of ownership, and that ownership is symbolic of the ownership not by an individual, but rather by a moral community.

Certain patterns are established in this text on King Mu: the museum text makes a claim that the Han Chinese moral community has an epistemological ownership over the region. In other words, the Han Chinese moral community (or members of it) are the ones who see and discover the region, and therefore the region belongs to the Han Chinese moral community. This is why, for the rest of the discussion of the museum, historical personages represented by the museum will be of a particular profile: they will be Chinese, and they will move from the imperial center to the imperial periphery. In this way, their ethnopolitical status will allow them to claim that the Han Chinese moral community has a political claim to the region. The ethnically defined moral community is equated to the state, and the ethnostate thus owns the region because, in ancient times, members of the ethnomoral community traveled to the region to visually survey and thus claim ownership over the region. It is in this way that the museum narrative begins to construct a moral community centered on the Han Chinese moral community.

As we move on to one of the next texts in the history section of the museum, we see many of these patterns reappear. This section is titled "Han-Tang Shule City":

In 128 B.C.E., Zhang Qian arrived in Shule (today's Kashgar).–Book of the Han, Commentary on the Western Regions—Impressively, it is recorded that the country of Shule had a market street. In 73 C.E., Ban Chao was sent out to the Western Regions. He arrived at Kashgar and built Pantuo City. During the Six Dynasties, official records indicate that Shule's name was changed to Qisha and Jiecha. During the Sui and Tang Dynasties, there also appeared the names of Jiashi, Jiashizhili, Jiashijili, etc.

There are several important things to note about this text. First is that the characters featured in this text, Zhang Qian (?–114 BCE) and Ban Chao (32–102 CE), are historical characters, unlike King Mu, who is a historical-cum-mythological character. Zhang Qian was a diplomatic envoy from the Han Dynasty[9] to the region, while Ban Chao was a military general sent to subdue the local non–Han Chinese peoples in the region through violence (Wills 1994, 91–95). It is important to note that, once again, Kashgaris play no role in the epistemological claims over their region. Zhang Qian and Ban Chao, as members of the Han Chinese moral community, come to the region and claim epistemological ownership over the region. They "know" the region and "discover" the region, and therefore the Han Chinese moral community gains ownership over the region.

Local Kashgaris, as they are not members of the Han Chinese moral community, are imagined out of the history of the region, even though they made epistemological claims over the region before Zhang Qian and Ban Chao arrived. However, the Kashgaris and their epistemological claims over the region are not authorized for discussion in the space of the museum's narrative. A discussion of Kashgaris would interrupt that imagined continuity of Han Chinese control that the Chinese state is utilizing to legitimize its claim over the region and thus to legitimize the moral community's claim over that region.

To claim Kashgar for the Han Chinese moral community requires the excision of Kashgaris from their own history. In other words, Kashgaris are excluded from the history of Kashgar because Kashgaris are not part of the Han Chinese moral community. Thus, the KUPEH's narrative presents a Kashgar without Kashgaris. This excision of the Kashgaris from the narrative is nearly total. Only once is the word "Uighur" used in the entire space of the museum. Neither the words "Islam" nor "Muslim" are ever used in the text of the museum, even though the Uighur community is almost entirely Sunni Muslim. Additionally, many of those non-Uighurs living in Kashgar are still Muslim.

The region can only be claimed by the Han Chinese moral community if the Uighurs and other nonmembers of the moral community are excluded from the narrative. The museum becomes a textual vehicle to construct an understanding of the history of Kashgar that excludes Kashgaris and thus creates a vehicle for the Han Chinese to claim that the region is the space over which the Han Chinese moral community exercises uncontested ownership.

Here, the museum narrative strives to avoid a discussion of the local because any discussion of the local Kashgari Uighurs would call into question the claim that Kashgar is a space in which the Han Chinese moral community exercises ownership. In the above examples, avoiding the local was done by excising locals from local history. But what happens when the museum is not able to avoid discussions of localness? The following passage, titled "Ethnic Folk Customs," demonstrates that, even when localness has to be discussed, the narrative seeks to avoid discussing it. The text below is a long passage worth quoting in full because it demonstrates the lengths to which the museum narrative will go to avoid this discussion:

> "If entering the marsh, get advice from the shepherd boy. If entering the river, get advice from the fisherman." "Every ten miles a different style, every hundred miles a different tradition." This style is intense. In the long river of history, this city where many ethnic groups have assembled, due to its unique social, historical and natural environment, its modes of production, its living customs, its architecture, its clothes, its cuisine, its etiquette, its wedding and burial customs, its taboos and what is not taboo, its handicrafts, etc. are all full of the thick scent of the local customs of the Western Regions. These unique distinguishing specialties are the best explanation of the local folkways of Kashgar.

In a passage that is supposedly about the local, this text avoids discussion of the local by avoiding discussion of anything concrete. Though the title is "Ethnic Folk Customs," this passage says nothing about the specific ethnic or folk who occupy the city, nor does it mention any specific customs. Rather than discussing concrete examples of customs, the text engages in a kind of legerdemain, discussing localness only as a category. There is nothing about the local Kashgar style, the kinds of wedding and burial customs it has, or its architecture.

The Uighurs are a Central Asian people who speak a language similar to modern-day Turkish, and their architecture, customs, and culture were drawn from shared experiences with the Kazakhs, Kyrgyz, Turkmens, Mongolians, and others. But any discussion of these Central Asian influences would implicitly be a rejection of the museum's ideological thrust that Kashgar is a space owned by the Han Chinese moral community. At the beginning of this section of the chapter, I pointed out that the museum's architecture itself is a rejection of any kind of localness, appearing more like the Sydney Opera House than a Central Asian Mosque or other standard architecture from the region. The architectural statement that this museum makes is as clear as the above passage is ambiguous. In order to claim Kashgar as a space of the Han Chinese moral community, any connection to local Uighurs and their Central Asian culture has to be excised.

This museum is the product of an ideological tension. The museum narrative is supposed to both discuss Kashgar and construct an imagined version of Kashgar located within the Han Chinese moral community. This tension is irresolvable, and the irresolvability of these two tasks is on display in the above passage. In a passage where the museum essentially asks, "What is local?" it answers that question by only discussing what localness is as a category rather than giving concrete examples of the local Kashgari customs.

Buchanan defined the moral community as a single cohesive unit that offered moral recognition of the in-group members but not those outside the group. Since 1989, the PRC has been seeking to construct this single cohesive unit along nationalistic lines, envisioning the entire country as a moral community organized around the Han Chinese identity. But to do this, the state has to excise all non–Han Chinese out of the museum narrative. Uighurs and other non–Han Chinese Kashgaris are excised from history. Within the museum narrative, the history of Kashgar can only be told from the perspective of the Han Chinese because the Han Chinese are the only ones who are treated as moral equals—those authorized to construct history. All non–Han Chinese are outside the moral community that the museum is constructing and thus are not authorized as subjects of history. Their voices are not allowed to be heard because the museum text is univocal. Kashgar's history, as constructed in this museum, is how the Han Chinese saw Kashgar and what the Han Chinese did in Kashgar. History is only found within the purview of the moral community, and only the members of the moral community are authorized to speak within the museum space.

As Hayek pointed out, all collectivist regimes require a common *weltanschauung*—a common narrative for those in-group members of the collective. Most museums in the PRC function as ideological agents constructing this common weltanschauung. What makes the KUPEH distinct is that few museums do so good (or bad) of a job of exposing the mechanics of the construction of a moral community. Because there is such a large gap between the imagined moral community and the facts on the ground, this museum demonstrates the lengths to which the Chinese state will go to use museum narratives to construct moral communities.

# KETAGALAN MUSEUM

Now, we turn to another museum, one that is similar in some ways but vastly different in other ways. This museum, Taiwan's Ketagalan Museum, along with the similarities and differences between it and the KUPEH, will demonstrate how museums operate differently when they are part of a Buchananian moral order rather than a moral community.

In the north of Taiwan, just a short half-hour subway ride away from Taipei's Presidential Palace, sits the Ketagalan Cultural Center—a museum dedicated to the history of the Ketagalan people, one of the ethnic groups who used to occupy the region around Taipei before the Han Chinese ethnic groups migrated to the region. Since the fifteenth century, various Han Chinese subethnic groups have occupied the region, pushing the Ketagalans and other indigenous ethnic groups to intermarry with Han Chinese and abandon their Ketagalan identity. Today, few Taiwanese people identify as fully Ketagalan, though some have adopted this identity. Even those who do identify as Ketagalan maintain little in the way of separate cultural traditions or living spaces.

Despite the fact that only a few Taiwanese citizens still identify as Ketagalan, the Ketagalans' contributions to Taiwanese society have been recognized in a variety of ways. In 1996, the street in front of the Presidential Palace was renamed Ketagalan Street in honor of their contributions to Taiwanese society. Numerous place names in the Taipei area are also derived from the Ketagalan language, and several museum exhibits have been built to reflect the Ketagalans' contributions to the northern Taiwan region, including the dedication of an entire museum to the group, the Ketagalan Cultural Center.

The contrast between this museum and the KUPEH will be the focus of the following pages. If the narrative constructed by the KUPEH focused on the construction of a Han Chinese moral community by allowing only Han Chinese to speak in the museum narrative and excising any local Kashgaris from the narrative, the Ketagalan Cultural Center contrasts that by not only discussing local Ketagalans but also allowing the local Ketagalans to speak for themselves in parts of the museum. This allowance of multiple voices to speak within the space of a single museum is the aspect that marks Taiwanese museums as belonging to a remarkably democratic museum culture and a sign that they are attempting to construct a moral order that includes all groups and all voices.

The Ketagalan Cultural Center is a quietly polysemous museum. Though the museum does not announce this anywhere in the museum narrative, the museum space itself hosts two separate narratives within the space of a single museum. These two separate narratives were written by two separate groups, yet they sit side by side within the same museum space. One of these narratives was created by a group of Ketagalans themselves, and another one was created by a group called the Beitou Environmental Museum Group, a regional government organization that has created museum exhibits for multiple museums. First, we will analyze the narrative created by the Ketagalans themselves. Next, we will analyze the narrative created by the Beitou Environmental Museum Group.

In the KUPEH, the entire narrative pointed toward demonstrating rightful ownership of the region by the Han Chinese moral community. The message in Kashgar was that Kashgar belongs to the Han Chinese. Because the nation of China was, by the state's definition, a moral community founded on the Han Chinese ethnic group, the entire narrative had to point to the legitimacy of the rulership of the Han Chinese ethnic group (and thus the legitimacy of the nation), upholding the moral community. The Ketagalan Cultural Center stands in stark contrast to the KUPEH. In the Ketagalan Cultural Center, narratives compete. Two narratives—two understandings of what the Ketagalans' role in local history was—are competing with each other. The museum's maker does not decide which narrative is the correct one. Both narratives are offered as equally legitimate and equally possible.

In the half of the museum narrative constructed by the Ketagalans themselves, the narrative frames the Ketagalans as having historical subjectivity. The Ketagalans are not conceptualized as a part of any national framework, but rather they are conceptualized as independent actors. Throughout this half of the museum, rather than a single frame being forced by an authority figure, multiple frames are utilized to understand the Ketagalans' positionality in history. The Ketagalans are framed by the text in their relationships within the Ketagalan ethnicity and within a broader transnational history. The museum narrative has passages examining how Ketagalans understood themselves and divided themselves up into small groups within the larger Ketagalan ethnic group. A quote from the text created by the Ketagalans demonstrates how this is done:

> [Scholarly research] indicates that Ketagalans probably split into three sub-ethnic groups, and it is only [upon understanding these three groups] that their richness can be reflected. These are the Masai people, who occupied the territory from the Jilong River Valley east all the way to the North Sea Coast, the Bianlu Leilang people (sometimes called the real Ketagalans), who occupied the territory from the West to Linkou Taidi, and the Culun people, who occupied the territory from Linkou Taidi to Taoyuan.

This long, descriptive text is, when contrasted with the KUPEH, quite striking. Here, the Ketagalans are discussing their own group, in the terms under which the Ketagalans understood themselves. Ketagalans are given the opportunity to define what it means to be Ketagalan. They are focused on the differences among themselves—the differences within the group. This is not how outsiders would discuss a group, but rather it is the kind of esoteric identification that all group dynamics are subject to. In other words, this museum narrative begins with this passage that insists on the museum visitor adopting a narrative position that requires visitors to see the Ketagalans on the terms that the Ketagalans saw themselves.

Now, we will look at a passage from a text that discusses the role that perspective plays in our understanding of Ketagalan history:

> It was on the island of Taiwan that this group of people entered the tide of the Great Age of Navigation. When they stepped onto the world stage, what kinds of stories did they have? We can only portray them through the perspective and pens of those on the sidelines, discovering little bits drip by drip. Afterwards, we also cannot forget the perspective of the "other," although that perspective has left a deep historical imprint on their descendants, but they are also filled with the subjective perspective and stereotypes [of the sideline observer], and that the "true treasure" of the history and culture of the indigenous people is still awaiting discovery and understanding.

In some ways, this passage is as devoid of content as the Kashgari text titled "Ethnic Folk Customs."[10] What makes this text different is the framework that it adopts in its conceptualization of the relationship between the minority and majority groups. In the KUPEH, the museum text never allowed the visitor to adopt the perspective of the local Kashgaris. Just as in the first passage we discussed from the Ketagalan Cultural Center, this passage encourages us to think about how local Ketagalans would have approached their own understanding of their role in history. The narrative gives the Ketagalans something that the historian Prasenjit Duara calls "historical subjectivity," that is the Ketagalan people become an authorized site from which to narrate history (Duara 1995, 25). The Ketagalans' perspectives become an acceptable way to narrate history. Note how different this is from the KUPEH, where the only acceptable perspective from which to narrate history was the Han Chinese moral community's perspective.

In reminding the reader that history, and thus the perspective that the museum narrative can offer, is the perspective of specific individuals and that our historical perspective is "filled with the subjective perspectives and stereotypes," the passage is making the point that the museum narrative is not the only possible way to understand the Ketagalans' role in history. In fact, the museum text is inviting us to think about the Ketagalans' perspective. Rather than creating a single voice through which history can be narrated, this half of the museum acknowledges that there are competing narratives that are also valuable for the visitor to consider. This idea of a polysemous narrative, a narrative with multiple voices constructed out of competing narratives, is something that is characteristic of this museum.

This half of the museum offers a narrative that does not situate the Ketagalans in relation to the Han Chinese colonizers of the island (those who dominate the island's population today). Rather, in the Ketagalans' own narrative, they situate Ketagalan history in terms of the "Age of Navigation," that is, in terms of a global history dominated at the time by European navigators. The KUPEH situated Kashgari history in terms of the nation and the moral community that made up that nation. If a fact did not support the moral community's claim over Kashgar or if information was not framed in terms of the nation, it was excised from the narrative. The Uighur people, being a Turkic-speaking ethnic group, have had a long history of intercourse with the peoples of Central Asia. Those Central Asian customs, architecture, and culture were drawn from shared experiences with the Kazakhs, Kyrgyz, Turkmens, Mongolians, and others. But, in the KUPEH, that history of intercourse with Central Asia was repressed in order to offer a narrative that represented Kashgar only in terms of the Chinese nation.

Here, Ketagalan identity is not only being framed in terms of the nation,[11] but it is also being framed in terms of the global. In other words, the Ketagalans are being authorized by the museum text to participate in world history as Ketagalans, not in reference to any national framework. Ketagalans are conceiving their history as a part of world history. In this passage, they see their history, and themselves, as acting on the world stage. There is no need to frame the Ketagalans in terms of the nation of China or the nation of Taiwan. With their historical subjectivity, Ketagalans are free to participate in the Age of Navigation as Ketagalans with no need to be mediated via the nation.

The museum narrative offered by this half of the Ketagalan Cultural Center has several characteristics. It acknowledges that history is made up of competing narratives and that no single narrative or frame is the correct one. It makes a Foucauldian point that knowledge is produced within institutions that have their own interests and that when the museum text, produced by those institutions, produces history, it necessarily does so in a manner with the "subjective perspective" of an observer. That is to say that the museum text is claiming that there are multiple ways to view history and that each of these perspectives has value. For the Ketagalan Cultural Center, the role of the museum is not to foreclose discussion and determine which perspective is correct, but rather to present competing perspectives and let the individual museum visitor decide what is correct. Thus, the museum is what Hooper-Greenhorn calls polysemous, with multiple understandings of Ketagalan history competing.

So far, I have discussed the half of the museum created by Ketagalan museum creators. But one of the things that is so fascinating about this museum is that it not only acknowledges that there are multiple ways to understand history, but it also actualizes that by allowing two narratives written by two different groups. The narrative discussed above was written by a group claiming to be Ketagalans,[12] but the museum also has a narrative written by the Beitou Environmental Museum Group. The Beitou Environmental Museum Group is a municipal group that has designed several museums in the region just north of Taipei's city center. The museum narrative offered by this group is remarkably different from the one offered by the Ketagalans themselves. The understanding of the Ketagalans offered by the Beitou Environmental Museum Group's narrative is one that is similar to the understanding of the Kashgaris offered in the KUPEH. Despite being in the Ketagalan Cultural Center, the narrative offered by the Beitou Environmental Museum Group does not talk about the Ketagalans specifically. Rather, it offers a narrative that discusses "indigenous peoples" as a single class. Epistemologically, the Beitou Environmental Group's narrative divides its story along the lines of two groups: Han Chinese and indigenous islanders.

In a series of historical passages presented along the same wall, the Beitou Environmental Museum Group's narrative discusses Taiwan's history and the role that indigenous peoples played in that history:

> In 1895, Taiwan was ceded by the Qing Empire to Japan. The indigenous peoples fought against the foreign authority during the Japanese rule. Since the Japanese government intended to colonize Southeast Asia, it developed the economic resources in Taiwan and suppressed the indigenous peoples. As a result, the tribes and clans often defended themselves or rebelled against the Japanese rule.

Though it may be obscure to those less familiar with Taiwanese history, what is happening in this passage would be clear to most Taiwanese readers; indigenous groups are being framed in terms of the history of the Chinese nation. This passage utilizes a vague notion of indigenous people as a single, homogenous category, even though the island's indigenous peoples were constituted by more than a dozen ethnic groups, each conceiving of themselves as separate. This passage conceptualizes these different groups as all fighting against the Japanese to suggest that the Ketagalans and other indigenous groups resisted foreign colonizers because they believed themselves to be part of the Chinese nation.

In terms of basic facts, this passage is quite misleading. Although it is true that during the half century of Japanese rule resistance to the Japanese was, at times, particularly fierce among some of the indigenous Taiwanese ethnic groups, other ethnic groups cooperated with the Japanese. The Beitou Environmental Museum Group's narrative says nothing about the specifics of which groups rebelled against the Japanese and which groups cooperated. Doing so would have required them to seriously discuss the agency that the Ketagalans and other indigenous groups had in history. But the goal of this narrative is to frame the Ketagalans and other groups in terms of how they contribute to the Chinese nation. By paving over any historical specificity, this passage exhibits similarities to the KUPEH in the way that it tries to frame the locals in terms of the nation.

In imagining all indigenous groups as a single, uniform category, this half of the museum demonstrates that it is not understanding the Ketagalans as they would have understood themselves. In the texts produced by the Ketagalans in the other half of the museum, we saw that the text could be quite specific in terms of how the Ketagalans organized themselves in different, smaller groups. This Beitou Environmental Museum Group narrative is offering the museum visitor the less focused perspective of the outsider looking at the indigenous groups and seeing them as all essentially the same. This passage understands the Ketagalans, not on their own terms, but as Han Chinese colonizers to the island would have understood them. In this way, the narrative offered by the Beitou Environmental Museum Group is similar to the narrative offered by the KUPEH, though the former narrative does not go to the extremes that the latter does. If the KUPEH excised Uighurs and other locals from the history of Kashgar, completely replacing Kashgaris with outsiders in the museum narrative, the Beitou Environmental Museum Group's narrative simply adopts the perspective of the outsider when discussing locals.

Finally, this text from the Beitou Environmental Museum Group conceptualizes the Ketagalans and other groups as lacking any historical subjectivity. The Ketagalans' own narrative positioned the Ketagalans as a part of the "Age of Navigation," while this text situates all indigenous groups in terms of Chinese/Taiwanese national resistance to the Japanese. The framework this text offers is the same one that textbooks in Taiwan have offered for years: In 1895, Japan took Taiwan from its rightful owner, the Qing Dynasty, but the Taiwanese, both Han and indigenous groups, resisted this colonialism. Eventually, in 1945, Taiwan was restored to China, where it belonged. The Beitou Environmental Museum Group's narrative offers a form of this narrative. Framing the narrative in this way demonstrates that the Beitou Environmental Museum Group conceptualized the indigenous people as just another part of the Chinese/Taiwanese nation, not as a group with autonomy and historical subjectivity.

In all these elements, the narrative offered by the Beitou Environmental Museum Group seems redolent of the KUPEH. It offers a factually challengeable reading of history, one that paves over differences between local indigenous groups and conceptualizes all these groups in the frame of the nation. Like the narrative offered in the KUPEH, the narrative offered in the half of the museum written by the Beitou Environmental Museum Group denies any historical subjectivity to the Ketagalans, even going so far as to avoid mentioning the Ketagalans as an individual group in most of their text. These characteristics of this narrative contrast quite starkly with the Ketagalan-created narrative in the first half of the museum, which constructs the Ketagalans as an autonomous group with historical subjectivity. The differences between these two narratives might seem to undercut my thesis that Taiwanese museum narratives reflect the moral order, since the former narrative has so many of the elements of the Kasghari museum's construction of a moral community.

In fact, both the narrative offered by the Ketagalans and the narrative offered by the Beitou Environmental Museum Group reflect Taiwan's status as a moral order. As I mentioned in the historical background section of the chapter, Taiwan, before the 1980s, was constructed as a moral community, and, certainly, many elements of the latter half of the museum are remnants of that ideology built on the moral community. But the fact that this narrative is presented alongside the Ketagalans' own narrative establishes the museum as a space of the moral order, not the moral community. The juxtaposition of these two narratives, competing with each other in a shared space, is emblematic of the moral order that Taiwan is building. The Taiwanese state and society are the products of multiple competing understandings of the world and Taiwan's place in that world. As a moral order, no narrative is imposed from above. Competing narratives can exist because there is no need, as in an illiberal state, to impose a common weltanschauung for the state's legitimacy. Ideas can compete with each other side by side, allowing the visitor to decide which narrative they find most convincing.

## CONCLUSION

These two museums, the KUPEH and the Ketagalan Cultural Center, are emblematic of many of the museums in China and Taiwan. In China, museums have become one of the most important mechanisms for imposing the collectivist narrative in order to construct the moral community. The KUPEH offers only a single voice—a single narrative of its history and its people. The museum narrative must be a text that forecloses other interpretive possibilities because to allow for any interpretive freedom would quickly undermine the moral community and jeopardize the ideological claim that the museum is making: the region is, always has been, and always will be owned by the Han Chinese moral community. In the Ketagalan Cultural Center, multiple voices and multiple narratives are authorized to speak within the space of the museum. Reflecting Taiwan's democratic society, there is no single right answer. Rather, visitors are allowed to move through the narrative as if they were voters; each is presented with multiple claims by competing narratives, and the visitor is allowed to choose what they think is most correct. In this way, these museums become what Umberto Eco calls "epistemological metaphors" (Eco 1989, 78). In their formal aspects, these museum texts reproduce aspects of the society that forms them. The differences between these two museums are emblematic of the differences between China and Taiwan.

China is a moral community—in which all politics and economics are controlled by the state—where political expressions must be in line with the views expressed by the Han Chinese moral community (as embodied institutionally in the CCP). In the Chinese museum, the ways of interpreting Kashgar's history are severely circumscribed. The CCP's interpretation of Kashgar's history is the only "correct" version of that history. If that understanding flies in the face of the lived facts that any visitor could see walking outside the museum—that the region is a Central Asian society—then so be it. The KUPEH replicates the Buchananian moral community in the narrative form of the museum. Because the Chinese state is representing all of China as a Han Chinese moral community, the museum narrative erases the Uighur populace of Kashgar from the narrative of Kashgar's history, discussing only the few Han Chinese figures who have come to Kashgar to conquer it. This move is the kind of move a Buchananian moral community would make; a single group offers moral recognition to those in the group but not those outside the group.

Conversely, Taiwan is a moral order, in which both politics and economics are relatively free, political parties compete for the support of the individual voter, and businesses compete for the individual consumer. By allowing for narratives to compete within the same space, the Ketagalan Cultural Center replicates that dynamic, allowing the narratives to compete in the marketplace of ideas. The Ketagalan museum exemplifies the moral order of Taiwan's democracy. This is not a dictatorial narrative style, where a top-down authority is instructing museum visitors on what to think. Rather, this museum allows for multiple narratorial voices to contest each other in the same museum. Different perspectives on this ethnic group's role in Taiwanese society are allowed to compete with each other for the visitors' attention, mirroring the moral order present in democratic societies, where leaders compete for the attention and loyalty of voters.

The broader implication of this chapter is that the museum has become a space where two conceptualizations of society, the moral community and the moral order, are competing in China and Taiwan. China's use of museums to construct a moral community increasingly threatens the liberty of its citizens, particularly minority citizens like the Uighurs. What Hayek called "the freedom to be different" is increasingly reduced. As China has increasingly become an authoritarian society, the museum has become the medium by which the state inculcates Chinese nationalism into its citizens.

The past half decade has proved Buchanan and Hayek's expectations that a moral community will descend into violence against minorities as correct. The CCP is increasingly closing off any expression of identity in Xinjiang that does not fit within the CCP's vision of the Han Chinese moral community. In the past three years, the CCP has constructed a gulag archipelago to house one to three million Xinjiang Muslims. Most of the gulag prisoners have been imprisoned for little more than expressing religious belief: having a beard, wearing a veil, or refusing to drink alcohol or eat pork. These acts have all become criminalized because they are acts the state has deemed not to fit within the moral community. The museum, and the moral community it sought to instantiate, was a prelude to the genocide we are witnessing today.

Likewise, Taiwan increasingly uses museums to embody the democratic ideals of a moral order. In Taiwanese museums, polysemous narratives allow the museum visitor to evaluate the facts presented and make their own decision based on the evidence. Although Buchanan and Hayek never discussed museums as institutions that could embody their liberal ideals and their illiberal fears, this chapter has sought to demonstrate that, in China and Taiwan, museums are the space where the moral community and the moral order are most clearly articulated.

## NOTES

1. For the sake of clarity, I would like to specify that I am using the word "nation" in its Weberian sense. "A nation is a common bond of sentiment whose adequate expression would be a state of its own, and which therefore normally tends to give birth to such a state." My understanding of the nation does not conceive of nations as always manifest in the form of a state, and oftentimes the state is quite different from the nation, something that common usage's equation of the state with the nation paves over. For more discussion of the Weberian sense of nation, see Smith (1999, 105).

2. For more on the discussion of the shift to nationalism and its relevance to museums see Varutti (2011, 306). For more on the general shift toward nationalism after 1989, see Zha (1998, 20), and Langfitt (2019, 157).

3. The KMT is the standard way to refer in English to this political party. This is the name still used by this party today. The abbreviation is the romanized version of the Chinese word "国民党" or the "Kuo Min Tang." Sometimes, this is abbreviated

as GMD, and sometimes they are referred to as the "Nationalist Party." Because of the many names used to refer to this political party, I have used the most common form of this party's name.

4. Note here, that I am not claiming that I believe that China is the state with the legitimate claim to Taiwan. I am only claiming that, in 1945, the United States claimed that China was the sole state with the right to exercise sovereignty over Taiwan. In 1943, the United States government affirmed that it believed that Taiwan was rightfully the property of the Chinese when it, as a part of the Cairo Declaration, stated that United States and United Kingdom policy was that "all the territories Japan has stolen from the Chinese, such as Manchuria, Formosa [Taiwan], and the Pescadores, shall be restored to the Republic of China." See Roy (2003, 56).

5. This statistic is drawn from the museum itself and is also the only time the word Uighur is used in the museum text.

6. All texts from museums that are discussed in this chapter are drawn from my personal visits to the museum and the photographic archive of museums that I hold.

7. The state is the king's body.

8. Of course, in the records of Xinjiang, there are numerous reports of locals talking about their oasis cities. These are, not surprisingly, significantly more numerous than those Chinese-language sources talking about these oasis cities. For more discussion of this, see Valerie Hansen's (2016) discussion of the matter.

9. Confusingly, the Han Dynasty is a historical dynasty from which the ethnic designation Han Chinese is derived. The Han Dynasty does not necessarily map neatly onto the Han ethnic group, although many contemporary Han Chinese nationalists imagine that the two terms are equivalent.

10. This is not a full quote of the passage on the Taiwanese sign. In other passages of the sign quoted above, the text provides more concrete examples of Ketagalan Culture.

11. Other passages discuss the Ketagalans' relationships with Han Chinese colonizers, but, due to limits of space, I will not quote those passages.

12. Keep in mind, few Taiwanese people identify as fully Ketagalan, as the ethnic group intermarried heavily with Han Chinese colonists for the past two centuries.

# REFERENCES

Aronsson, Peter. 2011. "Explaining National Museums: Exploring Comparative Approaches to the Study of National Museums." In *National Museums: New Studies from around the World*, edited by Simon J. Knell, 29–54. New York: Routledge.

Buchanan, James M. 2001. *The Collected Works of James M. Buchanan, Volume 17: Moral Science and Moral Order*. Indianapolis: Liberty Fund.

Duara, Prasenjit. 1995. *Rescuing History from the Nation: Questioning Narratives of Modern China*. Chicago: University of Chicago Press.

Eco, Umberto. 1989. *The Open Work*. Cambridge, MA: Harvard University Press.

Elliott, Jeannette Shambaugh. 2005. *The Odyssey of China's Imperial Art Treasures*. Seattle: University of Washington Press.

Hansen, Valerie. 2016. *The Silk Road: A New History with Documents*. Oxford: Oxford University Press.

Hayek, F. A. [1944] 2008. *The Road to Serfdom: Texts and Documents: The Definitive Edition*. Edited by Bruce Caldwell. New York: Routledge.

———. 1988. *The Fatal Conceit: The Errors of Socialism*. Edited by William Warren Bartley, III. Chicago: University of Chicago Press.

Ho, Dahpon David. 2006. "To Protect and Preserve: Resisting the Destroy the Four Olds Campaign, 1966–1967." In *The Chinese Cultural Revolution as History*, edited by Joseph Esherick, Paul Pickowicz, and Andrew Walder, 64–95. Stanford, CA: Stanford University Press.

Hooper-Greenhill, Eilean, ed. 1995. *Museum, Media, Message*. London: Routledge.

Kashgar City Network. 2015. "Kashgar East Lake, you have completely changed (喀什东湖，你彻底变了)." December 25. https://www.toutiao.com/i6232182206677123586/.

Langfitt, Frank. 2019. *Shanghai Free Taxi: Journeys with the Hustlers and Rebels of the New China*. New York: Public Affairs.

Millward, James. 2009. "Positioning Xinjiang in Eurasian and Chinese History: Differing Visions of the Silk Road." In *China, Xinjiang and Central Asia: History, Transition and Crossborder Interaction into the 21st Century*, edited by Colin Mackerras and Michael Clarke, 55–74. London and New York: Routledge.

Moses, Dirk. 2010. *Empire, Colony, Genocide: Conquest, Occupation and Subaltern Resistance in World History*. New York: Berghahn.

Newby, Laura. 1996. "Xinjiang: In Search of an Identity." In *Unity and Diversity: Local Cultures and Identities in China*, edited by Tao Tao Liu and David Faure, 67–81. Hong Kong: Hong Kong University Press.

Roy, Denny. 2003. *Taiwan: A Political History*. Ithaca, NY: Cornell University Press.

Smith, Anthony. 1999. *Myths and Memories of the Nation*. New York: Oxford University Press.

Teng, Emma. 2006. *Taiwan's Imagined Geography: Chinese Colonial Travel Writing and Pictures, 1683–1895*. Cambridge, MA.: Harvard University Press.

Varutti, Marzia. 2011. "The Aesthetics and Narratives of National Museums in China." In *National Museums: New Studies from around the World*, edited by Simon J. Knell, 302–312. New York: Routledge.

Wills, John. 1994. *Mountain of Fame: Portraits in Chinese History*. Princeton: Princeton University Press.

Xinhua News Agency. 2019. "2018年我国新增1亿多人次'打卡'博物馆." May 18. http://www.gov.cn/xinwen/2019-05/18/content_5392777.htm.

Zha, Jianying. 1998. *China Pop: How Soap Operas, Tabloids, and Bestsellers Are Transforming a Culture*. New York: New Press.

Zhou, Guoxing. 2005. "The Rise, Fall and Resurrection of the Nantong Museum (南通博物苑兴衰与复兴)." In *Nantong Centennial Celebration Documents* (I南通博物苑百年苑慶紀念文集), edited by Yihai Wang, 70–83. Beijing: Wenwu Chubanshe.

*Chapter 9*

# The Haider Phenomenon and the Rise of Austrian Neoliberalism

Valentina Ausserladscheider

During the late 1980s and throughout the 1990s, the leader of Austria's far right party was described as "the most controversial politician in Austria today—Jörg Haider, leader of one of the most successful right-wing parties in Europe" (Sully 1997, ix). Due to the attention that Haider received as the leader of the party, media and other commentators spoke about the "Haider party" instead of its actual name: the Austrian Freedom Party (FPÖ). While the party alone is subject to much debate due to its Nazi founders and its connections to the neo-Nazi fringes, the so-called "Haider phenomenon" (Sully 1997) stirred the controversy further. The ascribed "charismatic personality" of the party leader is often interpreted as the main reason for the success of far-right parties (Wodak, KhosraviNik, and Mral 2013, xviii). Indeed, scholars speak about the "Haiderization of Europe," whereby they describe the way in which Haider's forms and styles of political rhetoric have been adapted by other European far-right parties and thus led to their increasing electoral success (ibid., xvii).

Haider introduced new policy positions into the party competition of Austrian politics in 1986–1999 and applied new models of political communication (ibid., xxii). Literature on political entrepreneurship (e.g., De Vries and Hobolt 2020) would identify Haider's electoral success of 1999 in bringing the FPÖ, traditionally an opposition party, into government as a successful *political entrepreneur*. Applying the existing conceptualizations of political entrepreneurship onto "the Haider phenomenon" implies that Haider was able to most efficiently capture votes with the goal of maximizing his rent-seeking opportunity (Tullock 2004, 52; McCaffrey and Salerno 2011, 553). Simultaneously, findings of recent scholarship argue that the success of far-right politics is due to a cultural backlash against globalization, immigration, and multiculturalism. This means that Haider's entrepreneurship manifested in offering the "right" nationalist, culturally conservative, and anti-immigration policy positions at the right time to capture voters. This, theoretically, enabled him to pursue his vested interests in the 2000 Austrian government.

The newly established government should also mean the end of Austria's exceptionally strong welfare state, protection against international competition, and extensive market regulations; Austria can now be categorized as "neoliberal mainstream," which in comparison to other European countries presents a latecomer to the neoliberal policy era. The transformation toward neoliberalism was slow and started when the first austerity package was decided in 1987 under social-democratic leadership. Further facilitation of changes to these institutional arrangements happened due to Austria's accession to the European Union (EU) in 1995. This led to further Europeanization and internationalization, and Austria's capital profited immensely from the access to Eastern markets (Hermann and Flecker 2012, 121–22). Yet, the "turn-of-century-coalition" signifies the arrival of neoliberalism in Austria most clearly (Preglau 2001).

The rise of neoliberalism has been studied extensively and scholarship made an important contribution in identifying the role of ideas in changing political economies. Neoliberalism did not simply succeed prior models of governance such as the communist regime in Eastern Europe (Aligica and Evans 2009) or the "embedded liberalism" in Anglo-Saxon countries (Hall 1993; Hay 1996). Instead, neoliberal ideas slowly spread across epistemic communities as economic theory and throughout political rhetoric as doctrine, which suggested the normative value of neoliberal policies. Eventually the neoliberal policy paradigm found its implementation across most European and American countries. While studies have shown that neoliberalism was also institutionalized in Austria, there is no account of how neoliberal ideas were initially introduced.

This chapter suggests that the Haider phenomenon and the rise of Austrian neoliberalism are deeply intertwined phenomena. I will show this based on Haider's political entrepreneurship that lay in the discursive construction of "the winning formula": authoritarian, nationalist, and nativist values combined with a neoliberal agenda (Kitschelt 2004). By highlighting the often-neglected neoliberal ideas in the FPÖ's program, I show how Haider's entrepreneurship goes beyond the capture of voters' cultural backlash and paved the way to Austria's neoliberal turn. The contributions of this chapter are twofold in seeking to answer *how and when particular cultural and economic far-right programs become successful through the political entrepreneurship of their far-right politicians*. I first show the importance of the ideational context and ideas more generally for far-right political entrepreneurship. Second, I show the usefulness of applying the concept of political entrepreneurship to the understanding of ideational change.

The chapter proceeds as follows. The next section explores literature on political entrepreneurship, the rise of the far right, and the role of ideas in changing political economies. Then, the chapter explains how we can build a theory of ideational political entrepreneurship by studying successful far-right party discourse. After discussing the methodological approach of a descriptive analysis, the chapter provides two empirical sections that identify the pattern with the discourse of Haider's FPÖ from 1983–1999, shortly before its election into government. A concluding section summarizes the findings and draws once again on the connections between political entrepreneurship, ideational change, and Haider's rise to power.

## FAR-RIGHT POLITICAL ENTREPRENEURSHIP AND THE ROLE OF IDEAS

### The Cultural Element of Far-Right Political Entrepreneurship

> Culture is the language in which past events are interpreted, future circumstances are anticipated, and plans of action are formulated. Although not a language in the sense of a static set of words and grammatical rules, culture is a discourse. (Lavoie 2015, 49)

Scholars such as Don Lavoie and Virgil Storr successfully disenchant the rationalist dream of economists who sought to conceptualize economic development through entrepreneurship that simply finds the "best" solution, good, or organizing principle (Grube and Storr 2015). Instead, culture refers to "the subjective meaning that goods have to people, not the objective economic circumstances and causal processes with which economic science is concerned" (Lavoie 2015, 50). Lavoie and Storr show how the process of entrepreneurial action is necessarily one that is deeply embedded in culture through language, interpretation, anticipation, and formulation (see Grube and Storr 2015). The authors, thus, successfully enrich the understanding of entrepreneurship in the context of economic markets by explaining that culture and economic rationale are not mutually exclusive.

Even though it is well established that culture is a constitutive element of economic entrepreneurship, literature on political entrepreneurship remains set on its rationalist assumption: politicians' activities are "targeted at increasing the likelihood of being reelected and improving their standing in the political system" (Trofimov 2017, 2). These politicians thereby "go about acquiring income through the perception and exploitation of rent-seeking opportunities" (McCaffrey and Salerno 2011, 553). In this reading, politicians articulate their program in order to capture more votes to gain political power and subsequently pursue rent-seeking opportunities more effectively. This is what scholars of the Virginia School of Political Economy find most worrisome about majority voting in democracy (Tullock 2004). Gordon Tullock problematizes that "the 'entrepreneurs' who offer candidates or programs to the voter make up a complex mix of policies to attract support" while keeping "firmly in mind the fact that the voter may be so interested in the outcome of some issue that he will vote for the party which supports it, although the party opposes him on other issues" (Tullock 2004, 52). Especially economic policies, which promise increasing wages and redistributive measures for "the people"—often described as economic populism (Dornbusch and Edwards 1991; Rodrik 2018)—are argued to seek the mobilization of more voters in order to gain greater political power.

This notion of political entrepreneurship is based on the assumption that political entrepreneurs predominantly orient their program to capture public opinion. While "political parties follow a vote-maximizing logic" (de Lange 2007, 413), their electoral success and strategies are not solely determined by voters' ideological positions. Instead, "they position themselves in a distinct part of the competitive space" (ibid., 413), and thus, their positions are also dependent on the ideological spectrum of the broader party competition. Therefore, political entrepreneurs cannot be assumed to operate in a political vacuum. They navigate existing "ideological fields" in which they try to fill "voids in the competitive space" (ibid., 413).

Let us consider the recent phenomenon of far-right parties gaining electoral support across the globe. Successful far-right political parties have been shown to use all sorts of economic policies to mobilize a broader spectrum of voters (Mudde 2007; Rovyn and Polk 2020). Far-right economic programs are chaotic and combine seemingly immiscible positions: free markets, privatization, deregulation, lower taxation, and welfarism as well as anti-welfarism (Mudde 2007, 119). These programs also exhibit an "opaque economic profile" (Rovny and Polk 2020, 248). Scholars subsequently have argued that the main political entrepreneurial strategy of far-right parties is their cultural program. Their nationalist and nativist core ideology (Mudde 2007) is their main "selling point" because it speaks to a cultural backlash from voters against globalization, immigration, and the perceived threat to their cultural identities (Inglehart and Norris 2016).

Cultural backlash theorists make an important contribution in identifying the centrality of cultural values, national identities, and traditional norms in far-right parties' programs and success. Cultural backlash scholars conclude that economic policy positions in far-right programs and the socioeconomic context of voters are therefore secondary to the phenomenon of rising far-right politics (Inglehart and Norris 2016, 21). This approach to the study of far-right parties places selective emphasis on immigration and other cultural issues. Far-right parties are, however, no "single-issue organizations" and "strenuously endeavor to come across as credible actors in different policy areas" while bringing "new attention to socioeconomic issues" (Pirro 2017, 339). Additionally, cultural values and economic actions are not disparate variables, but instead, "culture shapes and is shaped by economic activity" (Aligica and Matei 2015, 295). Hence, we cannot assume that far-right political entrepreneurship is purely based on economic programs to suggest economic populism or cultural programs to capture cultural backlash sentiments.

This raises the question of *how and when particular cultural and economic far-right programs become successful through the political entrepreneurship of its far-right politicians*? This question I seek to answer by investigating "the winning formula" that many scholars attributed to the success of far-right parties in the 1980s and 1990s: the combination of authoritarian, nationalist, and nativist positions with neoliberal policy advocacy (Betz 2002; Kitschelt 2004; Kitschelt and McGann 1997). These positions are measured on two-dimensional scales: socialist-capitalist and libertarian-authoritarian (de Lange 2007). On the first dimension a party position that is socialist would favor "political redistribution of economic resources," while a capitalist party position would favor "market allocation" (ibid., 419). Indicators such as privatization, attitudes toward the public sector, the welfare and social security systems, the labor market, taxation, budget and financial deficits, and trade and enterprise policies should measure parties' positions on that scale. For the second dimension, indicators such as citizenship and ethnocultural relations, individual freedom, and collective decision modes are assessed to measure parties' positions on the libertarian-authoritarian scale (de Lange 2007, 420). Following this research design, far-right parties are placed closer to the capitalist and authoritarian poles. While this research design is still prevalent in political science studies to measure party positions, I find that political discourse is more complex than those indicators suggest. Often the interpretation of discourse through these indicators would place the FPÖ on both scales on contradicting poles. Yet, there is a clear pattern in the FPÖ's discourse and the indicators are a helpful guide to contextualizing the FPÖ's position in the broader ideological landscape.

Jörg Haider, the leader of the far-right FPÖ, enjoyed unprecedented success with this "formula" throughout the 1990s culminating in the 1999 electoral win and the subsequent governmental participation from 2000 to 2006. His political style and success have been described as "the Haider phenomenon," a narrative seeking to capture his character as "the Gladiator" and "the Entertainer" (Sully 1997). A broader conceptualization of far-right political entrepreneurs describes the "agility" with which these entrepreneurs are "defying traditional ways of doing politics" (De Vries and Hobolt 2020, 7). Political science scholars credit him with "the Haiderization of Europe," by which they describe how his political style, charisma, and strategy in rhetoric were adopted by far-right politicians across Europe (Wodak, KhosraviNik, and Mral 2013)—a real political entrepreneur, if you will. The success of Haider's FPÖ happened during a time of economic instability (Sully 1997), the dismantling of the Keynesian policy era of demand management (Hall 1993; Hay 1996), changing electoral constituencies (Plasser, Ulram, and Sommer 2000), and the rise of neoliberalism across Europe (Aligica and Evans 2009).

## Political Entrepreneurship and the Role of Ideas

The demise of Keynesianism and the subsequent rise of neoliberalism (Hall 1993; Hay 1996) have been studied extensively as fundamental societal transformation. These transformations are always preceded and accompanied by specific sets of ideas that formulate a particular policy paradigm (Hall 1993). While focusing on specific epistemic communities in Eastern European countries at the end of the communist regime, Aligica and Evans (2009) seek to answer how and why "economic ideas spread or die?" (Aligica and Evans 2009, 2). The authors convincingly show how the "change in the realm of beliefs was the precondition and one of the major forces that set into motion the changes leading to the collapse of the communist regime and the emergence on its ruins of the liberal order" (ibid., 1). This is not only important in the context of Eastern Europe, but more generally, "in order to understand institutional change it is crucial to explore why and how actors change their explicit or implicit views about what they see as a problem and its solution" (ibid., 2). Hay (1996) notes that this change of view requires an active discursive intervention, which renders the existing institutional arrangement useless and that in "such a moment of crisis, a particular type of decisive intervention was called for" (ibid., 253).

Similar to the need of going beyond the rationalist assumption on entrepreneurship, Aligica and Evans (2009) go beyond the rationalist equilibrium assumption of institutional change. In the Eastern European case, many scholars argue that the transformation to a liberal order is "self-explanatory" because the communist regime fared poorly economically. Instead, the work of Aligica and Evans (2009), "while accepting this simple but robust interpretation, goes beyond it and focuses at a deeper level by taking a closer look at a number of complex institutional and ideational processes involved" (2). It is not simply the "best" idea that becomes dominant, but instead, specific sets of ideas have to be institutionalized. The institutionalization of new ideas happens through the process of *normativization* followed by *normalization*

(Hay 2004, 500). In the first step, political actors present ideas as normatively superior by suggesting their problem-solving capacities in political rhetoric (ibid., 502). The second stage is concerned with the practical implementation of specific policies in the "normal" policymaking process (Hall 1993).

Aligica and Evans (2009) place special importance on social scientific and philosophical ideas in this process, which is why the authors study epistemic communities or "professional scholars dealing with economic theory and policy issues" (Aligica and Evans 2009, 7). Despite their theoretical and social scientific nature, these ideas also "inform and shape the way politics is done" (ibid., 2). They define "the interests that political actors articulate and the strategy they use to defend these interests" (ibid., 2). This has an important implication for a theory of political entrepreneurship: political entrepreneurs do not operate in a political vacuum. They operate in a "marketplace of ideas" (ibid., 83–105), in which they choose from a range of ideas to advance their political ambition. These entrepreneurs act in the context of institutional arrangements that have particular sets of ideas attached. The "entrepreneurial act" lies in the attempt to change these arrangements in articulating new or different ideas.

The set of "new" ideas in which Aligica and Evans (2009) are interested have "been labeled in various ways: Economic Rationalism, Monetarism, Thatcherism, Reaganomics, Neoconservativism, Managerialism, Contractualism, Washington Consensus, and Market Fundamentalism." These labels "have been condensed under the banner of 'neoliberalism'" (ibid., 3). While these various labels reflect some ideological biases and analytical assumptions, all of them capture a particular relationship between markets and the state. In this relationship, economic and social problems are suggested to "have a market solution, with the corollary that state failure is typically worse than market failure" (ibid., 3). Neoliberalism as a doctrine and practice thus undermines the legitimacy and efficacy of "big government." It also advocates for market deregulation, state decentralization, minimizing state intervention in the economy, and privatizing state industries and public services, thereby abolishing "dependency cultures" (ibid).

Aligica and Evans (2009) make an important contribution in showing the role of epistemic communities in spreading these ideas throughout Eastern European countries toward the end of the communist regime. But they remain on the "theoretical level" because they study the political economy theories popular among the communities in question—the "academic entrepreneurship," if you will. This chapter takes their insights as a point of departure and seeks to highlight the role of political entrepreneurs in the rise of neoliberal ideas based on the program of Haider's FPÖ from 1986 to 1999. While Haider's entrepreneurship is often based on its culturally exclusionary, nationalist, and nativist policy positions or his rhetorical style only, this chapter illustrates how his neoliberal agenda complemented the party program in constructing the "winning formula": the combination of neoliberal and authoritarian appeals (Kitschelt and McGann 1997). Ultimately, this program presents the process of *normativization* of neoliberalism, which paved the way for the neoliberal turn and *normalization* of neoliberal policymaking in Austrian politics through the 2000–2006 government.

## Building a Theory of Ideational Political Entrepreneurship

This chapter provides a theory of ideational political entrepreneurship by offering a descriptive account (Gerring 2012) of Haider's program during his leadership of the FPÖ. Instead of the "traditional interpretation" of political entrepreneurship, which emphasizes the potential rent-seeking opportunities that Haider might have pursued with his program, I provide an account of the ideational novelty that his program exhibited. With access to the archives of the manifesto project, I apply text analysis to the party manifestos of 1986– 1999 and other publications from the FPÖ's website. The empirical section showcases some of the analyzed material for exemplification of the FPÖ's discourse, which I have translated from German into English.

In addition, I describe the contextual factors to highlight that this entrepreneurial act is situated and potentially enabled through a time of rapidly changing foundations of the international political economy: the demise of Keynesianism and communism and the rise of neoliberalism. In doing so, I offer an empirical account of the advent of neoliberal ideas in Austrian politics. Even though this study is of descriptive nature, it is also analytical as it builds on the theoretical framework of Aligica and Evan's (2009) account on the role of ideas and Hay's (1996) approach to institutional change as decisive discursive intervention. This allows me to pinpoint which ideas are constitutive of Haider's entrepreneurship. To be clear, I do not attempt building a causal relationship as to *why* Haider took particular positions or *why* these positions were electorally appealing, but instead seek to understand *which* ideas and *when* they became entrepreneurially successful.

## THE CRISIS OF AUSTRO-KEYNESIANISM AND THE CONSTRUCTION OF THE WINNING FORMULA

Before Haider's accession of FPÖ leadership in 1986, Austria's political economy experienced the tail end of the Keynesian policy era. While the paradigm shift to more restrictive monetary policies and supply-side economics happened in the late 1970s in most countries (most notably the United Kingdom and the United States), Austria held onto its own brand of Keynesianism under the socialist Chancellor Kreisky until the mid-1980s. The so-called "Kreisky era" with its "Austro-Keynesian" strategy shaped the dominant policy paradigm from 1970 until 1983, when the Socialist Party of Austria (SPÖ) lost majority in government and Kreisky stepped back from his roles in Austrian politics. The "Austrian way" of Keynesianism prioritized, just like "conventional Keynesianism," full employment through countercyclical budget politics. Instead of accepting high inflation rates, however, Austria pursued price stability through fixed exchange rates and the involvement of the Austrian central bank and social partners (Mesch 2018). The central bank was a supporter of Austria's "hard currency policy" (Gnan 1994, 5) and the social partners ensured that wages remained competitive and production oriented (Mesch 2018). This strategy is assumed to have allowed Austria to hold onto the Keynesian strategy for longer despite the international economic turmoil at the time (ibid.).

However, Austria did not endure the economic turbulences of the 1970s and 1980s without consequences. The dollar depreciation in 1971, the breakdown of the Bretton Woods system, the first oil shock in 1973, the subsequent economic recession of 1974–1975, the second oil shock of 1979–1981, the next ensuing recession in 1981–1982, and multiple currency exchange shocks also affected Austria severely (ibid.). The first oil shock led to an inflation rate of 9.5 percent in 1974. Kreisky's countercyclical budget policy led to immense amounts of debt, especially in the years of recession. Austria's indebtedness grew from 18.5 percent of GDP in 1970 to 43.5 percent in 1983, which was above the European average at the time (ibid.). In addition, strongly subsidized sectors such as the steel industry remained nationalized, which led to great disadvantages in the increasingly international market competition due to the lack of innovation (ibid.). Eventually, the increasing debt, the mounting inflation, and the uncompetitive nationalized industries marked the beginning of the end for Austro-Keynesianism.

In September 1986, Jörg Haider took over the party leadership of the FPÖ while Austria underwent some fundamental changes to its political economy. The fear of inflation drove most OECD countries as well as the Austrian government to exercise restrictive monetary policies (WIFO 1983, 145). Austria's unemployment rate was on the rise and the Austrian government attempted to reduce its debt through the "Mallorca package"—an austerity package introduced in 1982. Public opinion of this mixture was poor, and it led to the end of the SPÖ's majority government (Zöllner 1990, 552). Even though GDP grew by 2.9 percent in 1985 based on exports as well as domestic demand (WIFO 1986, 220), Austria's economic situation remained difficult. State-owned companies reported high losses demanding partial privatization (Zöllner 1990, 552), and the unemployment rate increased further (WIFO 1986, 220). The dissatisfaction among voters and the continuing economic turmoil presented the perfect window of opportunity for political and electoral change. It was the FPÖ under Jörg Haider that understood this window of opportunity to effectively mobilize upon and persuade many formerly socialist constituencies as the table 9.1 shows.

Table 9.1.   Compiled List of General Election Outcomes FPÖ 1983–1999

| Year | 1983 | 1986 | 1990 | 1994 | 1995 | 1999 |
|---|---|---|---|---|---|---|
| Election Result | 5% | 9.7% | 16.6% | 22.5% | 21.9% | 26.9% |

*Source:* Bundesministerium für Inneres

## Instrumentalizing the Crisis of Austro-Keynesianism

When Jörg Haider assumed leadership of the FPÖ, commentators spoke about a "swing to the right" (Zöllner 1990, 552). The FPÖ itself celebrates this development in its leaflet depicting the party's history as the "start of the rise to a major party" (Info-Compact 2017, 6). Others describe the change of leadership as the introduction of a "new brand of right radical populism with its sound-bite rhetoric which went directly to the heart of people's needs and worries" (Sully 1997, 1). Under Haider, the FPÖ started to gain electoral support "in provincial elections and later bit into depressed industrial areas with rising unemployment. . . . Many workers, especially in run-down nationalized industries, felt they had been left in the lurch by the socialists" (ibid., 4). It was especially the "traditionally loyal working-class districts" where "the socialists suffered humiliating defeats" (ibid., 5).

Haider's FPÖ was able to capitalize on this window of opportunity presented by the slow demise of "Kreisky's era" and its Austro-Keynesian policy paradigm. This electoral development clearly reflects the ideational entrepreneurship, with which Haider "reformed" the FPÖ. The disillusioned voters "warmed to the aggressive class-warfare language of the Freedom Party which stood up against the 'penthouse trade unionists' with their fat salaries" (ibid., 4). Haider's ideas systematically constructed a crisis around the different dimensions and the ideas associated with the dominant Austro-Keynesian policy paradigm: the socialist government, the strong unions, the taxation regime, governmental debt, and the grand coalition that followed the socialist government. Simultaneously, Haider's FPÖ used this context and the critical framing of the socialist government to introduce new policy positions on immigration and European integration.

## The Socialist Government as Ideological Threat

Haider's critique of the socialist government that was in power from 1970 to 1983 rests on a deliberation about its underlying ideology and the threats of such. Even though the discursive critique is rooted in this particular era, the critique extends beyond the period of the socialist government and is visible in the FPÖ's discourse throughout Haider's leadership. While the socialists remain the primary source of crisis, similar discursive attacks also extend to the conservative party known as the Austrian People's Party (ÖVP) that forms the government with the SPÖ from 1987 to 2000. In order to construct this crisis of Austria's socialist government, the FPÖ's discourse during Haider's leadership makes use of narratives, collective memories, frames, and normative arguments. Collective memories legitimize policy actions through memories of previous events. Narratives shape the understanding of events. Frames establish different guideposts for knowledge that "serve to orient different understandings and actions" (Schmidt 2014, 191), and normative arguments "attach values to action and serve to legitimize ideas" (Schmidt 2014, 193).

> We stand at the end of the 20th century. It was a century of totalitarian wrong tacks and inhumane doctrines of salvation. One could believe that with the breakdown of the real socialism in Eastern Europe the last evil has been buried and freedom as well as peace are therefore automatically granted. This is a great misconception. The probation for democracy and liberal constitutions is coming only now. George Orwell with his book "1984" warned us in time. Totalitarianism, threats to freedom and autonomy, and authoritarian oppression of freedom of speech no longer need monopoly over violence, secret agents, police states, and concentration camps such as the archetypal gulag. The methods are different, they became more subversive. The threat of the freedom of the citizens is not obvious, but therefore much more effective. The threat also for our democracy today lies in the creation of a standardized society, in which politically prescribed standardization carries validity. Is this not the case? Whoever has access to mass media, access or manifested its power. "THE ONE WHO DEFINES THE TERMS, CONTROLS THE THOUGHT." The one who defines the terms, controls the thought. There, prejudices are built, "misnomers" are societally ostracized, important things are made politically taboo, and untruths become dogmas. . . . the socialism in Austria is captured by its power trip. Why shouldn't it be possible for the socialists to establish themselves as leading power as a united party and direct the democracy towards their imaginations? (FPÖ 1994)

The introductory narrative of the 1994 manifesto illustrates the ideological critique of the socialist government well. In this narrative of the twentieth century and its authoritarian and totalitarian ideologies, the socialist government's leading power is framed through the collective memory of the threat and the decline of Eastern European "real socialism." Thereby, the discourse establishes a direct equation of the possibility of the Austrian socialists to enact similar authoritarian oppression, capture the monopoly over violence, and build concentration camps. The narrative continues in showcasing how the power capture of the socialists is more subversive in that day due to the misconceived belief that freedom and democracy solve all these ills. Finally, the frame of "control" orients the understanding of socialist policies to be policies that do not allow for counter arguments or other ideologies and are based on prejudices.

> Our liberal ideas stem from the protest against authoritarian relations. The abso-lutism led to democracy over the year of 1848, where we have our ideological roots. Just like at that time, we protest today for the liberties of our citizens. And this liberty is in danger, even if some in welfare mentality do not want to see it. The socialism has the power in government, in ORF, in the constitutional court, in law, in the Austrian central bank, in postal services, in housing cooperatives, in cultural politics, in unions, and social insurances. And after the dramatic fail-ure of nationalized industries, they build [banks, holdings]. . . . All of this needs to be paid by taxpayers. (FPÖ 1994)

The "subversive" power capture is here exemplified and applied to the social-ists' economic policies: the way the Austrian central bank, housing, nation-alized companies, and unions are organized. The taxpayers are presented to be the ones who have to pay for this malfunctioning organization. Through the framing of "control" that takes away citizens' freedom and liberties, the FPÖ accuses the socialists of selling their policies under the guise of "welfare mentality." This narrative proves to be powerful due to the noticeable policy anomalies that Haider successfully blames on the "socialists" (who changed their name to the Social Democratic Party of Austria in 1991) despite their coalition with the conservatives. However, the key is the link within the nar-rative whereby Haider suggests that it is the Austrian taxpayers who suffer from this. This shows the way in which Haider's discourse seeks to mobilize bottom-up legitimacy for his vision of Austria.

> The ideological coordinates have moved so far to the left in recent years, that the position in the middle seems right today. Today there is a lot of space in the middle and right of the middle.
> The Marxist ideology of redistribution has failed. The Christian-socialist ideology has, just like the national and international socialism, ended in dictator-ship, in fascism. (FPÖ 1994)

The framing of the crisis of socialism through ideology allows Haider's FPÖ to position itself on the "ideological landscape." In equating the socialist government as being "so far left," the FPÖ positions itself as being "right of the middle." This frame allows the FPÖ to refute any accusation of being undemocratic due to its history of being founded by former Nazis or having questionable ties to neo-Nazism (Sully 1997, 2–3). In addition to the ideological equation of Austria's socialist party with Eastern European socialism, the FPÖ's discourse also indirectly compares the redistributive policy of socialists with that of the "Marxist ideology," which is narrated to have failed. Similarly, the grand coalition that followed the Kreisky era is described as "Christian-socialist ideology," which is more directly placed on a level with dictatorship, socialism, and fascism. In constructing a crisis around the previously dominant socialist government and the subsequent grand coalition, the FPÖ clearly claims the necessity of decisive intervention that none of the other parties are able to provide due to their misled ideological biases.

## The Grand Coalition as the Broken Promise

Not only does the ideological attack extend beyond the critique of the socialist government to its successor, but the grand coalition between the SPÖ and the ÖVP is another key dimension of the FPÖ's ideational entrepreneurship in constructing a crisis around Austria's policy paradigm at the time. This allows the FPÖ to position itself as the only alternative within Austria's party competition. These ideas landed on fruitful ground. The SPÖ and ÖVP entered a grand coalition in 1987 with the main goal of consolidating the state's budget while also lowering taxes, which presented itself as an almost impossible task. The cooperation between the two parties suffered immensely from blaming each other for failing to deliver election promises. These discrepancies were immediately reflected in regional and local elections by an increase of swing voters and a decrease in voters generally (Zöllner 1990, 553).

> The grand coalition is much indebted. The promised reforms remained lip service. Even if the grand coalition takes this path further, the political structures of the post-war period fall apart in Eastern Europe. Also in our republic has the specific way of making politics in party, cooperatives, and unions found its end in its political and creational capabilities. Grand coalition and cooperatives can no longer handle the challenges that the changing basics for society's life pose.
>
> How ridiculous does the attempt to conserve the political structure of the post-war period appear because of vested interests. The socialist control and redistribution state is in the same way at its end as the ÖVP politics of the smallest common denominator of multiple interest representatives. For decades did citizens "function" within the party and union-statist power apparatus. Now this state can no longer "bind" its citizens with soft violence. (FPÖ 1990)

The narrative of the Eastern European decline is also applied to frame the critique of the grand coalition. The narrative holds stories of broken promises and the inability of the political structures to face societal challenges. The political structure criticized relates to the dominant organization of interest representation through social partnerships, strong unions, and cooperatives. These structures have a great tradition across the SPÖ and ÖVP "with strong emotional, ideological, and organizational ties" (Plasser, Ulram, and Sommer 2000, 4). Their reach was described as "party-political colonization of the administration, public economy, and education sector." This "expanded the reach of camp-oriented relations and mentalities, which were then duly stabilized through the award of material benefits" (Plasser, Ulram, and Sommer 2000, 4). This is another example of how Haider's critique mobilizes on existing structures by offering a critique of such. The grand coalition is accused of abusing these structures to pursue its own vested interests. The narrative equates this structure to "soft violence" that is suggestive of taking away citizens' freedom similar to the framing of "control."

> The Austrian tax law is no longer adequate for the changing economic challenges of the modern industry and service society. High taxation, a barely transparent system of exemption rules, and privileges have led to a hindrance of efficient activities, a hard-felt protest against taxation, and the creation of a shadow economy. (FPÖ 1986)

> The states' indebtedness per capita has risen from 87,000 to 170,000 under Vranitzky. . . . Those who sack the state's budget simply destroy hard worked-for money. (FPÖ 1994)

> Austrians have been lied to by the governing parties SPÖ and ÖVP in the past. Promises, prior to the EU referendum and since the general elections of 1986, have been made and have been broken: from budget-rehabilitation to pension reform, administrative reform, health care reform to transit reform. (FPÖ 1995)

The FPÖ's discourse successfully mobilized the grand coalition's conflicts by framing them as "broken promises" regarding policy reforms that were felt to be necessary in the face of international economic turmoil and Austria's mounting debt. In the 1994 manifesto, Haider directly addresses the chancellor of the grand coalition, Vranitzky, and the rising debt, which is suggested to "sack" the money of hardworking people. Here, there is a direct link to the FPÖ's critique of Austria's tax system, which allows for privileges and the creation of a shadow economy. Taxation, governmental debt, political structures, interest representation, and the SPÖ and ÖVP's influence are presented as sources of crises, which need decisive intervention to lighten the burden put on Austrian citizens.

## Immigration as Problem of Marxist Ideology

The ideological critique that the discourse of Haider's FPÖ articulates does not only seek to mobilize given societal tensions such as the widely felt period of stagflation that Austria underwent toward the end of the SPÖ government. But the critique also utilizes this momentum of unrest to introduce a new policy position, which the 1990 FPÖ manifesto depicts as the "foreigner question" or the 1994 FPÖ manifesto as "multicultural experiment." Aside from the polarizing nature of Haider's discourse (Wodak, KhosraviNik, and Mral 2013) in criticizing the grand coalition and the SPÖ government, this policy position is another novelty that Haider introduced to the FPÖ's discourse. Haider's FPÖ introduced the topic during a period in which immigration became an explosive topic after the fall of the Iron Curtain (Sully 1997, 77). Seizing the moment yet again, Haider's hardline position on immigration proved electorally successful, especially in regions where "teachers were confronted with classes where 80 percent of pupils were immigrants" (Sully 1997, 77).

> Multicultural experiments with open borders serve old ideologies. This is hidden because it is the reverse approach: it is nothing else but the old Marxist theory of redistribution. Only this time around it is not about redistributing the money to the people, but the people to money. Redistribution has always led, how history proves to us, to more poverty for all. If one were to redistribute the people, this is much more dangerous. Because this leads to social tensions and violence. (FPÖ 1994)

The discourse presents a cognitive argument that is used to "offer guidelines for political action justified through reference to (social) scientific principles and interpretations, often with interest-based logics and invocations of necessity" (Schmidt 2014, 193). Applied to the excerpt above, multiculturalism is interpreted as an experiment that serves only particular actors—here, Marxists—with the (scientific) reference to a "theory of redistribution." The Marxists addressed here are an indirect reference to the SPÖ. This theory is argued to be wrong by offering the collective memory of how this has failed in the past. The history addressed is the continuing frame of the Eastern European development.

> THE FOREIGNERS QUESTION—In a Europe of regions
> The breakdown of communism as a political, economic, and social system in Eastern Europe as well as the unsolvable problems of the southern development countries in the short term will lead to an immigration tendency that will pose political challenges for all Western European states in the future.

AUSTRIA MUST NOT CLOSE ITS EYES TO THE NEGATIVE CONSE-
QUENCES OF ILLEGAL IMMIGRATION, PEOPLE SMUGGLING, BLACK
MARKETS, AND ILLEGAL TRADE . . .
The socialist politicians that demanded for immigration into Austria took
qualified workforce away from these countries that are necessary to build the
market economy. Plans to balance out population decrease through "import" of
foreigners is decidedly negated. (FPÖ 1990)

The "foreigner problem" that Haider describes is presented as a consequence
of the breakdown of communism and as an advancement of the interests of
Austria's socialist politicians following the logic of cognitive argumentation.
Thus, the political action that is discursively legitimated is the "import of foreigners." While it is often argued that this anti-immigration rhetoric is the key
to Haider's success and part of his entrepreneurial ingenuity, the discursive
embedding in the broader critique of socialism and its ideology suggests that
the anti-immigration position is mobilized to further advance the discursive
construction of a crisis of Austro-Keynesianism.

## The EU as Maastricht Superstate

Next to the FPÖ's anti-immigration position, the FPÖ's position on Austria's
accession to the EU also changed radically under Haider's leadership. Haider
turned the self-ascribed FPÖ tradition of being pro-Europe on its head. Sully
(1997) describes how "Haider railed against the 'Maastricht superstate'"
with its "faceless bureaucrats" and stoutly defended the interests of the nation states against "meddling and interference" from Brussels (92). While the
1986 manifesto can still be identified as pro-European, Haider strategically
changed the position once Austria became part of the EU in 1995 (Bundeskanzleramt, n.d.). During this time, the governing parties still struggled to
find common ground on the state budget. Despite the fact that the access to
the EU would make Austria's budget planning even more intricate due to the
ongoing Austrian budget deficits. The governing parties praised Europe and
fostered high expectations: "jobs would appear and goods would be cheaper"
(Sully 1997, 95). The SPÖ Chancellor Vranitzki "made a fatal pledge not to
raise taxes because of the EU, a position which became increasingly unten-
able with the need to balance the budget deficit" (ibid., 95). Six months after
Austria's accession, EU polls indicated rising skepticism, which Haider was
able to instrumentalize through the change of FPÖ's position on Europe.
Hence, Haider was able to entrepreneurially capture the atmosphere and once
again depict the governing parties as the major sources of crisis, especially in
regard to their state budget management.

Solving the lack of democratic procedures remains on the long agenda of over-due reforms. But the Euro-fanatics continue to accelerate the pace of integra-tion, regardless of the cost to democracy or the people [Maastricht was], one treaty too many and one step too far. . . . Anyone who has a vision of freedom for Europe should know that the new democracies of Eastern Europe have a profound distaste for the specter of centralism. It was not for nothing that they threw off the stifling mantle of a jaded bureaucratic superstructure. Maastricht is the wrong signal for today's Europe. A Europe which is divorced from its citizens is unthinkable and will go the way of despotic empires before it. (Haider 1995, 81–83)

The framing of pro-Europeans as fanatics who are willing to give up democ-racy and the people allows Haider to construct a discourse to mobilize bot-tom-up legitimacy for his Euroskeptic program. The continuation of utilizing the collective memory of the Eastern European transformation presents the link to the ongoing critique of socialist governance and ideas associated with it; the framing of the Maastricht treaty as "the specter of centralism" indi-rectly reminds of the critique of Marxist ideology and communism. Haider's discourse continues attacking the coalition's European policy that will put "an unacceptable burden to the Austrian taxpayer who had to fork out 100 million Schillings a day for the privilege of membership" (Sully 1997, 95). Similar to earlier discursive frames about the burden on Austrian taxpayers due to state budget mismanagement, the mobilization for Euroskepticism also rests on this bottom-up legitimization strategy.

## The Constructed Crisis of Austria's Dominant Policy Paradigm

After a period of economic turbulence from the start of the 1970s until the mid-1980s, Western democracies experienced more stable growth, which is linked to increased private investments and better profit expectations in export markets. Most commentators at the time link this development to the "regime change" from Keynesian demand management to a stronger emphasis on supply-side economics through deregulation and privatization of nationalized companies (Breuss 1989, 372). Even if not to the same extent as the United States, the supply-side role model (Breuss 1989, 372), Austria started to lean away from the so-called "Austro-Keynesianism" (Kausel 1998, 8). The slow demise of Austro-Keynesianism started in 1983 and was accompanied by the mounting budget deficit, intra-coalition conflicts between the ÖVP and SPÖ, nationalized sectors suffering losses, and the rise of the FPÖ's electoral sup-port. Haider's discourse actively uses this moment of economic and political uncertainty by constructing a crisis of the governing parties, the SPÖ and ÖVP, and the policy paradigm they pursue. The political structure of interest representatives, the taxation regime, the governmental debt management, and

**Table 9.2. Summary FPÖ Crisis Construction**

| Source of Crisis | Forms of Ideas |
|---|---|
| **The socialist ideology**<br>Context: end of Kreisky era (1970–1983), slow demise of Austro-Keynesianism (1983–1999) | • Frame of control that takes away citizens' freedom<br>• Collective memory of oppression and authoritarianism in Eastern Europe's "real socialism"<br>• Narrative of control over political structure for rent-seeking purposes of socialists |
| **The grand coalition**<br>Context: increasing budget deficit, mounting debt, uncompetitive nationalized companies | • Narrative of broken promises<br>• Narrative of political structure for rent-seeking purposes<br>• Frame of socialist ideology<br>• Story of taxation regime inadequate<br>• Framing debt management as "sacking taxpayers' money" |
| **Immigration**<br>Context: fall of Iron Curtain | • Narrative of Marxist ideology<br>• Narrative of immigration for vested interest<br>• Collective memory of increasing poverty |
| **European integration**<br>Context: Austria's accession to EU 1995 and rising Euroskepticism in public opinion | • Frame of EU fanatics<br>• Narrative of socialist specter of centralism<br>• Narrative of bureaucratic super structure |

the underlying ideologies of the governing parties are presented as sources of crisis, as table 9.2 summarizes, which only decisive intervention from the FPÖ's side can solve.

## The Construction of the Winning Formula

In constructing this crisis of the dominant policy paradigm, Haider's FPÖ establishes the necessity of decisive intervention. In doing so, the discourse clearly suggests that it is only the FPÖ that is able to successfully intervene and solve this crisis. For all scrutinized policy ideas, the FPÖ offers a solution, which resembles that of the "winning formula": neoliberalism and authoritarianism. Different ideas associated with both dimensions of this formula are suggested to solve the problems that the governing parties and their policy paradigm present. Even though the full-fledged Austro-Keynesian era was slowly declining from 1983 onward, the neoliberal era had not yet arrived in Austria. The promise of crisis solutions in authoritarian values and neoliberal policies *normativizes* those positions, which later culminates in the *normalized* neoliberal policymaking from 2000 onward.

## Freedom Instead of Socialism

FREEDOM IS OUR IDEOLOGY . . .

It is about intelligent dialogs in a liberal society. It is about the right answer to the left failure. It is about a fundamental reckoning with leftist hedonism, which has experienced the breakdown of the real socialism in the East, however could not manage the challenges of freedom. . . .

We want freedom without coercion instead of coercion without freedom. We want the strengthening of rights instead of the right of the stronger. We want responsibility for the weak instead of weak responsibility. We want opportunities for all instead of protection for the few. We want success through the market economy instead of chaos through mismanagement. (FPÖ 1994)

Instead of the failed ideologies of the socialists and the conservatives, Haider's FPÖ announces that freedom is its ideology, which is the "right answer to left failure." This framing allows constructing freedom as the opposite to the crisis-prone governing ideologies. The narrative of coercion and freedom, rights, responsibility, and opportunities plays with the same dichotomy: the crisis-prone other ideologies versus the winning one of freedom. The last sentence of this excerpt implies that the "ideology of freedom" is best lived in a market economy free from management. Here, there is a clear link to the neoliberal notion that all economic and political problems have a market solution (Aligica and Evans 2009, 3).

## Fulfilled Promises and Trust

At least in the voting booth did the citizens start to break through this system—more so since 1986. The SPÖ and ÖVP do not only ignore the running away of its voters, but even more extreme is their unwillingness and incapability to tackle the real and inevitable life questions of Austrians—even with the promised "rehabilitation-partnership." The winners of this awakening of the voter mobility since 1986 are the FPÖ . . . first the grand coalition tried to vilify the FPÖ as the neo-Nazi party as if the ghosts of yesterday would do anything good. A second counter strategy served the accusations of populism, of permanent quarrel, of lack of program, until the local elections in Carinthia where a FPÖ member got to the top of the local government, who has since proven that the FPÖ fulfills its promises. (FPÖ 1990)

In line with the continuous crisis construction, the FPÖ tells a story of people starting to "break the system" as well, which has become a great support for the FPÖ. This story is praising the voters for their reckoning of the broken system and how the system has failed to deliver its promises. It continues to praise the voter for seeing through the governing parties' strategy in accusing the FPÖ of neo-Nazism and populism. The reference to the local elections provides the narrative of fulfillment of promises, which stands in stark contrast with the governing parties that are presented as constantly breaking promises.

> We, the FPÖ, have not abused the citizens' trust. We are obliged, also without signature, for the future: We, the FPÖ, are obliged to make room for the interests of our homeland Austria and our programmatic goals. These build the binding foundation for a liberal problem solution. The citizens can take us by our word. (FPÖ 1995)

The narrative of trust that is embedded in the accusation of the governing parties having abused the voters' trust helps the FPÖ's positioning as crisis solution. The frame of "interests of our homeland Austria" acts as link to the FPÖ's anti-immigration position as well as its newly found Euroskepticism. By truly committing to the "interests of the homeland," the FPÖ would solve issues that arise from immigration and European integration. The narrative of a "liberal problem solution" explicates the FPÖ's discursive dynamic of constructing a crisis that only the FPÖ is able to solve. The notion of "homeland" as ethnocultural exclusivity in combination with the "liberal solution" illustrates the discursive construction of the winning formula well.

## Immediate Immigration Stop Is the Only Way

> We therefore demand:
>
> - Immediate immigration stop
> - No new citizenships
> - Strong intervention against organized crime
> - Stricter punishment for drug crime and smuggling
> - Fight against social security abuse
> - Consequential deportation of criminal foreigners
> - Repatriation of refugees after war has ended
> - No EU East expansion as long as they do not fulfill the entry requirements for EU membership (FPÖ 1999)

The 1999 manifesto first describes how the "old parties SPÖ and ÖVP" are responsible for millions of foreigners living in Austria—thousands of them illegally—and uncontrollable growth of organized crime. Thereafter, the manifesto continues with "therefore the FPÖ demands" as the excerpt above shows. The "solutions" reflect more authoritarian and nationalist anti-immigration positions that rely on ethnocultural exclusivity and strong executive enforcements against immigration that will reinstate that "Austria is no immigration country" with the claim of "Austria First" (FPÖ 1999). This policy position, especially, explicates the FPÖ's authoritarian ideas well.

## A National-Liberal Europe

A successful political economy is the foundation of political action. Almost every political decision affects the economy. On the other hand, only a healthy economy can provide the financial means for multiple necessary reforms. The FPÖ works for a European community, which is oriented toward federalism and self-reliance of its regions under the maintenance of the national-liberal perspective of the self-determination of the people. We negate a bureaucratic centralized organization for its own sake. Especially the recent events with the Eastern countries have shown that liberal economic programmatic, with its demand to roll back the state and the bureaucratic influence, is the right way. The FPÖ demands a European community that is open to the developments of Eastern Europe and offers entrance possibilities for countries of Eastern Europe, obviously based on the same rules of the game. A wrong East-euphoria must not result in "Eastern privileges" and disadvantage our domestic economy. (FPÖ 1990)

Austria first also counts for us within the EU. (FPÖ 1994)

Through the FPÖ's EU position, Haider "urged structural reforms in the Austrian economy before entry to avoid a sell off of Austrian economic interests and to prevent a budgetary catastrophe" (Sully 1997, 96). Strengthening capital resources, reducing secondary wage costs, overhauling the tax system, depoliticizing the Austrian central bank, and structurally reforming the banking and insurance sectors were among those reforms. As these reforms and the excerpts above suggest, the FPÖ's EU position also illustrates the winning formula that solves the crisis of the governing parties. The narrative of the "successful political economy" lies within the frame of the "national-liberal perspective," which opposes a centralized and bureaucratic institution. Therefore, the FPÖ's solution is to "roll back the state," which is another neoliberal policy idea reminiscent of ideas such as minimizing state intervention and supporting state decentralization (Aligica and Evans 2009, 3). Thus, the FPÖ's EU position can be interpreted as being solved through and feeding into the FPÖ's neoliberal agenda.

## The National-Liberal Solution

With the slow demise of Austro-Keynesianism and the international shift to supply-side economics, Haider's FPÖ uses this momentum to mobilize for its self-ascribed "national-liberal perspective." The ideas associated with this perspective are suggested to solve all dilemmas that the FPÖ puts on the SPÖ and ÖVP's governance. The perspective constitutes a mix of ethnocultural exclusivity and strict executive power with minimizing the state's involvement in the market and a free market economy. The first positions fix the discursively constructed problems of immigration and the "Austrian homeland's" interest representation within European integration. The latter solves described issues of state budget management, unfair privileges of politicians, and other actors within Austria's political structure of social partnerships, unions, and cooperatives. Table 9.3 summarizes these positions as well as the ideational format they exhibit in discourse. Scholars describe this mix of policy positions as the "winning formula" of far-right parties in the 1980s and 1990s (Kitschelt and McGann 1997; de Lange 2007). What these

**Table 9.3.   Summary of FPÖ Crisis Solutions 1983–1999**

| Sources of Crisis | Crisis Solution | Forms of Ideas |
|---|---|---|
| Socialist government's ideology | **Ideology of freedom** | • Frame of freedom versus failed ideology of governing parties<br>• Narrative of coercion, freedom, rights, responsibility, and opportunity<br>• Narrative of market economy without mismanagement |
| The grand coalition | **The vote for the FPÖ** | • Story of voters seeing through lies and breaking the system through FPÖ voting<br>• Narrative of governing parties accusing FPÖ for neo-Nazism and populism<br>• Story of promise fulfillment of voted FPÖ politician<br>• Narrative of trust in the FPÖ<br>• Frame of representing interests of the Austrian homeland<br>• Narrative of liberal problem solution |
| Immigration | **Immigration stop** | • Frame of old parties, the ÖVP and SPÖ, and what the FPÖ demands<br>• Narrative of Austrian is no immigration country<br>• Frame of "Austria First" |
| European integration | **A national-liberal European community** | • Narrative of budgetary catastrophe<br>• Narrative of successful political economy<br>• Frame of national-liberal perspective<br>• Narrative of rolling back the state<br>• Frame of "Austria First" |

scholars have overlooked, however, is that this formula was winning because the discourse of far-right parties suggested that it presents solutions to the crisis of the Keynesian policy paradigm. In showing how this formula seemingly solves the sources of the constructed crisis, far-right parties *normativize* neoliberal ideas as well as complementary authoritarian ideas.

## HAIDER AND THE WINNING FORMULA

To conclude, I have examined the FPÖ's discourse from 1986 to 1999, the time of Jörg Haider's leadership. The discourse of Haider's FPÖ was organized in a pattern. First, it constructed a crisis of the governing parties, the SPÖ and ÖVP, and their Austro-Keynesian policymaking, which necessitated decisive neoliberal and authoritarian intervention. Second, this intervention served to solve this crisis, which only the FPÖ was able to provide. Haider thereby successfully mobilized a moment of transformation and economic turbulence. His political entrepreneurship laid in the ability to capture this moment by providing explanations on who was to blame for these turbulences and offering solutions to them. These solutions were a mixture of "traditional" FPÖ positions, newly introduced positions, and a new rhetorical style that often polemically polarized the FPÖ's rhetoric. While the "national-liberal perspective" was not a novelty to Haider's FPÖ, in introducing new positions such as anti-immigration and Euroskepticism, Haider seemed to complement the national-liberal perspective with ethnocultural exclusivity and authoritarian sentiments. Organizing this discourse through the crisis construction and crisis solution logic and constantly linking this to the Austrian citizens or the Austrian taxpayers allowed Haider to mobilize bottom-up legitimacy and thereby normativize his vision for Austria.

Haider's vision for Austria was embedded in a context of international economic transformation from Keynesianism to neoliberalism. Not only was he able to capture the moment of transformation in his favor but he was also part and parcel of the same transformation in Austria. The national-liberal perspective represented an advocacy of neoliberal ideas that found its institutionalization through the 2000–2006 governmental coalition between the conservatives and the FPÖ. Haider's discourse normativized neoliberal ideas and thus played a central role prior to the neoliberal turn of Austria's political economy. The political entrepreneurship of Haider can therefore be understood in two ways. First, the FPÖ, the otherwise traditional opposition party, managed to access governmental participation under Haider. This is the most common reading of political entrepreneurship (e.g., De Vries and Hobolt 2020) as the literature review explains. Second, Haider provides an example of ideational entrepreneurship in introducing and successfully mobilizing for "new" policy ideas that challenge the dominant policy paradigm.

Thus, the rise of the far right with its "winning formula" can be understood through the lens of political entrepreneurship. This interpretation, however, necessitates taking economic and cultural ideas seriously. In doing so, we cannot assume that the "best" ideas will become dominant, but instead, we have to take into account how political entrepreneurs are able to capture contextual circumstances and appeal with new or different ideas. Put differently, the political entrepreneur needs to be able to seize moments where institutional change can be achieved through changing actors' "explicit or implicit views about what they see as a problem and its solution" (Aligica and Evans 2009, 2). Haider successfully seized the moment of the demise of Austro-Keynesianism, depicts the problem within the governing parties' Austro-Keynesian strategy, and offers the solution in the neoliberal and authoritarian policy paradigm.

The rise of the far right is no longer a phenomenon of the 1980s and 1990s only. The recent rise of far-right politics across the globe means that the study of far-right politics remains a key area of research for scholarship in sociology, political sciences, and political economy. Scholarship in this area suggests that far-right parties have adopted an economic nationalist policy program (Ausserladscheider 2019), provides an interpretation of entrepreneurship of parties that were recently successful (De Vries and Hobolt 2020), and investigates the contextual circumstances such as the financial crisis of 2008 (Hopkin and Blyth 2019). Yet, a detailed analysis of the far right's ideational entrepreneurship and its "new winning formula" remains unexplored. A study of recent events that takes ideas in discourse seriously could potentially provide important insights into the generalizability of ideational entrepreneurship of far-right political actors.

## REFERENCES

Aligica, Paul Dragos, and Anthony J. Evans. 2009. *The Neoliberal Revolution in Eastern Europe: Economic Ideas in the Transition from Communism.* Cheltenham, UK: Edward Elgar Publishing.

Aligica, Paul Dragos, and Aura Matei. 2015. "National Cultures, Economic Action and the Homogeneity Problem: Insights from the Case of Romania." In *Culture and Economic Action*, edited by Laura E. Grube and Virgil Henry Storr, 295–317. Cheltenham, UK: Edward Elgar Publishing.

Ausserladscheider, Valentina. 2019. "Beyond Economic Insecurity and Cultural Backlash: Economic Nationalism and the Rise of the Far Right." *Sociology Compass* 13 (4): e12670.

Austrian Parliament. n.d. "Bundesregierungen seit 1918." https://www.parlament. gv.at/WWER/BREG/REG/index.shtml?FUNK=ALLE&requestId=63522483 79&LISTE=&RESS=ALLE&STEP=&listeId=16&ascDesc=ASC&SUCH=& feldRnr=3&FBEZ=FW_016&REG=0&pageNumber=1&xdocumentUri=%2- FWWER%2FBREG%2FREG%2Findex.shtml&jsMode=.

Betz, Hans-Georg. 2002. "The Divergent Paths of the FPÖ and the Lega Nord." In *Shadows over Europe: The Development and Impact of the Extreme Right in Western Europe*, edited by Martin Schain, Aristide Zolberg, and Patrick Hossay, 61–81. New York: Palgrave Macmillan US.

Breuss, Fritz. 1989. "'Sanfte Landung' Der Konjunktur in Den Westlichen Industriestaaten." *WIFO*.

Bundeskanzleramt. n.d. "25 Jahre Volksabstimmung Über Den EU-Beitritt Österreichs - Bundeskanzleramt Österreich." https://www.bundeskanzleramt.gv.at/the men/europa-aktuell/25-jahre-volksabstimmung-uber-den-eu-beitritt-oesterreichs .html.

Bundesministerium für Inneres. n.d. "Historischer Rückblick." https://bmi.gv.at/412/ Nationalratswahlen/Historischer_Rueckblick.aspx.

De Vries, Catherine E., and Sara B. Hobolt. 2020. "Challenger Parties and Populism." *LSE Public Policy Review* 1 (1): 3.

Dornbusch, Rudiger, and Sebastian Edwards, eds. 1991. *The Macroeconomics of Populism in Latin America*. Chicago: University of Chicago Press.

FPÖ. 1986. "Eine Politik ohne Privilegien."

———. 1990. "Präambel Für Österreichs Zukunft."

———. 1994. "Österreich Erklärung."

———. 1995. "20 Punkte für den Vertrag mit Österreich."

———. 1999. "Einer, der für Österreich arbeitet."

———. 2017. "Info-Compact."

Gerring, John. 2012. "Mere Description." *British Journal of Political Science* 42 (4): 721–46.

Gnan, Ernst. 1994. "Austria's Hard Currency Policy and European Monetary Integration." *De Pecunia* 6 (3).

Grube, Laura E., and Virgil Henry Storr. 2015. *Culture and Economic Action*. Cheltenham, UK: Edward Elgar Publishing Limited.

Haider, Jörg. 1995. *The Freedom I Mean*. New York: Swan Books.

Hall, Peter A. 1993. "Policy Paradigms, Social Learning, and the State: The Case of Economic Policymaking in Britain." *Comparative Politics* 25 (3): 275–96.

Hay, Colin. 1996. "Narrating Crisis: The Discursive Construction of the 'Winter of Discontent.'" *Sociology* 30 (2): 253–77.

———. 2004. "The Normalizing Role of Rationalist Assumptions in the Institutional Embedding of Neoliberalism." *Economy and Society* 33 (4): 500–527.

Hermann, Christoph, and Jörg Flecker. 2012. "The Austrian Model and the Financial and Economic Crisis." In *A Triumph of Failed Ideas: European Models of Capitalism in the Crisis*, edited by Steffen Lehndorff, 121–36. Brussels: ETUI.

Hopkin, Jonathan, and Mark Blyth. 2019. "The Global Economics of European Populism: Growth Regimes and Party System Change in Europe (The Government and

224     *Valentina Ausserladscheider*

Opposition/Leonard Schapiro Lecture 2017)." *Government and Opposition* 54 (2): 193–225.

Inglehart, Ronald, and Pippa Norris. 2016. "Trump, Brexit, and the Rise of Populism: Economic Have-Nots and Cultural Backlash." Working Paper, Harvard Kennedy School.

Kausel, Anton. 1998. "Ein halbes Jahrhundert des Erfolges - Der ökonomische Aufstieg Österreichs im OECD-Raum seit 1950." *Finanznachrichten Wochenschrift für Wirtschaftspolitik*, Sondernummer.

Kitschelt, Herbert. 2004. *Diversification and Reconfiguration of Party Systems in Postindustrial Democracies*. Bonn, Germany: Friedrich Ebert Stiftung.

Kitschelt, Herbert, and Anthony J. McGann. 1997. *The Radical Right in Western Europe: A Comparative Analysis*. Ann Arbor: University of Michigan Press.

Lange, Sarah L. de. 2007. "A New Winning Formula?: The Programmatic Appeal of the Radical Right." *Party Politics* 13 (4): 411–35.

Lavoie, Don. 2015. "The Discovery and Interpretation of Profit Opportunities: Culture and the Kirznerian Entrepreneur." In *Culture and Economic Action*, edited by Laura E. Grube and Virgil Henry Storr, 48–67. Cheltenham, UK: Edward Elgar Publishing.

McCaffrey, Matthew, and Joseph T. Salerno. 2011. "A Theory of Political Entrepreneurship." *Modern Economy* 2 (4): 552–60.

Mesch, Michael. 2018. "Wirtschaftspolitik in der Kreisky-Ära: erfolgreiche keynesianische Globalsteuerung." *Arbeit&Wirtschaft Blog*, July 23. https://awblog.at/wirtschaftspolitik-in-der-kreisky-aera/.

Mudde, Cas. 2007. *Populist Radical Right Parties in Europe*. Cambridge, UK: Cambridge University Press.

Pirro, Andrea L. 2017. "Hardly Ever Relevant? An Appraisal of Nativist Economics through the Hungarian Case." *Acta Politica* 52 (3): 339–60.

Plasser, Fritz, Peter A. Ulram, and Franz Sommer, eds. 2000. *Das Österreichische Wahlverhalten*. Schriftenreihe Des Zentrums Für Angewandte Politikforschung, Bd. 21. Wien: Signum.

Preglau, Max. 2001. "Rechtsextrem oder postmodern? Über Rhetorik, Programmatik, Interaktionsformen und ein Jahr Regierungspolitik der (Haider-)FPÖ." *SWS-Rundschau* 41 (2): 193–213.

Rodrik, Dani. 2018. "Is Populism Necessarily Bad Economics?" *AEA Papers and Proceedings* 108: 196–99.

Rovny, Jan, and Jonathan Polk. 2020. "Still Blurry? Economic Salience, Position and Voting for Radical Right Parties in Western Europe." *European Journal of Political Research* 59 (2): 248–68.

Schmidt, Vivien A. 2014. "Speaking to the Markets or to the People? A Discursive Institutionalist Analysis of the EU's Sovereign Debt Crisis." *The British Journal of Politics and International Relations* 16 (1): 188–209.

Sully, Melanie A. 1997. *The Haider Phenomenon*. New York: East European Monographs.

Trofimov, Ivan D. 2017. "Entrepreneurship and Policy Dynamics: A Theoretical Framework." Working Paper, University Library of Munich, Germany.

Tullock, Gordon. 2004. *The Selected Works of Gordon Tullock, Volume 1: Virginia Political Economy*, edited by Charles K. Rowley. Indianapolis: Liberty Fund.

WIFO. 1983. "Analyse Der Wirtschaftsentwicklung in Österreich 1982." *WIFO*.

———. 1986. "Die Entwickling Der Österreichischen Wirtschat Im Jahr 1985." *WIFO*.

Wodak, Ruth, Majid KhosraviNik, and Brigitte Mral. 2013. *Right-Wing Populism in Europe: Politics and Discourse*. London: A & C Black.

Zöllner, Erich. 1990. *Geschichte Österreichs: Von den Anfängen bis zur Gegenwart*. 8th ed. Wien: Oldenbourg Wissenschaftsverlag.

## Chapter 10

# Law, Crime, and Emergent Dis/order

## *Reading Hayek with and against Durkheim*

### Brandon Hunter-Pazzara

"I don't try and make friends at work," Miguel said bluntly. "I just keep to myself, wait in line for rides, and do my best not to bother anyone. This is not the kind of job where you want to make friends because friendship always comes with a price."

After working for nearly a decade and a half as a bread delivery driver for the Bimbo Corporation, Miguel made the decision to purchase a new Nissan Sentra, painted it white with turquoise stripes, and applied to become a driver with the Sindicato de Taxistas Lazarro Cardenas—the official, and only, taxi union operating in the municipality of Solidaridad. His brother-in-law got him a spot with a group of taxis serving several high-end resorts just north of Playa del Carmen, a decent gig that would give him access to wealthy, and hopefully high tipping, tourists. A single ride from the resort into town could be as much as Mex$500 (about US$25 at the time), but in addition to paying his union dues, a fee to rent a taxi medallion, he was also required to give a small portion of each ride's earnings to the group leader.

Within just a few months of his new career move, Miguel found himself in a strange dispute with an older taxi driver. "He said I had looked at him funny and that he was offended. I had never interacted with the guy in my life, but all of the sudden he was saying that I offended him. He threatened me, said he wanted to fight me. And so the group captain intervened. I explained that I hadn't done anything, but the guy was more senior, so I was told that I had to leave the group, or I had the pay the guy Mex$4,000 [about US$225]. I didn't want to pay. I didn't think it was fair. But my brother-in-law convinced me to just pay because these guys are dangerous, and you never know what they'll do. So, I paid and after that I kept my head down. I don't try to make friends at work," Miguel sighed.

Miguel is not the only taxi driver with a story like this. During more than eighteen months of fieldwork in the town of Playa del Carmen, I met dozens of drivers who complained about abuse, intimidation, and threats they received from other drivers; drivers they believed were connected to any one of the criminal organizations operating in this part of Mexico. Even in the privacy of their taxis, drivers would whisper quietly when talking about the criminal elements that controlled the taxi union, a sense of fear and frustration audible in their voices.

Crime, or more specifically the prospect of being a victim of crime, was on the minds of most locals I met. Contrasting the current moment to a previous time of tranquility and peace, locals described a town now besieged by crime and violence in which authorities seemed either indifferent to their plight or powerless to do much about it. And yet, crime was also integral to the local economy, particularly the trade in drugs and prostitution but also the small ways locals swindled tourists, paid bribes to agents of the state, engaged in suspicious land deals, skirted environmental protections, or mistreated their workers. "Crime," a local historian declared to me, "was always here from the start, was always part of the order, or disorder, of things. The sort of economy that developed here [tourism] is rooted in crime."

In this chapter, I trace the history of this criminal "order/disorder." My aim is to illustrate how crime shaped the micro-social relations of Playa del Carmen and functioned as part of an "emergent order" that economically benefited those who came to the region looking for work. Crime functioned as a kind of "invisible hand," or what Martin and Storr (2008) call a "perverse emergent order" that implicated a diverse range of institutions and individuals. Crime operated at various levels, from the bribes paid by large multinational hotels securing land along the Caribbean coast to the acts of intimidation and extortion described in the opening vignette.

Whereas Martin and Storr (2008) draw a distinction between the positive and negative attributes of perverse and non-perverse orders as a way of distinguishing and categorizing them, I argue that a more challenging problem exists around the process of categorization itself. While a utilitarian calculus of perverse emergent orders might offer an answer, such an analysis betrays Hayek's (1976) warning that emergent orders are not utilitarian in nature, since by definition they serve no common purpose. In a complex society made up of different groups of individuals, the question of order and disorder can be perceived and experienced differently within the same social context, placing the social scientist and her analysis in a position of judgment. Whereas the notion of perverse emergent orders helps in naming negative social phenomena, I argue that the process of recognizing and naming an order as perverse produces a discursive site of social contestation and social scientific judgment that exposes a gap between law and justice often not shared across different classes of people within complex societies.

Hayek's answer to the problem of crime rests on the idea that emergent orders are held together by rules of just conduct that apply equally to everyone. Criminal law should intervene insomuch as it prevents the use of coercion in taking someone's property or in forcing them to act against their interests. Hayek maintains that such an order provides the means for individuals to act in accordance to their preferences, yet this produces a tension. Contrary to Martin and Storr's (2008) claim, individuals are free within this system to discriminate against others for any range of reasons, including gender and race. Hayek, of course, insists on rules of just conduct that are predicated on legal equality between individuals (a feature of the liberal project), yet he is unclear as to whether individuals who wished to discriminate together against other individuals would betray this project. Reconciling this tension moves us from the place of objective assessment to normative judgment, something Martin and Storr acknowledge (2008, 86) but with very little guidance from Hayek as to how to proceed. In this chapter, I turn to Émile Durkheim, and his specific theorization of crime and social solidarity, to bridge this conceptual gap.

Durkheim and Hayek are interesting intellectual interlocutors to pair together as both take seriously the emergent social complexity that comes about through the division of labor in society. Yet, they differ on several key points that reveal certain limitations in Hayek's thinking of emergent social orders. For Hayek, emergent orders epistemically come into being "between instinct and reason," which is to say that such orders are the result of purposeful activity by differentially situated individuals connected to one another through the mutual interdependence created by the complex division of labor. Hayek believes this order is best held together when basic rules of conduct are put in place that do not specify a telos to this system but allow individuals to pursue their multiple and distinct ends.

Hayek's notion of emergent order is similar, though not the same, to Durkheim's notion of "organic solidarity." For Hayek, an emergent order is a byproduct of the respect for basic rules of conduct, whereas for Durkheim it is held together through an elaborated notion of individuality. For Hayek, such rules can exist at the level of legal codification, but they are also the result of norms, customs, and traditions whose survival up to any point reveals their durability (and correctness).

Durkheim, however, is skeptical of this view, and this is because he believes that social solidarity cannot simply emerge from following uniform social rules. Law is an index of particular kinds of solidarity for Durkheim, its existence making partially visible the order, or disorder, of society. A consequence, then, is that law's normative value is indeterminate. Its existence is an outcome of political power that can too easily be taken for granted. This is why, for Durkheim, crime, both as a legal sanction and a socially shared sense of wrongdoing, requires a critical skepticism from the social scientist since the existence of criminal sanctions always carries the potential of reaffirming relations of injustice rather than correcting them.

Moreover, for Durkheim, complex emergent orders are best achieved when rules become relational rather than statically held. This is because what is meant by "just conduct" is different for different groups. According to Durkheim, though as I argue, for Hayek too, the social solidarity reflected in complex, emergent orders must be thought of as something more than the uniform rules of just conduct. They instead require an elaborated sense of individual consciousness and conscientiousness predicated on mutual recognition, a respect for difference, and the freedom to move across distinct and multiple moral communities.

To make this argument, I draw from ethnographic research on labor and crime in the Riviera Maya. I begin by placing this part of Mexico into a socio-historical context that describes how tourism development began and evolved from the late 1960s to the contemporary period. Departing from conventional narratives, I highlight how various forms of criminal activity became entangled in the region's economy. Next, I shift to the micro level, detailing the stories of two different interlocutors employed in the tourism economy in Playa del Carmen. I use their stories to draw attention to the way crime became part of an emergent order that implicated locals who found themselves both participating in crime and worrying about becoming the victims of crime.

Their stories also serve as a jumping-off point for the next section in which I critique Hayek by reading his theories with and against Durkheim. I argue that Hayek's claim that uniform rules of just conduct are necessary for emergent orders offers an insufficient answer to effectively assessing whether that order is positive or perverse. Durkheim's critical approach to crime and his theory of the individual within complex social orders provides a stronger analytical tool for making such evaluations. A critical approach to crime, I argue, complements rather than contradicts Hayek since it rests more comfortably with Hayek's ultimate aim of liberty and his elaborated notion of individuality.

## TOURISM AND CRIME: A STORY OF DEVELOPMENT

Just as the Nixon administration was beginning to inaugurate the War on Drugs through the creation, and eventual passage, of the Controlled Substance Act (1970), Mexico's President Luis Echeverria initiated an ambitious tourism development scheme in the Yucatán Peninsula. The project would be one of Echeverria's most important legacies, leading to the founding and construction of the city of Cancun; the addition of two new states into the Mexican Republic, Quintana Roo and Baja California Sur; and the formation of part of a broader set of economic development strategies aimed at moving Mexico away from Import Substitution Industrialization and toward a globalized and export-oriented economy.

From the late 1970s to the early 1990s, Cancun was part of what Torres and Momsen (2005) call "Fordist tourism development," a term used to describe the coordinating role the Mexican federal government played in securing loans, building infrastructure, and shaping Cancun's urban design. Because of Quintana Roo's sparse population, both the state and private sector recruited thousands of Mexicans from other parts of the country to work in construction and then eventually take work in the hotels and other businesses connected to the tourism economy. The state's population grew rapidly. In 1974, eighty thousand people lived in Quintana Roo—the minimum needed to become an official state in the Mexican Republic. By the mid-1990s, that number reached over one million. In 2015, over two million resided in Quintana Roo with officials estimating that thousands of long-stay tourists from Euro-America and thousands of undocumented migrants from Latin America called Quinitana Roo home (INEGI 2015).

At first, Cancun served as a destination for the international elite, capturing a small segment of the tourist market (Torres 2002). As the city's reputation grew, more tourists visited, and the market shifted to include lower-budget travelers from North America and Europe. Soon, tourists began to venture away from Cancun's "hotel zone" and traveled south along the coast to smaller cities like Puerto Morelos, Playa del Carmen, and other sleepy fishing villages. By the early 1990s, Cancun still drew the majority of tourists. But other destinations began to build a reliable market, and investors started turning their attention to this area.

In 1993, the state government made the decision to create the municipality of Solidaridad (Solidarity), splitting off this area from the municipal district of Cozumel and placing the seat of government in the small—but quickly growing—town of Playa del Carmen. The decision made it easier for local leaders living in this area to begin making deals with investors and divide land along the coast to sell to large resort companies eager to take advantage of Quintana Roo's pristine beaches. Such deals were also made possible by changes in Mexican law that began in the 1980s but reached their full development in the mid-1990s. These changes permitted foreigners to invest in the country and purchase land held collectively through Mexico's ejido system— a land reform system put in place after the Mexican Revolution.

While the role of crime in the state's development took many forms, two distinct phenomena help to capture the way crime became embedded in the region's political economy—drugs and land deals.

## Drugs

Since the 1980s, Quintana Roo's coastline served as a trafficking route for cocaine and other narcotics from Colombia to the United States. Drugs would wash along the state's shores in large packets that were then picked up by cartels before being delivered by land over the U.S. border. Quintana Roo was considered a favorite smuggling route for Colombian cartels and Pablo Escobar even built a house in what is today the bustling destination of Tulum (the house is now a boutique hotel). As tourism expanded, a local drug market catering to the needs of tourists expanded as well. Cancun, and later the rest of the Riviera Maya, took on a reputation as a place where it was easy to purchase drugs and officials tolerated drug use by tourists. Police enforced drug use laws arbitrarily, often singling out tourists they knew were purchasing drugs as a means of securing bribes but never enforcing the law in a manner that disrupted the local market.

Rumors surfaced alleging that the system of trafficking reached the highest levels of state government, and by the end of the 1990s, federal prosecutors launched an investigation of then-governor Mario Villanueva Madrid. After an interview with the state's attorney before he was set to finish his term, the governor went into hiding two weeks before transferring power, fearing his immediate arrest upon losing his immunity. In 2001, two years after his term ended, Villanueva was captured during a routine vehicle inspection and from there was prosecuted for money laundering (though cleared of drug trafficking charges). Upon serving his initial six-year sentence, the United States filed papers to extradite Villanueva to the United States to face charges for drug trafficking (Esposito 2010). While awaiting the proceedings, Villanueva was saved from extradition when a Mexican federal judge found Villanueva guilty of drug trafficking and extended his original sentence to thirty-six years in prison—a move that many rumored was orchestrated by Villanueva to avoid serving time in U.S. prisons.

Though extraordinary, Villanueva would not be the first high-level politician from Quintana Roo suspected of organized crime. In 2010, the former mayor of Cancun, Gregorio Sanchez, faced drug trafficking charges that ended his run for governor (Cortazar 2010). In 2015, prosecutors filed a number of charges against then-governor Roberto Borge, whom they accused of operating an elaborate corruption scheme from the governor's mansion in Chetumal. Borge would eventually find himself arrested in the Panama City airport in 2018 just before attempting to board a flight in a daring attempt to evade authorities and extradition (Lemos 2018).

Regardless of one's feelings about drug selling and drug use, the profits made from drugs proved an essential component to the economic development of Quintana Roo. As Playa del Carmen grew, drug money was responsible for the city's construction boom and was laundered into hundreds of other businesses in the city. During the course of fieldwork, locals regularly pointed out the large souvenir stores featuring an endless array of products that seemed to go unsold while workers, inattentive to the tourists passing by, simply milled about. In answering the question "Where does all the profit from drug money go?," those living in Quintana Roo believed their state was one recipient of this money.

While it is difficult to measure the extent of the drug trade (Hakim 2014), conservative estimates suggest it accounts for about 1 percent of global gross domestic product (GDP) (Chawla 2005), yet this figure is obviously not spread evenly. In Mexico, the illicit drug trade constitutes a much larger share of the country's economy, employing tens of thousands of individuals directly, while drug profits provide the capital for a range of investments and business ventures (Lange 2010).

Though individual cartels are believed to operate via a highly organized and hierarchical system of decision making, the global drug trade is composed of thousands of large and small operations acting with and against each other in what we might call a spontaneous order. Eduardo Arias's (2006) research illustrates that criminal organizations can operate differently even across neighborhoods in the same city, as gangs deploy networked approaches to manage their relations with politicians, police, and other criminal groups; market and move their product; maintain relations with customers; and launder their money into the licit economy. This produces distinct social norms within each operation as well as identifiable "criminal cultures," like the Sicilian Mafia in Italy. Like other commodities, drugs are prone to booms and busts, as market speculation can drive overproduction, highly potent or novel products can foster new demands, and violence between gangs and the arrest of gang leaders can alter leadership and quickly shift market control and power (Watt and Zepeda 2012).

## Land

Tourism development in Quintana Roo would not be possible without important, though often times illegal, changes in land ownership.

As noted above, Mexico's shift to an export-oriented economy entailed legal changes in its foreign direct investment rules that included allowing foreigners to purchase "Ejido land"—land previously held in common and provided to peasants as part of a series of land reform policies enacted after the 1910 Mexican Revolution (Kelly 1994). Unlike Cancun, which sat on federal land and thus did not need to be expropriated by the state in order to begin development, much of what is now the Riviera Maya, including the town of Playa del Carmen, was on ejido land.

This required private investors to begin negotiations with ejido stakeholders, a process that led to shady land dealings and social conflicts over land sales. This is in part because of the collective nature of ejido land, which requires all stakeholders to be included in the negotiation process before land titles can be transferred to private actors. In the rush of tourism expansion, land deals took place by ignoring the law. Officials often approved land deals without all stakeholders present. Leaders regularly forged signatures, and holdouts were forcibly removed from their plots by state agents or hired thugs (Guardado 2015). Fearing being the victim of coercion, many gave up their land rights quickly, often selling below market value simply to avoid receiving nothing at all. While much of the Riviera Maya's land sales occurred in the 1990s and early 2000s, these practices continued as development moved south with more recent reporting by U.S. news outlets on the land sale system in Tulum and other parts of the state (Guardado 2018; see Semple 2016).

While the vast majority of these land deals occurred between large resort companies and ejidos, the most notorious land controversy happened early in Playa del Carmen's history. In 1994, hundreds of migrants invaded and asserted squatters' rights over a large parcel of land located north of the city center (Manuel-Navarrete and Redcliff 2012).

With the growth of Cancun in full swing and investors poised to begin construction in a number of resorts within the Riviera Maya zone, thousands of new inhabitants found their way to Quintana Roo looking for work. In Playa del Carmen, the city's population jumped from three thousand inhabitants in 1990 to sixteen thousand in 1993, leading to exorbitant rent prices that placed economic strains on workers. Eventually, workers began settling closer to unoccupied land. Finally, in April 1994 "*la invasión*" (the invasion) took place and hundreds of migrants settled, cleared, and claimed parcels of the forested land for themselves.

What made the invasion challenging for authorities was that both the state government and the Rangel Castelazo family claimed title to the area (Manuel-Navarrete and Redcliff 2012). The government of Quintana Roo asserted control over the land based on a decree of transfer made by President Luis Echeverria in 1973, yet the Rangel Castelazo family asserted land title based off a series of land transactions occurring much earlier. Because of the limited presence of the federal government in Quintana Roo before 1974, no recordings of the land deals existed. Yet, after paying the secretary of the Agrarian

Reform Agency Mex\$2 million, the Rangel Castelazo family received a "receipt" from the Agrarian Reform Agency issued in 1980 certifying their title to the land (Manuel-Navarrete and Redcliff 2012).

At the time of the invasion, the notorious governor Mario Villanueva Madrid was in charge. His government looked the other way as the invasion took place and, only after some time had passed, asserted that the state was powerless to reverse the invasion. Others suspected that Villanueva had ordered the invasion as a populist effort to build political patronage with newcomers. Invaders carved out plots and set up a grid layout and Villanueva named the area after assassinated populist presidential candidate Luis Donaldo Colosio—a close friend of Villaneuva's (Manuel-Navarrete and Redcliff 2012). Villaneuva's government established a payment plan for squatters to regularize their land holdings, but Villanueva's successor canceled the program after taking office. The government refused to return payments to the squatters, and many were left in a legal limbo, as the Rangel Castelazo family successfully asserted their claim in federal court. There, it was believed by many that they bribed federal judges to receive favorable judgments.

Despite squatters not being granted formal land rights, many went on to sell the land as demand increased and new workers arrived in Playa del Carmen. In some cases, two or three workers asserted possession of the same parcel of land. The irregularities regarding land titles still exist today with the Rangel Castelazo family unsuccessfully attempting to collect rents from current inhabitants. Despite the lack of clarity surrounding ownership, the Colosio had steadily developed from a thick forest to an area with paved roads, electricity, and water and sewage service. It is also increasingly the site of new tourism ventures, including vegan cafes, vacation rental properties, posh boutique hotels, and trendy bars.

As Manuel-Navarrete and Redcliff (2012) claim, the sketchy land dealing practices that characterized the Riviera Maya during its initial growth period set the stage for a culture of unscrupulous land dealings across the region. Local lawyers grew adept at helping investors skirt regulations in the name of economic pragmatism—a pragmatism largely extended to business owners. Though as the Colosio example reveals, workers were also the beneficiaries of these legal shortcuts (Guardado 2015). While it might be easy to point to these practices as necessary in the face of burdensome regulatory regimes, I highlight them simply to point out that the question of what to do, given the illegality of these practices, is less clear cut.

Justifications to bypass legal rules can always cut in multiple and indeterminate directions, especially if they are done in the name of economic growth and progress. While there is no telling what kind of tourism opportunities might have developed had the rules been followed, what is clear is that breaking the rules helped move things along quickly and generated growth in Quintana Roo that was uncharacteristic in relation to the rest of Mexico.[1]

In a 2019 documentary titled "La Invasión," produced by a local historian in Playa del Carmen (Tineo 2019), a member of the Rangel Castelazo family asserts that the invasion was illegal and that those who still reside on the land are criminals. While attending the opening screening for the documentary, a discussion regarding the legality of the invasion took place among locals. One man raised his hand to make a point that best captures the crux of the issue of crime explored in this chapter. He asked, "If the people of the Colosio are criminals because they took land that did not belong to them, what do we make of the resorts, hotels, and businesses who took ejido land from the indigenous? What do we call these people, who we know did not follow the rules, and what should we do about their land now?"

As a practical matter, little can be done. Even with broad agreement in the room, evidenced by the nods and claps following his rhetorical question, officials made no formal attempts to right the recent wrongs. Yet, to refuse to recognize these wrongs is equally unsatisfactory, since doing so would make the mistake of believing that the current economic order sprang from and operated along principles of just conduct.

In Hayek's (1976) writings on social justice, he concedes the point that economic gain derived from wrongdoing ought to be corrected whenever it remains possible to locate the individuals that produced that harm. At the same time, he also argues that the Great Society and its accompanying spontaneous order, more exemplified to him by the political economies of the United Kingdom and the United States, is not itself the result of explicit acts of coercion and theft that still persist to this day.[2] Such apparent blindness to the realities of history, as the next section shows, does not escape everyday people who come to understand how the economy "really" works via an acknowledgment and replication of this history in their individual dealings.

## EVERYDAY CRIMINALITY IN PLAYA DEL CARMEN

### Oscar

"I was born at the wrong time," Oscar says during our first interview. The last of eight children, he was just two when his father died of a heart attack, leaving his mother and older siblings to support the family. Oscar's father was a midlevel employee in the state electricity utility and made a decent wage, but when he died his generous salary was reduced to a modest pension and hardship followed. "We would often go without dinner or have to ration loaves of bread," Oscar recalled, "and it was only on rare occasions like Christmas or New Year's when we got something sweet, like a liter of Coca-Cola." His older sister was the first to leave for the United States in the late 1980s, and as soon as Oscar turned eighteen, he followed, crossing the border in the dark of night and swimming across the Rio Grande.

From Texas he made his way to the Northwest where he took a job on an apple farm in rural Oregon where his sister lived. He worked and saved his money for about five years until one day he was caught by immigration officials and deported back to Mexico. This was before Clinton's 1996 immigration reform bill, the Illegal Immigration Reform and Immigration Responsibility Act, that set strict penalties on deportees, and so after Oscar was deported, he used the money he saved to purchase forged documents that allowed him to obtain a tourist visa. He used the visa to go back and forth between the United States and Mexico. "Americans claim they don't want immigrants coming across the border, but I always found work. It was easy. In fact, I worked so well I received raises and learned a lot of new skills on the farm. Eventually, I was making fifteen dollars/hour—a good wage at the time, even in the U.S."

Things continued smoothly for Oscar until around 2002. After the September 11 attacks, immigration enforcement increased, and immigration officers began raiding workplaces while local police ramped up their harassment of migrants across the United States. Oscar became a victim of this harassment when he was pulled over by a police officer in Oregon for what he describes as "simply looking like an immigrant." When the officer ran Oscar's plates, it was discovered that the vehicle was registered to his sister, who by that time had become a legal resident through marriage, and so the officer detained Oscar.

> When I tried to explain to the officer, who I might add was Mexican like me, he ignored me and said I had broken the law. Frustrated, I looked him in the eye and said, "You're going to do this to your people? You're going to act just like the Gringos?" He didn't appreciate that, so he arrested me. The prosecutor gave me two options: I could leave the United States voluntarily and avoid trial, or I could face trial and risk going to prison for two years, after which I might face further penalties for violating immigration law. I decided to leave. I had had enough of the United States and the disrespect I received.

At first Oscar returned to his hometown in Veracruz, but he soon learned that a cousin of his was working in Playa del Carmen making decent money in the tourism industry. Oscar's time in the United States allowed him to acquire a high level of English proficiency, and his cousin promised him it would be easy to find work given his skills. "So I got on the next bus, and I left." Oscar's first job was for an American car rental company where he processed orders, checked the cars after they were returned, and handled other odds and ends.

Speaking lightheartedly, he says, "It was during this job that I learned my first scam." When tourists returned their rentals, workers at the company would, in "Oscar's" terms, "take a little off the top," charging the customer's credit card to refill the gas tank, put air in the tires, or have the car cleaned after use. "The charges were always small enough that no one would notice or fight about it, but if you had thirty cars in one week and you were taking thirty pesos here, fifty pesos there, things would add up." When I pressed Oscar about the scams and whether he felt bad for stealing from the company, or stealing from the tourists, he smiled.

> Everyone steals to get by! You think those Americans cared about theft when I first worked on their farms for such little wages? No. You think the companies care about theft when they refuse to pay our pensions or give us insurance, as required under the law? In the resorts, I hear that a can of Coca-Cola can cost four times as much as it does here in town. It doesn't cost four times as much to drive a crate of Coca-Colas to the hotels, does it? Everyone takes off the top, but people only get mad when "*los pobres*" [the poor] do it.

I nodded in agreement.

After a few years, Oscar saved enough money to leave his job at the car rental company and become a taxi driver. He purchased a Volkswagen Jetta but rented a "*placa*" (medallion) from a senior driver. At the time of our conversation, he was the de facto "*sitio*" (taxi stand) captain of a group of taxis operating in the Walmart parking lot. Despite the existence of local ordinances dictating the prices of taxis, Oscar informed me that he often charged more than the required fare, especially when it came to tourists.

> The city fare rates haven't been changed in years, and in that time the value of the peso has dropped about 20 percent while the cost of living in Playa has increased steadily. So, if the legal fare is forty pesos, I charge seventy.

Oscar added, laughing:

> Even when I raise rates, I have to remind myself that to the tourist it's usually just a dollar or two more, which is less of a markup than those resort sodas.

Unlike other taxi stands, Oscar's stand did not affiliate with a local criminal organization and so, from Oscar's perspective, was more in accordance with the law than the other taxi stands in the city. "On the Quinta, where you have the narco taxi stands, they'll charge 300 pesos when the ride should cost forty pesos, so at least we're better than that."

## Miguel

According to Miguel (from the opening vignette),

> I probably get asked about where to find drugs or prostitutes by forty percent
> of the tourists who visit Playa del Carmen. I used to think it was because the
> tourists thought they could do whatever they want in Mexico, and maybe that's
> part of it. But I realize now after watching American television on Netflix that
> Americans do a lot of drugs and hire a lot of prostitutes in the United States
> too. I guess doing drugs by the beach is more fun than doing drugs back in your
> home.

Like Oscar, Miguel immigrated to Playa del Carmen in the early 2000s from
the state of Veracruz. Younger than Oscar, Miguel left for Playa del Carmen at the age of eighteen, first landing a job at a hotel doing grounds work
before quickly being transferred to transportation. It was in that capacity that
he learned how to drive large vehicles and earned his commercial driving
license. With the certification, a cousin connected him to a job as a bread
delivery driver with the Bimbo Corporation. The job paid well, and it came
with a slate of benefits. But it also meant that Miguel worked long hours, took
weekend shifts, and often missed holidays and his kids' birthday parties. His
wife told him he needed to choose "either the job or your family." Miguel
picked his family.

When I met Miguel, he had been a driver for about a year, working out of
a taxi stand that serviced a set of resorts about twenty minutes north of Playa
del Carmen. His brother-in-law, a more senior driver, vouched for him, and
he soon found himself waking up every morning at three o'clock to shuttle
tourists to the airport, Playa del Carmen, or in rare cases, far off destinations
in the state. Despite the taxi stand's affiliation to nefarious elements and the
occasional tiff with older drivers, Miguel liked the group and appreciated the
professionalism.

Drivers unaffiliated with a taxi stand often worked just as hard as he did
when he worked as a bread delivery driver, zooming around the city in search
of smaller fares that would hopefully add up to a decent wage. The stand,
however, controlled prices, so after two or three rides Miguel would make
his daily quota and have time to return home to pick his daughters up from
school or spend time with his wife. Where a standard trip to the airport cost
Mex\$650, from the resort that ride would cost Mex\$1000 plus the occasional
tip. While sitio rules meant that fare prices were hiked up, something that occasionally bothered tourists, sitio drivers were encouraged to practice "*buen
servicio*" (good service), an ethos that included hard work and commitment to
customer care. In practice, this meant breaking the law. "If the tourist wants
drugs, you find them. If the tourist wants to meet women, you help him do

that. If the tourist is running late, and you can get away with it, you speed," Miguel explained.

Since the resorts and the taxi sitios worked together, an expectation formed that drivers were part of the full resort experience. "The resorts know that we help the tourists find drugs," Miguel stated plainly.

> Often the drivers and the resort staff work together. If a tourist asks a bellboy for drugs, he'll come to the taxi stand and some drivers who work directly for the cartel will hand him the drugs, and the bellboy will get a small finder's fee. As long as the tourist doesn't cause trouble or get hurt, no one cares.

While the system mostly worked smoothly, the illegal nature of the drug market occasionally put drivers in harm's way. Drivers sometimes found themselves indebted to cartels—debts that if left unpaid could produce serious consequences. The real danger, however, came from the realization that the drug market itself could not be controlled. When Playa del Carmen was smaller and only a handful of cartels operated in the city, gangs could broker peaceful business arrangements among themselves. But as the Riviera Maya region grew, more actors attempted to enter the market, often using violence to stake out a position.

Following a string of skirmishes between cartels in the fall of 2018, I received a text message from Miguel around eleven o'clock at night—a screenshot of a message from one of the sitio leaders advising drivers to immediately head home after their shifts. A rival cartel issued a public threat stating it would start targeting drivers from all sitios affiliated with the other cartel. At the time, Miguel stated that he was not worried, since he assumed his marginal position in the sitio would spare him from direct retaliation. Later, over pizza, he confided in me that the threat left a profound impact on him. "What if I was taking my daughters to school and they attacked me? I use this car for my personal needs too, so for a whole week I drove as carefully as possible, hoping I wouldn't get caught up in the mess."
Despite his fear of the cartels, Miguel realized prohibiting drugs would be even costlier.

> If they somehow were able to ban the drugs, I don't think it would help us because then a lot of the tourists would stop coming. There are lots of places around the world where you can do drugs, drink cocktails, and sit by the beach, and if this part of Mexico is no longer an option, the tourists will find somewhere else to go.

Though I take Miguel's estimation that 40 percent of tourists come to the region looking to participate in illegal activity with some degree of skepticism, his broader point that the Riviera Maya competes with other parts of the world for tourists is well taken. The region's competitive advantage is not just its beautiful, white sandy beaches, but its permissiveness when it comes to illicit activities—activities that other parts of the world, and indeed other parts of Mexico, are happy to provide. The pragmatic challenges of eradicating drugs are also worth noting, especially because the war on drugs has gone on for longer than Quintana Roo has been a state with absolutely zero progress made in prohibition.

In Latin America, contemporary scholarship highlights the numerous problems created as states empowered the police and military to join the United States in combating drug production and shipment. In the frenzy of eradicating drugs and demonizing those affiliated with drugs, police across Latin America, especially in Mexico, regularly use excessive force, target particular groups and individuals on racial and class grounds, solicit bribes from criminal organizations, and on occasion work on behalf of those criminal organizations. The movement of drugs cannot be controlled, yet attempts to do so have eroded the public's trust of law enforcement and the state as the excesses of the war of drugs have, to borrow Coyne and Hall's (2018) insight from another context, brought tyranny home (for certain classes of people). Miguel says over beers,

> I think 'cause I see the people who use drugs, I'm not that scared of a world where drugs are legal. In Mexico, many people here are very conservative and have a very negative view of drugs. They think drug users lack education, that they're poor and misbehaved, but the majority of drug users I see are rich tourists who spend more money a night at a resort than I do in a month.

Miguel's insight around drugs helps to make clear a conclusion made by scholars of the drug war—prohibitions around the sale and use of drugs are not about controlling drugs, but rather they are about controlling certain kinds of people affiliated with drugs. From Miguel's perspective, drugs are effectively legal for some people but illegal for others. During the same conversation, he remarked, "If I wanted to go buy lots of drugs and then do all those drugs, I could. I know the people who sell them, I have a house I can do them in, and there's not much anyone could do about it. And why should they? I am not hurting anyone, and if I want to hurt myself to get a little high, why shouldn't I?" He exclaims this before taking a large gulp of his beer and gesturing the glass in a way to draw the connection between the legal drug he's allowed to partake in, alcohol, and the illegal ones the law forbids him (but cannot stop him) from consuming.

To be clear, Miguel does not consume drugs, nor does he want to. He tried marijuana as a young man, and it just made him sleepy. He prefers beer if he plans to cut loose, which is not all that often. Even so, he knows the drug war is not working, and the prohibitions against drugs only create more problems than they solve. What Miguel helps to demonstrate is not simply that the way society manages drugs needs reform. That case is well established at this point. Rather, he demonstrates that by taking the prohibition against drugs for granted as an equally applied rule misses not just that the rule can be applied unequally but that even in its equal application it can produce emergent orders that generate both harm and benefit, depending on where one finds themselves in that particular order. If everyone who ever did drugs were prosecuted to the fullest extent of the law, our current mass incarceration crisis would look tame.

This is not just true of drugs. Even more basic rules of just conduct require elaborate and robust enforcement schemes that, if implemented, might usher in an era of authoritarianism and state control that would betray the very liberal principles both Hayek and Durkheim subscribe to.

Take the crime of fraud, which globally is at an all-time high. Globalization makes it possible for criminal networks across the world to pursue fraudulent schemes via the internet and telephone, tricking thousands of people each day into giving up their private information, which scammers then use to steal billions. Combatting this problem seems next to impossible without serious global cooperation, limitless resources invested in security measures, and a robust and uniform criminal justice system that can investigate, prosecute, and punish these complex operations. The history of the war on drugs tells us that regardless of the state's motives, power given to the state in the name of crime prevention runs a real risk of abuse. Uniform rules of just conduct, whether embedded in social relation or codified into law, are ultimately indeterminate in content and unenforceable as a matter of practice. Such rules must be internalized in one's conscience to have any efficacy, but this demand for ethical uniformity runs into tension with the liberal pillar of difference.

This tension within Hayek's theory of emergent order requires resolution. Following Durkheim, I argue that rules in a complex order must be relational, rather than uniform, and that their value as rules is dependent on their ability to foster and maintain a heightened sense of individuality necessary for liberty.

## EMERGENT ORDERS, ORGANIC SOLIDARITY, AND CRIME

Order, for Hayek, refers to "a state of affairs in which a multiplicity of elements of various kinds are so related to each other that we may learn from our acquaintances with some spatial or temporal part of the whole to form correct expectations concerning the rest" (Hayek 1973, 35; emphasis omitted). Social order, then, is not "exogenous," that is, coming from an external force delivering discrete commands regarding what people should do. Instead, it is an "endogenous" system created not through direct design but through the relational interactions between different elements of the order (ibid., 36).

In distinguishing "made orders" from spontaneous orders, Hayek uses the term "taxis," which refers to "deliberate arrangements" that are "relatively simplistic" and "serve a purpose of the maker" (Hayek 1973, 38). Spontaneous orders, or kosmos, go beyond "what a human mind can master," and they are instead orders based on "abstract relations which we can only mentally reconstruct" (ibid., 38). Though not all spontaneous orders are complex, according to Hayek, spontaneous orders can achieve a degree of complexity that made orders cannot (ibid., 38). Society, the market, and even things like international relations might be said to be spontaneous orders, as the specific multitude of relations that comprise these orders would be far too numerous and complex for any one person to understand. No single, discernable purpose characterizes these orders, yet as Hayek makes clear, the multitude of relations within these orders produces the orders themselves—a process that develops through evolutionary trial and error (ibid., 41). As a consequence, the more complex a spontaneous order, the less power any individual or even group of individuals have to alter it, at least not without "upsetting the overall order" (ibid., 42). Hayek maintains that at best we may be able to discern general rules from the observance of certain spontaneous orders that allow us to make certain predictions as to how an order will unfold. Such predictions are not certain, as complex spontaneous orders, such as the market, always contain a degree of uncertainty simply unknowable to any particular person. Yet, it is this degree of uncertainty that generates the possibility and regularity of change within that order.

All spontaneous orders are held together through rules of conduct. These rules, for Hayek, are often unknown to those who subscribe to the rules, making such rules akin to custom, cultural practices, or what Bourdieu calls "habitus" (Bourdieu 1977; Hayek 1973, 43). In spontaneous orders characterized by the existence of market exchange, Hayek posits that certain implicit rules exist, such as preferring more profit over less. But simple profit-maximizing activities are not sufficient for Hayek, since he argues that for "a resulting order to be beneficial people must also observe conventional rules . . . which do not simply follow from their desires and their insight into relations of cause and effect, but which are normative and tell them what they ought or ought not to do" (Hayek 1973, 45). Though such rules are often tacit, as complex spontaneous orders emerge and gain form, rules may be explicitly stated and codified into law (ibid., 46).

Hayek contrasts rules of organization with rules of spontaneous orders, suggesting that rules of organization are designed to complement organizational commands and serve distinct and direct purposes. In contrast, "rules governing a spontaneous order must be independent of purpose and be the same," as it is through their sameness that individuals can pursue their distinct ends within the parameters of the rules. This is because in complex societies, the complexity of a society is wholly unknowable to individuals, but individuals within that society possess knowledge that they act upon in the service of their interests or ends. Any attempt to supplement the rules governing that order with commands meant to direct that order will be "impossible," but more importantly, it might disrupt the usefulness of the knowledge people already possess and might act upon (Hayek 1973, 51). This does not mean, for Hayek, that rules within a spontaneous order cannot be improved, even deliberately so, but only that what makes a particular rule good will depend on its separation from the aims of particular individuals or groups.

At the base of Hayek's preference for spontaneous orders is his ultimate belief in the cause of liberty. Liberty, however, is not a natural condition of individuality, since Hayek rejects natural law. But instead, it results from people engaged in an order (like society) and being allowed to act upon the knowledge they receive from their particular place in that order. Individual knowledge, Hayek reminds us, is a consequence of being in a social order, meaning individuality is less a product of being human and more a state of consciousness and a disposition of conscientiousness that allows one to act in their interests, but not if those interests conflict with rules or principles of just conduct (Hayek 1973, 56–57). Thus, for Hayek, freedom must be the "supreme principle" that guides spontaneous orders. Hayek likens this principle to ideology, a system of principles (discursively constructed) that makes apparent to individuals their very individuality.

It is only briefly stated by Hayek where criminal law should reside, though what might comprise criminal law is left unstated. Crime, under Hayek's framework, is an element of "private law," which is a misleading term, as it refers not to the law of private domains but to the rules of conduct between private individuals (whereas public law refers to the procedural operation of government) (Hayek 1976, 34–35). Private law encompasses rules of just conduct, which comprise a set of negative obligations that determine how individuals ought to treat one another (ibid., 37). The outcomes that flow from following such rules are not important to Hayek insomuch as the rules themselves are just, since a spontaneous order necessitates winners and losers as each pursues their respective preferences under the risk that such pursuits may not be rewarded. Thus, while the specific rules of just conduct may be different depending on the spontaneous order in question, we learn from

Hayek that they share two general principles: (1) they are negative obligations that (2) apply equally to everyone within that order.

Hayek's minimal foundation of rules of just conduct for a spontaneous order stems in large part from his suspicions that particular groups might build positive obligations into the law that serve particular ends. As a matter of principle, this relates to the non-interference maxim Hayek believes is necessary for a spontaneous order to unfold, but as a pragmatic issue, comes from the recognition of the law's coercive power and its potential to subject particular groups and individuals to great harm for the benefit of others. For this reason, both the rules of just conduct and the assessment of their just nature are evaluated in the negative, thereby making the correction of injustice the task of any system (Hayek 1976, 44). This produces an asymptotic relationship to justice, in which a just social state is never explicitly defined but simply comes into being through the correction of injustices that might occur through the violation of the rules. This leaves open the possibility of many different kinds of rules of just conduct that might adhere to the negative conception of justice that Hayek posits (1976, 56).

This last element of Hayek's theory becomes important since a spontaneous order capable of including difference represented through the liberty individuals have to pursue their ends is central to Hayek's liberalism. Adherence to a positive conception of justice frustrates the possibility of difference, leaving the door open for state coercion in the service of someone else's interests.

Though Hayek is convinced of the moral wrong such coercion might entail, his ultimate point is that pursuing our interests, through some minimal negative check on our actions, is the only way in which we might all enjoy the benefits of liberty. Indeed, even while Hayek is one to praise the existence of morals and customs learned over time and integrated into specific spontaneous orders, his ideal rests with the eventual formation of what he calls an "Open Society." Such a society, he laments in volume two of *Law, Legislation and Liberty*, exists in a not-yet-achieved horizon in which "national boundaries have ceased to be obstacles to the free movement of men" and a global sense of equal treatment between different individuals is achieved (Hayek 1976, 57). It is here that one understands Hayek's concern is not really about rules of conduct. It is instead a notion of individuality in which a person pursues their interests not in a selfish and unchecked manner but via the recognition of their relationship to others. This is distinct from individuals acting in accordance to a common end or in the spirit of altruism. Rather, it is a kind of recognition of the value of others and the basic degree of respect they deserve. Hayek, of course, cautions against the state instilling such a moral order, as such ways of being together cannot be coerced without the fear of backlash. Instead, this form of individuality is a state of consciousness set against and above a sense of self allied to one's particular group membership.

For Durkheim, the complex social order made possible by the division of labor and the development of the market similarly requires a sense of elaborated individuality. In the three books that comprise *The Division of Labor in Society* (2013), Durkheim pursues an answer to the questions "How does it come about that the individual, whilst becoming more autonomous, depends even more closely upon society? How can he become at the same time more of an individual and yet more linked to society?" (Durkheim 2013, 7).

Like Hayek, Durkheim does not view individuality as set apart from the social order and existing in a state of nature that society must tame. Instead, he views individuality as springing from society, its possibility a result of exchange (economic and otherwise) that allows movement across distinct moral communities, which generates difference.

Durkheim famously sets up a distinction between what he calls mechanical solidarity and organic solidarity, terms that refer to distinct social orders rather than states of social development. Mechanical solidarity, or the solidarity of similarities, presumes a society held together under a single moral framework such that an individual sees herself in relation to that framework. Similar to Hayek's point that individuality emerges as a state of consciousness, mechanical solidarity denotes a social order held together through a singular and well-defined set of rules, or criminal sanctions, that repress the possibility of difference or deviance from that order.

Durkheim's iconic statement about crime is worth repeating here: "We should not say that an act offends the common consciousness because it is criminal, but that it is criminal because it offends that consciousness" (Durkheim 2013, 64). This line is often misread and interpreted to suggest an uncritical relationship between crime and a shared sense of social opprobrium, such that criminal law reflects society's judgment. Yet, Durkheim's point is more nuanced. His statement suggests not a direct relationship between crime and society's judgment, but rather that it is society's judgment, as a singularly conceived moral order, that determines what is criminal. In the same chapter, Durkheim offers a number of examples that push his reader to shed the idea that crime and social harm are inextricably linked. In one place he writes,

> Even when the criminal act is certainly harmful to society, the degree of damage it causes is far from being regularly in proportion to the intensity of repression it incurs. In the penal law of most civilized peoples, murder is universally regarded as the greatest of crimes. Yet, an economic crisis, a crash on the stock market, even a bankruptcy, can disorganize the body social much more seriously than the isolated case of homicide. Assuredly, murder is always an evil, but nothing proves that it is the greatest evil. (Durkheim 2013, 58)

Where mechanical solidarity is a somewhat clunky term, it might be better understood as illiberal. In illiberal societies, uniform rules of repression become the highest order of law, as these societies cannot tolerate difference. This is not to say that within illiberal societies individuals do not recognize themselves as individuals, but rather that the social order does not allow for the full expression of individuality to the extent it departs from the established moral order.

Durkheim's observation regarding crime runs parallel to Hayek's (1976) caution against societies organized around discrete claims of social justice. So long as society insists its members act toward a singular purpose, deviation from that purpose is sanctioned at the cost of individuals freely pursuing their desired ends. This social order might be understood as an ideal, similar to Hayek's "Great Society" (see note 2), and is characterized by a political economy reliant on the division of labor, increasing specialization, and the formation of an individuality both conscious of itself and conscientious of others.

Durkheim, like Hayek, conceives of the complex social order that springs from the division of labor as an abstract phenomenon that surpasses any one individual's ability to know it fully. For Durkheim, this social order holds itself together not through a singular moral code (from which repressive law coerces people into compliance), as that would undermine the difference the division of labor relies on, but through the interconnected systems of exchange that produce an interdependence between members of society. It is for this reason that Durkheim maintains that within an organic social order, repressive or criminal law recedes, and a relational and restorative law takes over. Since an organic social order implies an abstract social order composed of many interlocking and overlapping societies, or many different ways of being, basic rules of just conduct are incompatible so long as those rules, even framed within the negative, presume a distinct way of being, or living, reminiscent of mechanical, or illiberal, social orders.

For this reason, organic social orders can never act toward a particular end but must instead make room for the members within that order to negotiate their differences, repair and restore past harms, and find peaceful ways of living together. This process is not a state-led endeavor. Instead, it entails the formation of what Durkheim calls "professional ethics," or the distinct rules of conduct that are unique to particular moral communities and their members and yet relational to other moral communities in a complex social order (what the Ostroms might call polycentricity). Foundational to this social order is the same idea of individuality that marks Hayek's dream of an "Open Society," an individuality that is both conscious and conscientious of others and includes the freedom to move across moral communities. Crime is thus an object of critical intervention for Durkheim—its existence as a codified sanction worthy of scientific scrutiny and the judgment that comes with it.

Returning to Oscar and Miguel, a critical examination of crime reveals a social order not in need of new criminal sanctions but in need of repair. Oscar's swindling of tourists is in direct response to the mistreatment he received as a migrant in the United States—his own dreams squashed at the hands of an immigration-restriction system marked by racial discrimination and irrational fears of migrants. When he charges above the legal rate set for cab fares, he is not just questioning the outdated regulations that govern taxi ride prices in Playa del Carmen. Rather, as he stated to me, he is mimicking those large resorts who upcharge tourists for a can of Coca-Cola (something they are legally allowed to do).

In Miguel's case, we see the absurdity of criminal sanctions surrounding the sale and use of drugs and their unequal enforcement, but also the real danger that follows when state entities are empowered through the law to enforce as they please. The point, of course, is that what is legal and what is sanctioned can never be taken for granted. Even uniform and basic rules of just conduct, when applied equally to different sets of people, can produce relationships of mistrust and exacerbate previously existing prejudices that can become entrenched in social relations over time.

Durkheim warns of what he calls "abnormal" forms of solidarity that might emerge when the division of labor and specialization exist, but such relations are held together through the coercive and repressive force of criminal sanction. The racial discrimination that still persists in the United States is one example where a market society is present, and yet the dominant players continue to harbor racially prejudicial feelings toward particular members of that society carried over from centuries of marginalization rooted in slavery, extended during Jim Crow, and maintained through mass incarceration—a phenomenon caused in part by the War on Drugs. In this form of solidarity, some individuals are free to pursue their ends as they please, but some are not—locked out through legal sanction or social custom from enjoying the fruits of liberty.

Greenhouse (2003) argues that Durkheim's critical approach to crime, like Martin and Storr's (2008) critical approach to perverse emergent orders, places the social scientist in a position of normative judgment. This means resisting descriptive reification and instead challenging society's justification for criminal sanctions. Objectivity emerges not from a position that resists bias but through a presentation of facts and an openness to fairness and argumentation that might draw us closer to understanding. In an organic social order, difference cannot be so easily disregarded, both by society and especially the social scientist, meaning any assumption made about crime in the absence of inquiry should be suspended. This provides us not with a guarantee that we might come closer to devising what the proper rules of just conduct ought to be but only offers a possibility—one that, as society changes, forces upon social science the endless task of revision and reinvestigation.

For those living and working in the Riviera Maya, such questions once loomed in the background, but now they sit squarely in the foreground as the profit from crime (from drugs, land deals, and other misdeeds) sits next to the pain (the violence, social relations of deceit, and broad sense of mistrust), necessitating not more rules to follow but the ritual of restoration and repair.

## CONCLUSION

If during the course of Hayek's writing the greatest threat to liberty resided in the prospect of a totalitarian, socialist state coming into being, it may now be said that the greatest threat to liberty is crime (Milhaupt and West 2000). This does not just entail being the victim of crime but also becoming the subject of states' measures to control crime (Wacquant 2009). We are regularly confronted with the extent of a global economic order seemingly marked by illegal activity and nefarious wrongdoing. This is not only evidenced in the global trafficking of drugs, weapons, and people across state borders or the rise of complex and elaborate scams made possible by globalization, but as the Panama Papers (to cite just one example) revealed, it includes the actions of powerful elite actors and their use of tax loopholes and tax havens to hide money and skirt domestic laws (Comaroff and Comaroff 2008, 2016).

At the same time, coordinated security measures increasingly empower state, and even non-state, actors to invade our privacy, subject us to abuse, or place us into authoritarian contexts that limit our freedom (Coyne and Hall 2018). Whereas Hayek warned of the dangers of distinct groups advancing claims of "social justice" as a means of hijacking the state for their own interests, ordinary citizens now grow weary of governments and private institutions they view as victims of institutional capture by corporate and criminal interests. In some cases, such state capture is used to protect criminal wrongdoing, and in others it is used to create new criminals (the migrant, the terrorist, the "super predator"). Crime threatens the confidence people have in market relations, eroding the trust necessary to engage in fair dealing and sparking a pattern of swindling and deceit viewed as necessary to get ahead. Yet, as Oscar observes, legality can do the same. The challenging question posed by the integration of criminal activity into state, corporate, and individual practice is whether wrongdoing is an outcome of the law or is instead best viewed as legal violation.

A form of this question sits on the minds of people living in the town of Playa del Carmen. In that context, the tourism economy appears held together through the normalization of criminal activity. Yet, the harm of crime produces a shared sense of vulnerability that leaves locals both frustrated and eager for legal compliance yet also willing to bypass the law for their own gain. Would tourists from Euro-America still visit Playa del Carmen if it were impossible to purchase recreational drugs, solicit sex workers, and engage in other illicit activity? Conversely, what value do legal sanctions against recreational drug use, prostitution, or other criminal activities have when no one wishes to follow them? Is a law that applies equally to everyone, like prohibiting drug use and dealing, an example of a legal order in the service of liberty, or is it the state overstepping its bounds and restricting liberty? Hayek's framework, while offering some clues, is ultimately unable to definitively offer answers.

Yet, it is Hayek's commitment to individuality and liberty that provides us a path forward, a path carved out by a fellow liberal, Émile Durkheim. To follow this path, however, is to abandon the search for a set of uniform rules of just conduct. Society's multiplicity of difference requires a relational approach to crime and law, one that allows different groups and different individuals to undertake the challenge of repair and restoration produced both through the enforcement and violation of criminal sanctions. The place of social science in this process must be a critical one that refuses to take for granted society's judgment but instead examines it by holding in the same space both the perspective of those that judge and those who are judged. To do so is both to commit to the kind of individuality that both Hayek and Durkheim believe is necessary for the Great Society and organic solidarity, respectively—an individuality rooted in a heightened sense of consciousness and conscientiousness and keenly committed to the full expression of difference.

## NOTES

1. Since the founding of Cancun, Quintana Roo's economic statistics make it an exceptional case in relation to the rest of Mexico. The state's economic growth has, on average, been double the national average. It has maintained low unemployment levels, and the medium income of workers is considerably higher than the Mexican average (Gobierno de Quintana Roo 2020).

2. While a recounting of all the coercive practices that defined the United States and United Kingdom's economic development cannot be fully elaborated in this chapter, please see Taylor (2019) on the role of real estate industry in abusing government programs to exploit African American lenders, Coates (2014) on similar

private-public collusion against African Americans in the real estate industry, Coates (2014) on the role of private settlers in the taking of indigenous land, and Stuesse (2016) on the exploitation of migrants in the Deep South. For an account of the British slave trade and subsequent efforts at abolition see Hochschild (2005). For a history of private and state-sponsored colonial theft in India see Tharoor (2017). And see Inikori (2002) on the role of economic coercion and exploitation of Africans during the late 1700s and 1800s.

## REFERENCES

Arias, Enrique Desmond. 2006. *Drugs and Democracy in Rio de Janeiro: Trafficking, Social Networks, and Public Security.* Chapel Hill, NC: University of North Carolina Press.

Bourdieu, Pierre. 1977. *Outline of a Theory of Practice.* Cambridge, UK: Cambridge University Press.

Chawla et al. 2005. "2005 World Drug Report." *United Nations Office on Drugs and Crime.* https://www.unodc.org/pdf/WDR_2005/volume_1_web.pdf.

Coates, Ta-Nehisi. 2014. "The Case for Reparations." *The Atlantic*, June. https://www.theatlantic.com/magazine/archive/2014/06/the-case-for-reparations/361631/.

Comaroff, Jean, and John L. Comaroff. 2008. "Introduction." In *Law and Disorder in the Postcolony*, edited by Jean Comaroff and John L. Comaroff, 1–56. Chicago: University of Chicago Press.

———. 2016. *The Truth about Crime: Sovereignty, Knowledge, Social Order.* Chicago: University of Chicago Press.

Cortazar, Jose. 2010. "Mayor of Mexico Resort Arrested for Drug Gang Ties." *Reuters*, May 26. https://www.reuters.com/article/us-mexico-mayor/mayor-of-mexico-resort-arrested-for-drug-gang-ties-idUSTRE64P5ST20100526.

Coyne, Christopher J., and Abigail R. Hall. 2018. *Tyranny Comes Home: The Domestic Fate of US Militarism.* Stanford, CA: Stanford University Press.

Durkheim, Émile. 2013. *The Division of Labor in Society.* 2nd ed. London: Palgrave Macmillan.

Esposito, Richard. 2010. "Mexican Governor Charged with Helping Cartel Smuggle Tons of Cocaine Is Extradited to U.S." *ABC News*, May 10. https://abcnews.go.com/Blotter/mexican-politician-charged-helping-drug-cartel-smuggle-200/story?id=10604656.

Ford, Lisa. 2010. *Settler Sovereignty: Jurisdiction and Indigenous People in America and Australia, 1788–1836.* Cambridge, MA: Harvard University Press.

Gobierno de Quintana Roo. 2020. "Quintana Roo Ocupa el Tercer Lugar Nacional en Crecimiento Económico." Accessed April 29, 2020. https://qroo.gob.mx/portal/quintana-roo-ocupa-el-tercer-lugar-nacional-en-crecimiento-economico/.

Greenhouse, Carol J. 2003. "Solidarity and Objectivity: Rereading Durkheim." In *Crime's Power: Anthropologists and the Ethnography of Crime*, edited by Philip C. Parnell and Stephanie C. Kane, 269–92. New York: Palgrave Macmillan.

Guardado, Gustavo Marín. 2015. "Turismo: Espacios y Culturas en Transformacion." *Desacatos* 47: 6–15.

———. 2018. "Tourism Development and Land Appropriation: The Role of Agrarian Mafias in Tulum, Mexico." *Norois* 247: 31–47.

Hakim, Danny. 2014. "Sex, Drugs, and G.D.P." *The New York Times*, June 16. https://www.nytimes.com/2014/06/17/upshot/sex-drugs-and-gdp.html.

Hayek, F. A. 1973. *Law, Legislation and Liberty, Volume 1: Rules and Order*. Chicago: University of Chicago Press.

———. 1976. *Law, Legislation and Liberty, Volume 2: The Mirage of Social Justice*. Chicago: University of Chicago Press.

———. 1988. *The Fatal Conceit: The Errors of Socialism*. London: Routledge.

Hochschild, Adam 2005. *Bury the Chains: Prophets and Rebels in the Fight to Free an Empire's Slaves.* Boston, MA: Houghton Mifflin.

INEGI. 2015. "Numero de Habitantes por Municipio, Solidaridad." Accessed April 29, 2020. http://cuentame.inegi.org.mx/monografias/informacion/qroo/poblacion/.

Inikori, Joseph E. 2002. *Africans and the Industrial Revolution in England: A Study in International Trade and Development.* Cambridge, UK: Cambridge University Press.

Kelly, James J., Jr. 1994. "Article 27 and Mexican Land Reform: The Legacy of Zapata's Dream." *Columbia Human Rights Law Review* 25 (2): 541–70.

Lange, Jason. 2010. "From Spas to Banks, Mexico Economy Rides on Drugs." *Reuters*, January 22. https://www.reuters.com/article/us-drugs-mexico-economy/from-spas-to-banks-mexico-economy-rides-on-drugs-idUSTRE60L0X120100122?fbclid=IwAR2o4Uw8bHyu8wqxDmv5WeU8FnmiXfPhlU2odhc8OXrIiZS8T_Oz-mHo020.

Lemos, Carlos. 2018. "Panama Extradites Former Mexican Governor Accused of Corruption." *Reuters*, January 4. https://www.reuters.com/article/us-panama-crime-mexico/panama-extradites-former-mexican-governor-accused-of-corruption-idUSKBN1ET1Z5.

Manuel-Navarrete, David, and Michael Redclift. 2012. "Spaces of Consumerism and the Consumption of Space: Tourism and Social Exclusion in the 'Mayan Riviera.'" In *Consumer Culture in Latin America*, edited by Sinclair J. Pertierra, 177–93. New York: Palgrave Macmillan.

Martin, Nona, and Virgil Henry Storr. 2008. "On Perverse Emergent Orders." *Studies in Emergent Order* 1 (1): 73–91.

Milhaupt, Curtis J., and Mark D. West. 2000. "The Dark Side of Private Ordering: An Institutional and Empirical Analysis of Organized Crime." *The University of Chicago Law Review* 67 (1): 41–98.

Mintz, Sidney W. 1985. *Sweetness and Power: The Place of Sugar in Modern History*. New York: Viking.

Semple, Kirk. 2016. "Evictions by Armed Men Rattle a Mexican Tourist Paradise." *The New York Times*, August 17. https://www.nytimes.com/2016/08/17/world/americas/mexico-tulum-corruption-evictions.html.

Stuesse, Angela. 2016. *Scratching Out a Living: Latinos, Race, and Work in the Deep South*. Berkeley, CA: University of California Press.

Taylor, Keeanga-Yamahtta. 2019. *Race for Profit: How Banks and the Real Estate Industry Undermine Black Homeownership*. Chapel Hill, NC: University of North Carolina Press.

Tharoor, Shashi. 2017. *Inglorious Empire: What the British Did to India*. London: Hurst & Company.

Tineo, Raymundo. 2019. "Invasión ¿justicia social o negocio." YouTube [video], June 21. https://www.youtube.com/watch?v=MxI1BzkBLg4.

Torres, Rebecca. 2002. "Cancun's Tourism Development from a Fordist Spectrum of Analysis." *Tourist Studies* 2 (1): 87–116.

Torres, Rebecca Maria, and Janet D. Momsen. 2005. "Gringolandia: The Construction of a New Tourist Space in Mexico." *Annals of the Association of American Geographers* 95 (2): 314–35.

Wacquant, Loic. 2009. *Punishing the Poor: The Neoliberal Government of Social Insecurity*. Durham, NC: Duke University Press.

Watt, Peter, and Roberto Zepeda. 2012. *Drug War Mexico: Politics, Neoliberalism, and Violence in the New Narcoeconomy*. London: Zed Books.

*Chapter 11*

# A Pluralistic Approach to Corruption

## Principal-Agent, Collective Action, and Hayek

### Mario I. Juarez-Garcia

The clarity of the high-modernist optic is due to its resolute singularity. Its simplifying fiction is that, for any activity or process that comes under its scrutiny, there is only one thing going on.

—James C. Scott (1998, 347)

In 1996, James D. Wolfensohn, the president of the World Bank, declared war against the "cancer of corruption."[1] It was the first time that the president of a major international organization spoke openly about widespread corruption, a topic previously considered taboo.[2] From then on, the World Bank declared corruption "public enemy number one" in developing countries.[3] Economists are at the forefront of this war because their theories are used to design anti-corruption policies. This chapter focuses on the importance of theories for grasping the problem of corruption. Because they are simplified versions of reality, theories allow us to perceive, grasp, and predict behaviors by reducing the noise of details. They aim to grasp the essence of the phenomenon by reducing it to its bare bones. Theories are like maps: they provide a particular approach to the terrain—the subject matter—by underlining some of its characteristics and hiding some others depending on the interest of the traveler.[4] This chapter shows that we require (at least) three approaches to depict the complex terrain of corruption.

Anti-corruption experts usually employ the principal-agent theory to grasp corruption (World Bank 1997; United Nations 2004). Due to the failures of this map, recently, a different one appeared. The new map put forward the understanding of corruption in developing countries as a collective-action problem (Bicchieri and Xiao 2008; Persson, Rothstein, and Teorell 2013;

Mungiu-Pippidi 2015; Bicchieri 2016). Both charts share a key assumption: laws must be enforced. Those who use these maps intend to find strategies that promote law compliance. Conversely, I argue that our understanding of corruption will remain incomplete—and anti-corruption policies will remain ineffective—as long as we discard the possibility that some cases of corruption indicate that certain laws must not be enforced. Employing insights from mainline economists,[5] this chapter advances a third map that is sensitive to the role of the inadequate laws in the proliferation of corrupt practices and makes it salient that when laws ban practices that are not considered morally wrong, people prefer corrupt public officials over honest law enforcers. I call this third approach Hayekian.

The Hayekian approach has an advantage over the principal-agent and collective-action frameworks: it grasps the influence of culture on corrupt practices. The principal-agent and collective action–based approaches prioritize what the law says. Conversely, the Hayekian approach emphasizes what people do over what the law says—it focuses on the cultural practices. Since "there is relatively little written on how culture affects rent seeking" (Choi and Storr 2019, 103), widening the study of the relation between corruption and culture is one of the aims of this chapter. However, my main objective is not to defend or argue for any particular anti-corruption approach. On the contrary, I believe there is no one-size-fits-all map for the complex terrain of corruption. Each approach is effective in its appropriate context, and each one is unfruitful in inappropriate contexts. The contribution of this chapter is to show that, depending on the details of the situation, corrupt practices can be the result of deviant moralities, undesirable social norms, or cultural responses to inadequate laws. A complete theory of anti-corruption policies includes the three maps, constituting a pluralistic approach to corruption.

The chapter proceeds as follows. First, I briefly show the blind spot of current approaches to corruption. The next section analyzes the typical principal-agent approach, underlining its virtues and its limitations. Then, I will articulate the scope and limits of the collective action–based approach. The last section presents the Hayekian approach. I conclude that only a pluralistic approach will account for the different kinds of corruption.

## THE BLIND SPOT OF ANTI-CORRUPTION THEORIES

Corruption—understood as the use of public office for private gain—is operationalized in different ways with the goal of designing efficient anti-corruption policies. This section briefly states the blind spot of the principal-agent and collective action–based approaches and shows how a Hayekian perspective opens up new ways to understand corrupt practices.

The principal-agent theory is the standard approach to corruption. It aims to eradicate corruption by designing an incentive structure that motivates public officials to comply with their legal obligations. Some scholars hold that this approach is insufficient to solve the problem in developing countries where corruption is the norm (Persson, Rothstein, and Teorell 2013). A different approach conceptualizes corruption in such societies as collective-action problems and designs policies to abandon the undesirable norm of corruption. The following sections will deal with these two approaches in more detail. For now, it is sufficient to note that these two approaches share an underlying assumption: the law must be enforced. There is no theory that tracks the cases of corruption in which both citizens and public officials prefer corruption to law enforcement, all things considered. This is an important blind spot. When citizens and enforcers prefer corrupt to honest public officials, all things considered, one can interpret that corruption is a signal that the law that is being violated *must not* be enforced. To be sensitive to this dimension of corruption, we need a new approach that removes the assumption that laws must be enforced.

A way to build an anti-corruption approach that is sensitive to these cases is to put at its basis the distinction between informal and formal norms. Mainline economists embrace the three following propositions: "(1) there are limits to benevolence that individuals can rely on and therefore they face cognitive and epistemic limits as they negotiate the social world, but (2) formal and informal institutions guide and direct human activity, and, so (3) social cooperation is possible without central direction" (Boettke, Haeffele-Balch, and Storr 2016, 4). As proposition (2) states, the distinction between formal and informal institutions is key for mainline economists. If both kinds of institutions contradict each other and, at the same time, both guide human action, we can predict a conflict in practice. I argue that one way to avoid the conflict is corrupting the officials in charge of enforcing formal institutions to preserve informal norms.

In *Law, Legislation and Liberty*, F. A. Hayek, one of the primary mainline economists, distinguishes between law and legislation. Law exists prior to legislation since it refers to the "common rules [that] make the peaceful existence of individuals in society possible" (Hayek 1982, 72). Legislation, on the other hand, is "the deliberate making of the law" (ibid., 72). Since peaceful cooperation exists before the invention of formal mechanisms of legislation, societies observe laws long before legislation. Within this framework, Hayek concludes that, in a free society, people observe the legislation that closely maps the law; on the contrary, in a despotic society, the ruler imposes legislation that corresponds uniquely to her own capricious will. In the fourth section of this chapter, I will use New Development Economics theory to construct a novel approach to corruption of Hayekian inspiration.

The Hayekian approach shows that legislation promotes corruption when it runs afoul of the informal norms of a society, in which case citizens tend to find a way to violate formal rules without being punished; an easy way to do so is, for example, to offer a bribe to the law enforcer.

The Hayekian approach is just one map to certain kinds of corrupt practices, not to all. When corruption arises in societies with legislation that actually coincides with the law, the Hayekian approach tells us next to nothing about effective strategies to eradicate such corrupt behaviors. A principal-agent approach seems more adequate to deal with corruption in those cases. The point is that the different anti-corruption approaches presented in this chapter have virtues and limits. But they have points of connection as well: where an approach fails, another succeeds. Corruption is a complicated phenomenon. The same action can be understood in different ways. I hold that each approach helps us to understand the same act of corruption in a different way, depending on the context. Therefore, we need a pluralistic approach to discover which map better tracks particular cases of corruption. We can only perceive the full picture of corruption when we consider the three approaches together. The idea is that we need to experiment with different theories and their strategies until finding the correct one. The correct one would be the one that allows us to design successful strategies to eradicate "the cancer of corruption."

## THE PRINCIPAL-AGENT APPROACH

Consider the following hypothetical case:

> *Speeding*: Avital drives above the speed limit. Paul, the police officer, sees the violation, follows her, and asks her to stop. She obeys. Paul is looking for a bribe. Avital reads the signs and bribes him. Paul lets her go.

When thinking about *Speeding*, our first intuition is to think that there is something wrong with Paul's action. Every public official who uses her power for personal benefit violates a fiduciary obligation toward the citizens. The principal-agent theory models this intuition.

The principal delegates a task $\Phi$ and the means to fulfill $\Phi$ to an agent. In exchange, the principal provides incentives—rewards or punishments—to the agent for fulfilling $\Phi$. The agent, then, acquires a fiduciary obligation to the principal. As in many economic models, the principal-agent framework assumes that actors are rational maximizers. If the rewards for being honest and the threat of punishments for not being honest are enough, the agent calculates that it is in her interest to comply with the obligation. If the incentive structure does not provide sufficient rewards or punishments, the agent calculates that her utility is maximized when she violates her fiduciary obligations. Corruption, then, is a problem of insufficient incentives for the agent to act honestly. The principal-agent approach recommends that, to correct the corrupt practices of the agent, the principal must design better incentive structures.

The political scientist Robert Klitgaard is one of the pioneers of this approach to corruption. Yet, he proposed a slightly different model: the principal-agent-client model (Klitgaard 1988, 69). The example of tax collectors illustrates his interpretation of corrupt practices. The principal is the politician who wants to collect taxes. The agent is the bureaucrat who actually collects taxes, and the client is the taxpayer. The agent only has two options: collecting taxes from the client according to the principal's instructions or taking a bribe from the client to disregard her taxes. The agent acts corruptly if the payoff of taking the bribe is higher than the payoff of fulfilling her fiduciary obligation. The components of the expected utility calculations are of different kinds: money, moral gains, the severity of the sanctions, the probability of being punished. For Klitgaard, when the agent is deciding whether to do her job or taking a bribe, she says to herself, "I will be corrupt if: the bribe minus the moral cost minus [(the probability I am caught and punished) times (the penalty for being corrupt)] is greater than my pay plus the satisfaction I get from not being corrupt" (1988, 69). From this approach, corruption is the result of insufficient material or moral incentives to be honest. The problem lies in the institutional design when it does not provide sufficient material incentives to act honestly.

Other scholars have simplified Klitgaard's model (Besley 2006; Persson, Rothstein, and Teorell 2013, 452; Schmidtz 2015, 53). In a functional democracy, citizens are the principals, and the government comprises the agents. The citizens delegate their power to the government, so it can be used in the public interest. In this framework, citizens must design an incentive-compatible structure for the government so that their interests and the public officials' interests are aligned, and corruption is prevented. This simplification, however, does not change the essence of Klitgaard's calculation: a public official will be corrupt if the bribe minus the moral cost and the expected utility of punishments is greater than the moral reward for being honest plus the pay.

Briefly, if we see corruption through the lens of principal-agent theory, the issue is that individuals respond to incentives and the structure of incentives is poorly designed. The strategy against corruption is, then, to construct a better incentive structure that includes severe punishments for engaging in corrupt practices, efficient monitoring of public officials, and increasing the wages of public servants, among other measures. Briefly, as the main strategy to eradicate corruption, the principal-agent approach recommends improving the institutional arrangement so as to provide enough incentives to be honest.

## The Anti-Corruption Toolkit: Success and Failure

The principal-agent approach has been a major influence for international organizations (Persson, Rothstein, and Teorell 2013, 451; Johnston 2005). In 2004, the United Nations published "The Anti-Corruption Toolkit" to promote their policies against corruption in developing countries (United Nations 2004). The influence of the principal-agent view is clear in its policy recommendations: better monitoring systems, autonomous anti-corruption agencies, stronger judicial powers, increased transparency in the government, laws for protecting whistleblowers, strict government hiring procedures, education to raise awareness about the problem of corruption, more severe punishments, and better compensations for honest public officials, among others.

The anti-corruption toolkit has been tried in several countries. Its successes and failures have provided some lessons about the theory itself. The toolkit yields good results in developed countries. An example of success is South Korea. Kyoung-sun Min (2019) studies the implementation of the policies of the anti-corruption toolkit in South Korea and compares its results with a national measurement of honesty. Because there is a positive correlation between the implementations of anti-corruption policies and the level of integrity in the public servants, Min concludes, "the implementation of anti-corruption policies has a positive effect on curbing corruption in public organizations. . . . In South Korea at least, the success of anti-corruption policies is not elusive" (2019, 237). These observations, as Min acknowledges, are limited to the South Korean case.

Conversely, in developing countries, the results of the anti-corruption toolkit are disappointing (Brinkerhoff 2000; Mungiu-Pippidi 2011). Nigeria is a case in point. The economist Ngozi Okonjo-Iweala, a high-level official at the World Bank, returned to her birthplace in 2011 to enact reforms following the anti-corruption toolkit and eradicate generalized corruption (Okonjo-Iweala 2017). She reformed the economic institutions and built better monitoring systems in spite of resistance and numerous menaces. She left office in 2015 satisfied with the policies that she implemented. Unfortunately, there is no evidence that the new institutions actually reduced corruption. The Corruption Perception Index of Transparency International indicates that the levels of perception of corruption in Nigeria remain as high as before she took office. On a scale where zero denotes the highest level of corruption and 100 denotes no corruption, after 2011, Nigeria has fluctuated between 24 and 28 points.[6] In other words, after Okonjo-Iweala's reforms, Nigeria did not experience a significant change regarding generalized corrupt practices. Corruption remains a dominant concern for Nigerian society.

The key lesson of these paradigmatic examples is that recommendations of the principal-agent approach to corruption are often effective in *open access orders* (societies with a solid rule of law and low levels of corruption) yet ineffective in *limited access orders* (where there is a general disregard for the law).[7] In limited access orders, bribery is a common and normalized practice among the population.[8] In essence, when corruption is part of the daily routine, it is not seen as an anomaly that must be corrected (Ashford and Anand 2003, 11).

If one treats the principal-agent approach as a testable hypothesis, one concludes that the explanatory power of this approach has clear limitations: it tracks the issue with corruption in open access orders but fails to understand the phenomenon in limited access orders. Some argue that this limitation is the result of the theoretical assumptions of the principal-agent model (Persson, Rothstein, and Teorell 2013, 454; see Rothstein and Varraich 2017, 20). The model assumes that the interest of the principal is to hold the agent accountable; it is taken for granted that the honest principal is interested in the agent's honest fulfillment of her fiduciary obligations. Nevertheless, it is argued that the principal's honesty is not to be taken for granted in limited access orders. In those societies, corruption is normalized and tolerated. Most of the time, not only public officials but also citizens benefit from corrupt practices (Olivier de Sardan 1999; Okonjo-Iweala 2017). Therefore, "we cannot assume the existence of 'principled principals' who are willing to hold corrupt officials accountable" (Persson, Rothstein, and Teorell 2013, 405). To fight against corruption in limited access orders, we must revise our theoretical approach. We need another map to understand corruption in limited access orders.

## THE COLLECTIVE ACTION–BASED APPROACH

Consider *Speeding+*, which is a description of *Speeding* in a limited access order:

> *Speeding+*: Avital drives above the speed limit. Paul, the police officer, stops her. Avital bribes Paul and leaves. Avital is not surprised since bribery is a normalized practice in their society. Later that day, Ben drives beyond the speed limit. Paul stops him, as well. Like Avital, Ben bribes him and leaves. Avital and Ben would prefer to live in a society where police officers were honest; however, they both know that unilateral honest actions would not change the generalized corruption of their society.

The principal-agent theory deals with the actions of the agent, but it does not say anything about how to correct a principal that acts corruptly. To grasp the particularities of corruption in limited access orders, we need a theory that allows us to understand the action of the *principal*. Therefore, regarding *Speeding+*, before thinking about Paul's incentives, we need to comprehend why Avital and Ben tolerate corrupt behaviors.

### Corruption as a Norm

Some scholars revisit the "principled-principal" assumption—namely, the idea that the *principal* prefers agents that fulfill their fiduciary obligations—and propose a different conceptualization of the phenomenon: corruption in limited access orders is analogous to a collective-action problem (Bicchieri and Xiao 2008; Persson, Rothstein, and Teorell 2013; Bicchieri 2016; Hoffman and Patel 2017). Enter the collective action–based approach. The point of departure of this approach is that corruption is normalized yet morally condemned by the overwhelming majority of the members of the society.[9] As the anthropologist Olivier de Sardan noticed, in some developing countries, "corruption is . . . as frequently denounced in words as it is practised in fact" (Olivier de Sardan 1999, 29).

The *principals*—the citizens—prefer honest agents, but no one wants to unilaterally pay the cost of being honest when a unilateral action does not solve the problem, that is, no one wants to be the only one who pays a fine when everyone else pays a lower bribe. Yet, it is assumed that if each citizen knew that everyone else pays their fines, they would pay their own fine instead of bribing, which would force law enforcement to be honest. This indicates a coordination problem (Bicchieri and Xiao 2008). The collective action–based approach conceptualizes the problem in game-theoretical terms to highlight the strategic reasoning of the citizens. One can understand this approach within the framework of the principal-agent theory. The individuals that constitute the *principal* are not passive as in the principal-agent model: each member of the principal has a strategy to maximize her own expected utility. The goal of this approach is to coordinate different "principals" so they behave as a unified *principal* with a common goal—namely, monitoring the honesty of the agents.

Consider *Speeding+* in game-theoretic terms. The two players, Avital and Ben, decide whether to accept the fine (*cooperate*), or to bribe Paul (*not cooperate*). As in any game-theoretic model, assume that Avital and Ben are rational maximizers and that bribes are cheaper than fines. Avital and Ben would maximize their utility if they can enjoy the advantages of an honest society—in which everyone acts honestly—while unilaterally giving a bribe with impunity; in other words, their first preference is to *free ride* (i.e., not cooperate while the other cooperates). If they cannot free ride, they prefer an *honest society* where everyone pays their fines and enjoys the advantages of honest police officers (that is, Avital and Ben cooperate). If this is not possible, they prefer a society where nobody respects the law, and everyone bribes (in other words, no one cooperates). In a state of *generalized corruption*, at least they pay cheaper fines. However, they hate being honest and paying an expensive fine when everyone else is bribing law enforcers; in other words, they hate being *the fool* (i.e., cooperating while the other does not cooperate).

In brief, the ranking of preferences for both Avital and Ben, where > denotes strict preferences (i.e., "is strictly preferred to"), is as follows: free riding > honest society > generalized corruption > the fool. Table 11.1 represents their strategic interaction, where $\alpha > \beta > \gamma > \delta$.

**Table 11.1. Corruption as a Collective-Action Problem**

| | | Ben | |
|---|---|---|---|
| | | Cooperate | Not cooperate |
| Avital | Cooperate | $\beta$ | $\alpha$ |
| | | $\beta$ | $\delta$ |
| | Not cooperate | $\delta$ | $\gamma$ |
| | | $\alpha$ | $\gamma$ |

Thus, in a limited access order, the problem of corruption has the form of a Prisoner's Dilemma (PD). For both Avital and Ben, noncooperation—bribing—is a strictly dominant strategy. The Nash equilibrium is the state of generalized corruption (not cooperate, not cooperate). The equilibrium is suboptimal because an *honest society* improves both players' payoffs. In simple words, Avital and Ben see that they both can do better than bribing; however, neither has a reason to act differently in a strategic context.

The collective action–based approach frames the problem of corruption in terms of norms. Norms are equilibria in coordination problems (Brennan et al. 2013, 15–18; Vanderschraaf 2018). Within this framework, Avital and Ben adopt the norm of corruption due to their strategic reasoning. Even if they would rather live in an honest society than a limited access order, they are stuck in an undesirable norm. Framed as such, the questions about how to eradicate corruption change. The new quandaries are the following: How can a society act collectively to eradicate corruption when there is no individual reason to do so? How can an undesirable norm be abandoned?

## Anti-Corruption Strategies of the Collective Action–Based Approach

The PD has been studied in depth. Several theoretical strategies can move the players from the suboptimal to the optimal equilibrium in this cooperation game (Ullmann-Margalit 1977; Axelrod 1984; Bicchieri 2006; McKenzie 2007). If corrupt practices in limited access orders are correctly characterized as PDs, one can try different theoretical strategies. Unlike the principal-agent theory, which focuses on material and moral incentives, the collective action–based approach stresses open communication as a tool to trigger cooperation among the members of the *principal*. Bicchieri (2016) and Hoffman and Patel (2017) developed two main strategies: open deliberation and trendsetters. In the following, this chapter studies how these strategies help individuals to abandon the norm of corruption in limited access orders and their possible limits.

### Deliberation

Undesirable norms are often grounded in pluralistic ignorance, which refers to "a cognitive state in which each member of a group believes her personal normative beliefs and preferences are different from those of similarly situated others, even if public behavior is identical" (Bicchieri 2016, 42). When political corruption in limited access orders is the result of pluralistic ignorance, each individual acts corruptly because they expect that everybody else acts in the same way, but each one ignores that everyone else condemns corruption. The undesirable norm, then, results from incomplete information about the normative beliefs—what people think is right or wrong—of everyone else.

In cases of pluralistic ignorance, people abandon an undesirable norm once open and sincere deliberation reveals that everyone's preferences and normative beliefs are the same: everyone condemns corruption. This is, in part, an insight from an iconic mainline economist, Elinor Ostrom, who highlighted that in actual PDs, people are not prisoners—they can talk, deliberate, reach agreements, and act upon themselves (Ostrom 1990, 184). If people are candid, distribute information, debate, and reach a consensual disavowal of corrupt practices, the society can collectively move the equilibrium to an optimal state (Bicchieri and Mercier 2014, 43). The essence of this strategy is to understand that people change their actions by changing their beliefs about what other people approve or condemn. Once consensus is reached, a new problem arises: guaranteeing that people comply with their promises without a central authority that sanctions noncooperators.[10] Yet again, Ostrom reminds us that a central authority is not necessary to enforce social agreements (Ostrom 1990, 185). Real people use different strategies to punish those who violate public consensus, for example, damaging their reputation, ostracism, and public shaming. In the collective action–based approach, no central monitoring is needed, as argumentation and a certain capacity for imposing social sanctions are sufficient to correct expectations and abandon undesirable norms.

However, there are reasons to believe that when corruption is the norm, actual deliberation may not solve the problem. The unique characteristics of corrupt practices make it more difficult than other undesirable norms to abandon. I provide two reasons to be skeptical about the efficiency of these strategies. First, publicizing that the majority of the people actually engage in corruption can be counterproductive (Bicchieri 2016, 86). People normally have rough approximations or beliefs about other people's corrupt actions but lack precise knowledge of this. After an honest and informed discussion, people can become certain that corrupt practices are actually as extensive as they thought—or even more. Such a certainty hinders norm change. The certainty that everyone is corrupt reinforces the expectation that nobody would act honestly, even when the consensus is reached. If this happens, people become certain that, in the PD, they will be *the fool* if they act honestly (Köbis, Iragorri-Carter, and Starke 2018, 44). In other words, the undesirable norm is strengthened once everyone knows that people systematically defect. In this sense, open debate ends up being counterproductive.

Second, deliberation about corruption is seldom honest because admitting a corrupt behavior represents a major social cost. Admitting one's corruption in public is extremely difficult for several reasons. The obvious one is that, when corruption is illegal, nobody will incriminate herself. Furthermore, admitting one's corruption is difficult because signaling virtue grounds social cooperation. People want to communicate that they are trustworthy moral agents who deserve reciprocation from their peers. Confessing one's corruption is difficult because of the social stigma that it carries. If this is true, sincere debates about corruption are unlikely to occur. Moreover, admitting one's corruption becomes even more unlikely due to another layer of the complexity of social cooperation. Generally, people would publicly sanction someone who openly admits to engaging in corrupt behavior. People signal their honesty not only by denying their own corruption but also by sanctioning corrupt individuals.[11] Therefore, it is not only difficult to confess one's corrupt actions, but it is also difficult to refrain from penalizing the confession of the corrupt actions of others. Everyone wants to show trustworthiness by hiding their own corrupt actions and by sanctioning corrupt individuals. This might explain why people invest so much in keeping their own corruption a secret (Rose-Ackerman and Palifka 2016, 58). Briefly, in limited access orders, open deliberation might reinforce corruption, and sincere deliberation is unlikely to occur.[12]

## Trendsetters

Another lesson of the research on PDs is that trendsetters can lead the way to abandon an undesirable norm (Bicchieri and Fukui 1999, 143; Bicchieri 2016, 163).[13] A first mover can modify people's expectations by setting the example of how to act in accordance with one's true preferences and transgress the undesirable norm. When information spreads about the possibility of acting according to one's preferences, observers change their actions. Trendsetters trigger an informational cascade that eventually leads to the abandonment of the undesirable norm (Bicchieri 2006, 196). The classical example of this phenomenon is the bystander effect. When someone is injured in public, people typically do not help right away, even if they truly want to assist; everyone's inaction makes each one believe that nobody wants to help the injured individual. It takes a first mover to trigger the informational cascade that leads the others to assist. Examples of successful trendsetters include the empowering of women in India thanks to Latin American soap operas (Hoffman and Patel 2017, 30), the end of footbinding in China (Mackie 1996, 1011), or the promotion of family planning in Mexico through *telenovelas* (Bicchieri 2016, 202). Trendsetters can be real people, such as politicians, businessmen, or police officers (Hoffman and Patel 2017, 28), but they can also be fictional characters in the mass media. They serve as role models for those who do not dare to act on their true preferences (Bicchieri 2016, 195; Köbis, Iragorri-Carter, and Starke 2018, 43). Trendsetters make people realize that they should not be afraid of modifying their own corrupt practices. In limited access orders, a just president, decent businessmen, or honest police officers tend to modify the behavior of citizens and help them to abandon the norm of corruption.

Even though there are several cases of successful trendsetters, I am skeptical of the effectiveness of relying on trendsetters to combat corruption, especially when corrupt practices are related to highly productive activities that people considered justified. Frequently, corrupt practices enhance efficiency and productivity, at least in the short term (Nye 1967; Huntington 1968; Tullock 1996; Munger 2018). Even if there is some consensus that corruption is harmful for political legitimacy in the long run, one can make the case that, given certain circumstances of poverty or severe need (characteristic of limited access orders), the immediate benefits of corruption can be somehow justified (Alatas 1990; Rose-Ackerman and Palifka 2016; Rothstein and Varraich 2017). In other words, sometimes the corruptor has justification for her actions. As Olivier de Sardan reminds us, "the briber, embezzler or corrupter

often has 'good reasons' for his actions and carries them out with a clear conscience. Their attitude is not illegitimate as far as they are concerned, but is
only perceived as such by those on the outside, or by participants who might
stand to lose in the transaction, or by those who are placed at a disadvantage"
(1999, 35). This phenomenon is especially clear in cases in which corruption
dismantles a prohibition of highly productive activities (e.g., the commerce
and production of illegal drugs in an impoverished society). In those cases,
people may even consider corruption legitimate.[14] If poor people realize that,
thanks to a corrupt law enforcer, they can get a job and their lives are improved (at least in the short-term), it is unlikely that they imitate some far-off
trendsetter who supposedly enjoys a prosperous life without being corrupt.
It is simplistic to think that role models can change the norms of corruption
in limited access orders, especially when wealth creation depends on corrupt
behaviors that allow the production of illegal commodities.

### The Limits

The collective action–based approach is fairly recent, and there is not strong
evidence about the efficiency or inefficiency of these anti-corruption strategies. This section, nonetheless, provides reasons to be skeptical: open deliberation is unlikely, and trendsetters are useless when corruption is somehow
justified for the corruptor. These are the limitations of the collective action–
based strategies. Some undesirable social norms might be abandoned, but
it is unlikely that the strategies of the collective action–based approach are
useful for all the instances of normalized corruption. It is different to bribe a
bureaucrat to have access to one's school documents, to bribe a police officer
to look the other way in a traffic violation, or to bribe politicians to allow a
drug business to grow. The first two are cases in which people are better-off
when public officials fulfill their fiduciary obligations. In these cases, corrupt
practices might be changed with the strategies of the collective-action theory.
However, the last one is a case of corruption that brings substantial benefits
to the participants of the corrupt act. In those cases, the corrupting element
is the law since the actors are better without it than with it. Corruption is a
way to deactivate the law and enact the real preferences of the participants.
However, the principal-agent and the collective-action theories assume that
the law must be enforced. Current theories of corruption aspire to make citizens respect the law, but they cannot be used to assess whether the law must
be observed in the first place. This blind spot hinders anti-corruption efforts.
A complete approach to corruption should be able to distinguish between the
laws that must be enforced and the laws that must not.

The next section deals with corruption that is somehow justified for both
the citizen and the public official. Bribery that increases economic efficiency

and material well-being in a poor society is a case in point. When the anti-corruption strategies of the principal-agent and the collective-action theories cannot eradicate corruption, we need yet another map.

## THE HAYEKIAN APPROACH

Consider another description of *Speeding*:

> *Speeding\**: Avital speeds, and Paul stops her. This is the fifth time in two weeks that Avital is stopped. She thinks the new speed limits are absurd. The legislators recently changed the limit from 60 to 30 miles per hour on a highway. These strong regulations are done to protect drivers, they argue. Paul is tired of stopping cars at 35 miles per hour and dealing with angry drivers who complain about the unreasonable new speed limits. Avital cannot afford to pay any more tickets this month, so she offers a bribe to Paul on the condition that he does not stop her again when she drives below 50 miles per hour. Paul is generally honest. But he is tired of enforcing absurd speed limits, so he accepts the bribe. Avital leaves. Paul decides that this will be his new policy: accepting bribes from those who drive between 40 and 60 miles per hour and giving tickets to those who drive faster than 60 miles per hour. This would make his tedious work more worthy of his time. And, anyhow, he knows that driving below 60 miles per hour on a highway is safe for everyone, no matter what the legislators say. Later that day, when Ben drives at 45 miles per hour, Paul stops him and applies his new policy.

Paul acts corruptly because it is justified for both Avital and him. This is a different situation than the one presented in *Speeding* and *Speeding+*, even if, on the surface, they look the same. *Speeding\** tracks a case in which corruption results from a law that everyone finds unreasonable. So how can corruption that is justified for everyone be eradicated? Should it?

Our current approaches are unfitted to face this situation. The principal-agent approach argues that Paul is blameworthy. Therefore, he needs to be held accountable; however, Avital lacks strong reasons to hold him accountable.[15] The collective action–based approach recommends either asking Avital to confess her corrupt behavior—which, as said, is unlikely—or imitating the honest citizens who pay tickets—yet her decision has nothing to do with her expectation about other people and everything to do with her lack of money. So, if principals and agents prefer the corrupt act, how can it ever be eradicated? I hold that these two maps in Speeding* miss the key element: the speed limit.

## Corruption as a Problem of Legislation

*Speeding\** exemplifies one case in which the law must not be enforced because people believe that the low speed limits constitute an unjustified imposition. Legislators, then, are accountable for imposing unreasonably low speed limits, which runs afoul of what citizens and law enforcers consider a justifiable limit and, hence, promotes corrupt practices that aim to deactivate an unreasonable law. To eradicate this kind of corruption, it is fruitless to attempt to correct the individuals; one must correct the speed limits. As said in the first section, to understand why there is a misuse of public office in cases like *Speeding\**, we need to draw a different map whose basis is the Hayekian distinction between law and legislation.

The Hayekian distinction influenced several mainline economists. Building on this insight, Boettke, Coyne, and Leeson (2008) developed New Development Economics (NDE). Even though NDE is obviously conceived as a contribution to development theory since it focuses on the transplant of institutions from one country to another one, it provides a general framework for grasping the adequacy of formal institutions in general (i.e., NDE can be used to assess the pertinence of enacting formal institutions, regardless of whether the policymakers are locals or foreign). In this sense, NDE provides a general framework to study the relation between legislation that is obeyed and legislation that is not. Yet Boettke, Coyne, and Leeson do not use Hayek's terms to refer to the distinction between law and legislation. Instead, they talk about formal and informal institutions. They divide institutions into three kinds: indigenously introduced endogenous institutions (IEN), indigenously introduced exogenous institutions (IEX), and foreign-introduced exogenous institutions (FEX). IEN are spontaneous orders, practices that emerge in a community through time; they are what Hayek calls laws. IEN are basically the formal rules imposed by the local authorities—what Hayek calls legislation. A foreign political actor—for example, the IMF or the UN—that enacts legislation in a host society, imposes FEX (Boettke, Coyne, and Leeson 2008, 334–36). Furthermore, the foundation for every institution (formal or informal) are "skills, culture, norms, and conventions, which are shaped by the experience of the individuals" (ibid., 338). This is what the political scientist and anthropologist James Scott (1998) calls *mētis*. Scott recovers the Greek term *mētis*, which "represents a wide array of practical skill and acquired intelligence in responding to a constantly changing natural and human environment" (1998, 313), to refer to practical and local knowledge. Any institutional arrangement that a society adapts must make sense within the framework of *mētis*. NDE's main thesis is that institutions that are observed and followed are grounded in *mētis*: "*Mētis* can be thought of as the glue that gives institutions their stickiness" (Boettke, Coyne, and Leeson 2008, 338).

*Stickiness* is the fundamental concept for NDE since it refers to "the ability or inability of new institutional arrangements to take hold where they are transplanted" (Boettke, Coyne, and Leeson 2008, 332). Since they are spontaneous orders, IEN are firmly grounded in *mētis*. Institutions that *stick* closely map IEN. IEX and FEX are the real subject of NDE because these institutions can either make sense or not to the people and can either be close or far to IEN. If IEX and FEX are close to IEN, they will stick, and people will observe them; if they are far from IEN, people will not obey them. In Scott's words, "formal order . . . is always and to some considerable degree parasitic on informal processes, which the formal scheme does not recognize, without which it could not exist, and which it alone cannot create or maintain" (Scott 1998, 310).

An example that illustrates NDE's theoretical framework is money. The practices of economic exchange in a community (*mētis*) shapes a barter economy and "only over time do agents find certain media of exchange more useful for facilitating exchange than other media" (Boettke, Coyne, and Leeson 2008, 337). The emergence of some currency as a unit of account and exchange constitutes a spontaneous order, an IEN. A national currency guaranteed by a government constitutes an IEX. The dollar, for example, is an IEN that *stuck*. The U.S. government imposed it as a medium of exchange and people accepted it. However, "if the US government decided that ashtrays should circulate tomorrow as the new legally mandated medium of exchange, this institutional change would not stick. People would simply refuse to use ashtrays for this purpose" (Boettke, Coyne, and Leeson 2008, 341). Formal institutions that do not parasitize informal institutions do not last.

A formal institution—legislation—that does not *stick* results in generalized and frequent disobedience, which can be expressed through different reactions (e.g., criminality, protests, institutional decay, conflict, and, most importantly for this chapter, corrupt practices). When studying the privatization efforts in post-Soviet Russia, Boettke, Coyne, and Leeson hold that economic reforms failed because they did not *stick*: "The result was widespread corruption, crony capitalism, and the prevalence of organized crime" (Boettke, Coyne, and Leeson 2008, 352). Widespread corruption is, in some way, a response from *mētis* to an institution that does not map the IEN. Or, in Hayekian terms, corrupt practices result from the imposition of a legislation that contravenes the law. Paying public servants to not do their work is a way to deactivate the compulsory force of formal institutions that do not correspond to *mētis*.

A Hayekian approach to corruption, whose basis is NDE, captures the cases in which corruption signals that legislation does not *stick*. Some cases of corruption are, in a way, a feedback mechanism. The inadequacy of a legislation, I argue, can be measured by the frequency of corrupt behaviors that it provokes. If public officials in charge of enforcing a particular legislation are systematically corrupt, it must be taken as an indication that legislation promotes corruption because it is not grounded in *mētis*. In these cases, to eradicate corruption, one must revise the formal laws.

## Hayekian Anti-Corruption Strategies

Consider *Speeding\** through the Hayekian approach. How could corruption be eliminated in that case? The new perspective illuminates the blind spot of the other two approaches: ultimately, neither Avital nor Paul are accountable for the corruption. Rather, the legislators are accountable for imposing absurdly low speed limits that lead police officers to prefer a bribe to their fiduciary obligations and citizens to prefer corrupt to honest law enforcers. If lawmakers decide that the speed limit in a highway is 30 miles per hour, they ought to be attentive to the consequences of such legislation. If, like in *Speeding\**, the legislation results in systemic bribery, lawmakers must conclude that this is a rule that leads to widespread corruption. Legislators committed to eradicating corruption would raise the speed limits to a reasonable point that citizens and police officers accept to obey.

It is a truism that corruption is eradicated when the formal law that is violated disappears. However, truisms should not be discarded as solutions. The Hayekian approach conceptualizes systemic corruption as a reason for removing a rule; it provides criteria for detecting inadequate legislation. When a law contravenes *mētis*, it makes it impossible for people to legally pursue practices that they consider justified. An easy and inexpensive way to break the law is bribery. The unreasonable law is *de facto* abolished.

If lawmakers experiment with the strategies of the principal-agent and the collective action–based approaches and corruption remains, they should be ready to accept failure and remove the formal law. No matter how ideal and perfect the formal law might look on paper, good lawmakers must conclude that a legislation that promotes corruption is inadequate and that it must not be enforced. For honest lawmakers, there is no shame in backing up.

## Case 1. Corrupting Legislation: The Prohibition Era

On January 17, 1920, alcohol became illegal on American soil. During the Prohibition years, corruption was pervasive, reaching unprecedented levels in U.S. history. "Cynics predicted that corruption would accompany Prohibition, but even they were surprised by the massive scope of the graft and malfeasance" (Funderburg 2014, 340). Prohibition agents made fortunes.

Their low wages—as low as $1,200 per year—were compensated by massive bribes. Corruption made it impossible to enforce prohibition laws. People who wanted alcohol were eager to pay the mafia to have a drink, and the mafia was eager to pay off law enforcement agencies to give the people what they wanted. "In Chicago an investigation by the district attorney's office exposed 'systematic graft on a very large scale' among the Prohis. Windy City bootleggers paid dry agents $1 per gallon for permits to withdraw alcohol from bonded warehouses" (Funderburg 2014, 341). People who wanted alcohol praised those who provided it and condemned those who enforced the unreasonable formal laws. What was the right strategy to eradicate massive corruption in that case?

Thinking in terms of the principal-agent approach, in 1927, Congress improved the hiring process of police officers and imposed exams to increase the quality of the agents. As we know, this measure did not eliminate corrupt practices. The dry law was such a great opportunity for easy graft in that it transformed honest law enforcers into venal public officials. A collective action–based approach would further the idea of public deliberation as a way to make people aware that a healthier life and a society without alcohol is better for everyone. I would argue that people knew that drinking alcohol was not healthy, and yet they still gladly paid bribes to enjoy a refreshing beer after a hard day's work.

The Hayekian approach provides the historical answer to this widespread corruption. Taking into account the failure of past strategies to improve law enforcement, lawmakers concluded that Prohibition cannot *stick* and, hence, that the formal law should be removed. Dry laws were simply not grounded in the American *mētis*. A society that values individual freedom condemns politicians controlling people's consumption and preferences. On April 7, 1933, America could drink legally again. The legislature ultimately acknowledged that Prohibition was an error, even if, for a moment, it seemed like a beneficial project in favor of the health of Americans.

## Case 2. The Uncertain Outcomes of the Kim Young-Ran Act

It is easy to see that *mētis* triumphed over the Prohibition because we know how the story ended. However, when implementing policies in the present, it is not easy to determine whether *mētis* will prevail or the legislation will change *mētis*. Concluding that certain anti-corruption policies are not adequate for *mētis* takes time. The following case of anti-corruption legislation illustrates what happens when we do not know the end of the story.

In 2015, South Korea passed the "Improper Solicitation and Graft Act" (also commonly referred to as the Kim Young-Ran Act, named after the former

head of the Anticorruption and Civil Rights Commission) . . . which makes
it illegal for public officials, certain private individuals (e.g., journalists and
private school teachers) and their spouses to accept monetary gifts over 50,000
South Korean Won (roughly US$47), with higher limits set for gifts given at
weddings or funerals. It also limits the amount that can be spent taking these
officials to dinner (roughly US$28). . . . Furthermore, public employees must
report any gifts that they receive; otherwise, both the gift recipient and giver are
prosecuted. (Choi and Storr 2019, 120)

The Kim Young-Ran Act clashes with at least two deeply rooted cultural
practices that act as "social lubricants in Korean culture" (Choi and Storr
2019, 120): gift-giving and dining norms. First, Korean people use gifts to
express appreciation; for example, parents thank their kids' schoolteachers
with expensive presents at the end of the year. Another example is *chuseok*
(Korean thanksgiving), during which families, friends, and business connections exchange numerous gifts. The Kim Young-Ran Act disrupts these cultural practices and limits the level of appreciation that one can show. Second,
this act conflicts with the informal norms of networking. Business relations
and social networking become more difficult to develop when the limits for
taking officials to restaurants are set at US$28. Businessmen cannot treat their
clients, partners, or employees with dinner, entertainments, or shows as they
used to. Since the Kim Young-Ran Act contradicts *mētis*, the question becomes whether the legislation will stick or *mētis* will find the way to prevail.

Choi and Storr are optimistic about the Kim Young-Ran Act. Korean people widely respect the rule of law, which indicates the existence of a "social
norm of legal obedience" (Mackie 2017, 319) that makes it easier to modify
cultural practices. When the people embrace a social norm of legal obedience,
they tend to prioritize following legislation. Furthermore, Choi and Storr
(2019, 121) hold that the culture of gift-giving had become an undesirable
social norm, as it involved significant expenses and sacrifices. By cutting the
social pressure to buy presents, they argue, the Kim Young-Ran Act would
lower the price of living for many Koreans. As an example, Choi and Storr
(2019, 121) mention parents who used to buy luxurious gifts for their kids'
teachers while buying inexpensive products for themselves only to comply
with social norms. If Choi and Storr are correct, prohibiting expensive gifts
might actually help Korean people abandon an undesirable gift-giving norm
and foster the creation of a new and less expensive social norm to express
gratitude. If this is the case, the Kim Young-Ran Act has good chances of
sticking in South Korea.

However, the Kim Young-Ran Act might yield unexpected consequences
in the case that strong cultural practices adapt to such prohibitions. First, if
the gift-giving norm is an irreplaceable social lubricant, its disruption might

harm the levels of social trust in Korean society.[16] One might fear, for example, that teachers feel less economically and emotionally recognized after the Kim Young-Ran Act. This act forces people to find new ways to develop the social networks that resulted from the Korean gift-giving norms. But, if they fail to find these new ways to promote social trust, prohibiting these norms might create social problems. Nonetheless, these new ways might be used to avoid the legislation (e.g., the use of third parties for bribing might increase, generalize, and become normalized), which would create further layers of corruption more difficult to detect and eradicate. The Hayekian approach predicts that surreptitious practices will emerge to avoid the Kim Young-Ran Act if these cultural practices are so deeply ingrained in Korean culture that people prefer to violate the legislation to follow the social norm.

Only time will tell whether Choi and Storr are correct. However, from the perspective of the Hayekian approach, it is fundamental to keep an eye on the possibility of failure so as to remove the anti-corruption legislation before it becomes corrupting.

## Limitations of the Hayekian Approach

Some might worry that the Hayekian approach is too relativistic. It seems that the only good legislation is the legislation that sticks; this would give prevalence to social norms over the deliberate formal law. One could argue that the Hayekian approach can serve the status quo. Yet, sometimes we expect more from formal laws, and sometimes we expect that they help societies reach moral objectives to improve the customs and behaviors of the citizens. Conversely, the Hayekian approach would favor the status quo, no matter how damaging and unjust it might be.

To illustrate the limits of the Hayekian approach, consider the following hypothetical case of moral reform in a society where it is a tradition to hunt human beings for sport.[17] In this society, citizens in general think that human hunting is justified, except for the liberal and educated ruling elite, who believe that this practice is abhorrent. The elite, disregarding citizens' opinions, use their public power to prohibit human hunting simply because it is the right thing to do. Human hunting is, however, still part of the common practices of this society, despite what the rulers mandate (i.e., it is grounded in *mētis*). Then, people systematically bribe those officials who try to enforce the prohibition to deactivate it. Since law enforcers share the social norms of the populace, they do not consider this kind of bribe morally condemnable. Legislation against human hunting leads citizens to widespread corruption. According to the Hayekian approach, the formal prohibition of this practice must be removed to eradicate corrupt practices. But *hunting human beings for sport is indeed abhorrent!* Should legislators give up on a moral law just because people have repugnant informal norms? Does the Hayekian approach lead us to conclude that unjust informal institutions are preferable to moral legislation, all things considered?

The Hayekian approach might be accused of grounding legal normativity in the actuality of informal norms. But these accusations would be misleading. Per se, there is nothing normative about legislation that *sticks*. As a matter of fact, it is not uncommon that informal norms are oppressive, unjust, or resulting from coercion. The Hayekian approach is neutral regarding the desirability of legislation.[18] The new approach only holds that imposing a formal rule that contradicts *mētis* leads to systemic corruption. As an approach to corruption, it only asserts that corruption can be eliminated by removing the rule. Yet, it does not say that one must prefer *mētis* to a morally good law, all things considered. The desirability of legislation is simply beyond the purview of the Hayekian approach—it is its blind spot. The Hayekian approach, however, allows for arguments in favor of imposing rules that contradict *mētis*. Perhaps a society would accept some level of corruption if imposing legislation is the only way to reach some moral objective. Perhaps the moral elite ought to double the efforts to prohibit human hunting, despite growing corruption of law enforcement, because every human being has rights. These kinds of arguments are strong. Nonetheless, they fall beyond the scope of the Hayekian approach. Moral debate, at this point, is unavoidable.[19] It might be that approaches to corruption open up a new front in moral debates about legislation, but they do not settle the question. However, the Hayekian approach's claims remain exact: sometimes, corruption is a result of legislation, not of deviant people; in those cases, corruption can be eliminated when the legislation is removed.

Yet, if lawmakers are sure of doing the right thing and are willing to pay the cost of enforcing legislation that contradicts *mētis*, then designing incentive-compatible institutions to impose the formal law might be the right way to proceed. In other words, if the legislators intend to enforce a corrupting but morally good legislation, then the principal-agent approach can orient them better than the Hayekian approach in their endeavor. The limitations of the Hayekian approach are addressed with the tools of the principal-agent approach.

## CONCLUSION

Political corruption appears in different forms. It may be a moral problem of public officials, but sometimes, it is a social problem resulting from undesirable norms; yet it can also be a cultural response to inadequate laws. The main contribution of this chapter lies in showing that there is no one-size-fits-all theory of corruption. Solving the problem of corruption requires taking into consideration insights from morality, sociality, and culture.

Current approaches to corruption grasp well the morality and social sides of the issue. The principal-agent approach underlines the insufficiency of incentives to act honestly as the problem of corruption, in which case anti-corruption lawmakers should design better incentive structures to correct individual behaviors. Yet, these strategies fail to eradicate corrupt practices in limited access orders. For these situations, we need the collective action–based approach to perceive that the problem lies with uncoordinated citizens who fail to hold their government accountable due to undesirable social norms. This approach aims to coordinate the citizens so they can hold the government accountable. Yet, this strategy might be fruitless if citizens sincerely prefer corrupt public officials to honest ones because legislation contravenes justified practices. The secondary contribution of this chapter is to construct an approach that accounts for the cultural dimension of corruption. The Hayekian approach fills the gap that the other two theories left. When the attention shifts from corrupt individuals to legislation, we realize that corruption may not be a problem but rather a social solution to the imposition of formal laws that people cannot live with. In these cases, the only anti-corruption measure that would work is to revise, amend, or even remove formal laws that promote corruption. And yet, this approach has its own limitation: it does not tell us whether the legislators must prefer a morally good formal law or a repugnant informal norm. If they prefer the latter, they must remove the legislation; if they prefer the former, they may redesign a better system of law enforcement using the principal-agent approach's tools. The three approaches together constitute a pluralistic approach to corruption.

# NOTES

1. Thanks to Ginny, Paul, and Virgil for all their work and support. Thanks also to all the contributors of this volume for their very helpful feedback. I'm grateful to David Schmidtz, Allen Buchanan, Tom Christiano, Tauhidur Rahman, Jerry Gaus, and Lauren Beall for numerous suggestions, encouraging comments, and heated discussions. Finally, my deep appreciation to all the people at the Mercatus Center for making this wonderful program possible.

2. There are other conceptions of corruption. Some of them are more comprehensive and define corruption as the violation of a norm. I do not deal with these conceptions of corruption in this chapter because the approaches studied here operationalized the standard conception of political corruption as the misuse of public office for

private gain to design anti-corruption policies. The classical definition of this kind of corruption is given by Joseph Nye: corruption is a "behaviour which deviates from the formal duties of a public role because of private-regarding (personal, close family, private clique) pecuniary or status gains; or violates rules against the exercise of certain types of private-regarding influence" (Nye 1967, 419).

3. As said by Jim Yong Kim, former President of the World Bank (2012–2019).

4. For the idea of theories as maps, see Schmidtz (2006, 21–28). For more on how theoretical models shape the way we reason about problems in social sciences, see Ostrom (1990, 7–8), Scott (1998, 342–57), Morgan (2012, 30–38), Rubinstein (2012, 34–37). For the use of theoretical models that shape anti-corruption policy, see Rothstein and Varraich (2017, 19–20).

5. Peter J. Boettke writes, "the core idea in [mainline economics] is that there are two fundamental observations of commercial society: (1) individual pursuit of their self-interest, and (2) complex social order that aligns individual interests with the general interest" (Boettke 2012, xvii). To be clear, Boettke also contrasts mainline economics with mainstream economics: "mainline is defined by a set of positive propositions about social order that were held in common from Adam Smith onward, but mainstream economics is a sociological concept related to what is currently fashionable among the scientific elite of the profession" (2012, xvii). For more on mainline economics, see Boulding (1971), Boettke, Haeffele-Balch, and Storr (2016).

6. It is certainly an index about perception, not about factual corruption. However, because it is really difficult to have clear knowledge of corruption levels, perception is usually accepted as the standard measurement of corruption. For the history of Nigeria in the index, see https://tradingeconomics.com/nigeria/corruption-index. For the 2018 index, see https://www.transparency.org/country/NGA.

7. The distinction between open and limited access is originally in North, Wallis, and Weingast (2009, 18–25). Mungiu-Pippidi (2015) recovers the distinction in the context of anti-corruption theories. Open access orders are "individualistic, with political equality, high personal autonomy, and high civic participation. The state is autonomous from private interest, and allocation and policy formulation are achieved on the basis of ethical universalism and transparency" (2015, 30). On the contrary, limited access orders are characterized by particularistic norms, unequal distribution of political power, informal clientelist networks for protection, and a thin Rule of Law, which results in normalization of corrupt practices. See Mungiu-Pippidi (2015, 30–31).

8. "Over time, constant exposure to a culture of bribery or extortion can lead to the normalization and entrenchment of a tolerant environment in which such practices flourish." (Hoffman and Patel 2017, 12). See also Olivier de Sardan (1999, 36), Rose-Ackerman and Palifka (2016, 233), and Choi and Storr (2019, 105).

9. For information about surveys in Nigeria about massive condemnation of corrupt practices, see Hoffman and Patel (2017, 13).

10. They cannot count on a central authority because they must assume that the central authority is corrupt, given that that's the problem that they are trying to solve in the first place.

11. For the importance of norms as signaling devices, see Brennan et al. (2013, 156–58).

12. A good case for studying the different results of sincere debate about corruption is the case of *Ipaidabribe.com*. This program worked well in India, but failed in China, which gives us reason to be skeptical about this kind of strategy. See Ang (2014).

13. Game theory aside, the importance of leaders for leading social reform is a lesson of political science as well. See Fukuyama (2011, 86), Rose-Ackerman and Palifka (2016, 415), and Okonjo-Iweala (2017, 135).

14. "In societies where there is a [Culture of Rent Seeking], some members of those societies will view certain rent-seeking activities as acceptable or legitimate paths for achieving economic success. For instance, a definite [Culture of Rent Seeking] can be said to exist in societies where bribing public officials is an acceptable and routine part of doing business" (Choi and Storr 2019, 112).

15. Avital could have a weak reason for holding Paul accountable, namely blind observance of the law. Yet, if blind obedience to the law was the norm in this society, this situation would not appear in the first place.

16. Gift-giving norms, as the anthropologist Marcel Mauss (1950) holds, are fundamental for social cohesion, reciprocation, and trust.

17. I thank Lauren Beall for suggesting this example.

18. This is true for the Hayekian approach to corruption as presented here. The actual position of Hayek (1982) on the issue of the priority of the law over legislation might be debatable. For example, Raz holds that Hayek mistakenly identifies "the rule of law with the rule of the good law" (Raz 1979, 227). This chapter takes no stance in the exegetical question about Hayek's position.

19. The fact that the rule of law is only one virtue of the law among others is a fairly common point. As Raz says "conflict between the rule of law and other values is just what is to be expected" (1979, 228).

## REFERENCES

Alatas, Syed Hussein. 1990. *Corruption: Its Nature, Causes, and Functions*. Aldershot, UK:Avebury.

Ang, Yuen Yuen. 2014. "Authoritarian Restraints on Online Activism Revisited: Why 'I-Paid-A- Bribe' Worked in India but Failed in China." *Comparative Politics* 47 (1): 21–40.

Ashford, Blake, and Vikas Anand. 2003. "The Normalization of Corruption in Organizations." *Research in Organizational Behavior* 25: 1–52.

Axelrod, Robert. 1984. *The Evolution of Cooperation*. New York: Basic Books.

Besley, Timothy. 2006. *Principled Agents: The Political Economy of Good Government*. Oxford: Oxford University Press.

Bicchieri, Cristina. 2006. *The Grammar of Society: The Nature and Dynamics of Social Norms*. Cambridge, UK: Cambridge University Press.

———. 2016. *Norms in The Wild: How to Diagnose, Measure, and Change Social Norms*. Oxford: Oxford University Press.

Bicchieri, Cristina, and Yoshitaka Fukui. 1999. "The Great Illusion: Ignorance, Informational Cascades, and the Persistence of Unpopular Norms." *Business Ethics Quarterly* 9(1): 125-55.

Bicchieri, Cristina, and Hugo Mercier. 2014. "Norms and Beliefs: How Change Occurs." In *Complexity of Social Norms*, edited by Maria Xenitidou and Bruce Edmonds, 37–54. Cham, CH: Springer.

Bicchieri, Cristina, and Erte Xiao. 2008. "Do the Right Thing: But Only If Others Do So." *Journal of Behavioral Decision Making* 22 (2): 191–208.

Boettke, Peter J. 2012. *Living Economics: Yesterday, Today, and Tomorrow*. Oakland CA: The Independent Institute.

Boettke, Peter J., Christopher J. Coyne, and Peter T. Leeson. 2008. "Institutional Stickiness and the New Development Economics." *American Journal of Economics and Sociology* 67 (2): 331–58.

Boettke, Peter J., Stefanie Haeffele-Balch, and Virgil Henry Storr. 2016. *Mainline Economics: Six Nobel Lectures in the Tradition of Adam Smith*. Arlington, VA: Mercatus Center at George Mason University.

Boulding, Kenneth E. 1971. "After Samuelson, Who Needs Adam Smith?" *History of Political Economy* 3 (2): 225–37.

Brennan, Geoffrey, Lina Eriksson, Robert E. Goodin, and Nicholas Southwood. 2013. *Explaining Norms*. Oxford: Oxford University Press.

Brinkerhoff, Derick W. 2000. "Assessing Political Will for Anti-Corruption Efforts: An Analytical Framework." *Public Administration and Development* 20 (3): 239–52.

Choi, Ginny Seung, and Virgil Henry Storr. 2019. "A Culture of Rent Seeking." *Public Choice* 181 (1–2): 101–26.

Fukuyama, Francis. 2011. *The Origins of Political Order: From Prehuman Times to the French Revolution*. New York: Farrar, Straus, and Giroux.

Funderburg, J. Anne. 2014. *Bootleggers and Beer Barons of the Prohibition Era*. Jefferson, NC: McFarland & Company.

Hayek, F. A. 1982. *Law, Legislation and Liberty: A New Statement of the Liberal Principles of Justice and Political Economy*. London: Routledge.

Hoffmann, Leena K., and Raj N. Patel. 2017. "Collective Action on Corruption in Nigeria: A Social Norms Approach to Connecting Society and Institutions." London: The Royal Institute of International Affairs. https://www.chathamhouse.org/2017/05/collective-action-corruption-nigeria.

Huntington, Samuel. 1968. *Political Order in Changing Societies*. New Haven, CT: Yale University Press.

Johnston, Michael. 2005. *Syndromes of Corruption: Wealth, Power, and Democracy*. Cambridge, UK: Cambridge University Press.

Klitgaard, Robert. 1988. *Controlling Corruption*. Berkeley, CA: University of California Press.

Köbis, Nils C., Daniel Iragorri-Carter, and Christopher Starke. 2018. "A Social Psychological View on the Social Norms of Corruption." In *Corruption and Norms:*

*Why Informal Norms Matter*, edited by Ina Kubbe and Annika Engelbert, 31–52. Cham, CH: Palgrave.

Mackie, Gerry. 1996. "Ending Footbinding and Infibulation: A Convention Account." *American Sociological Review* 61 (6): 999–1017.

———. 2017. "Effective Rule of Law Requires Construction of a Social Norm of Legal Obedience." In *Cultural Agents Reloaded: The Legacy of Antanas Mockus*, edited by Carlo Tognato, 313–34. Cambridge, MA: Harvard University Press.

Mauss, Marcel. 1950. *Essai sur le don*. Paris: Presses Universitaire de France.

McKenzie, Alexander J. 2007. *The Structural Evolution of Morality*. Cambridge, UK: Cambridge University Press.

Min, Kyoung-sun. 2019. "The Effectiveness of Anti-Corruption Policies: Measuring the Impact of Anti-Corruption Policies on Integrity in the Public Organizations of South Korea." *Criminal Law and Social Change* 71: 217–39.

Morgan, Mary S. 2012. *The World in the Model: How Economists Work and Think*. Cambridge, UK: Cambridge University Press.

Munger, Michael C. 2018. "On the Contingent Vice of Corruption." *Social Philosophy and Policy* 35 (2): 158–81.

Mungiu-Pippidi, Alina. 2011. "Chasing Moby Dick across Every Sea and Ocean? Contextual Choices in Fighting Corruption." Berlin: Norad. https://pure.au.dk/portal/files/42016541/HSOG_Norad_Draft_report_Contextual_choices_in_fighting_corr.pdf.

———. 2015. *The Quest of Good Governance*. Cambridge, UK: Cambridge University Press.

North, Douglass, John J. Wallis, and Barry Weingast. 2009. *Violence and Social Orders: A Conceptual Framework for Interpreting Recorded Human History*. Cambridge, UK: Cambridge University Press.

Nye, Joseph. 1967. "Corruption and Political Development: A Cost-Benefit Analysis." *The American Political Science Review* 61 (2): 417–27.

Okonjo-Iweala, Ngozi. 2017. *Fighting Corruption is Dangerous*. Cambridge, MA: MIT Press.

Olivier de Sardan, J. P. 1999. "A Moral Economy of Corruption in Africa?" *The Journal of Modern African Studies* 37 (1): 25–52.

Ostrom, Elinor. 1990. *Governing the Commons: The Evolution of Institutions for Collective Action*. Cambridge, UK: Cambridge University Press.

Persson, Anna, Bo Rothstein, and Jan Teorell. 2013. "Why Anti-Corruption Reforms Fail—Systematic Corruption as a Collective Action Problem." *Governance: An International Journal of Policy, Administration, and Institutions* 26 (3): 449–71.

Raz, Joseph. 1979. *The Authority of Law: Essays on Law and Morality*. Oxford: Oxford University Press.

Rose-Ackerman, Susan, and Bonnie J. Palifka. 2016. *Corruption and Government: Causes, Consequences, and Reform*. 2nd ed. Cambridge, UK: Cambridge University Press.

Rothstein, Bo, and Aysha Varraich. 2017. *Making Sense of Corruption*. Cambridge, UK: Cambridge University Press.

Rubinstein, Ariel. 2012. *Economic Fables*. Cambridge, UK: Open Book Publishers.

Scott, James C. 1998. *Seeing Like a State: How Certain Schemes to Improve the Human Condition Have Failed.* New Haven, CT: Yale University Press.

Schmidtz, David. 2006. *Elements of Justice.* Cambridge, UK: Cambridge University Press.

———. 2015. "Corruption: What *Really* Should Not Be for Sale." In *Performance and Progress: Essays on Capitalism, Business, and Society*, edited by Subramanian Rangan, 49–64. Oxford: Oxford University Press.

Tullock, Gordon. 1996. "Corruption Theory and Practice". *Contemporary Economic Policy* 14 (3): 6–13.

Ullmann-Margalit, Edna. 1977. *The Emergence of Norms.* Oxford: Oxford University Press.

United Nations. 2004. "The Global Programme against Corruption: UN Anti-Corruption Toolkit." Vienna, AT: Office on Drugs and Crimes. Accessed October 2019. https://www.un.org/ruleoflaw/blog/document/the-global-programme-against-corruption-un-anti-corruption-toolkit/.

Vanderschraaf, Peter. 2019. *Strategic Justice: Conventions and Problems of Balancing Divergent Interests.* Oxford: Oxford University Press.

World Bank. 1997. "Helping Countries Combat Corruption: The Role of the World Bank." Accessed October 2019. http://www1.worldbank.org/publicsector/anticorrupt/corruptn/corrptn.pdf.

*Chapter 12*

# Reconsidering the Reproductive Justice Framework

## *The Priority of Bodily Integrity over Parental Privileges*

### Samantha Godwin

The shift from framing the right to abortion and contraception as a "a right to choose" or "reproductive rights" to what has been termed the "Reproductive Justice Framework" has been widespread among pro-choice[1] and feminist advocates and academics.[2] This shift in frame has so far gone without substantial criticism in academic spheres. As a critique of the "reproductive *rights* framework," the "reproductive *justice* framework" makes a number of distinct contributions. These contributions are presented as radically progressive. I argue in this chapter that this is mistaken: the pivot to Reproductive Justice often amounts to an illiberal[3] revival of patriarchal family values at the expense of the truly liberating elements of the pro-choice movement. The Reproductive Justice Framework's central claim is that the "choice paradigm's" focus on rights to abortion and birth control should be replaced by advocacy recognizing the equal importance of "(1) the right to have a child; (2) the right not to have a child; and (3) the right to parent the children we have" (Ross 2007, 4). This central claim, in its application, has the effect of asserting that parental rights over children and the right to control one's own body are morally equivalent. This has several damaging implications. First, it falsely links conservative "family values" to rights that liberals are bound to defend in a manner that provides fresh cover to social conservatism and neutralizes would-be critics of patriarchal family values. Second, it denies the distinctiveness of bodily integrity rights and, ironically, reduces them to the mere exercise of consumer choice.[4] Third, it obfuscates the significance of formal legal rights held against the state in a manner that makes them more difficult to articulate and defend and appear less worthy of defense. While the Reproductive Justice Framework is a political project motivated by the values of liberty and equality, its effect is to undermine the pro-choice movement's ability to coherently argue for those values—the movement's philosophical and political entailments are contrary to its apparent motivations.

The principal contributions of the Reproductive Justice Framework can be understood as consisting of both a positive project and a critical project. The critical project of the Reproductive Justice Framework is to correct the allegedly conservative shortcomings of the pro-choice movement's focus on preserving formal legal rights in favor of recentering advocacy toward providing the financial ability to make meaningful choices, including financially costly choices to have and raise as many children as desired in the manner desired (Ross 2006). The Reproductive Justice Framework is presented as an intersectional, critical rejoinder to the supposedly "neoliberal" (Solinger 2007) choice framework and formal rights rhetoric (West 2009, 1413). In advancing this critical project, the prior pro-choice movement's focus on the moral imperative of specific bodily integrity rights is partially displaced by demands for a cultural shift within the pro-choice movement.

The positive contribution of the Reproductive Justice Framework is to define the political demands of the pro-choice movement in an ostensibly more wholistic fashion: rather than concerning only the bodily integrity and self-ownership rights to prevent, terminate, or carry pregnancies to term without being subject to force or coercion, the Reproductive Justice Framework defines reproductive rights to also include the right to "have children . . . and parent the children we have in safe and sustainable communities" (SisterSong Collective n.d.). The positive project of the Reproductive Justice Framework in this way includes linking the right to prevent or end a pregnancy as the morally equivalent other side of the coin to parental rights over children, including rights against child protective services (Roberts 2007) and opposition to population planning (Ross 2006).

The first section of this chapter will describe general problems with the Reproductive Justice Framework's shift away from a discourse focused on specific formal rights to a discourse focused on the "ends" of justice.[5] While politically attractive as a means of bypassing the highly charged questions of abortion,[6] framing questions in terms of the ends of social justice abandons the legal, ethical, and policy questions that are actually subjects of contention and reflects a basic misapprehension about social processes and social change. An implication of this discursive move is to unnecessarily cede the moral debate over women's bodily integrity rights to the anti-abortion movement and, in turn, to shift the pro-choice movement's argumentative terrain from the ethical case for women's bodily integrity rights to less distinctive public health, utilitarian arguments. This has the effect of undermining the Reproductive Justice movement's stated objectives and reducing the pro-choice movement's ability to effectively advocate for its philosophical and policy commitments.

A second implication of the incoherence of this discursive shift from rights to justice is to grant social conservative policy positions cover via the language of Reproductive Justice—and in doing so, legitimate traditionalist cultural values with liberals and leftists. By tying these social conservative policy positions to the project of correcting the allegedly privileged perspectives said to dominate liberal and left-wing politics through an appeal to an intersectional perspective, these social conservative positions are further insulated from serious critical examination since very few liberal or leftist activists or academics would want to criticize positions that are thought to be essential to the broader project of intersectionality theory. The second part of this chapter makes the case that the distinctive positive contributions of the Reproductive Justice Framework go against the foundational liberal and egalitarian commitments broadly shared by the pro-choice and Reproductive Justice movements. These distinctive policy contributions are not themselves consistent with those shared commitments.

The third part of this chapter then turns to the Reproductive Justice Framework's critical contributions. While the Reproductive Justice Framework's advocates argue that it provides a corrective to the prior pro-choice movement's exclusive "neo-liberal" fixation on formal legal rights meaningful only to a privileged class of women (Solinger 2007; Price 2010, 46), I argue that these critiques generally fail. Rather than expanding the scope of the pro-choice movement's concern from rights afforded only to women with racial and class privilege, the Reproductive Justice Framework intervention actually has the opposite effect: financially precarious people are those with the greatest need for formal rights and the least ability to vindicate their interests within the vague, ends-oriented politics of social justice. Ironically, people with greater financial and social resources are less reliant on formal legal rights, at least up to a certain point, since they have greater alternative avenues for vindicating their interests (such as the abilities to travel to other jurisdictions or make use of the informal economy).

Redirecting the pro-choice movement's principal subject away from a defense of the distinctive negative right to bodily integrity at stake in the capacity to prevent or end a pregnancy in favor of the positive right to pursue one's preferred life choices, reliant on financial and legal assistance,[7] is to actually propose a model of reproductive rights reducible to a mere choice between options that are universally regarded as limited in scope, rather than a fundamental element of respect for persons as persons. As a consequence, the Reproductive Justice Framework's critical case against the "choice framework" is actually more aptly directed against the Reproductive Justice Framework's positive case itself. The Reproductive Justice Framework's logic is self-undermining: someone who finds the alleged problems of the "choice framework" troubling should actually prefer the formal negative rights emphasis that is ostensibly a feature of the "choice framework" over the Reproductive Justice Framework since those problems are more acutely applicable to the philosophical and political implications of the Reproductive Justice Framework's commitments.

## HOHFELDIAN RIGHTS CONTRASTED WITH HAYEK'S CRITIQUE OF THE RHETORICAL USE OF SOCIAL JUSTICE

Rights are matters of endless controversy between entrenched political positions. Justice, however, is universally regarded as desirable. Demands for a given *right*, whether rights to abortion, rights to guns, rights to free speech, rights to healthcare, or rights to discriminate according to one's religious beliefs, are all controversial matters subject to disagreement since they entail specifying exactly what persons and the government should and should not be permitted to do. As described by Wesley Newcomb Hohfeld, to assert a right is to assert a corresponding duty on another person or entity—whether other private persons, institutions, or a government—to refrain from an action or to perform an action (Hohfeld 1917, 1). In contrast, a demand for *justice* within a given sphere is, absent additional content, rarely controversial since everyone is in favor of justice, and without further specification, justice on any of the previously mentioned topics could accommodate the full range of views. "There ought to be a right to assault rifles" is a controversial statement since it entails a duty (either absolute or partial) of the government to refrain from banning and seizing assault rifles. "There ought to be justice in assault rifle policy," however, is uncontroversial since it can accommodate the full range of views, ranging from a policy of criminalizing assault rifle possession (i.e., no right to assault rifles) to a policy prohibiting the government from interfering with assault rifle possession (i.e., a negative right to possess assault rifles) or even requiring the government to provide people with assault rifles on demand (i.e., a positive right to possess assault rifles).

These features of rights claims make it clear how appealing it can be to shift rhetorical registers from discussions of rights to discussions of justice because doing so provides a means of circumventing deeply held, emotionally charged political convictions. The sleight of hand that gives "justice" terminology its appeal over "rights" terminology, however, purchases far less political leverage precisely because of its under-specification, vagueness, and ability to avoid offense by avoiding (without eliminating) questions about how to allocate power among people and between people and the state.

This problem can be better understood by considering F. A. Hayek's analysis of what he termed "social justice." Hayek regarded the emergence of "social justice" as the chief moral imperative appealed to by the full breadth of the political spectrum as problematic for several relevant reasons. First, "social justice" as a concept seems to refer to the distributive results of spontaneous social processes, while the proper subject of the demands of justice, according to Hayek, is the conduct of persons toward each other (Hayek 1998, 31–32, 62–65). Second, "social justice" as a term is widely thought to have a definitive, mutually understood meaning, but as it is used, the term "social justice" is so vague as to be meaningless without supplying additional controversial contents, leading to a false sense of apparent agreement and shared objectives when none are present (ibid., 65–67).[8] Third, nearly any political demand can be rhetorically fashioned into a demand for "social justice," and this rhetorical maneuver has the effect of eroding opposition to that demand since "social justice" is regarded as a moral imperative by virtually everyone regardless of their other values and commitments (Hayek 1998, 65–67). These three claims are useful for understanding the way the rhetorical shift from a "means"-centered reproductive rights discourse to a "results"-focused Reproductive Justice discourse both abandoned essential features of the pro-choice agenda and enabled the smuggling in of socially conservative values into the otherwise liberal pro-choice political movement.

Elements of this critique have drawn substantial criticism. First, some of the basic conceptual claims that Hayek advances do not seem to sustain criticism. Andrew Lister argues that Hayek's claim that it does not make sense to label a market economy's distribution just or unjust is flawed in two ways. First, even if no one can be identified as responsible for a distribution of resources in a market economy, people can still be held responsible for failing to correct for a maldistribution—people may be morally culpable for a failure to rectify an inequality even if they are not culpable for the inequality arising (Lister 2013, 412).[9] Second, even without personal duties to rectify inequalities, there may be collective duties to ensure that institutions are designed consistent with principles of distributive justice (ibid., 413). Adam Tebble suggests that even if no one agent or group intentionally brought about a consequence, there is nothing conceptually incoherent about saying that we might hold ourselves as a political society responsible for unjust consequences (Tebble 2009, 591). Given the fact that voters and governments can reasonably predict that our economic system will produce inequalities, their choices in maintaining that system and failing to correct for it are meaningful targets for complaints of injustice (ibid., 591).

It is debatable whether unintended social processes can be proper subjects of inquiries into justice, and it is further debatable to what extent the distribution of wealth and resources in society is the result of unintended and spontaneous social ordering. It might be argued that, regardless of the merits of spontaneously self-ordered free market societies, we certainly do not live in a social order resembling Hayek's idealized free market society. All contemporary societies with states have legal orders chosen by persons with foreseeable and often intended distributive effects. Some clear examples are found in tax codes, which are knowingly designed to incentivize some behavior and disincentivize other behavior; in the vast amount of government spending that directly and indirectly foreseeably impacts the distribution of wealth; and in the immense amount of commercial, business, and labor regulations present in all developed economies. This is also more subtly seen in the common law and statutory law of property, contract, tort, and crime, where explicit and implicit negotiations between people take place against the backdrop of legal rules that allocate bargaining power unequally between people (see Hale 1923).

Stefanie Haeffele and Virgil Storr have responded to Hayek's critique of ends-based social justice rhetoric by noting that actual socioeconomic systems in the United States and other Western countries differ substantially from the idealized accounts assumed by Hayek in his critique of "social justice"—the rules governing economic life in any real-world context are likely to be weighted against some participants. (Haeffele and Storr 2019, 150). Such "games" themselves can be properly described as unjust for that reason (ibid., 150). Additionally, even with procedurally and substantially fair rules, enforcement is often governed by people and institutions who act unjustly (ibid., 150–51). Both of these factors undermine Hayek's apparent contention that distributive results are not a proper subject of justice claims.

What remains of Hayek's first observation, however, is what is most relevant to the shift in focus from Hohfeldian rights to vague social justice rhetoric: regardless of the status of social processes and outcomes, only persons, whether acting in a private or official capacity, and institutions[10] controlled by identifiable persons are capable of responding to others' demands of justice and modifying their behavior accordingly. Lister notes that with regard to Hayek's specific claims about distributive justice, his "premise about the interpersonal nature of claims of justice . . . does not advance his case against social justice very far" (Lister 2013, 413). But it is precisely Hayek's effective criticism of claims of justice that are *not* interpersonal in nature that serves as a corrective to the specific style of claims that do not make demands on identifiable persons or institutions. "People should have more money" is a statement about a desired change in the state of affairs that is not itself a policy prescription or political demand that can be responded to and fulfilled in the way the following proposition can be: "the Treasury Department should mail everyone a stimulus check."

To more effectively demonstrate this, consider as an example a political movement that regards it morally desirable for people to be safe. In order to effectuate this aim, it is necessary for the movement to specify what act or omission people or institutions should perform. Safety in the abstract as an end cannot be willed into existence—it can only be pursued through the acts or omissions of people and institutions. Political contestation takes place largely in disagreement about what means people and institutions ought to adopt in order to achieve a desired state of affairs. For instance, some people think that pursuing the goal of safety requires that government officials maintain a nuclear deterrence and invade supposedly menacing countries, while other people think that the goal of safety requires that government officials dismantle their nuclear arsenal and refrain from attacking potentially threatening countries. A political movement that insists that, while safety is the end it wants to achieve, it would rather not focus on what is required to achieve that end, has opted out of politics with any real-world impact, including the political questions that must be addressed in order to pursue its stated ends.

## SHIFTING FROM REPRODUCTIVE "RIGHTS" TO REPRODUCTIVE "JUSTICE"

The Reproductive Justice Framework has taken the pro-choice movement toward just such an adoption of vague and under-specified justice rhetoric at the expense of well-articulated demands for Hohfeldian rights. Loretta Ross, one of the Reproductive Justice Framework movement's most prominent founding advocates,[11] describes the Reproductive Justice Framework's distinctiveness from the prior "pro-choice movement" as thus:

> Instead of focusing on the means—a divisive debate on abortion and birth control that neglects the real-life experience of women and girls—the Reproductive Justice analysis focuses on the ends: better lives for women, healthier families, and sustainable communities. This is a clear and consistent message for all social justice movements. . . . We also fight for the necessary enabling conditions to realize these rights. This is in contrast to the singular focus on abortion by the pro-choice movement that excludes other social justice movements. (Ross 2007, 4)

Shifting from the "divisive debate on abortion and birth control" in favor of the uncontroversial widely shared desire to have "better lives for women, healthier families, and sustainable communities" does not make those debates go away—it is simply to opt-out of participating in them. This problem with the Reproductive Justice Framework's discursive turn is an instance of the general problem posed by attempting to shift the locus of demands from the means, or actions of persons and institutions, to ends and processes (see Hayek 1998, 31–32, 62–65). The Reproductive Justice Framework's aspirations are also less divisive precisely because they are less action guiding. Everyone wants "better lives," "healthier families," and "sustainable communities." These ends are not actual matters of political disagreement, and so the apparent common ground found within these ends is not progress in favor of pro-choice positions but orthogonal to them. This issue with the Reproductive Justice Framework's rhetorical pivot is a case of the general problem of the vagueness of social justice rhetoric as sufficiently unconstraining that it can include the full array of possible political and policy preferences—and as such, gain acceptance at the cost of effectively advancing any specific program.

Gaining support and decreasing controversy by recentering a movement on ends that are universally thought to be desirable has the effect of giving up on attempting to influence what people and institutions actually do—which is the extent of what people can control. To achieve any desired end, it is necessary to adopt a means, not merely to lobby for that end in the abstract. The religious right has not lost its interest in pursuing the means of lobbying specific politicians to appoint judges who believe that it is constitutionally permissible to ban abortion, pass "targeted restrictions against abortion provider" laws (Guttmacher Institute 2020) or invest heavily in public messaging campaigns against the morality of rights to abortion to move public political debates in their direction. Adopting a discursive focus on mutually desired ends fails to confront the anti-abortion and anti-contraception movement's means of achieving its ends.

Ross's characterization of the remainder of the pro-choice movement as focusing on debates that "neglect the real-life experience of women and girls" seems aimed at not only encouraging her preferred form of activism but discrediting that of pro-choice advocates who aim to defend the formal legal rights that are actively jeopardized. By arguing that the pro-choice movement should abandon its "singular focus on abortion" that "excludes other social justice movements," Ross has, in effect, proposed that concern for the specific injustice of state laws against abortion and contraception should be redirected toward causes that "other social justice movements" are already concerned with. Part of the bite of this rhetorical device is a contemporary version of the way Hayek observed opposition to a preferred position erodes in the face of social justice rhetoric: the accusation that someone is "excluding" other "social justice" concerns is, especially following the current dominance of intersectionality criticism within feminism, sufficient to silence opposition within many feminist activist circles (see Pluckrose 2017). This would imply that there ought to be no set of organizations or political actors *focused* on defending rights to abortion and contraception, even while their opponents continue to focus on depriving people of these rights. When resources are redirected from tackling challenging, controversial, potentially unpopular issues toward addressing less controversial, more popular issues, it is reasonable to expect that the former set of issues will go comparatively under-addressed.

## THE POSITIVE PROJECT:
## THE CONSERVATISM OF REPRODUCTIVE
## JUSTICE AND LOST RADICALISM OF "CHOICE"

By reworking the pro-choice movement with a specific, limited, distinct agenda into a movement for social justice generally, without philosophically coherent limits,[12] the Reproductive Justice Framework distorts the philosophically coherent pro-choice position[13] into a wider set of core commitments. This new set of commitments are both less defensible than those of the prior pro-choice movement and actually undermine the philosophical case for what had been the pro-choice movement's core commitments. The Reproductive Justice Framework's new framing of its core commitments as "fight[ing] equally for (1) the right to have a child; (2) the right not to have a child; and (3) the right to parent the children we have" (Ross 2007, 4) is problematic in its implications in several ways that I will address in this section. First, recasting the right to prevent or end pregnancy as the "right not to have children" equal to, rather than distinct from, the "right to have children" and "the right to parent" distorts the stakes of the abortion debate in a manner that makes the right to abortion less philosophically defensible by denying the basis for its special solicitude. Despite the Reproductive Justice Framework's self-presentation of a politics beyond the merely liberal "politics of choice," equating right to control one's own body with the right to parent reduces the self-possession and bodily integrity interests at stake in the right to control one's own body to *merely* the right to choose between two life preferences. The mere fact that someone has a certain preference is not normally regarded as sufficient grounds for granting them a positive right to fulfill that preference or even a negative right against governmental interference with that preference when majoritarian or utilitarian reasons would otherwise argue in favor of that interference.[14] Second, the Reproductive Justice Framework's commitment to parental rights as government-conferred rights over children and to government assistance for parenting is much closer to an illiberal family values position than a position reconcilable with the liberal and egalitarian commitments of the pro-choice movement. In so doing, it legitimates these illiberal positions with the pro-choice movement and therefore with liberals and leftists. Third, the Reproductive Justice Framework's assertion that the right to have children and parent those children is equivalent to the right "not to have children" is either philosophically incoherent or philosophically inconsistent depending on its interpretation. If the rights to "have children" or "not have children" are interpreted as positive rights distinct from negative bodily integrity or self-ownership rights, then these cannot be universal rights, since making them universally available would require denying them to some (or many) people.

Loretta Ross and Rickie Solinger summarize the "primary principles" and "basic claim" of the Reproductive Justice Framework as follows:

> Reproductive justice is a contemporary framework for activism and for thinking about the experience of reproduction. It is also a political movement that splices reproductive rights with social justice to achieve reproductive justice. The definition of reproductive justice goes beyond the pro-choice/pro-life debate and has three primary principles: (1) the right not to have a child; (2) the right to have a child; and (3) the right to parent children in safe and healthy environments. . . .
>
> The case for reproductive justice makes another basic claim: access to these material resources is justified on the grounds that safe and dignified fertility management, childbirth, and parenting together constitute a fundamental human right. Human rights, a global idea, are what governments owe to the people they govern and include both negative rights and positive rights. Negative rights are a government's obligation to refrain from unduly interfering with people's mental, physical, and spiritual autonomy. Positive rights are a government's obligation to ensure that people can exercise their freedoms and enjoy the benefits of society. (Ross and Solinger 2017, 9–10)

By asserting that the "right to have children," "the right to parent children," and government provision of material resources necessary for parenting are all "fundamental human rights" equivalent to the right "not to have children," the Reproductive Justice Framework improperly frames the abortion and contraception debates. The basic claim of the pro-choice movement is that the government has no right to compel women to continue a pregnancy, even if it has an electoral mandate to do so, serves other public interests, or maximizes aggregate utility. This is the assertion of the right to abortion and contraception as a right in the "rights as trumps" sense,[15] where the right asserted is not one consideration among many prudential considerations, or one interest or desire among many competing interests and desires, but rather a prerogative with a moral force that overrides others' preferences and interests that lack the same moral force.

The central claim of the Reproductive Justice Framework is precisely the denial of the distinctiveness of the claim that the right against compelled pregnancy by equating it to a preferred pattern of resource allocation. This implies either that the right against compelled pregnancy is not a "trumping right" but just one set of people's preferences that might be weighed against another set of people's preferences, or that government provision of the resources needed to parent as many children as desired (see Ross 2006) in the way a person prefers is also a "trumping right." If the first interpretation is correct, this implies that the core pro-choice claim is not a right requiring special consideration beyond the reach of a democratically elected government, such that a legislature or majority should be free to ban abortion and contraception just as they are free to prioritize funding for highways over funding for railroads—this would essentially be a full repudiation of the pro-choice position that Ross and Solinger seemingly seek to augment rather than repudiate. If the second interpretation is correct, this implies that by accepting the core pro-choice claim, "justice" requires also accepting as a "trumping right" a specific and highly controversial fiscal policy that would seemingly entail massive redistribution of wealth toward people who want many children on the same basis—a position seemingly implied elsewhere by Ross (2006) and Solinger (2007). Whether or not this fiscal policy is itself desirable or even morally obligatory, this is not a position that logically follows from the belief that it is morally impermissible for the government to compel someone to continue a pregnancy. The fiscal policy requires independent argumentative grounds for adopting it, and it is not necessarily likely to be adopted by people who adopt the core pro-choice claim. It is also not even clear that it is possible to deliver without given limits to a given society's resources.

The negative rights to abortion and contraception are, on the best formulated accounts, subsidiary rights to the right to bodily integrity or self-ownership—to exercise control over one's own body and what is done to it. This is well described by Justice Blackmun in his concurrence to *Planned Parenthood v. Casey*, the current controlling case on the constitutional right to abortion in the United States. Justice Blackmun writes,

> The Court today reaffirms the long recognized rights of privacy and bodily integrity. As early as 1891, the Court held "[n]o right is held more sacred, or is more carefully guarded by the common law, than the right of every individual to the possession and control of his own person, free from all restraint or interference of others . . . the compelled continuation of a pregnancy infringes upon a woman's right to bodily integrity by imposing substantial physical intrusions and significant risks of physical harm . . . restrictive abortion laws force women to endure physical invasions far more substantial than those this Court has held to violate the constitutional principle of bodily integrity in other contexts." (Blackmun 1992)

As Justice Blackmun notes, bodily integrity and possession and control of one's own person is not, in American constitutional law or Anglo-American common law, just an ordinary entitlement that the government can grant or take away as it pleases the way the government can change the tax code. Sovereignty over one's own body is essential to being treated as a full person with an agenda of one's own rather than an instrument of reproduction or someone whose personhood is discounted in relation to the putative personhood of another.[16] This same set of principles is found in the law and philosophy of self-defense, where it is recognized as permissible to use violence to protect one's body from an assailant, *even if* the assailant suffers more than the person exercising a right to self-defense and *even if* the assailant is an "innocent aggressor." This is because someone should not have to endure a violation of their bodily integrity, or deprivation of their self-possession, by another person, even if doing so would maximize aggregate utility.[17] Bodily integrity rights, are, in other words, widely recognized as deontic rights that place constraints on democratic preferences or utilitarian calculations. The right to abortion, on Justice Blackmun's account then, is best conceptualized as a right against "compelled continuation of a pregnancy," which is necessary in order to extend pregnant women the same bodily integrity rights that are extended to men and women in other contexts.

The strongest philosophical defenses of the right to abortion all follow from this conceptualization of the right as a right to bodily integrity and/or self-possession. These include Judith Jarvis Thomson's argument from involuntary bodily servitude and risk (Thomson 1971, 47–66), Maggie Little's argument from nonconsensual intimacy (Little 1999), and Eileen McDonagh's argument from self-defense and consent (McDonagh 1996). Each of these arguments provides moral grounds for special protection from state-imposed compulsory pregnancy and childbirth that exceed the moral and political consideration owed by governments to each person's ordinary preferences for states of affairs beyond what happens to their bodies.

Crucially, these bodily integrity and self-possession arguments provide no equivalent moral grounds for equally fundamental rights to control the upbringing of as many children as desired, let alone for state subsidies for those preferences. These arguments do not so much advance a "right to choose" as such, but rather a right against the government's encroachment on one's body. While the Reproductive Justice Framework's self-presentation is that of a politics beyond the ostensibly neoliberal "politics of choice," the equation of the right to control one's own body with the right to parent as simply the choice to have or not have children recasts the self-possession and bodily integrity interests at stake in the right against compelled continuation of a pregnancy as *merely* the right to choose between two life preferences. It is in fact the Reproductive Justice Framework and not the "choice paradigm" that understands reproductive rights as a matter of consumer preference.[18] A person's desire that the government provide them with resources sufficient to pursue an expensive way of living is not normally thought to enjoy special rights that supersede other people's preferences—and in a world of limited resources, a demand for a large share of those resources will often be incompatible with other people's similar demand for those resources.

To illustrate this problem by way of a hypothetical example, if a person would like to be a Formula One race car driver and needs a $15 million grant from the government to finance this ambition, others would reasonably question why this expensive life preference should be prioritized above their own life preferences when limit resources prevent everyone from receiving similarly generous grants from the government. The aspiring Formula One race car driver either needs to provide an argument for why this particular interest is special among the array of ways people might like to spend tax revenue on themselves or concede that they are demanding a greater-than-equal consideration from the state—a position in conflict with the most basic liberal and egalitarian commitments against discrimination and in favor of equal basic rights.[19] The Reproductive Justice Framework's apparent insistence on the priority of parents over non-parents, and parents of large numbers of children over parents of small numbers of children, in conditions of scarcity is likewise, in effect, an insistence that some people deserve a greater suite of rights than other people do. In contrast, bodily integrity rights can be construed as compatible with the equally extensive rights of others: everyone possesses decisional authority over just one body, their own.[20]

Adopting a framework for reproductive rights that has, as an implication, the denial of the strongest moral arguments in favor of a right to abortion and treating abortion rights as a lifestyle preference of the sort that would not ordinarily attract special consideration carries the obvious risk of reducing the argumentative resources for defending abortion rights. Ross and Solinger are at least aware of the potential for objections along some of these lines. They write,

> some people were skeptical about this new framework, worrying that it improperly minimized the focus on abortion or, too often, avoided mentioning abortion altogether. Other skeptics thought reproductive justice was too broad a concept and a claim. By bringing together the right to have children and the right to parent them in safe and healthy environments, these skeptics claimed, reproductive justice included everything, even the kitchen sink. Women of color pushed back, pointing out that both historically and in contemporary America, ubiquitous and persistent white supremacy and population control efforts have clarified that the motherhood rights of all women are not equally valued and neither are all children. (Ross and Solinger 2017, 70)

Although this historical account is not necessarily meant to be a counter-argument, it is clearly nonresponsive to the objections they are describing. Instead, it points to a very concerning tendency, observed by Hayek and discussed earlier, that simply appealing to the label of social justice can be rhetorically effective in silencing opposition to a position (Hayek 1998, 62–65).

The vagueness and under-specificity of social justice discourse enables the expansion of the rights grounded in bodily integrity to include rights without similarly rigorous moral grounding—having the effect of both obscuring abortion rights' basis in bodily integrity rights arguments and lending its moral and political force to completely distinct rights claims. Through transforming the "divisive," controversial pro-choice movement's rights claims (Ross 2007, 4) into a movement able to broaden its appeal by potentially offering all things to all people, the Reproductive Justice movement took on as one of its major planks the major plank of the conservative family values movement: state-enabled parental control rights over children.[21]

Ross and Solinger describe the Reproductive Justice position on parental rights as a "radical departure from the privacy arguments of abortion rights advocates" where "reproductive justice activists are demanding *public* support for *private* actions" (Ross and Solinger 2017, 180; emphasis original). This amounts to two positions: a demand for state financial assistance to parents and a demand for government-conferred legal privileges to parent as one chooses without scrutiny regarding abuse and neglect. Ricki Solinger describes the first element of "[a] woman's right to be the parent of her child" as "the right to economic resources sufficient to be a parent" (Solinger 2007). Dorothy Roberts explains that the second plank includes "extend[ing] our struggle for reproductive justice to challenge the foster care system because it violates thousands of women's right to parent their children (Roberts 2007, 29). She says this on the grounds that

> most cases of child maltreatment involve parental neglect, which is usually difficult to disentangle from the conditions of poverty . . . [the] child welfare system reflects a political choice to address the startling rates of child poverty in communities of color by punishing parents instead of tackling poverty's societal roots [where] government policy has intensified its focus on "freeing" children in foster care for adoption by terminating parental rights rather than preserving families. (Roberts 2007, 29)

Both positions are frequently combined in identifying any limits to or conditions of state subsidies for parenting as the deprivation of parental rights for poor parents—such as Khiara Bridges's view that "poor mothers have been deprived of family, informational, and reproductive privacy rights," such as the Temporary Assistance for Needy Families (TANF), "family cap policies," and requirements for beneficiaries to engage in minimum work activities depending on family structure (Bridges 2017).

The general set of presumptions by Reproductive Justice advocates rejuvenates the misapplied private/public distinction used to shelter intra-family power from political critique. Feminist legal scholars such as Frances Olsen have previously argued that characterizing power as "private" is an analytically incoherent means of naturalizing and legitimating the power against "public" action that might interfere with it (Olsen 1983).[22] The power that parents have over children (and that husbands historically had over wives), in the context of a state society, can be understood as state delegations of authority, legal privileges, and immunities to particular individuals over others (see Olsen 1983). The suspicion of state action in the "private realm" of the family in ways that modify the authority that parents exercise over their children regards that previously established authority as if it were a natural and presumptively legitimate baseline, when in the scope and extent of parental power is historically and socially contingent and variable, determined by law and enforced by state action (see Godwin 2015, 14). In this regard, the Reproductive Justice Framework's insistence on "public support for private actions" involves a failure to see state action as a background condition of current intra-family power dynamics and adopts a deeply conservative theory of the family that is characteristic of thinking prior to the development of the feminist critique of legally enforced family roles.[23]

The view that limits to public support referred to as "family cap" laws amount to deprivations of reproductive rights, and that any minimum requirements for receiving these benefits likewise amount to deprivations of reproductive rights, is a conceptual framework that would not make sense if applied to any other personal interest. In no other case would the government's failure to pay *unlimited* subsidies to fund a select group of people's lifestyle choices be characterized as a coercive "cap" on their choice. Ordinarily, when the government pays people any amount of money if they engage in a particular activity, these payments are understood to incentivize that activity. That these payments may not follow a schedule of linear progression would not in any other context count as coercively preventing the recipients from engaging in the incentivized activity.

If maximum family grants were viewed the way similarly structured laws were, they would seem like a non-linear incentive to have a family rather than a coercive cap preventing poor people from having more children. Given that TANF, the Special Supplemental Nutrition Program for Women, Infants, and Children (WIC), public housing, the earned income tax credit, the child tax credit, and other financial benefits are income contingent, the effect is to grant low-income people a pro-natalist option rather than to coerce low-income people in an anti-natalist direction, as Bridges argues (Bridges 2017). Likewise, the claim that low-income families "have no privacy rights" (Bridges 2017, 11) because some welfare programs are formally or informally contingent on providing the government with additional access to personal information would not make sense if the same analytic framework were applied to any other rights relationship. Ordinarily, if someone has a Hohfeldian legal right that they can waive at their option in exchange for payment from the government, we would not say that they have been deprived of that right, but that they have been given an additional privilege right to sell it.[24] For example, if we apply the general structure of the following proposition that "if the government pays X for Y and 2X for 2Y but not 3X for 3Y, the government is coercively limiting Y" to small business incentives that have phase out levels, no one would argue that this was a sinister sort of coercion. Likewise, with regard to the privacy claims, the fact that sole proprietors need to provide extensive details about their work and life to the government in order to obtain maximum tax deductions would not be taken seriously as a basis for the claim that sole proprietors have no privacy rights.

The demand for government-conferred legal privileges to parent as one chooses without ordinary scrutiny regarding abuse and neglect is also indefensible. Once actually born, children are not mere extensions of their parents but separate persons with their own rights and interests that cannot be conflated with those of their parents (as social conservatism often insists on doing).[25] Children's interests are often consistent with collectivist desires to elevate community and family units above individuals,[26] but as separate individuals they will also often have separate interests. They are not the property of their parents, and their interests are often at odds with strong parental rights, such as those that the Reproductive Justice Framework often argues for (e.g., making it more difficult to terminate the parental rights of children in foster care so that they can be adopted by their new families—leaving children in longer states of legal and relational limbo).[27] If the "choice paradigm" limits its claims to rights to govern one's own body, the Reproductive Justice Framework's parental control rights are rights to govern other people.

There are also more fundamental, philosophical problems with construing the rights to "have children" or "not have children" as positive rights: if the right to have children is a universally applicable positive right, this would require denying the same rights to other people since a person's ability to have children is contingent on another's participation. If a pregnant woman has a unilateral right to decide to have a child, then her male partner has no right against "having children" against his wishes. If a pregnant woman has a unilateral right to decide not to have a child, then her male partner has no right against "not having children" against his wishes. The reason for prioritizing a pregnant woman's decisional autonomy over her male partner's cannot be simply the preference for women over men, which would be arbitrary and discriminatory, but rather the recognition that a pregnant woman's bodily integrity and self-ownership is at stake in pregnancy in a way that a male partner's is not. If it is bodily integrity and not mere reproductive preference that is the normative foundation of a pregnant women's decisional priority over their male partners, it follows that parenting choices are also not equivalent to choices during pregnancy, since parenting choices are not contingent on bodily integrity.

## WHAT IS LOST IN THE TURN
## AWAY FROM THE "CHOICE PARADIGM"

The critical project of the Reproductive Justice Framework, as a critique of "rights talk" generally and the "choice paradigm" specifically, is also self-defeating. The Reproductive Justice Framework is presented with intimations (or, direct accusations) that the "choice" movement ignores or fails to care about meaningful choice and economic framework that confines people's reproductive choices. This is generally a false accusation, at least as of recent decades: every significant pro-choice organization opposes targeted regulation of abortion providers (TRAP) laws designed to impose extraneous financial costs on abortion clinics and restrictions on the use of health insurance to pay for contraceptives and abortion. Rickie Solinger writes,

> "What happens when women's special guarantee—the promise that all women can decide for themselves whether and when to have children—is expressed by the individualistic, marketplace term "choice"? For one thing, the term "reproductive choice" invites many people to distinguish, in consumer-culture fashion, between a woman who can—and a woman who can't—afford to make a choice—even when we're talking about issues that seem to refer to fundamental human dignity and human rights. The language of choice masks issues of safety and potential danger at the heart of women's special guarantee. . . .
>
> The underlying assumptions of "reproductive choice" refer to the individual woman's economic suitability and even to her eugenic suitability as a mother of future citizens. According to politicians and public policy, choice-making should be associated with—and typically reserved for—women with resources: only a woman with a sufficient bank account (and other personal resources such a "normal" genetic profile or a "normal" IQ) has the makings of a legitimate mother. According to the Hyde Amendment, only a woman with enough money to pay can "choose" abortion. By extension, then, engaging in heterosexual sex is a class privileges as well, reserved only for women in a position to make—and pay for—appropriate reproductive choices. Pursuing fertility treatments is

a class privilege. The Supreme Court—and public opinion—asserts that women
do not have a right to decide whether and when to become mothers; they merely
have a consumer's choice. (Solinger 2007)

Here, Solinger has taken the language of "choice," which she rejects, and uses
it to refer to the choice that the Reproductive Justice Framework proposes
between having a child and parenting that child or not having a child. The
"choice" referred to in the phrase "pro-choice" and vindicated in the U.S.
Supreme Court's precedents discussed earlier in this chapter, however, is the
choice of what to do with a pregnancy without government interference—a
limited negative right over one's body against interference. Few people in the
pro-choice movement would think to propose that this is a "positive" right,
even with regard to pregnancy—the pro-choice movement does not assert a
right to another person's gametes required for pregnancy or a right to force a
doctor to perform an abortion. In both cases, the other required party's participation must be obtained voluntarily.

Next, Solinger implicitly attributes to the pro-choice movement the Hyde
Amendment's restriction on U.S. federal Medicaid funds for abortions. The
Hyde Amendment is universally opposed by all major pro-choice groups
in the United States. It is not a product of the pro-choice movement but a
product of the opposition to the pro-choice movement. Representative Henry
Hyde, the amendment's namesake, would have liked to have banned abortion
generally if it was constitutionally permissible and politically possible—since
it is not, the Hyde Amendment represented an anti-abortion rights position
within the realm of what is permitted under current U.S. constitutional law
and possible in U.S. politics.

Solinger's framing of fertility treatments as "class privilege" is likewise
adopting her preferred choice paradigm in place of the bodily integrity–based
negative rights paradigm of the prior pro-choice movement. The Supreme
Court's negative rights jurisprudence on abortion and contraception is, as
argued earlier, not really about "choice" at all, but rather a restraint on the
government's ability to compel someone to remain pregnant: a negative right,
not a choice. Ironically, Solinger's view that there should be a positive right
to make the full array of "reproductive choices" is closer to the consumerist model she disparages. The notion that someone should be able to select
among a menu of reproductive goods is close to the way people exercise
consumer choice. However, someone merely possessing a right against in-
trusions on their body is more in line with the way people exercise rights of
self-defense. Solinger has, in effect, disparaged the "pro-choice paradigm"
as consumerist for its failure to deliver the consumer options she would
advocate for, even though it was the failure of the "pro-choice paradigm" to

advocate for the same choice model that sparked the Reproductive Justice critique in the first instance.

More substantially, formal legal rights are not insignificant or meaningful only to people with financial resources. Formal rights do not only confer rights on the wealthy and powerful, but it is actually quite the reverse: formal rights that restrain the government against interfering with anyone's liberty are most significant to people who lack the power to vindicate their interests absent those formal rights. As aptly illustrated by Patricia Williams's criticisms of the Critical Legal Studies rejection of "rights talk," while already powerful people might be able to more effectively exercise their legal rights, in the absence of formal rights, those who are more socially vulnerable are placed more squarely at the mercy of inequalities in social power since they cannot as easily bargain and navigate arrangements in the absence of rights (Williams 1987). The formal right against state prohibition of abortions serves as a clear example of this dynamic: abortion bans chiefly prevent poor (or young) women from obtaining abortions since women who are financially secure can always travel to jurisdictions where abortion remains legal (or even in the absence of such jurisdictions, wealthier, well-networked women have historically been able to obtain *safe* illegal abortions not available to poorer women).

Solinger's presentation of the problem of one where "women's special guarantee . . . is expressed by the individualistic, marketplace term 'choice' . . . the term 'reproductive choice' invites many people to distinguish, in consumer-culture fashion, between a woman who can—and a woman who can't—afford to make a choice" (Solinger 2007, 39) is potentially revealing in another way. A major component of the complaint levied by Solinger is one of *terminology* and *expression*, of a "consumer-culture" implied by the language of "choice" and how, Solinger fears, this invites an adverse distinction to be drawn against "women who can't afford to make a choice." This is a complaint not about the actual distribution of rights, power, or resources but of the type of culture conveyed by the language of choice. It is also a complaint about what kinds of women are most centrally represented in the pro-choice movement. It is a demand for recognition of less privileged women in pro-choice discourse. These criticisms may very well be valid—"choice" language can invite confusion about which rights are actually in question: bodily integrity or the multiplicity of genuinely consumer-like choices, some of which are potentially reactionary, that the Reproductive Justice Framework's proponents insist on. Dropping the language of "choice" in favor of rights necessary for basic equality between persons would make the stakes in the abortion debate less ambiguous. Shifting the movement's focus from moral disagreements that carry with them policy imperatives to the politics of cultural recognition within the movement itself may risk expending energy on self-critique while the anti-abortion movement actively works to deprive marginalized women of their most basic rights to their own bodies.

While the Reproductive Justice Framework presents itself as the intersectional correction to the choice paradigm's focus on formal legal rights, this is not how it has been received outside of the American context in which it was developed. Lynn Morgan, a U.S.-based anthropologist, recounts her experience presenting at a conference in Argentina on abortion rights where she proposed adopting Reproductive Justice language in response to the backlash against reproductive rights:

> Reproductive justice, I told my audience, was quickly becoming the favored framework for reproductive and sexual rights activists in the United States and elsewhere. The concept was introduced in 1994 by SisterSong, a collective of US women of color who found "reproductive rights" to be too focused on privacy, autonomy, and abortion; the movement, they said, was inattentive to the concerns of immigrants and women of color. . . . If the language of rights had been co-opted by religious conservatives, I reasoned, perhaps the Argentines would consider substituting the concept of reproductive justice. I did not expect my proposal to be particularly controversial. . . . The justice framework, I concluded, was preferable to rights. My audience did not agree. The murmuring began even before I finished speaking. I knew I had struck a nerve. As the house lights came back up, people whispered animatedly to their neighbors and hands shot up. "Absolutely not," was the overwhelming response. "We have fought long and hard for the government to grant us the rights we deserve, and we are not giving up now." One after another, members of the audience rose to declare their allegiance to the language and framework of human rights. Honestly, I could not fathom why they were so passionate[;] . . . the Argentine feminist anthropologists [clung] so tenaciously to the language of human rights, and they insisted on *abortion* rights even while they are clearly cognizant of the structural and strategic connections between reproductive governance, equity, and justice. (Morgan 2015, 137–38)

It might be suspected that the value of formal rights is most apparent when they are absent, as they are in Argentina where abortion remains criminalized. Discussions of the language of social justice may make the most sense within contexts where activists and academics are seeking recognition from each other rather than specific rights against the government.

Legal and economic barriers to exercising meaningful choice are also not neatly categorically divisible because legal rights and legal impediments are equivalent to economic subsidies and "taxes." Enough money will usually allow a person to access that which is legally prohibited, whereas a sufficiently extensive legal rights provision with regard to a particular question can remove economic barriers by creating an entitlement to services. The formal legal restrictions on abortion and contraceptive funding and provision are in effect financial tolls that increase their cost. Presenting a false tension between legal rights and economic justice and wrongfully casting the "choice" framework as being on the "conservative" side of the dichotomy undermines and demoralizes work to protect and expand formal rights. Given the current composition of the U.S. Supreme Court, the formal right to abortion and contraception is in real jeopardy of being lost. If it is lost, wealthy women will still be able to navigate around this impediment just as they did prior to the legalization of abortion and contraception in the United States—it will instead be poor and marginalized women who will functionally lose their rights.

## CONCLUSION

More than two decades after Loretta Ross and her colleagues launched the Reproductive Justice movement through the SisterSong Women of Color Reproductive Justice Collective as a critique of and corrective to the what they saw as the inadequacies of the pro-choice paradigm, the pro-choice movement in the United States has largely adopted its preferred terminology and philosophical position.[28] This discursive dominance was achieved in part through elements of Reproductive Justice rhetoric that parallel the kind of "social justice" discourse that Hayek previously analyzed as superficially appealing but ultimately undermining substantive political reform. These rhetorical elements include the Reproductive Justice Framework's demands for ambitious, but vague, justice rather than actionable demands for legally enforceable rights. The widespread agreeability of the Reproductive Justice rhetorical claims that render them palatable, inoffensive, and politically impossible to object to have the simultaneous effect of undercutting the pro-choice movement's capacity to articulate its principles in their most morally powerful forms. The Reproductive Justice Framework has effectively displaced the pro-choice movement's morality-focused case for specific rights with a culture-focused appeal for recognition. Despite this success in pivoting the pro-choice movement's discursive focus, the Reproductive Justice Framework's principal proponents continue to frame themselves as radical critics of the conservativism and elitism of the mainstream pro-choice movement. This is neither a fair representation of the wider pro-choice movement nor an accurate representation of the Reproductive Justice Framework's contributions. The current pro-choice movement, heavily modified by the Reproductive Justice Framework, has seemingly shied away from its radical, controversial focus on the rights under active threat—women's rights to bodily integrity— in favor of more accommodating advocacy for vague social justice. This has not been to its advantage. What remains of the pro-choice movement after the intervention of the Reproductive Justice Framework, as argued in this chapter, amounts to a position that is both less desirable and less defensible.

## NOTES

1. Throughout this chapter, I will use the term "pro-choice" to describe the position and movement that holds that rights to abortion and contraception should be protected. The "Reproductive Justice Framework" is "pro-choice" in this sense. I will use the phrase "choice paradigm" to refer to the formal rights–focused target of the Reproductive Justice Framework's criticism within the pro-choice movement.

2. I would like to thank the editors and contributors to this volume for their helpful comments and recommendations—in particular, I greatly benefited from a conversation with Virgil Storr.

3. In this chapter, I am using the term "illiberal" to refer to the rejection of individual liberty on the "most extensive system of equal basic liberty compatible with a similar system for all" (Rawls [1971] 1999, 220), which I take to be a central commitment of both "classic liberals" and "left liberals." I will use the term "liberal" to refer to both "classic liberals" and "left liberals," and part of my critique of the Reproductive Justice Framework, popular with both self-identified left liberals and leftist progressives, is that it is deeply at odds with other fundamental commitments of left liberals.

4. Ironic because this is part of what advocates of the Reproductive Justice Framework accuse the prior "choice paradigm" of doing. See Price (2010).

5. For example, "Instead of focusing on the means—a divisive debate on abortion and birth control that neglects the real-life experiences of women and girls—the Reproductive Justice analysis focuses on the ends: better lives for women, healthier families and sustainable communities. This is a clear and consistent message for all social justice movements" (Ross 2007, 4).

6. Which was part of the intent (Ross 2007).

7. Leading Reproductive Justice Framework figures Loretta Ross and Rickie Solinger expressly describe their project in terms of augmenting the negative rights framework of the prior pro-choice movement with positive rights to resources, which they describe as "the government's obligation to ensure that people can exercise their freedoms and enjoy the benefits of society" (Ross and Solinger 2017, 10). I will use the term "positive rights" in this way when specifically discussing the Reproductive Justice Framework's philosophical position, but I will otherwise use the terms "negative rights" and "positive rights" in the manner of Isaiah Berlin's (1969) account of negative and positive liberty since I do not think that that Ross and Solinger's account of "negative rights" as "a government's obligation to refrain from unduly interfering with people's mental, physical and spiritual autonomy" is quite what is typically meant by negative rights.

8. Hayek was specifically concerned that giving effect to the demands of "social justice" and rendering the term meaningful requires demanding that greater power is vested in the state to compel some ordered ends incompatible with individual liberty.

9. Lister notes here that while libertarians might argue that people should not be required to aid others or share the benefits of cooperation, this does not seem to be Hayek's position, since Hayek elsewhere argues in favor of state provision of income for people who are unable to adequately support themselves through the market (Lister 2013, 412–13).

10. By institutions, I mean the government agencies, courts, legislative bodies, firms, and other private and public organizations that are directed by specific individuals and discrete groups of people. A prison or a church is an institution on this definition. Discrimination and Christianity have pervasive social impacts that effect people's lives in ways that might be properly described as "systemic," but they are not institutions in this sense.

11. "Loretta Ross, a founder of the modern-day 'reproductive justice' movement . . . was one of the creators of the term 'reproductive justice' which African-American women coined in 1994" (Sorensen 2019).

12. This is, I think, a fair reading of Ross's intent: "The Reproductive Justice analysis offers a framework for empowering women and girls relevant to every family. Instead of focusing on [abortion and birth control] the Reproductive Justice analysis focuses on the ends: better lives for women, healthier families, and sustainable communities. This is a clear and consistent message for all social justice movements. Using this analysis, we can integrate multiple issues and bring together constituencies that are multi-racial, multi-generational, and multi-class in order to build a more powerful and relevant grassroots movement. . . . We also have to build the social, political and economic power of low-income women, Indigenous women, women of color, and their communities so that they are full participating partners in building this new movement. This requires integrating grassroots issues and constituencies that are multi-racial, multi-generational and multi-class into the national policy arena, as well as into the organizations that represent the movement" (Ross 2007, 4).

13. By which I mean the negative right to determine what happens to one's body.

14. Of course, many would argue that interfering with a person's preferences should ordinarily require identifying the harm that that person is doing to another (see Mill 1859), but what constitutes a "harm" is itself hotly contested (see Feinberg 1984, 245).

15. For a discussion of the concept of "rights as trumps," meaning that the assertion of a "right" is the assertion of a consideration that trumps consequentialist considerations, see Dworkin (2009, 335).

16. A well-known argument to this effect was developed by Judith Jarvis Thomson (1971).

17. For a philosophical account of this position on self-defense, see Thomson (1991). For a summary of current U.S. law on self-defense, including the proposition that killing an assailant is lawfully privileged in self-defense even if the defender would not expect to die absent the defense but instead merely expects to sustain serious bodily injury, see Torcia (2020, § 127).

18. Contrary to Solinger's (2007) contestations.

19. For example, see Dworkin (2013), Hart (1979), and Blake (2001). With regard to the specific race car driver example, it would not be persuasive for the aspiring

race car driver to say "the right to drive a race car for one's enjoyment is analogous to the right not to be forced to drive a race car against one's wishes—the choices are both equally valid," since the apparent equivalence of the two "choices" ignores that the former is a matter of one's personal aspirations that cannot be guaranteed, and the latter implicates the right against involuntary servitude that we would defend in all other contexts.

20. Anti–abortion rights advocates will, of course, frequently take issue with formulation on the grounds that fetuses should also have their own bodily integrity rights that are incompatible with a right to abortion. This argument is particularly well addressed by McDonagh (1996).

21. For discussion of the centrality of parental rights claims to the conservative family values movement, see Dowland (2015). For discussion of the tension between conservativism and classical liberalism regarding the appropriate scope of parental rights, see Lessard (2002).

22. "On the second level of criticism, 'public' and 'private' are shown not to be analytic categories at all. On this level of critique, the problem is not just that private actions can be made to look like state action and vice versa, but rather that there really is no way to say that certain action is private action. . . . For most of us, what we want to do and be left alone to do seems like private action. . . . The laws that facilitate the injury of one person by another seem like state action when they seem unjust, but go unnoticed or are treated as a neutral background of law to those who support the rules" (Lessard 2002, 319).

23. In various ways, Okin (1999), Firestone (1972), and Pateman (1988) all argued that the family is a space of social domination. For the earliest of such arguments, see Mill ([1869] 1911, 1859).

24. Using the terms "right" and "privilege" as developed in Hohfeld (1917).

25. See Dietz (1987) for critique of "maternalism."

26. An interest described by Ross (2007, 4).

27. A position advocated for by Roberts (2007).

28. All of the major pro-choice organizations in the United States, including Planned Parenthood (see Price 2016), the National Organization for Women (see National Organization for Women n.d.) the ACLU (see Foulkes 2009) and NARAL Pro-Choice America (see NARAL Pro-Choice Missouri 2020) have all expressly adopted the Reproductive Justice Framework's preferred terminology and agenda. Recently formed academic organizations have tended towards adopting "Reproductive Justice" language (e.g., the Program for the Study of Reproductive Justice at Yale Law, or the Reproductive Justice Project at Berkeley Law), and some smaller organizations have gone so far as to rename themselves (e.g., "Law Students for Choice" renamed itself "Law Students for Reproductive Justice"—later renaming itself "If/When/How, Lawyering for Reproductive Justice"). For their part, Ross and Solinger believe that reproductive justice "began to eclipse pro-choice language as the primary way many activists talked about reproductive politics" (Ross and Solinger 2017, 70).

# REFERENCES

Berlin, Isaiah. 1969. "Two Concepts of Liberty." In *Four Essays on Liberty*, 118–72. Oxford: Oxford University Press

Blackmun, Harry. 1992. Planned Parenthood of Southeastern Pennsylvania v. Casey 505 U.S. 833. (Concurrence in Part of Justice Harry Blackmun).

Blake, Michael. 2001. "Distributive Justice, State Coercion, and Autonomy." *Philosophy & Public Affairs* 30 (3): 257–96.

Bridges, Khira. 2017. *The Poverty of Privacy*. Stanford, CA: Stanford University Press.

Dietz, Mary. 1987. "Context Is All: Feminism and Theories of Citizenship." *Daedalus* 116 (4): 1–24.

Dowland, Seth. 2015. *Family Values and the Rise of the Christian Right*. Philadelphia, PA: University of Pennsylvania Press.

Dworkin, Ronald. 2009. "Rights as Trumps." In *Arguing about Law*, edited by Aileen Kavanagh and John Oberdiek, 335–44. London: Routledge.

———. 2013. *Taking Rights Seriously*. London: Bloomsbury Publishing.

Feinberg, Joel. 1984. *The Moral Limits of the Criminal Law, Vol. 1: Harm to Others*. Oxford: Oxford University Press,

Firestone, Shulamith. 1972. *The Dialectic of Sex: The Case for Feminist Revolution*. New York: Bantam.

Foulkes, Risha. 2009. "Reproductive Justice and Women's Rights." *ACLU Women's Rights Project*, December 24. https://www.aclu.org/blog/smart-justice/mass-incarceration/reproductive-justice-and-womens-rights.

Godwin, Samantha. 2015. "Against Parental Rights." *Columbia Human Rights Law Review* 47 (1): 1–83.

Guttmacher Institute. 2021. "Targeted Regulation of Abortion Providers." February 1. https://www.guttmacher.org/print/state-policy/explore/targeted-regulation-abortion-providers.

Haeffele, Stefanie, and Virgil Henry Storr. 2019. "Is Social Justice a Mirage?" *The Independent Review* 24 (1): 145–54.

Hale, Robert. 1923. "Coercion and Distribution in a Supposedly Non-Coercive State." *Political Science Quarterly* 38 (3): 470–94.

Hart, H. L. A. 1979. "Between Utility and Rights." *Columbia Law Review* 79 (5): 828–46.

Hayek, F. A. 1998. *Law, Legislation and Liberty: A New Statement of the Liberal Principles of Justice and Political Economy*. London: Routledge.

Hohfeld, Wesley Newomb. 1917. "Fundamental Legal Conceptions as Applied to Judicial Reasoning." *The Yale Law Journal* 26 (8) 710–70.

Lessard, Hester. 2002. "Liberty Rights, the Family and Constitutional Politics." *Review of Constitutional Studies* 6 (2): 213–61.

Lister, Andrew. 2013. "The 'Mirage' of Social Justice: Hayek against (and for) Rawls." *Critical Review* 25 (3–4): 409–44.

Little, Margaret Olivia. 1999. "Abortion, Intimacy, and the Duty to Gestate." *Ethical Theory and Moral Practice* 2 (3): 295–312.

McDonagh, Eileen. 1996. *Breaking the Abortion Deadlock: From Choice to Consent.* Oxford: Oxford University Press.

Mill, John Stuart. [1869] 1911. *The Subjection of Women.* New York: Frederick A. Stokes Company.

———. 1859. *On Liberty.* London: Longmans.

Morgan, Lynn M. 2015. "Reproductive Rights or Reproductive Justice? Lessons from Argentina." *Health and Human Rights* 17 (1): E136–47.

NARAL Pro-Choice Missouri. 2020. "Black Women and the Fight for Reproductive Justice." February 3. https://prochoicemissouri.org/2020/02/03/black-women-fight-reproductive-justice/.

National Organization for Women. n.d. "Reproductive Justice Is Every Woman's Right." https://now.org/resource/reproductive-justice-is-every-womans-right/.

Okin, Susan. 1999. *Is Multiculturalism Bad for Women?* Princeton, NJ: Princeton University Press.

Olsen, Frances. 1993. "Constitutional Law: Feminist Critiques of the Public/Private Distinction." *Constitutional Commentary* 10: 319–27.

Pateman, Carole. 1988. *The Sexual Contact.* Oxford: Polity Press.

Pluckrose, Helen. 2017. "When Intersectionality Silences Women." *Areo*, November 7. https://areomagazine.com/2017/11/07/when-intersectionality-silences-women/.

Price, Kimala. 2010. "What Is Reproductive Justice?: How Women of Color Activists Are Redefining the Pro-Choice Paradigm" *Meridians: Feminism, Race, Transnationalism* 10 (2) 42–65.

———. 2016. "Reproductive Justice: Beyond the Statistics." *Planned Parenthood of the Pacific Southwest*, January 6. https://www.plannedparenthood.org/planned-parenthood-pacific-southwest/blog/reproductive-justice-beyond-the-statistics.

Rawls, John. [1971] 1999. *A Theory of Justice Revised Edition.* Cambridge, MA: Belknap Press of Harvard University Press.

Roberts, Dorothy. 2007. "Foster Care and Reproductive Justice." In *Reproductive Justice Briefing Book: A Primer on Reproductive Justice and Social Change*, 29. SisterSong Women of Color Reproductive Health Collective and Pro-Choice Public Education Project.

Ross, Loretta. 2006. "Understanding Reproductive Justice." *SisterSong Women of Color Reproductive Justice Collective.* Updated March 2011.

———. 2007. "What is Reproductive Justice?" In *Reproductive Justice Briefing Book: A Primer on Reproductive Justice and Social Change*, 4–5. SisterSong Women of Color Reproductive Health Collective and Pro-Choice Public Education Project.

Ross, Loretta, and Rickie Solinger. 2017. *Reproductive Justice: An Introduction.* Berkeley, CA: University of California Press.

SisterSong Collective. n.d. "Reproductive Justice." SisterSong Women of Color Reproductive Health Collective. Accessed 2020. https://www.sistersong.net/reproductive-justice.

Solinger, Rickie. 2007. "The Incompatibility of Neo-Liberal 'Choice' and Reproductive Justice." In *Reproductive Justice Briefing Book: A Primer on Reproductive Justice and Social Change*, 39–40. SisterSong Women of Color Reproductive Health Collective and Pro-Choice Public Education Project.

Sorensen, Meghan. 2019. "Loretta Ross, Founder of the Modern-Day Reproductive Justice Movement, Speaks at Amherst College." *The Massachusetts Daily Collegian*, October 21. https://dailycollegian.com/2019/10/loretta-ross-founder-of-the-modern-day-reproductive-justice-movement-speaks-at-amherst-college/.

Tebble, Adam James. 2009. "Hayek and Social Justice: A Critique." *Critical Review of International Social and Political Philosophy* 12 (4): 581–604.

Thomson, Judith Jarvis. 1971. "A Defense of Abortion." *Philosophy and Public Affairs* 1 (1): 47–66.

———. 1991. "Self Defense." *Philosophy and Public Affairs* 20 (4): 283–310.

Torcia, Charles E. 2020. *Wharton's Criminal Law*. 15th ed. Toronto: Thomson Reuters.

West, Robin. 2009. "From Choice to Reproductive Justice: De-Constitutionalizing Abortion Rights." *The Yale Law Journal* 118: 1394–1432.

Williams, Patricia. 1987. "Alchemical Notes: Reconstructing Ideals from Deconstructed Rights." *Harvard Civil Rights–Civil Liberties Law Review* 22 (2): 401–33.

# Index

Italicized page numbers indicate tables and figures.

# About the Authors

**Ololade Afolabi**, PhD student in mass communications and media arts at Southern Illinois University Carbondale.

**Dr. Paul Dragos Aligica**, senior fellow, F. A. Hayek Program for Advanced Study in Philosophy, Politics, and Economics, Mercatus Center at George Mason University.

**Valentina Ausserladscheider**, post-doctoral researcher at the University of Vienna and research affiliate at the University of Cambridge.

**Jaime L. Carini**, PhD student in musicology and DM student in organ performance and literature at Indiana University Bloomington.

**Dr. Ginny Seung Choi**, senior fellow, F. A. Hayek Program for Advanced Study in Philosophy, Politics, and Economics, Mercatus Center at George Mason University.

**Samantha Godwin**, PhD student in science of law at Yale University.

**James Goodrich**, PhD student in philosophy at Rutgers, The State University of New Jersey and Stockholm University.

**Lewis Hoss**, PhD student in political science at Northern Illinois University.

**Brandon Hunter-Pazzara**, PhD student in anthropology at Princeton University.

**Mario I. Juarez-Garcia**, PhD student in philosophy at the University of Arizona.

**Rosaleen McAfee**, PhD student in anthropology at the University of British Columbia.

**Lee Moore**, PhD student in East Asian languages and literatures at the University of Oregon.

**Dr. Virgil Henry Storr**, associate professor of economics, George Mason University; Don C. Lavoie senior fellow, F. A. Hayek Program for Advanced Study in Philosophy, Politics, and Economics, Mercatus Center at George Mason University.

**Dr. Nicole Wu**, assistant professor of political science, University of Toronto.

www.ingramcontent.com/pod-product-compliance
Lightning Source LLC
Chambersburg PA
CBHW021808270326
41932CB00007B/105